DATE			

Readings in HUMAN COMMUNICATION

Russel R. Windes, *Consulting Editor*

To Cherie with love

Readings in
HUMAN
COMMUNICATION
an interpersonal
introduction

Thomas M. Steinfatt

Temple University

BOBBS-MERRILL EDUCATIONAL PUBLISHING
Indianapolis

P
87
.R4

First Edition
First Printing 1977
Design by Anita Duncan

Library of Congress Cataloging in Publication Data

Main entry under title:
Readings in human communication.
   1.   Communication—Addresses, essays, lectures.
I. Steinfatt, Thomas M.
P87.R4   301.14   76.25530
ISBN 0-672-61360-3

CONTENTS

v

Contents

EIGHT   **A Reminder: Communication is an Interacting Process**

pREfACE

Readings in Human Communication is intended to be used as either the main text in an introductory communication course for freshmen and sophomores or as a supplementary set of readings for such a course. *The selections are ordered so that the book can be read from cover to cover in a logical sequence;* or the selections can be read in any order that corresponds to the outline of a particular introductory course. The *Teacher's Manual* which accompanies this book contains suggestions for integrating the readings with a companion text, *Human Communication: An Interpersonal Introduction.*

The readings were selected both for what they have to say and how they say it. Each reading discusses an important aspect of the communication process in an understandable manner, though some readings will be more difficult for freshmen than others. Specifically, Five "Modelling the Communication Process," and Eleven "An Introduction to Categorizing," are written in a slightly more difficult style than are the remaining selections.

This anthology differs from other "readers" intended for basic communication courses in several respects. First, it is organized so that the student can begin on Page 1 and progress from reading to reading, with the knowledge obtained from one selection adding to the understanding gained from following selections. It is not simply a collection of readings about communication haphazardly bound between two covers. The introductions to each reading and the Questions for Discussion which follow help to achieve this organization.

Second, while several readings have been taken from books and periodicals in the fields of psychology, sociology, and anthropology, the majority of the articles included in *Readings in Human Communication* are written by people affiliated with a department or enterprise primarily concerned with some aspect of communication.

Third, seven of the twenty-four readings are being published for the first time, and an eighth, Craig Stark's "The Sense of Hearing," is usually neglected by anthologies in communication. Thus, much of the material printed in *Readings in Human Communication* is not readily available elsewhere.

Some departments of communication are fortunate enough to have two basic courses—one a performance course, and the other not. Many have a single course which tries to achieve some type of balance between the two approaches. With the rising cost per pupil of teaching an effective performance course, an increasing number of universities have begun to teach performance only in upper level courses with smaller enrollments. I believe that this is generally a healthy trend, yet I think it would be unfortunate if students, whose only exposure to communication is often through a single basic course, are never given any practical advice regarding communicative performance. Thus, while the emphasis of this book is heavily on the side of helping the student to achieve an understanding of the communication process, a section is included (Part Seven) which discusses the performance of communicative behaviors in work and family settings and includes articles on listening and basic public speaking.

I wish to thank each of the authors and copyright holders of the reprinted material. Russel Windes interested me in the project initially, and I thank him for his support. My wife Cherie helped me greatly in sending out requests for permissions to reprint. Andy Rancer, Deepak Pershad, and Randi Schneider Sherman also assisted me at various stages of the project, and I thank them for their help. The Department of Communication of Queens College merits special thanks for creating an atmosphere that both encourages and allows time for publication and research. Finally, the authors of the articles that have not been previously published deserve special thanks for their contributions to this effort. David Berlo, Louie Bender, John Hocking, Wayne Cowart, Dominic Infante, David Stang, Rick Crandall, and John Dimmick have produced a series of excellent articles introducing the student to various phases of the communication process. I thank them for their time and applaud their efforts.

New York City   Thomas M. Steinfatt
August 1976

Readings in HUMAN COMMUNICATION

ONE

introduction to theory and basic concepts

The author discusses two common misconceptions about communication: first, that problems in communication are primarily due to *communication break-downs* or *communication gaps*, and second, that communication is similar to the operation of a *telephone switchboard*. Neither of these ideas is especially useful to advance the study of human communication, as Mortensen points out. Replacing these ideas with concepts such as "relevant dialogue" and "I-Thou relationships" does not lead us to an improved understanding of the communication process. What is needed, according to Mortensen, is a "shift from a concern with general images of communication to more precise ways of approaching the assumptions underlying the complexities of communication behavior." Following his discussion of the dangers of these misconceptions, we shall begin to examine some of these more precise ways of approaching human communication behavior.

1

A FRAME OF REFERENCE

C. David Mortensen

The images men share about communication—and about its
possibilities—largely regulate what sort of encounters each person
will seek or avoid. Consider the alternative interpretations of the
following three social incidents. Each one approximates events experienced in the course of a single day. First, here is a description of a
conversation between an operator at a telephone-answering service
and a subscriber (Haber, 1969):

> "Hello . . . Hebert—ah, Harbart residence. Just a minute." (The voice
> goes off the phone for one minute, 55 seconds.) "Yeah?"
> "Hello, this is Miss Haber. I'm calling from Los Angeles. Are there
> . . . ."
> "Just a *moment*." (Off the phone 45 seconds.) "Un-huh?"
> "Are there any. . . ."
> "*Just a moment*." (Off the phone two minutes, 25 seconds.)
> "Yes?"
> "*Messages*! For Pete's sake. I'm calling from *California*!"
> "One *moment*." (Off the phone another two minutes.) "No mes-
> sage."
> "I've been away for *three* weeks. Do you mean to tell me that *no one*
> has called?"
> "Well, they didn't leave any messages."
> "Well, would you mind checking again? For what this call's cost-
> ing, I'd like to have at least one message to show for it."
> "Oh, wait a minute." (Forty seconds.)

C. David Mortensen is professor of communication at the University of Wisconsin,
Madison. This article is reprinted from Communication: The Study of Human Interaction, by C. David Mortensen. Copyright © 1972 by McGraw-Hill, Inc. Used with
permission of McGraw-Hill Book Company.

"Here's a couple. They were in the wrong box. Dolores musta' done that."

"Please!"

"Mr. Lackamoose called, Mr. Moorx and Dr. Fisher."

"I've never heard of any of them. Did they leave their numbers?"

"One *moment.*"

"*Wait!* Don't go off the line again. . . . "

The writer then commented:

Unfortunately, that conversation between me and my answering service was not imaginary. (Except for the names of my callers. I found out later, much later, that they were Mr. Bartholomew, Mrs. Morse, and Mr. Viser—old friends whose real names had lost something in the translation.) It's a sample of the kind of dialogue that takes place not infrequently between Manhattan's 175 telephone-answering services and their 50,000 subscribers.

The second incident is typical of the commentary about communication to be found in editorial pages of newspapers, journals, and books by social critics; it is taken from the editorial page of a Sunday newspaper (Elegant, 1970).

AMERICANS CAN'T COMMUNICATE

The past two weeks have not been the most comfortable time for a resident abroad to visit the United States, nor have they been the most illuminating . . . . Nonetheless, some shafts of light have pierced the clouds of rhetoric and the fog of emotion. They may be—indeed, they are probably—warped, for I have found that it is all but impossible for anyone to think clearly and dispassionately in the present atmosphere. Perhaps because of the confused background, first impressions do stand out clearly. . . .

The real issues appear to be: Discontent with the status quo, demands for instant gratification in instant solutions—and, *chiefly, failure of communication. The communication gap transcends the much-discussed generation gap. Americans obviously communicate with great difficulty, regardless of age; they're almost incapable of communicating with the outside world.*

Arriving in the United States is like climbing into a pressure-cooker, in part because of the tension stimulated by the President's decision [regarding Vietnam] but, in greater part, because of the tension inherent in American life. It is, therefore, not remarkable that *dispassionate analysis and communication are rare,* while emotion and isolation appear to be primary characteristics of American society.

Those tendencies are, of course, greatly magnified by a minority's deliberate intent.

Young people who cry out that older people do not "relate" to them are basically correct. *Many of their mothers and fathers do not communicate with each other. . . .*

The basic fault is the elders', since their obvious power over their children did not breed complimentary responsibility.

Belatedly aware of responsibility, some elders are now attempting to communicate. *The effort is often not merely belated, but impossible.* The wall of willful mutual incomprehension is too high [italics added].

The third incident is taken from a full-page newspaper advertisement sponsored by the Avco Corporation; it concerns the power of the mass media to foster communication:

**If
you have
something
important to tell
America,
we'll put you on
national television
to say it**

You read it right.

You.

Not a movie star or a noted author or a celebrated activist or an official spokesman for some lobby or pressure group. America hears from them.

It's you we're after. You, the ungrouped, individual American *with something to say and no place to say it.* We think what you believe, what you feel, what you like about this country, what you don't like about it, and what you'd like to see done with it, are vital.

Yet it's harder and harder to be heard.

There is a tendency, as life in America becomes more complex and our population keeps growing, for the individual to feel his voice is too small, is lost, that his opinions no longer count.

Why are we at Avco concerned? Simple enough.

This country's greatness has been achieved by individuals and the quality of her future depends on them equally. . . .

We cannot arrange for millions of Americans to talk on TV, but we have committed ourselves to do just as much as we can. Here's the plan.

Our time is your time

Beginning in August this year we are turning over our television commercial time—time we'd ordinarily spend talking about our divisions, the products they make and the services they provide—turning it over to individual Americans like yourself.

Americans who strike us as having something fresh and original to
say to their countrymen. . . .

The rest of America may not agree with you. We at Avco may not
agree with you. *The important thing is: we will all have seen and heard you.
One American speaking his mind* [italics added].

The three seemingly dissimilar incidents have two common
themes. First, each reflects how difficult it is to conceive of or to
describe communication in impersonal or neutral terms. In each case,
the image of communication is bound to the personal evaluation and
feelings that link attitudes toward self, the actions of others, and
culturally defined patterns of behavior. The subscriber to the
telephone-answering service suffered a sequence of minor indignities
merely to get some personally satisfying information. The writer of
the newspaper article found it impossible to separate his observations
about the difficulties of communicating in the United States from the
wider substrata of his political, social, and perhaps religious views.
And the newspaper advertisement also ties the import of communication to feelings of personal worth and democratic values. The second
common denominator of these three incidents is also striking: Each
excerpt reflects an unquestioning faith in the power and significance of
attempting to communicate, difficulties notwithstanding. Note again
the parallels. The subscriber in the abortive telephone conversation
refused to hang up the phone, even after the interminable delays,
interruptions, distortions, misunderstandings, and preoccupations of
a bungling operator at the other end of the line. To the end she
pleaded with the operator not to go "off the line again," thereby
expressing what is probably a universal need to have at least *something*
to show for every communicative exchange, regardless of costs and
frustrations. In a similar vein, the newspaper editor called on all sides
"to listen to each other," even after proclaiming the climate in the
United States too chaotic to achieve mutual understanding. The
newspaper advertisement, if taken at face value, also affirms the principle of being heard, even when "it's harder and harder to be heard,"
under circumstances where "one voice is too small, is lost, . . . and no
longer counts." The critical thing, the ad intones, is not the cost or the
number of people who, by implication, will not be heard, but that "we
will all have seen and heard you." What is revered here is the act of
communication divorced from its reasoned worth or social consequences.

Despite these common elements, the excerpts suggest two rather
distinct, and in some ways conflicting, assumptions about the essential

nature of communication. The implications of these images are worth pursuing in detail, for they reveal the consequences of conceiving of communication in alternative ways.

Misconceptions About Communication

The prevailing image in the newspaper editorial is one of the most commonly heard—the notion of a *communication gap* or *breakdown*. At its heart is the tendency to think of social malfunctioning and disruption as an abnormality that must be repaired or replaced. Further, the terms *gap* and *breakdown* imply that "normal" communication is a matter of bridging individual differences in viewpoint and interpretation—purely a semantic problem. By definition, then, so long as two parties "work" at talking and listening intently to one another, at seeking to "really communicate" by resolving their differences, the malfunction or gap between them supposedly will be eliminated. Less obvious, perhaps, is the tendency—once the language of "communication breakdown" is accepted—to reduce the complexities of verbal interchange to mechanistic operations and to search for tangible "obstacles," "barriers," and "roadblocks" to effectual communication (Smith, 1970).

An additional consequence of such reasoning is the tendency to see more and more evidence of malfunctioning until all social disruption and conflict is explained as a gap in communication. Once this happens, it is not difficult to take the final step, to dismiss altogether the possibility of establishing meaningful communication. In many quarters, this deeply seated pessimism toward the possibilities of communication is already much in vogue. Current despair over human misunderstanding seems a result of a wider sense of alienation and disaffection. Adherents of social protest groups, in particular, are prone to say that our unquestioning faith in the power of the written and spoken word is misplaced—that the business of human talk between young and old, between black and white, between the haves and the have-nots is but an empty and meaningless enterprise. People in positions of authority and high station do not listen to the disenfranchised. In short, the argument goes, talk is cheap, and the hope for "relevant dialogue" is a cruel delusion, an appeal for an exercise in futility. The idea of talk without communication is well underscored in these lyrics from "The Sound of Silence" by Simon and Garfunkel:

> . . . people
> talking without speaking, people hearing without listening . . .

Rarely is the notion of communication breakdown more in evidence than in the attempts to explain discord within families. In many quarters talk of a "generation gap" or "credibility gap" is now replaced by references to a "communication gap." Typical of what many take to be a growing disaffection among members of families is the conclusion drawn from a study of family relations in a small community in upstate New York after the seventeen-year-old son of a Methodist minister died from an overdose of barbiturates (Associated Press news release, Oct. 12, 1970). One recurring theme described was the total absence of communication between the parents and their teenage sons and daughters. A seventeen-year-old boy said, "I suppose I'd like them to understand me a little better, but there is a barrier on both sides. I don't listen to them; they don't listen to me." In similar context, a college student wrote the following in response to an essay "On Being an American Parent" (*Time*, Dec. 22, 1967):

> I could never tell my parents anything; it was always, "I'm too busy . . . too tired . . . that's not important . . . that's stupid . . . can't you think of better things, . . ." As a result, I stopped telling my parents anything. *All communication ceased.* I have only one important plea to parents . . . *Listen, listen, and listen again.* Please, I know the consequences and I am in hell [p. 7, some italics added].

In angry tones parents retorted (Toole, 1970):

> Too many youngsters are eccentric boors. They will not listen; they will only shout down. They will not discuss, but, like four-year-olds, they throw rocks and shout.

It indeed would be difficult to find strata of American life that are devoid of attempts to explain events with the language of "communication gaps," "barriers," "breakdowns," and "obstacles."

The Telephone Switchboard

In addition to the imagery of "communication breakdowns" is one that compares human interaction to the activities of a *telephone switchboard*. This notion identifies urban life with the activities of a vast and intricate switchboard where man is the communicator and the metropolis is a massive network of possibilities for communication. Not surprisingly, the switchboard image conceives of communication in technological terms—wires and switches, inputs and outputs, channels and transmitters, cross circuits and transmission lines. The idea of a switchboard gains credence from an almost universal faith in the power of technology to solve social ills and to promote public welfare. Most striking is the widespread acceptance of McLuhan's "global village," a vast electronic network that shrinks the space between West and East to that of a hamlet. McLuhan (1965) wrote.

> Today after more than a century of electronic technology, we have extended our central nervous system itself in a global embrace, abolishing both space and time as far as our planet is concerned. Rapidly we approach the final phase of the extensions of man—the technological simulation of consciousness, where the creative process of knowing will be collectively and corporately extended to the whole of human society, much as we have already extended our senses and our nerves by the various media . . . as electronically contracted, the global is no more than a village. Electronic speed in bringing all social and political functions together in a sudden impulsion has heightened human awareness of responsibility to an intense degree [pp. 3-5].

McLuhan went on to argue convincingly that "any medium has the power of imposing its own assumptions on the unwary." The same idea holds, it might be said, of all images—they impose assumptions that are far-reaching and not altogether obvious. For example, once we accept a switchboard image of communication, with all its technological overtones, we come to expect of human interaction what is tacitly expected of technological performance; unwittingly the astonishing advances of technology get superimposed on our ideas of efficiency in the fragile business of talking to each other. If a technological age compels, as McLuhan insisted, "commitment and participation," then it is not unreasonable to view involvement and relevance as the keys to any interpersonal encounter. If the electronic switchboard can be expected to create a vast and efficient network of extensions and connections, then McLuhan was right in insisting that "the aspirations of our time for wholeness, empathy and depth of awareness is the national adjunct of electronic technology [p. 5]."

The allusions to communication breakdowns and gaps or telephone switchboards certainly do not exhaust the possibilities. Communication can be represented in the abstract in any number of ways. Until recently the most popular conceptions have been mechanistic operations where communication is likened to the operations of telegraph and transportation systems, radio transmitters, conveyer belts, assembly lines, computer activity, and electrical gadgets. A more recent vogue is the psychologically oriented imagery of "turning on" and "rapping" or the states of "identification," "mystico," "I-Thou relationships," and "relevant dialogue."

The Dangers of Misconceptions

The above images of communication need to be brought into the open for a number of reasons. First, we must recognize that the business of creating analogies to represent experience is unavoidable and necessary. The very act of communicating with other people during the greatest part of our waking hours—some claim eighty percent of the time—inevitably creates idealized notions and assumptions about what is essential to communication and what is not. Obviously there is a tremendous difference between assumptions that bear out reality and those that give a grossly distorted impression of the requirements of effectual communication. Hence, much is to be gained by bringing the underlying assumptions into the open. We need to examine them in large measure because images constitute a set of ground rules for the way we handle ourselves and the way we interpret our communicative activities. Ordinarily, the ground rules are only vaguely understood, yet they are the determinants of communication and its adjudged significance.

For example, the notion of gaps and breakdowns automatically portrays communicative activity as a directional and linear sequence of events—much like electronic impulses traveling from beginning to end in a telephone system or digital computer. Once this linear, one-way analogy is accepted, it is almost impossible not to think of communicative difficulties as a result of some malfunctioning that occurs along the line. To correct a breakdown, one is tempted to search for the part or element that needs repair, much as a telephone repairman looks for a break in circuits along a row of telephone lines (Smith, 1970). Even worse, communication tends to be defined in all-or-nothing terms: Either the system works or it does not; the signals arrive at their destination, or they are blocked somewhere along the line. Running through the previous quotations about communication breakdown is an implicit and mistaken notion that "no" communication occurred. Supposedly, whenever people fail to arrive at an identical point of view, we can merely assume that they have—almost by definition— "failed to communicate." For example, the teenagers all spoke of certain "barriers" or "obstacles" that prevented *any* communication, even though a good deal of verbal exchange took place. And the editor used absolute terms when he referred to people as being "incapable of communicating" and to the "failure of communication" as though it were some "rare" or "impossible" state to achieve. As a consequence, those with an interest in improving communication are led to search for barriers, obstacles, gaps, and roadblocks that prevent communication from taking place . . . .

Communication does not necessarily stop simply because people stop talking or listening. To the contrary. The teenager who complained about his parents still "got the message," which he interpreted to be his parents' indifference and lack of respect.

The switchboard image also has consequences that need to be examined. Again, the tendency is to regard aspects of interpersonal relationships in technological terms that are, we presume, amenable to mechanical repair. Thus, if people feel isolated and lost, the answer is clear: Give them the enormous resources of computers (for dating purposes), telephone-answering services (to ensure interpersonal contact), and the mass media (as an outlet for their views). If it is "harder and harder to be heard," let representatives of the silent majority speak out. Never mind the cost of 62,000 dollars for one minute of prime television time; allow the forgotten man to unburden himself before a waiting nation. Similar "remedies" abound in all aspects of human affairs. Theologians can turn to Madison Avenue to create proper commercials on behalf of the church. Even the tough problems of politicians—particularly those lacking a proper image—can be handled by media specialists who know that political commercials are most effective when placed in a nonpolitical setting, next to a newscast if possible. And if the public does not want to hear a particular candidate, there is always the "voice over" technique, where the screen shows only a political problem—a polluted river or a crowded ghetto—and the candidate's face is never seen nor his voice heard. There are techniques for creating "canned spontaneity" and, with the help of a good lighting man, an image of warmth and congeniality.

But a less obvious problem with the switchboard concept is that of getting man to accept the switchboard as an extension of his self-image. All too often we are prone to regard the switchboard not as an extension of our ears and voice, but as an intrusion, a mechanical beast of burden. It extends us, but not always at the moment of our choosing. It also tyrannizes. The clamoring of the telephone demands instant attention, fractionalizing and dividing other activities, switching out some events while it switches in others. The added irony is that the switchboard itself has caused communication failure. For despite the complexity of a national switchboard system that spans an incredible 700 million miles of wires, cables, microwave relays, switches, and some 500 million billion interconnections, the system can and often does break down. The following account describes the situation well (*Newsweek*, Sept. 29, 1969):

> Using the telephone right now is like plugging into a mystery. Strange sounds, voices, and events greet the phone user each day, especially when he calls during a "peak" hour in any major American city. Dial Kansas City, for example, and you may get San Francisco. Talk several minutes to a friend and you may find yourself suddenly in the middle of somebody else's two-way conversation as well. Instead of a dial tone, there are bongs or gongs. Or perhaps nothing, no sound at all, sometimes for hours. The phone company's official line for such complaints is that the product has gotten too popular for its own good. Thanks to affluence, gabby teenagers, and the company's persuasive ad campaigns—which have convinced Americans, among other things, to long-distance dial rather than write a letter—circuits are overloaded, it says, beyond anybody's wildest forecasts [p. 70].

The breakdown and switchboard images deserve attention for still another, more significant reason. Despite their similarities, the two images presuppose conflicting views of communication. The notion of communication gaps, with its focus on disruption and malfunctioning, is essentially a negative one. On the other hand, the switchboard image is positive in outlook. It accentuates the marvels of technology and the ever-widening range of channels and connections made instantly available by electronic hardware. Taken together, the two images underscore what is a central dilemma, and perhaps irony, of contemporary times: in a period marked by unprecedented possibilities for communication, there is also an unprecedented expression of doubt about whether any "real communication" occurs. In an age of technological triumph and advanced communicative facilities, what William Ellinghaus called "one of the great natural resources," the public has become increasingly conscious of "people talking without speaking, people hearing without listening. . . . " Note that the editor cited earlier viewed communicative failure as the central problem of our day. This view can be seen also in a host of plays, novels, and poems that deal with the dominant themes of the decade: alienation, separateness, isolation, lack of understanding, despair. The irony is that all the questioning is occurring at a time when the advances of technology permit instantaneous, breathtaking view of the moon, and a satellite system makes global television possible by the flick of a dial.

Although the dilemma must be taken seriously, the conflict between the possibilities and limitations of communication may be more apparent than real. Perhaps the public today is generally more sensitive to the requirements of communication and takes them less for granted than in earlier times. Perhaps, too, this increased sensitivity is a direct by-product of our technological advances. On the other hand, some would insist that electronic hardware, switchboards, and relay systems have little to do with people's ability to engage in meaningful interaction on a one-to-one basis. In any case, the disparity between the possibilities and limitations of communication cannot be resolved so long as we attempt to account for it in idealized and abstract terms. Though images may be valuable in establishing the ground rules in our study, they are of little use in accounting for key problems in precise terms. The requirements and possibilities of communication can only be understood by examining what is fundamental to all communicative behavior and by gaining some understanding of the forces that determine the process and outcome of complex communicative events. The first requirement is to shift from a concern with general images of communication to more precise ways of approaching the assumptions underlying the complexities of communicative behavior.

QUESTIONS FOR DISCUSSION

1. Before reading Mortensen's article, would you have described problems in communication in terms of *communication gaps* or *communication breakdowns*? If you answer no, how would you have described such problems? How does your description differ from the *gap* or *breakdown* notion?
2. Do you think that the definition of communication you are using affects your interpretation of the article? Is *communication* a switchboard system? How does the idea of a telephone switchboard fit in with your meaning for the word *communication*?
3. How does *information* relate to *communication*?

References

1. Elegant, R. S. "Americans Can't Communicate," *Seattle Times* (Los Angeles Wireservice, May 17, 1970).
2. Haber, D. "For Whom the Bell Rings . . . and Rings," *New York* Magazine, (November 17, 1969), p. 68.
3. McLuhan, M. *Understanding Media: The Extensions of Man* (New York: McGraw-Hill, 1965).
4. Smith, D. R. "The Fallacy of the Communication Breakdown," *The Quarterly Journal of Speech*, 34 (1970), pp. 343-346.
5. Toole, K. R. *Seattle Times* (March 29, 1970) p. 16.

Before we can examine communication precisely, as Mortensen advocates, we must know something about the process we shall analyze. David Berlo provides an introduction to that knowledge. Berlo suggests that changes in matter or energy characterize all human behaviors. He asks us to view communication as both a *physical* process and a *symbolic* informational process so that we can understand both the physical nature of communication and the ways in which an understanding of communication must go beyond the physical level.

Berlo emphasizes that *information* is fundamentally different from most of the physical things we deal with in life. Meanings and information are not transferred in the physical signal that passes between persons when they communicate. The meanings must already be in the persons in order for communication to occur.

2

HUMAN COMMUNICATION: THE BASIC PROPOSITION

David K. Berlo

Everything man does involves some change in state of matter or energy. Given Mr. Einstein's expression of the relationship between matter and energy ($e = mc^2$) we can use the two terms interchangeably, and simply talk about matter-energy units. Communication includes human acts: therefore, human communication must involve matter-energy units. Yet, as we shall try to demonstrate, human communication cannot be understood unless we transcend matter-energy changes.

Hopefully, the three case studies using figures from your distant past that are described below will clarify for us the relationship between matter-energy and communication, and will emphasize both the "what" and the "why" of communication study.

Case Studies

1. **Run, Jane, Run.** A young woman (Jane) and her dog (Spot) rented a room. The room had a fireplace and a pile of logs. On the first night when Jane arrived home, it was chilly; therefore, she lit one of the logs in order to warm the room. Soon the log no longer existed. Instead, there were ashes, smoke, and the heat that made Jane warm. Jane did not pay any attention to the log while it was burning; how-

David K. Berlo is consultant-trainer for the Center for Communication Analysis in Rockville, Maryland, and is chairman of the Research Strategy Council for Market-Opinion Research in Detroit. This article was originally part of the reading material in an introductory communication course at Michigan State University. It appears in published form for the first time in this book.

ever, in retrospect, she thought that the burning log had been pretty, and she reminded herself to watch it burn the next time.

On the second night Jane was not chilly. Yet, she lit another log so that she could watch it burn. She did watch it and found it a pleasant experience. Meanwhile, across the street, Dick (who lived with his two roommates, Tom and Harry) had noticed each night that (a) sometimes Jane was home and sometimes she wasn't, and (b) sometimes there was smoke coming out of the chimney and sometimes there wasn't, and there was a relationship between presence of smoke and presence of Jane.

On the third night, Jane came home and started her fire. Dick did not see her come home; however, when he saw the smoke coming out of the chimney, he, Tom, and Harry sallied across the street to visit Jane. The four of them enjoyed the visit; however Jane perceived that "three" was, indeed, a crowd. She suggested the use of a blanket to control the smoke in the fireplace by making puffs. Finding that she could make puffs of smoke, she and the men agreed that one puff would stand for Dick, two for Tom, and three for Harry.

On the fourth night, Jane started her fire and used her blanket to make one puff of smoke. Dick saw the call, went over to Jane's alone, and. . . . actually, that's as much as we need to pry in order to analyze the situation for our purposes. What generalizations can we make from a comparison of the four nights?

A commonality across nights was the burning of the log. This change in matter-energy is a process which follows all of the rules of matter-energy change (viz., laws of thermodynamics). We will refer to it as an **action process.** It is necessary to any communication process; however, in itself it is not a communication process. Before we can develop a communication process, two properties have to be imposed on the matter-energy that is transferred. Those properties are *pattern* and *reference*.

Pattern began to become apparent in night two and was clearly apparent in nights three and four. Jane experienced and responded to patterning in the action process. Though she probably could not have described the pattern for anyone, she was reacting to variations in such things as hue and intensity of the light. As pattern is imposed on matter-energy transfers, we say that the action process also begins to become an information process. The burning of the log establishes minimal conditions of pattern or structure; therefore, it is, at best, minimally an **information process.** We can better understand the concept of information process by looking at the second night from Dick's point of view.

Dick did not see the fire, but he did see the smoke. He noticed that sometimes there was smoke and sometimes there was not. Over time, he could have developed a pretty good idea of the odds that there would be smoke, i.e., he could assess the probability of smoke and the probability of no-smoke. But, on night two, he was not limiting himself to observing smoke. He also observed another hunk of matter-energy, Jane. He observed her in two situations: present and nonpresent (again, he could have—but didn't—develop probability statements for each situation). The pattern he observed was: if smoke, then Jane; if no-smoke, then no-Jane. For Dick, we can call the changes in Jane and the log an *information process*; in addition, it was an action process. All information processes are also action processes; however, some action processes are only action processes.

Under what conditions would we use the phrase *information process*? The matter-energy change was separated into discriminable units of matter-energy. Various patternings of those units were specified, and some estimate of the probability of occurrence of each was made, i.e., a statement of the relationship among units was specified. Those are the necessary conditions for an information process; discriminable units of matter-energy, discernment of pattern, statement of the relationship among units.

This idea of information was more intuitively clear on night three. While Jane was enjoying the burning of her log, Dick saw the smoke. He had not seen Jane come home; however, the presence of the smoke gave him information that she was there.

At the risk of ruining an otherwise pleasant evening, let's suggest that the topic of conversation on night three turned to information processes. Dick explained to Jane that what had brought them together really was an explicably patterned matter-energy process. This excited Jane, and she began to explore how she could bring that information process under control, i.e., how she could use it to work for her.

If she were to use the fire—or its smoke—she realized that she must reduce that hunk of matter-energy to discriminable units. Using her blanket, she experimented and found that she could impose a pattern which we shall label as smoke or no-smoke. The state we call smoke was named "puff" by Jane. By imposing the concept of sequence, Jane could make an infinite series of puffs. When she and the men agreed that each puff would stand for or represent a different man, she had brought the action process under her control and could use it as a tool.

If we introduce a few concepts, we may terminate this discussion shortly. Let us agree that the matter-energy called Dick is the **referent** of the matter-energy called "one puff." We say that the puff refers to the man. When one unit of matter-energy refers to another, we call the first one a **symbol**. Given these terms, we can specify the minimal conditions under which we shall refer to a process as a **communication process**.

Communication is a process involving the transfer of matter-energy that carries symbolic information. That statement has many implications. For example, it implies that communication is always *about* something, i.e., that the matter-energy units refer to some other set of matter-energy. That is what is meant when we say that communication is vicarious experience or second-hand information.

Another implication is that communication is only one source of information. Dick obtained information through direct observation of smoke (present-absent) and Jane (present-absent). The fire certainly wasn't communicating with Dick, and, at that time, neither was Jane. In addition to the information Dick obtained when he saw smoke, Jane communicated with him via smoke when she called him. The presence of smoke *signalled* the presence of Jane. The occurence of one puff *symbolized* Dick.

A third implication is that all communication involves matter-energy transfer, and the patterning of that matter-energy. All behavior involves changes in matter-energy; however, *only some behavior is patterned explicably* (i. e., carries information), and *only some informational behavior is communicative.* That implication places the study of communication in some perspective vis-à-vis the study of behavior. It also implies that any matter-energy transfer could become informational if pattern were imposed; furthermore, any matter-energy transfer could become communicative if reference for pattern were imposed. To put it differently, we can communicate through any matter-energy, but we don't.

If you can analyze the following situation, you have grasped the main points. On the fifth day, Dick and Jane sallied forth for a picnic in the woods. They arrived in a small clearing, surrounded by tall pines. They made a fire to cook hot dogs. After the fire began to burn well, Dick sat back to enjoy watching it. He was quite surprised a few minutes later when a truckload of forest rangers arrived, with shovels and sand, to put out the fire. While assuring them that the smoke had not signalled a fire out of control, he was even more surprised when a pair of Indians appeared out of the woods and asked, "You called?"

It was at that point that Dick turned to Jane and said, "_____,_____,_____."[1]

2. **The Upset Coffee Upset**. Miss A is seated at a coffee table, pouring coffee for Mr. B and Mr. C. Mr. B leans across the table to reach the sugar. His arm hits a book which is standing on the table. The book falls on Mr. C's coffee cup. The cup falls off the table, and hot coffee is spilled on Mr. C's leg. Mr. C jumps, frowns, and says to Mr. B, "You stupid #$%;ct&@#."[2] Mr. B says, very quietly, "I'm terribly sorry." Meanwhile, on hearing Mr. C, Miss A blushes.

The problem is to account for this sequence of events. The first principle we use is direct matter-energy transfer. Setting technical details aside, we probably would agree that the energy in B's arm movement accounts for the energy in the book's movement (a straightforward example of energy transfer). Similarly, the book's movement can account for the change in the coffee cup, and the coffee can account for Mr. C's jumping behavior, although some would quarrel at that point with matter-energy transfer as a sufficient principle. Whether or not one believes that the coffee can account for the jump, one can agree that the energy in the coffee is not sufficient to account for Mr. C's frown, and certainly not sufficient to account for his production of the sounds, "You stupid #$%;ct&@#." Though there is some relationship between the amount of energy in the coffee and the energy used by the facial muscles (frown) and larynx, something else is needed to account for the frowning and talking. There was an interaction between the energy being transferred and the energy already existing in Mr. C.

Matter-energy transfer can be thought of as a sequence of actions, e.g., the falling of a row of dominoes. The energy input to a domino, when corrected for the mass of the domino, correctly predicts the energy output. Information processes do not allow such a simple set of predictions. For one thing, information occupies no space, has no mass. It is the transference of arrangement, of pattern. Information must be processed, and the energy outputs of the processor are a joint function of energy inputs and energy elicited from the processor by the information. To phrase it more simply, what a processor does is attributable to (a) the energy in what was done to it, and (b) the energy in the processor that was elicited by the information received. Information processing is more complex than matter-energy transfer. Sometimes the matter-energy being transferred accounts for much of the next event, sometimes for very little.

When the process becomes communication, it still requires matter-energy transfer; however, the amount of matter-energy being transferred is a very poor predictor of the next event. For example, one would not be very successful in predicting Mr. B's, "I'm sorry" from a matter-energy analysis of Mr. C's, "You stupid #$%;ct&@#." To understand communication processes, one must understand the matter-energy characteristics—and the patterning—of the processors as well as of that which is being transferred. And the information or patterning (in both message and processor) accounts for most of the subsequent events.

When I point out that the amount of matter-energy being transferred is a trivial predictor of the consequences of communication, I do not mean to imply that it is an irrelevant factor. The communication engineer is extremely interested in the fidelity of patterning and therefore is interested in the permanence and inflexibility of the matter-energy units being used. The economist of communication, interested in the efficiency of the system, is concerned with minimizing the amount of matter-energy being transferred to cut down on cost. Finally, the characteristics of the matter-energy being transferred do affect the nature of the information. As McLuhan correctly argues, the medium (i.e., matter-energy units) does affect the message (patterning or information).

Our third case study, hopefully, will clarify what is involved in analyzing the processor of communicative information and will lead to the basic proposition underlying human communication.

3. **Information Is Different from Most Other Commodities.** Let's suppose there is a pile of lead bricks in Bin A. Let's suppose there is also Bin B, and it is empty. You are given the task of getting the bricks from Bin A to Bin B.

This is an intellectually simple problem of moving hard-goods merchandise. Though it might entail large practical problems, theoretically it simply is a movement of matter-energy. It involves three steps: packaging, shipping, and receiving. The bricks must be removed from Bin A (packaging); they must be shipped (transferred, conveyed, moved, gotten across, or shipped by any of several other devices); they must be received and placed inside Bin B.

This is the nature of a matter-energy process involving movement of hard goods. The bricks were bricks when in Bin A, they remained intact during shipment, and they were still bricks when in Bin B. The matter-energy was equivalent in all three stages.

Let's suppose that a further restriction was given, namely, that the bricks could not be removed from Bin A in their present form. Given a fire under Bin A, a mold in Bin B, and a pipe through which the melted lead could flow, you still could transfer the bricks. The matter-energy during shipment would differ from the matter-energy in Bins A and B; however, principles of transformation of matter-energy provide a specific set of instructions which enable us to relate the matter-energy in the bins directly to the matter-energy in the pipe.

Now, let's change the problem. Bin A becomes Person A, Bin B becomes Person B, and the lead bricks become an idea that Mr. A has. His assignment is to get that idea into Mr. B. How is he going to do that?

The typical response is to define this problem as analogous to the first one, and to attempt to handle it the same way. We talk about packaging an idea. We talk about conveying it, getting it across, transferring it, or moving it. We talk about getting an idea or receiving it or implanting it in somebody's head. At times, we even talk about pounding it in. Typically, we talk about communication as if it involves somebody doing something to somebody else. Traditionally, we have looked on a communicative act as analogous either to a hypodermic needle, sticking information into somebody, or a dump truck, dropping information into somebody.

All of these metaphors, and many more, are consistent with the basic assumption that communication is only a transfer of matter-energy, and that information can be treated as any other commodity. That assumption is fallacious. Of course, matter-energy is transferred in communication, but there is little or no (usually, no) relationship between the matter-energy being transferred and the matter-energy inside the communicant. For example, there is nothing catlike about c a t, nothing beautiful about b e a u t y. It would not be productive to compare matter-energy inside my head as I write this, yours while you read, and that energy on the page itself. There is no relationship between the mass of a word and its effect or utility. In short, information is a commodity that can be moved around; however, that is not the defining condition of a communication process.

What is the defining condition? **Symbolic information:** *the patterning of matter-energy with reference.* Both the awareness of pattern and the awareness of referent are within the human who is processing the message. The significance or meaningfulness of a message does not lie in the message-medium, does not lie in the matter-energy. The meaning of a message lies within the participant, the person processing the message. To put it more simply, *meanings are not in words–they are in the people who use them.* Significance is only found in the eye of the beholder, the mind of the communicator.

Information, then, is different from most commodities in that it is a *potential.* Like electricity or human labor, it can be bought and sold, but only as a potential. A communicative act does not *transport* an idea—it *elicits* an idea from the receiver of the message. A communicative act does not consist of choosing the right word (the word that conveys the intended meaning), shipping the word and its meaning, and dumping both into the receiver. A communicative act consists of (a) selecting a set of matter-energy units which one participant uses to represent or stand for a set of references, patterning those units and transmitting them, and (b) receiving the patterned matter-energy units and assigning meaning to the units and their pattern.

Matter-energy is transferred. Pattern is transferred. Significance for that pattern is not transferred. Meanings for the matter-energy units are not transferred. Meanings are in people, and they are not transferable, not conveyable. Why? Because the only thing that can be conveyed is patterned matter-energy, and that is only arbitrarily related to what is going on inside each individual's head.

If meanings are in people, where do they come from? They come from experience. They are learned, personal, private. The meanings I have can only be understood in terms of the experiences I have had. Meaning is relative. It can be assumed that no two persons ever have exactly the same experience; therefore, no two persons ever have exactly the same meaning. Furthermore, each individual constantly is experiencing; therefore, no one person can ever have exactly the same meaning for anything at two different points in time.

This, then, is the basic communication proposition. Everything *is* relative. Relativity theory applies not only to physics, it applies to all of man's behavior. Meanings are in people, not in the matter-energy units they exchange. Meanings are dynamic, constantly under change, both within and between persons. Communication involves a transfer of matter-energy, but not a transfer of ideas, of meanings. Meanings can't be conveyed; ideas can't be "gotten across." You can't put ideas *into* people. Everything *is* relative.

The proposition that significance or meaning lies within the human and is experientially based has a very large number of serious implications for the nature of human behavior. We'll analyze several of them from time to time. For now, let's review a few of the more basic ones.

1. *The probability of perfect communication is zero.* All communication has less than perfect fidelity. If meanings are in people and come from experience, and if no two persons can have exactly the same experience and, therefore, the same meaning, then you and I can never mean the same about anything.

2. *There are prerequisites to meaningful communication relationships.* Sometimes we argue that anybody should be able to communicate with anybody if he is talented enough. Not so. Some commonality of

experience is a prerequisite to meaningful communication. If you and I share nothing, we shall not share meanings for any matter-energy unit.

3. *The meanings you want others to have must be in them*– before *you communicate*. If words can't carry meaning, I cannot select a word that will carry the "right" meaning. Rather, I must try to select symbols that will elicit from another the meaning I want elicited. To elicit such a meaning, it must be in the other individual prior to our moment of contact.

4. *You can't "tell it like it is."* As Einstein informed us, the observer is inherently a part of any observation. In observing, my own meanings are imposed on the data I observe. In communicating, my own meanings are instrumental in selecting particular matter-energy units and their patterns. At best, the only way I can tell it is as I see it. No one with any information can be completely objective because information itself introduces bias into the system. To put it differently, the only way to have a completely open mind is to have an empty head.

5. *The objectives of the poet, the journalist, the scientist, and the artist are quite similar.* Traditionally, we have looked at the poet and other artists as men who attempted to *create* reality, and we have looked at the journalist and the scientist as men who *discovered* and reported reality. But, if meanings are in people, and everything is relative, then reality can't be discovered; it must be created. What's real to you is real, to you. What's real to me is real, to me. And the question, "What's *really* real?" is nonsense.

6. *All knowledge gained through communication should be accepted only tentatively.* If you can't tell it like it is, then you can't hear it like it was. The Aristotelian notion of truth is not useful. "To say of what it is that it is, or to say of what is not that it is not, is true" doesn't help much if we accept the proposition that we can't "say of what is that it is." Every time information passes through human hands, it is altered. Reports that you receive have been altered by everyone involved in their preparation. The notion of a fixed reality external to man, awaiting discovery and available for complete and accurate reporting, is a fallacious notion. The only permanence is change. Thomas Wolfe said it: You can't go home again. Heraclitus said it: You can't step in the same river twice—the river isn't the same, your foot isn't the same, the context isn't the same, nothing is ever the same.

SUMMARY

This article has considered some of the implications of the basic communication proposition including the intellectual and philosophical context of our study of the processes of human communication. An awareness of that context and implementation of its implications should produce caution in communicating, tentativeness in acceptance or rejection of ideas, a tolerance for ambiguity and change, an openness in interpersonal relationships, a careful monitoring of those given the power to operate communication institutions and machinery—and a greater awareness of the interdependence of men.

QUESTIONS FOR DISCUSSION

1. What does Berlo mean by an *action process*?
2. What is necessary in order to change an action process into an *information process*? Why?
3. Is an information process necessarily a *communication process*? What is needed to make it a communication process? Why?
4. A currently popular phrase says that you *cannot not communicate*. Discuss this phrase in terms of Berlo's definition and discussion of communication. How would you have to define communication in order for the phrase to be correct?
5. Can information be transferred directly from person A to person B as one would move a pile of bricks? Why not? Be specific and show that you understand why this cannot be done.
6. What is transferred between persons during communication? What is *not* transferred?
7. How do meanings get inside of people?

NOTES

1.   How did you fill in the blanks? If you said "Run, Jane, run," ask yourself how the discussion we've just concluded would help explain that choice of words.

2.   "#$%;ct&@#" is used as a substitute for a sequence of four-letter words. To those who might question my artistic integrity or physical courage in making the decision to use a substitute, let me at least cite my three reasons: (1) the popularity of any given set of obscenities is transient, and the use of substitutes allows for the essay a possibility of timelessness; (2) some readers might be offended at a particular set, and this permits them to avoid recall; (3) readers who enjoy four-letter words are given a chance to participate in the essay by choosing any particular grouping that is satisfying to them.

Meanings are not in words. They are in the people who use those words. Meanings cannot be transferred directly between persons. Only messages, patterned matter energy, can be transferred. While you may (or may not) be willing to agree with those statements at this point, it is unlikely that you have the same meaning for them that Berlo has. If meanings are in people, and must be there before communication can occur, how do the meanings get there? And why doesn't the pattern that forms the message have meaning in it?

David Bender and John Hocking discuss the question of how meanings get inside people and why messages do not contain meaning. Their article is written in the form of a dialogue between two persons who hold "typical male attitudes" toward females, which provides much of the humor of the article. Some may be offended by the opinions expressed, and the method of expression, especially members of the feminist movement. If you feel offended when you read it, recall that in the early days of the civil rights movement, films of such great actors as Stepin Fetchit were not shown, and if they were shown, one was expected not to laugh. It is a sign of the maturity of the civil rights movement that black actors such as Fetchit can be applauded and enjoyed once again. The stereotype of the characters he represented can now be separated from the quality of his performances. A similar distinction should be made between the attitudes toward women of the characters in the following dialogue, and the value of their comments in the interest of an increased understanding of communication.

3

COMMUNICATION:
YOU ARE WHAT'S HAPPENED TO YOU
AND I CAN TELL BY WHAT YOU SAY

A dialogue in THREE ACTS

David C. L. Bender and John E. Hocking

ACT I

Setting: A tavern. Two men are seated side-by-side at the bar. To their left is a table at which a young woman is sitting. She is drinking gin and tonic. The men are drinking beer.

Louie: No, I really don't think she's good-looking.

John: You've got to be kidding. That's one of the best-looking women I've ever seen.

Louie: Well, then, it's obvious you've never seen any good-looking women.

John: Are you kidding? Have you ever seen my ex-wife?

Louie: Well, I wasn't going to say anything about her, but my statement still holds: you don't know what true good looks are.

John: I suppose you do.

Louie: Damn right I do. Did you see the woman I was with last night?

John: (Guffaws, slaps his thigh) This woman sitting behind us is ten times better looking than the girl you were with last night.

David C. L. Bender is instructor of communication at Rutgers, State University of New Jersey. John E. Hocking is assistant professor of speech communication, University of Georgia. This dialogue was originally part of the reading material in an introductory communication course at Michigan State University. It appears in published form for the first time in this book.

Louie: You know, John, I just can't understand this; you're normally a pretty reasonable person, and yet you don't recognize true beauty.

John: O.K., stud, what *is* true beauty?

Louie: Well, if you don't know . . .

John: I know. I'm not sure you do.

Louie: All right. True beauty, for example, is epitomized by the woman I was with last night.

John: So what makes you the expert on true beauty? Who are you to say what true beauty is or isn't?

Louie: I've obviously had more experience than you.

John: Horsefeathers. I've had just as much experience as you. Maybe more.

Louie: Well, if we've both had all this experience with true beauty, then why do we disagree about what true beauty is?

John: Well, for one thing, you know what they say: "Beauty is in the eye of the beholder."

Louie: What's that supposed to mean? Here we are trying to resolve an issue and you lay a cliché on me. Eye of the beholder, hell; beauty is in the body of the beheld.

John: If that's true, then we'd agree about whether or not that woman over there is beautiful.

Louie: If what you're saying is true, then there wouldn't *be* any true beauty.

John: Damn straight. Beauty is subjective. Beauty exists only in people's minds.

Louie: Now I've heard it all! You mean to sit there and tell me that beauty is different for you and for me?

John: Sure it is. Because of our different *past experiences*, we *perceive* things differently, we have different *expectations*, we have different *beliefs*, different *attitudes*, and different *values*.

Louie: How could having different past experiences make us perceive the same thing differently? If it's the same thing, we'll see it the same.

John: Not if we've had different past experiences with the thing or other things like it. If we go over to the baseball field right now and I pitch you some batting practice, what will you do?

Louie: Put a few over the fence for you.

John: You'd stand right up at the plate and swing away?

Louie: Sure.

John: And what if I all of a sudden burn one in and whap you in the ear with it?

Louie: What if you did?

John: Yeah. How would you perceive the situation then?

Louie: What do you mean?

John: Well, would you want to stand right up at the plate and swing away some more?

Louie: Maybe not right away. I might be a little shaky at first.

John: Why?

Louie: Because you just hit me on the ear with the baseball.

John: So you'd perceive the situation differently the next time you got up there? You'd perceive the situation as potentially dangerous?

Louie: I guess so.

John: Well, in the same way that you would perceive this situation differently before and after catching a baseball in the ear, any two different people, one of whom recently had been hit by a baseball and the other of whom had not, would perceive this situation differently at the same time, because of their different past experiences.

Louie: I guess that makes sense. You mean I'd perceive the situation differently after I got hit by the ball because getting hit had become a part of my past experiences by the time I got back up to the plate.

John: That's right. And as long as we're talking about baseball, have you ever seen a player argue with an umpire's decision in an important situation even when it was obvious to everyone else that the call was correct? The player *wants* the call to go the other way so badly that he might actually have perceived it differently from the umpire. I remember one case where a player even swore to his teammates that a called third strike was a ball. Later, when he was shown a videotape of the pitch, which was right down the middle, he couldn't believe it. He wanted it to be a ball so badly that he had *actually* perceived it to be a ball.

Louie: What you're saying is that what people *want* to see or *expect* to see can affect perceptions. Can't temporary moods affect perception too, like if I'm angry I might tend to perceive that someone else is trying to start an argument with me?

John: Right. The important point is that no two people have the exact same past experiences, so *everybody* perceives *everything* differently from everyone else. You know why I perceive that woman over there as good-looking?

Louie: I can't imagine.

John: Because she reminds me of Judy Collins. I sat in the front row at a Judy Collins concert one night and fell in love with my ex-wife. It was beautiful. Judy Collins was beautiful.

Louie: She doesn't look like Judy Collins to me. She kind of reminds me of Wanda Martin.

John: Who's Wanda Martin?

Louie: She was this girl who dumped on me when I was a senior in high school.

John: Y'see? You had a *negative* past experience with somebody who looked like that woman over there. You don't think she's good-looking. I had a *positive* experience associated with someone who looks like her. I think she's good-looking. A clear case of our past experiences shaping the way we perceive reality. See, like I told you, everybody's reality is different.

Louie: Well, that could explain part of it, I guess. What you're saying, then, is that these different past experiences get in the way of our perceiving "True Reality."

John: No, no, no. You're missing the point. Absolute true reality isn't there to *be* misperceived. Reality *is* what we perceive, and we all perceive it differently. Nobody's reality is any more or less legitimate than anybody else's.

Louie: That's a little heavy for me, especially since we're already on our ninth pitcher.

John: Look, since everybody has different past experiences, and since everybody perceives things differently, then *nobody* can say what *really* exists, what true reality is.

Louie: So you're saying that when we perceive our environment—all the people and horses and all the things they do—that your senses and my senses get it differently because of what's happened to us before? Because of the way we've perceived things in the past?

John: Right.

Louie: Now wait a minute, John. I believe that everyone has had different past experiences and I believe that because of this, everyone perceives the world differently. But don't we pretty much agree on many aspects of reality, especially if it's some aspect that we can directly observe?

John: What do you mean?

Louie: I mean that it seems that just about everyone agrees on things that are *empirically verifiable*. For example, these barstools we're sitting on are about three feet high. If you perceived them to be one foot high, we could easily measure them and determine that your perception of reality with respect to these barstools was wrong. Yet you've said that absolute true reality isn't there to be misperceived; what we perceive *is* reality. But the person who thought these barstools were one foot high would be misperceiving reality.

John: All right, I see what you're getting at and it's a good point. What we need to do to clarify this is to make a distinction between *agreed-upon* reality, and *absolute* reality. Most people in our culture have had a similar experience in that they have learned what a "foot" is. They also agree on what "height" is and would agree on what procedures are appropriate for measuring an object like a barstool. Since most everyone who has had these similar experiences *agrees* that barstools are three feet high, three-foot high barstools are reality for these people.

Louie: But not absolute reality?

John: Right, only agreed-upon reality. What if I said that I perceived the barstool to be one foot high?

Louie: You'd be wrong. People would think you're even weirder than you are.

John: Come on now, I'm being serious. What if I was surrounded by a bunch of people who all thought barstools were one foot high?

Louie: You'd all be wrong.

John: But, what if we were all twelve feet tall and had different standards for what a "foot" was? *Our* reality that *we* agreed on would be that these things you and I are sitting on are one foot high. •

Louie: I think I'm confused.

John: All right, in Columbus's time the world was thought to be flat. Just about everyone agreed on it. If you asked someone, "Sir, I'm doing a project for my communication class; could you tell me whether the world is flat or round?" they no doubt would have said that it was flat. In fact, they might have thought you pretty strange for even asking a question that suggested the possibility that the world might not be flat. For *them*, reality was a flat world and they had no way to know otherwise. In the fifteenth century, reality was a flat world. Note: not absolute reality but agreed-upon reality. Now *our* reality today—the one *we* agree on—is that the world is round, and it's hard to imagine anything that could happen to change this belief. But how do we know that many things that we agree to be true or real now won't be false in the future? We have no way of knowing that the reality that we agree on is true in any *absolute* sense.

Louie: OK, but how does this relate to my question about misperceiving reality?

John: It's necessary that we *agree* on a lot of things just to get along in the world. However, if *one* individual perceived some aspect of reality in one way, and everyone else perceived it another way, that wouldn't make it any less real for that one individual. But if what that one person perceived was radically different from what the majority perceived, the majority would say that this perception was wrong. This, of course, wouldn't make the reality that the majority perceived true or right in any absolute sense.

Louie: So if someone in the fifteenth century said that the world was round, he would have been wrong.

John: Right. He would be wrong in that he disagreed with agreed-upon reality. It's kind of like the mentally ill person who thinks he's Napoleon. *His* perception is that he really *is* Napoleon and it is no less real to him than is the perception of another person that he is *not* Napoleon. But because the would-be Napoleon's perception disagrees with the majority, he is defined as "sick."

Louie: So what you're saying is that even though reality is relative, that is, it is different for everyone, there is a sense in which we can talk about "wrong" perceptions of reality.

John: Right, but these situations are usually when the aspect of reality being "misperceived" is pretty much universally agreed on by most people.

Louie: And this usually occurs when the aspect of reality in question is directly observable, like the height of barstools.

John: Exactly.

Louie: Hey, it's about time for another pitcher, isn't it?

John: I don't know, Lou; we've already drunk nine. Nine pitchers is a lot of beer.

Louie: Not to me it isn't. I drink fifteen or sixteen every night. How many do you usually drink?

John: Only about five or six.

Louie: Well, that proves your point. Because of our past beer-drinking experiences, we have different perceptions of how much beer is a lot.

John: Lou, you're catching on. It's a matter of opinion how much beer is a lot of beer. People tend to agree much less on what *opinions* are correct or true than they do on things like how tall barstools are. It becomes kind of nebulous to talk about *agreed-upon* reality, let alone *absolute* reality, in terms of things like how much beer is a lot.

Louie: You know, that's funny; I guess it doesn't really matter. You think six pitchers is a lot of beer. I think sixteen pitchers is a lot of beer.

John: What do you mean, it doesn't matter?

Louie: I mean who's to say which one of us is right? Who's to say what *is* a lot of beer?

John: *Anybody* can say what is a lot of beer; and, for them, that *is* a lot of beer.

Louie: But, on the other hand, so what? I mean, it's kind of trivial: what's a lot of beer?

John: Or for that matter, how good-looking that girl is. But there are a lot more important things that work the same way. Like values, for instance.

Louie: You mean like a special on Budweiser?

John: No. A *value* is a generalized idea about what's right and wrong. And people have different values, too, because of their different past experiences.

Louie: What do you mean, a generalized idea of what's right and wrong?

John: Well, you could have an idea of good and bad that would apply across many situations. For example, you might think that honesty is a positive quality. That kind of general notion would be a value that you hold.

Louie: You mean a value is like when a person thinks that the Republican Party has a good philosophy, and he applies that to several situations.

John: Right. That would be a value.

Louie: But other people think that the Republican Party philosophy isn't at all worthwhile.

John: And those two types of people would obviously disagree about Republicanism as a value. And do you know where they get those differing values?

Louie: Sure, they think about it and they make their decision.

John: Well, maybe. But, with only a few exceptions, people whose parents are Republicans end up being Republicans, too. And people whose parents are Democrats end up being Democrats.

Louie: In other words, we're back to past experiences.

John: Right. And you obviously can't control who your parents are, or, for that matter, what *most* of your past experiences are. So how can you fault someone for having a different value from yours? Did you ever stop to wonder why there are so many Communists in the U.S.S.R.? Or why there are so many Catholics in Italy? Or why so many people who are paroled from prisons don't share our values for honesty and the sanctity of human life?

Louie: Don't tell me; those people hold those values because they're the values they've mainly been exposed to in their past experiences?

John: You got it. And if that's true, how can you fault someone for having a value different from yours?

Louie: All right, so our perceptions, values, and realities differ because we've had different past experiences. Why is it important to know this?

John: Look: If you believe that something is true *just* because you believe it, and you don't know why you believe it, that belief is dangerous.

Louie: I don't understand.

John: Well, lots of times people believe things just because they've always believed them, they've always known them to be true. The belief is so deeply ingrained in them that they've never even thought it might not be true. They've never questioned the belief. They believe it because . . . well, because they believe it.

Louie: OK, but why is that kind of a belief dangerous?

John: Because it's not subject to change. Things that you believe on faith are beyond your control to a large extent. On the other hand, if you recognize that you believe what you believe because of experiences you've had, such a belief is much more rational and under your own control.

Louie: Do you mean that we should be aware of how the environment affects us? Of how people and events shape our beliefs and values?

John: Exactly. If we know how all the many and varied influences that are impinging on us *affect us*, we're much less at the mercy of things beyond our control.

Louie: I'm not sure I understand.

John: OK, let's say that you are strongly opposed to nudity and sex in movies—as many people are—and you don't know why you are, just that you *are*. It's not very likely that you are going to change your views. On the other hand, if you understood why you felt the way you did, and that the only difference between you and someone else who disagreed with you was different past experiences, you'd be less likely to think your values were real, true values, and theirs were false and wrong. Maybe you grew up in a small, conservative town where everyone was against sex in movies, and the other person grew up in a city where there was a more liberal atmosphere. Each of you would have different values because the people you grew up with influenced you. But since you understood why you held the values you did, you'd be more likely to rationally question your position and possibly change your view. On the other hand, your examination might make you even more certain that your values are best and leave you in a better position to defend them.

Louie: And if the person who said sex in the movies was OK understood where his value came from, he would be less likely to be dogmatic or closed-minded in believing that his values were *the* "true" values.

John: Right! Both people have the right to their values. The reality that each experiences is different and who's to say which reality is correct or true?

Louie: So you're saying that if we realize that the only difference between these differing values and realities is different past experiences we are likely to be more tolerant of the view of others and more open-minded in questioning what we believe. Does this mean that if I run across someone who has a value that's different from mine, I should leave them alone? Even if it's one of my really important values?

John: Well, there's nothing wrong with trying to *change* their value, and thus become part of their past experiences. But whether they change or not, their value is still their value. It's a product of their past experiences, and they have every right to hold that value, without anyone passing judgments on the legitimacy of that value.

Louie: Good sermon there, Father John. But don't a lot of people behave as if their values are the only true values?

John: Well, nobody would hold the values they hold if they didn't think they were good values, right values. The problems come when people fail to recognize: one, that past experiences are the source of the reality they perceive and the values they hold; two, that everyone's past experiences are different; and three, therefore, no one should judge anyone else as a good or a bad person just because they perceive things differently or hold different values. Like the man said, there are no *absolute* right ways or wrong ways. There are just different ways.

Louie: Who said that?

John: I was afraid you'd ask. I did. Just now.

Louie: I'll drink to it anyway.

Curtain

ACT II

Setting: The following evening. John and Louie are again seated at the bar. John is reading the evening paper. They are on their fourth pitcher. The girl is not there.

John: I'll be damned.

Louie: What's that?

John: (reads aloud) "Dog Bites Man." You know, people shouldn't be allowed to have German shepherds.

Louie: Huh?

John: Says right here, "Dog Bites Man." I'm just saying I don't believe people should have German shepherds. They're always biting somebody.

Louie: What makes you so sure it was a German shepherd?

John: Well, it's right here in black and white: "Dog Bites Man." It's obvious to anyone who can read what happened: a German sheperd savagely attacked and bit a man. See for yourself. (Hands Louie the paper.)

Louie: (after reading the story) It doesn't tell what kind of a dog it was.

John: Are you telling me I can't read?

Louie: Maybe you can read too well. You seem to be reading something that isn't even there.

John: All I know is that when it says, "Dog Bites Man," it means a German shepherd.

Louie: It doesn't mean German shepherd. *You* mean German shepherd.

John: That's ridiculous. The source of the true meaning is in those words, right in front of your face.

Louie: If that's true, how come, when I read the same words, I don't get the same meaning you get?

John: I guess some people just don't know the true meaning of words.

Louie: Words don't *have* any meaning in themselves, let alone a *true* meaning.

John: Of course they do. If meanings aren't in words, then where are they?

Louie: In people. Meanings are in people, not words. People use words to represent things. Words are only *symbols* for things, not the things themselves. Words are like eagles.

John: Wanna run that by me again?

Louie: You know the eagle is the national bird of the United States? Well, it kind of *stands for* the United States, right? So when people look at an eagle, they're supposed to think of the United States.

John: Yeah?

Louie: Well, words are the same way. When I say certain words, you're supposed to think of what the words stand for. Like when I say, "I'm the greatest," what do you think of?

John: Muhammad Ali.

Louie: You think of *him*, right?

John: Yeah.

Louie: You don't think of the words, "I'm the greatest," right? You don't get a picture in your mind of the words, "I'm the greatest" on some big theater marquee, do you?

John: No.

Louie: Well, that's how words work. They stand for something else. They refer to something. You don't picture the words; you picture a prize fighter with arms uplifted, wearing boxing gloves.

John: So you're saying meanings are in people? And you're saying that's because words don't have meanings in themselves—people have meanings. So when people hear or see words, it triggers these meanings.

Louie: Right. Meanings are in people, not in words.

John: It's about time for another pitcher, isn't it?

Louie: It certainly is. We could use another pitcher.

John: At least that's one word that has meaning for both of us. Bartender, another pitcher over here.

Louie: Oh, *that* kind of pitcher. I thought you were talking about the guy on TV over there who just gave up two home runs and a double.

John: No, dummy. When I said, "pitcher," the word meant "beer pitcher"!

Louie: No, *you* meant beer pitcher. The word didn't mean anything. You've just illustrated the point I was making a minute ago. Meanings are in people, not in words. You used the symbol "pitcher" to mean one thing, and I thought it meant something else. If meanings were in words, then we wouldn't have misunderstandings or failures in communication like that one.

John: Hmmm.

Louie: Remember last night when you were talking about how everybody perceives the same things differently? How everyone's reality is different?

John: Yeah, because of their past experiences. But I don't see the relevance of that discussion to this one.

Louie: Don't you think words and symbols are parts of your past experiences? You can perceive things directly, or you can perceive them symbolically.

John: Like if you'd describe a girl to me that I'd never seen, I'd be perceiving her symbolically.

Louie: Right, but the important thing is that however you perceive things—whether directly or symbolically—you perceive them differently from everyone else.

John: It seems like using symbols must be about as complicated as trying to agree on whether or not somebody is good-looking.

Louie: It's even *more* complicated. We have different past experiences with things, and we have different past experiences with symbols. So when we use symbols to represent things, we have probably twice as much chance for disagreement.

John: So communication, or using symbols to transfer our meanings for things, is likely to cause even more disagreement between two people than when we look at the things or events themselves.

Louie: Right, except for one thing: Communication is not the transfer of meaning, it's only the transfer of symbols. No matter how closely you look at a symbol, or how hard you think about it, it still has no meaning in itself. The meaning is in the person who says or writes the symbol and in the person who hears or sees the symbol. Those meanings are always different, because the source and the receiver have had different past experiences associated with those symbols and the things they stand for.

John: Wait a minute, Louie. Hold it. Let me ask you one question.

Louie: Shoot.

John: Are we communicating right now?

Louie: Sure.

John: OK, then, you've just said that because of our different past experiences, that we perceive everything differently and that everybody has different meanings for symbols, right?

Louie: Right.

John: And we're using symbols right now, right?

Louie: Right.

John: Then, because meanings are in people, we can't be communicating, right?

Louie: Wrong.

John: That's inconsistent, and you know it. I got you now.

Louie: Well, there's one thing I haven't made clear. I'm saying we can't communicate *perfectly*. I'm *not* saying we can't communicate.

John: Explain.

Louie: Remember that woman who was in here last night?

John: Sure.

Louie: Well, when I just used the symbol "woman," you knew what I was talking about, right?

John: Of course. Everyone knows what a woman is.

Louie: Then you knew what it was I intended to communicate to you, right?

John: Well, yes. At least I *think* I know what you intended to communicate to me.

Louie: Why do you think that's so?

John: I guess we have pretty much the same meaning for the word "woman."

Louie: Right. That's the way I see it, anyway. Even though we can't understand perfectly, we've had enough similar past experiences with the symbol "woman," that we can figure we attach pretty much the same meaning to it.

John: So we haven't had the exact same past experiences, but they've been similar enough that we can get enough agreement so that we can communicate, even though it's not 100 percent agreement.

Louie: Right. Let me see if I can't make it more plain: Say you're a cop, a desk sergeant. And say I call you up at the station, and you answer the phone. What do you say?

John: Hi, Police Station.

Louie: Ummam umma, ggg,ggg.

John: What's the matter, there, sir?

Louie: Aak, aak.

John: Sir, you'll have to speak a little plainer.

Louie: Ugga, ugga, oh, God, it's awful.

John: What's awful, sir? You'll have to tell me what's awful before I can do anything about it.

Louie: Aaarrrgh.

John: Sir, are you hurt?

Louie: No, no. It's my wife.

John: What is it that's the matter with your wife?

Louie: She's choking on a yo-yo.

John: Louie, could we get this example over with?

Louie: I was done anyway.

John: What's the point?

Louie: Well, look, when I called the cops, I knew what was the matter, right?

John: I suppose so.

Louie: But you didn't.

John: No, I didn't.

Louie: But when I got done, you knew.

John: Yeah.

Louie: When I called, it could have been any one of a thousand things. I had to lay some symbols on you to activate your pile of meanings, and they had to be symbols that you had some meanings for.

John: Sure.

Louie: And all that ugga mugga crap when I first called didn't do you any good, even though those things stood for, or represented some of the things that were uppermost in my mind right then. But you didn't understand them.

John: No, I didn't understand them.

Louie: That's because we had never talked before and agreed that whenever I call you and say ugga mugga or whatever, it means my wife is choking on a yo-yo.

John: This is a really great example, Lou. I don't think I've ever heard an example that made anything quite so clear.

Louie: Look, all I'm trying to tell you is that by using symbols for which we both have a common, or agreed-upon, meaning, I can get you to have a meaning more like mine than you had when we started communicating.

John: Yeah?

Louie: Sure. When I first called, you didn't know anything. But when I was choking around, you knew something was the matter. But you didn't know *what* was the matter. So, to reduce that uncertainty what did you do? You asked me what was the matter.

John: Yeah. Well, what the hell'd you expect me to do?

Louie: Just that. And then I choked around some more and you took a stab at what might be the matter; you asked me if I was hurt. I told you, no, it was my wife. At that point you knew more than you had before—I had finally given you some symbols that we had a more or less common meaning for. And then, to reduce your uncertainty even more, you asked me what was the matter with her.

John: Yeah.

Louie: And I told you she was choking. At that point, because I gave you even more symbolic information, you were even less uncertain about what it was that I was perceiving. You were more or less symbolically experiencing the same thing I was, and you weren't even there. I had reduced your uncertainty to the point that, even though you didn't know exactly what was going on, you shared the important parts of the meaning I had for the situation.

John: And so we had communicated.

Louie: But imperfectly.

John: Because you can't transfer meaning, only symbols.

Louie: Exactly. And since we didn't have any common agreement about the gibberish, you had to remind me to use symbols that we'd both had past experiences with. Like "wife" and "choking."

John: Well, I haven't had too many past experiences with choking on a yo-yo, but "wife"—I could tell you things you wouldn't believe.

Louie: This isn't a romance comic book, John; it's a book about communication. Let's try to stick to the subject as much as possible.

John: OK, I'll do my best.

Louie: Let me summarize what I've been telling you. First of all, meanings are in people, not in words. Second, we can communicate, but only imperfectly. Third, when we communicate using symbols, we're trying to reduce uncertainties we have about things. Fourth, symbols don't do us any good if we haven't agreed on their meanings before we try to communicate.

John: I'm not so sure about that last one.

Louie: You don't believe we have to agree about what symbols are going to stand for before we can use them to communicate?

John: I'm not sure. Remember your stupid example about the Police Station?

Louie: Yeah.

John: Well, the guy who was calling? I'll bet he didn't call up the night before and tell the desk sergeant, "Look, if I call you up one of these nights and tell you my wife is choking on a yo-yo, that means that the woman I'm married to is heading for Croak City."

Louie: I think I see what you're saying. You mean, if we have to agree about what a symbol is going to represent before we use it to communicate, how can we communicate with a stranger who wants to know what time it is, right?

John: Yeah, I mean if he's a stranger, then we never agreed with him about what he means by time.

Louie: That's a good question, John. I've got a good answer for it, too, which I'm sure will make our readers out there in communication-land very happy. There's a thing called standardized usage, which is what you have when a whole society or culture agrees on how its members will use certain symbols. In other words, when we're little kids, we learn that the symbol for what you're sitting on is "barstool." And everybody in the whole society is taught that "barstool" is the symbol to use when they want to refer to one of those things you're sitting on. Where are you from, John?

John: California.

Louie: Who taught you that the symbol for what you're sitting on is "barstool?"

John: My mother.

Louie: Sure she did. Everybody's mother teaches them what the symbol "barstool" stands for.

John: But if you go back in time, there must have been some point when one guy said to another guy, "Barstool," and pointed to one.

Louie: Right, and that's how we came to agree on the uses of symbols. Of course, it's a lot easier to agree on how to use a symbol like "barstool" than it is to agree on how to use symbols which don't stand for things that we can point at.

John: What do you mean?

Louie: Well, words like "justice," "equality," or "freedom;" it's not easy to point at what they stand for. What a political conservative means by "freedom" or "equality" might be very different from what these words represent to a liberal. In general, there is more agreement about the meaning of words that have direct empirical referents than for abstract words.

John: Well, what would happen to some guy who didn't go along with this standardized usage thing?

Louie: What do you mean?

John: Well, say some guy thought that thing you're drinking out of should be called a lamp instead of a glass. I mean, what would be wrong with that?

Louie: Well, in one way, nothing. See, the assignment of symbols to things they represent is really arbitrary as hell. I mean, what kind of a bonehead would call *anything* a "lamp?" But people do. Almost everybody calls those things that light up their rooms "lamps." We could call them "borcks," but it's just that everybody kind of agrees that we'll all call them lamps.

John: You still haven't answered my question. What happens to the guy who won't play along with the arbitrary symbol deal?

Louie: He just wouldn't be able to communicate and they'd probably chuck him in the slammer. Since the majority of people in society want to call this a glass—even though it's kind of arbitrary—that's what goes.

John: But sometimes we kind of forget that the assignment of symbols to the things they refer to is arbitrary, huh?

Louie: Right. It's just that everybody is so used to using symbols according to the societal standardized usage that they get upset when someone doesn't.

John: How does everybody find out about what the standardized usage is?

Louie: Oh, their parents, their teachers, their friends. And if nobody else is around, they use the dictionary.

John: So you're saying that the dictionary is a good place to find out what a word means if you aren't sure, but you think you might want to use it to communicate?

Louie: Well, it's not quite that simple because there really are no meanings in dictionaries. After all, a dictionary only has words, that is, symbols, and we've already agreed that words don't have meaning: Only people do. A dictionary tells us, in symbols, how people have agreed to use other symbols. But unless the user of the dictionary already has some meaning in his head for the symbols which are used to define the particular word that he's interested in, he won't be able to get the meaning for that word from a dictionary.

John: OK then, but if you have meanings for enough of the words in the language in which the dictionary is written, you can use it to find the meaning of new words in that language that you don't have meanings for.

Louie: That's true, but you have to be careful because a dictionary only contains societal standardized usages. This is the meaning that most speakers of a particular language have kind of implicitly agreed that a word has. The dictionary *doesn't* necessarily tell us about the meaning that the person with whom we are communicating has for it. You've never seen anything in the dictionary like, "Be careful when you use this word around Homer Reynolds; he thinks it means something else," or "Don't use this word over at the Elks Club unless you want your clock cleaned for you!"

John: I'll have to admit that. Then the dictionary could be a useful tool in establishing agreement about what symbols stand for. But we shouldn't count on it, because everybody has probably had past experiences with the word that wouldn't be evident from the dictionary definition. Or they might belong to a group or an organization which uses the word differently.

Louie: I couldn't have said it better myself.

John: Isn't it about time to call it a night?

Louie: Well, you can call it a night if you want, but don't assume I'll share your meaning for it.

John: Are you trying to tell me you're still thirsty?

Louie: I'll drink to that.

John: Bartender, another lamp for me and my friend.

Curtain

ACT III

Setting: The same bar. The next night. The same two men. A new pitcher. No girl.

Louie: You up for some peanuts?

John: No way. I've got just exactly enough money for three more pitchers. You know how tough it is living on a grad assistant's salary.

Louie: Yeah, I know. You suppose they'd take food stamps for a bag of peanuts?

John: Probably not. You know, I still think that girl who was in here the night before last was damn good-looking.

Louie: Haven't we covered that ground before?

John: Well, yeah, but it's just hard for me to understand how our past experiences could be *that* different. I mean *most* people would have agreed that she was good-looking.

Louie: Don't bet on it.

John: I'd bet the bartender thought she was good-looking. Hey, bartender.

Bartender: Another pitcher already? That's six tonight, isn't it?

Louie: Five.

John: Say, help us settle an argument, will you? You remember a girl who was in here the night before last? She was sitting by herself over by the window.

Bartender: (ponders) No, I can't say I do remember her. We have a lot of people in here every night, you know.

John: Well, she was in here all night. She had black hair, kind of long, and I think she was kind of tall.

Louie: And warts all over her face.

John: Louie!

Bartender: I don't know. I think maybe I do remember a girl sitting over there.

John: Good. Tell us, how would you rate her physical attractiveness?

Bartender: Hell, I don't know. I don't remember what she looked like. We were pretty busy that night.

Louie: You don't remember anything about her?

Bartender: No...Oh, wait a minute. I do remember she was drinking gin and tonic. That's about it, though. Hey, maybe Lola remembers her. (Calls to waitress) Lola, come over here for a minute.

Lola: (Comes over to bar, winks at John) Yeah?

Bartender: Remember a girl who was in here two nights ago? She was sitting over by the window drinking gin and tonic. These guys want to know how attractive we think she was.

Lola: Oh, yeah, I do remember her. But I'm sorry; I really can't remember what she looked like. Oh, I do remember how she was dressed though. She was wearing really fine clothes. I wish I could find outfits like that.

John: OK, thanks anyway. (Bartender and waitress leave)

Louie: Gee, that's funny; they hardly noticed or remembered her.

John: Well, now, not really. Think about it a minute. This fits right in with what we were talking about the other night. The waitress saw the same girl that we did and yet she didn't notice whether the girl was good-looking or not. She *selectively perceived* some aspect of the situation. She was interested in the clothes other girls wear, so that's what she noticed.

Louie: You know, I don't remember what she was wearing.

John: I don't either. I just remember what she looked like.

Louie: Yet, if we talked to the waitress at the time the girl was sitting there, I'm sure we could have more or less agreed on what she was wearing. We could have seen the same things as the waitress, yet we missed it entirely. What she was wearing just didn't register for us at all.

John: In a sense the waitress "selected out" different aspects of the girl to notice. She could have noticed how tall she was, how old she was, what color her hair was, what she looked like, or anything, but she perceived features of that girl selectively, probably largely based on her interests: clothes in this case.

Louie: And you selectively perceived features of her based on *your* interests: lecherous, I presume.

John: Something like that.

Louie: And where do those interests come from? One guess.

John: So we're back to past experiences. So far we've said that our perceptions, our values, our meanings for symbols, our desires, and now our interests are all based on our past experiences. Anything else?

Louie: I'm afraid so. In fact, all of the problems we'll be discussing here in Act III are related to past experiences. See, the waitress has learned what her interests are from her past experiences, just as we have.

John: This all sounds good, Louie, but it seems more complicated than just selectively perceiving different aspects of a situation. Take the bartender—I'm *sure* that at the time the girl was here, he perceived more about her than just "gin and tonic." I mean, he at least knew that it went to a female in that part of the room.

Louie: You're right. He probably did perceive a lot more than he remembered, but most of it was so unimportant to him that he could only remember "gin and tonic."

John: You have a point. Not only do people selectively perceive things, they *selectively recall* them. Different aspects of an event are important to different people. They tend to recall only those things which are important to them.

Louie: Wouldn't selective perception and selective recall apply to information received symbolically, too?

John: You mean information received through communication?

Louie: Yes.

John: Well, sure. First of all, the person who perceived the event firsthand would selectively perceive certain aspects of it. Then when he came to describe the event to someone else, he would selectively recall only certain parts of it. He might gloss over certain details, which is called *leveling*, and focus in on certain others, which is called *sharpening*. In both cases, some information is lost. By emphasizing some aspects of the situation and glossing over others, he is likely to distort what occurred. We usually *say* that what *most* people *agree* on is what actually exists. In other words, his description would distort the information that other observers would agree occurred.

Louie: Continue.

John: *Assimilation* is a combination of leveling and sharpening by which the person kind of plugs in missing details that, based on his past experience, he thinks should have occurred given what he knows did occur.

Louie: Could you give me an example?

John: OK, let's say that two students in Comm 100 both had to read this chapter, but one fails to read it, so his friend tells him what's in it.

Louie: I like this example.

John: Good; why don't you continue it?

Louie: My pleasure. The student who read the chapter might focus on some unimportant details. He could describe the baseball example in great detail without ever mentioning the point that the example was illustrating. This would be *sharpening*. Or he might say that the chapter said "meanings are in people" without elaborating or giving any detail. This would be *leveling*. In both cases he would be distorting the emphases of the chapter.

John: How about an assimilation example?

Louie: Well, that's a little tougher since he has to have had a relevant past experience with which to assimilate the new information. Let's say that he had a communication course in high school and covered *information overload* at the same time *information distortion* was covered. But, since this person's past experience placed both these communication concepts together, he might think that "overload" had been covered here.

John: Sure, he might sharpen some details, level others, and fill in some of the gaps with knowledge he had gained from his previous course. He would thus assimilate what we cover with what he would expect to be covered in such a chapter. In short, he might distort information about the content of this chapter.

Louie: And if his friend were asked what was in this chapter by a third person in the class, the information distortion problem would be further compounded. All these same processes by which information is distorted would operate there, too.

John: It's sure easy to see why a newspaper sometimes has difficulty giving an accurate account of an event. Louie, didn't you once work on a newspaper?

Louie: Yes, John, I did.

John: How many people have to handle information before it appears in print?

Louie: Well, let's see. Say a reporter goes out to interview witnesses of a barroom fight. Each witness, even though he or she perceived the fight directly, would disagree about what happened. The reporter would try to get each witness's version and synthesize them. What most people tended to agree on, the reporter would probably call a fact, or an alleged fact, if a criminal act were involved.

John: The reporter might have certain expectations about what some of the details would be. And I guess he would have different meanings for the words the witnesses used to describe the fight.

Louie: That's right. He might sharpen some details, level others, and assimilate the information he was given with his past experiences. If a deadline was approaching, he would phone in the "facts" to the newspaper. Someone at the paper would write them down and give them to a writer who would write the story. The story would then go to an editor who might selectively delete some portions of it or even rewrite it. It might then go to a headline writer who would read it and write a headline which may or may not reflect the emphasis intended by the editor, which may or may not reflect the emphasis intended by the writer, which may or may not reflect the emphasis intended by the reporter, which may or may not . . .

John: (cutting in) Reflect what happened in the bar.

Louie: Right, and each of the processes through which information is distorted is in operation at each level. When the story finally appears in the paper, it will be read by people who also have widely differing perceptions, values, meanings for words, and so on. It's amazing that newspapers are as accurate as they are.

Bartender: (interrupting) Hey, Fellas?

John: Yeah?

Bartender: Look, I don't mean to interrupt or anything, but you guys have been at the bar here for three nights now, talking about all this crap, and I haven't heard anybody say anything yet that might help anybody communicate any better. Now is this chapter going to be just another one of those academic exercises that doesn't do anybody any good, or are you two going to get down to brass tacks and tell people something worthwhile?

Louie: That's a good question. As a matter of fact, I think John and I understand this stuff well enough now that we can discuss some possible applications of the concepts we've been talking about.

Bartender: It's about time. I'm ready whenever you are.

Louie: OK, here goes. One thing that's good to know is that your capacity for perceiving information has limits, so that the less information you put into a message, the less distorted it'll be at the other end.

Bartender: Can you be more specific?

John: Well, the point is that the less information in a message—or the shorter the message—the less distortion is likely to occur.

Bartender: I'm still not sure I understand.

Louie: Well, say for instance, the waitress comes up here and asks for a Scotch and Pepsi and a martini. Could you handle that?

Bartender: Yeah, I think I could make those drinks without any problems.

Louie: But say she came up and reeled off twenty drinks in a row. Could you keep track of that?

Bartender: I'm pretty good, but . . .

Louie: Well, that's all we mean by saying that the less information in a message, the less distortion in the reception of the message.

John: Yeah. Or like directions. If I tell you how to get to the men's room, you're more likely to get all of the message—and get it the way I intended it—than you are if I try to tell you how to get to my ex-wife's house in Bayonne, New Jersey.

Louie: That makes sense. But on the other hand, if you went to Bayonne with the bartender here, and rode in the front seat and told him where to go, one turn at a time, then he probably won't have any problem.

John: You wouldn't say that if you'd ever met my ex-wife.

Louie: I mean he wouldn't have any problem *getting* there.

Bartender: You're saying, then, that to reduce distortion, I should keep messages short?

John: Right. And if you have a lot of information to impart, try to break it down into smaller messages. You'll have a lot less distortion that way.

Bartender: That makes sense. It really works, huh?

Louie: Bank on it.

Bartender: All right, this one's on the house. (Slides pitcher down bar)

John: Thanks. (Pauses, drinks) That's not the only way to reduce distortion, you know. You can reduce the number of links in the communication chain, too.

Louie: I used to know a girl who was into chains.

John: That was probably a different kind of thing. What I mean is the fewer the links in the chain, the less the distortion. That is, as the number of people who transmit a message from its source to its ultimate receiver increases, the chance for error increases, and the probability of distortion increases.

Louie: You know, that makes sense, too.

John: Sure it does. Remember when you were a little kid? You used to play that game where about fifteen or twenty kids would get around in a circle. One kid—usually the kid whose birthday it was—would whisper a message to the kid next to him, and then that kid would whisper the message to the next kid, and it would go like that all the way around the circle. By the time it got back to the birthday boy, it was really different from the way he'd first said it.

Bartender: Sure, I remember that game. And what you're saying is that, if there had been only two or three kids passing the message on, there would have been less distortion.

John: Right.

Bartender: You know, that same sort of thing happens around here sometimes. Every now and then some woman will tell her date what she wants to drink; her date will tell the waitress, the waitress will maybe tell another waitress; the second waitress will tell me. I'll make the order, and by the time it gets back to the table, the woman's drinking a hard-boiled egg.

John: Sure, but you never have any trouble when we sit up here at the bar and just tell you face-to-face we want another pitcher.

Bartender: Makes sense. Here's another one on the house.

Louie: That's not all, either. Did you know that no matter what the message is, the source and receiver, just because of their past experiences, have a lot to do with how much distortion you're going to get in a message?

Bartender: There you go with your past experiences again. Tell me what good it does to know that.

John: Well, there are at least two parts to this: the first is similarity; the second is familiarity. Similarity is when two people have had quite a few past experiences that are very much alike. If two people are both male, twenty-one years old, black, from New York City, juniors at the same college, veterans, married, and poor—since they've shared a lot of past experiences, they'll be able to communicate with less distortion than two dissimilar people, even though they may never have met before.

Louie: The other interesting thing is that people who are familiar with each other, that is, people who have shared past experiences together, which almost always involves having communicated with each other before, will have less distortion in their communication than two strangers.

Bartender: That all seems obvious.

Louie: Right. But the point is, to reduce distortion, you want to be similar to the person with whom you're communicating, and you want to be familiar with that person, or have communicated with him or her before.

Bartender: Oh, thanks a lot. So what do I do if I'm not similar to the other guy and I've never seen him before in my life?

Louie: Well, everybody communicates with dissimilar, unfamiliar people every day. The thing to remember is that since you are dissimilar and unfamiliar, it increases the likelihood of distorted communication. You should be aware of it and try to overcome it.

John: What Louie's saying is, you can't automatically make yourself similar to or familiar with another person—nor do you always want to. But you *can* realize that being dissimilar and unfamiliar can leave your communication wide open to distortion, because you don't have so many past experiences in common with the other person.

Bartender: But what can I do about it? How do I overcome those obstacles to distortion-free communication?

Louie: Well, there are at least two important things to do. In fact, those two things are the most important things in *all* of the book.

Bartender: (Breathes heavily)

Louie: The first magic word is feedback.

John: The second is metacommunication.

Bartender: Well, it's really nice to know some six-bit words like those, but I still don't see how they can help me to communicate better.

Louie: That's because you're not supposed to know until now. John, do you want to tell him about feedback?

John: Sure. Feedback is simple. You understand what communication is, right?

Bartender: Sure.

John: Well, feedback is a kind of communication. It's communication that's actually an *effect* of another, previous communication. It's a *response* to the previous communication which gets sent—or *fed back*—to the previous communicator.

Bartender: You mean if you say something to me, and I say something back to you, what I said is feedback?

John: Right. And if I then respond to your feedback, that's feedback too.

Bartender: You mean like if I ask you a question, like right now, that's feedback?

John: Exactly. And if I'm communicating with you and you yawn, that's feedback. Or if you walk away, or crack me in the chops, or make some comment, or disagree, all that's feedback, too.

Louie: Right. Feedback is what makes communication an ongoing process, rather than a bunch of stop and start, source-to-receiver interchanges. If I say something to John, and he responds, his response is feedback. If I respond to John's response, my response is feedback. As long as we're communicating, we're laying feedback on the other guy.

John: And the key is, the more feedback that's available and attended to, the less distortion will occur.

Louie: If feedback isn't available, the sender never knows if his message got through, or if it was understood.

John: But if feedback is available, and the communicators respond to it in ways that reduce distortion, then you're likely to have good communication.

Bartender: Then feedback, if it's available and attended to, can reduce distortion.

Louie: Definitely. If you're looking and listening for it, the observation of feedback will tell you if the receiver is getting your symbols the way you're sending them, and if those symbols call up meanings similar to those you had in mind when you encoded your messages.

Bartender: Well, one way to assess feedback would be to ask the other guy if he understood what I said, right?

John: No, don't do that. Don't ask him *if* he understood; ask him *what* he understood.

Louie: Right. Because he'll almost always say yes, because he doesn't want to appear dumb—especially if he works for you.

Bartender: I stand corrected. Ask *what* the other person understood—not *if* he or she understood. Then if the other person hasn't called up the same meaning I had for the symbols I used, I'll be able to try again, right on the spot.

John: Right, thereby reducing distortion.

Louie: There are other ways to assess feedback—even if it's feedback you'd rather not receive. If the other guy stands there scratching his head or looking as if you just told him his ears were on upside-down, then you've got a pretty good nonverbal indicator that your message isn't being decoded the way you intended it to be.

Bartender: Well, at that point, I could ask him what he understands.

John: Good. If you suspect that the other person is getting a message different from the one you intended, it's time to check it out.

Bartender: But even if he or she *seems* to be getting the message the way I intended, I'd be better off checking anyway.

John: Sure. As long as feedback is available, you should use it. Also, if by chance you still aren't convinced that meanings are in people, go around sending messages and actively soliciting feedback for a day. You'll be astounded at how differently your communication is received from the way you intended it.

Louie: One more thing—the way we've been talking, it sounds like the responsibility for attending to feedback is mostly on the source. We want to make sure we don't allow that emphasis. The receiver should always actively try to provide feedback to a source.

John: That's true. For example, if you don't understand something, speak up. Ask the source to try again. Louie and I have been doing that right here at the bar. If one of us didn't understand something the other was trying to get across, we'd ask questions. If we disagreed, we'd do it verbally—out in the open where we could better identify problems—and we'd keep disagreeing or questioning until we could both pretty well understand each other's meanings.

Louie: People who are going to be good communicators can't be getting irritated every time somebody doesn't understand them on the first try.

John: Since people who are good communicators know that meanings are in people, they search out other communicators' meanings for symbols. The way they do it is by paying attention to feedback.

Bartender: That sounds like it takes some extra time; but the extra time is probably worth it.

Louie: Maybe the best example of all this can be found in schools. It seems to me that students who don't understand things should ask questions. Every time.

John: That's true. And students don't need to ask specific questions, either. A simple, "I don't understand," should be good enough to get the instructor to try again.

Louie: One thing instructors don't do enough of—and this includes me—is ask students *what* they understand, except on tests. I often find myself saying, "Is that clear?" or, "Does that make sense?" when I *should* be saying, "Jim, tell me what that means," or, "Would the girl in the forty-fifth row with the orange sweater please tell the class in her own words what I've just said."

John: Right. Using that technique in teaching would be worth the extra time it would take.

Bartender: Well, it seems to me that one of the main points about feedback is that everyone concerned with the communication has both a right and an obligation to actively solicit feedback and provide feedback. If everybody did that a lot of distortion problems would be wiped out.

Louie: For sure. John, what else is important about feedback?

John: Just that it's usually there, in one form or another, and the successful communicator is the one who uses it to reduce distortion.

Louie: OK, then, let me tell our friend about metacommunication. That is, I'll tell him if my voice holds out; my throat feels like Oklahoma.

John: Mine too.

Bartender: All right, all right. I guess being able to throw around a word like metacommunication is worth a pitcher.

Louie: Aaaah. Well, metacommunication is a kind of feedback. It's communication about communication. The difference is that feedback is mostly about the content of communication, and metacommunication is about the process of communication itself. Thus, metacommunication is a type of feedback.

Bartender: I've got the example this time: what you two have been doing here for the past few nights is metacommunicating.

John: In a way, yes. We've been communicating about communication. Communicating about the *content* of communication is the more general type of feedback. When two people talk about which of them is going to do the dishes, or about whether a girl is good-looking or not, or about who's going to type this chapter, that's communication about content, and there's bound to be feedback involved in the process.

Louie: But when people talk about the problems they have communicating, or about the communication process itself, then that's metacommunication. Of course, it wouldn't be entirely content-free, but the important part of the discussion would be things like, "One problem I have in understanding you is that you use words without defining them," or "Try to be more specific when you ask me to do things." That would be metacommunication. It might be accompanied by some things like, "What do you mean when you use the word *message*?" or, "I'm not sure I understand what you want me to do with this rifle, Sergeant. Could you please repeat what you just said?"

Bartender: I think I understand. You wouldn't necessarily need to refer to content when you're talking about general problems of communicating. For example, if I held a meeting with the waitresses to try to figure out a more efficient way to call in drinks, we wouldn't have to mention the name of a drink, except maybe to illustrate the new communication system.

John: Good example. See, you'd be benefitting from a meeting like that, but it's a different kind of feedback than you normally get. For one thing, you've got a better chance of communicating about communication problems without starting an argument about whether a specific drink should have an olive or a mint leaf in it.

Bartender: Somebody should teach my wife how to metacommunicate without starting an argument about the last time I got drunk.

Louie: That's a problem with metacommunication. Sometimes content, by way of innocent illustration, creeps into metacommunication discussions, and a content dispute will begin. At that point, one of the metacommunicators should remind the other people that metacommunication probably works best when it doesn't degenerate back to discussions of specific past events or specific past communications.

John: Right. In metacommunication, the emphasis should be on improving *future* communication.

Louie: There's another problem with metacommunicating, too. Metacommunication is subject to the same problems about which people are metacommunicating. What I mean is, you metacommunicate to talk over problems. But those same problems—poor feedback, distortions, different meanings—may well arise again, right during metacommunication and gum things up there, too. You've got to be on the lookout for that.

Bartender: I think I'm a little confused. Can we go back over feedback and metacommunication for a minute?

John: Well, to start with, you just provided us with feedback when you asked that question. Remember, feedback is a response that's sent back to a communicator. One of the effects of our communication with you was your response to it—namely, your asking for clarification. If we receive your communication, it's feedback. If we don't receive it, that's *attempted feedback*.

Louie: And if we *do* receive it, there are three things we can do with the feedback: one, we could ignore it; two, we could misinterpret it; three, we could attend to it by responding to your feedback.

John: And remember, our response to your feedback is feedback, too.

Bartender: If I receive it.

Louie: Right. If you don't, it's attempted feedback.

Bartender: So feedback isn't always received by the source?

Louie: Right. And sometimes it's ignored or misinterpreted, especially if it's nonverbal.

John: But if feedback is available, and attended to, then communicators can't help but improve their communication.

Louie: Remember, too, that not only should feedback be actively sought and asked for, it should be readily and freely given. If feedback were always immediately available and actively sought and freely provided by everyone concerned, we'd obviously be able to communicate with much less distortion. That's because we'd know better when the meanings we have for symbols used aren't the same meanings the others have, and we could try again.

Bartender: One question: when *wouldn't* feedback be available?

John: Very rarely. But there are many communication situations in which feedback can be delayed. When you watch Johnny Carson or read a newspaper editorial, that's obviously communication. But you can't mail your feedback out until the next morning, and it won't get to the other communicator for two, maybe three, days.

Bartender: If I'm lucky.

John: So that's one thing that's peculiar to mass communication, communication by mail, and communication in large organizations: the whole notion of delayed feedback.

Louie: Advertising is like that too. You don't really get good feedback from an advertising campaign until you see a sales report on your product.

Bartender: OK, I think I understand feedback. Now how about metacommunication?

Louie: Again, it's communication about communication, usually to make future communication better.

John: It could be a discussion about past communication, with the emphasis on the *process* of communication itself, rather than on specific content.

Louie: Making *rules* can be done by metacommunicating. And establishing provisions for regular feedback opportunities can be done by metacommunicating.

John: It's also useful for people who have to communicate together a lot. Like husbands and wives, or people in organizations.

Louie: It's hard to do, because a metacommunication session often gets content attached to it, and starts being communication and regular feedback about that specific content.

Bartender: So when you're communicating about communication, it's better to stay pretty much away from content.

John: Usually. Except you'll probably want to use some examples. As long as you don't get into discussing the examples themselves rather than what they're examples of.

Bartender: That's good stuff. We talked a long time about that.

Louie: That's because it's important.

John: I hope nobody got bored.

Bartender: We could use some metacommunication around here.

Louie: We could use some medication over here—how about some more beer?

Bartender: There you go. (Slides pitcher to Louie and John)

Louie: There's more to come.

Bartender: Shoot.

John: The better organized your message is, the less chance there'll be for distortion.

Louie: Another thing you can use to help reduce distortion is repetition.

Bartender: You mean the more times I repeat something, the less distorted it will be received?

John: Yes, but only up to a point. Things like the Pledge of Allegiance, and "Now I lay me down to sleep . . . ," get repeated so many times that, for many people, those messages lose any meaning they ever had. It gets so that the symbols don't activate any meaning at all.

Bartender: Or some TV commercials, like Mr. Whipple squeezing the Charmin?

Louie: Sometimes, yes. You'll just get irritated, and after that you'll try to tune it out.

Bartender: But all in all, with that qualification, repetition is a good way to reduce distortion?

Louie: Yes, but there's another qualification, too. Repetition has a high cost for communicators in money, time, and energy. Two newspaper ads cost twice as much as one. Sometimes it's not worth the extra resources.

John: That's true. Another thing, if the receiver or receivers are familiar with the topic, you're likely to have less distortion because the receivers may be acquainted with at least part of the content of your communication, or with similar content.

Louie: There's a catch there, too. If the receiver is *too* familiar with similar arguments or content, he may *assimilate*, or fill in details, depending on his or her past experiences.

John: Sure. Another example of that is a guy who goes to church every week. Every Sunday the usher hands him a program, which is communication. It lists the sermon topic and the hymns and everything. Now the guy is familiar with the topics being communicated in the program, so he understands the program very well, and there is little distortion. But the problem is that he is so familiar with it that he knows the service always ends up with Hymn 125. Chances are he's so familiar with that piece of information that he won't look at that part of the program very carefully. When they decide to sing 426 instead, he's going to stand up and start singing 125.

Bartender: So the communication in the program wouldn't be distorted by the guy until he starts assimilating some of the information in there with his past experiences.

John: And he's got so many past experiences with Hymn 125 that he *expects* it, and overlooks the change in the communication.

Louie: So we've talked about several ways to reduce communication distortion. Can you remember what they are?

Bartender: Let's see: for less distortion the ideal communication situation would, most importantly, include feedback and maybe metacommunication.

John: Good.

Bartender: You also wouldn't have too much information in messages, or too many links in the communication chain. The people communicating would be similar and familiar; the message would be well-organized; there'd be repetition—but not too much of it; and the receivers would be familiar with the topic—but not too familiar.

Louie: I think that's about all of it.

John: I hope so. I'm getting as drunk as this chapter is getting long.

Louie: We can't leave without wrapping it up, though.

John: I guess you're right.

Louie: You know what I'm talking about: Those two words that more or less cover everything we've talked about for three nights.

John: Right. Shall I lay those two important words on the bartender, or do you want to?

Bartender: You mean *receiver orientation*?

Louie: How'd you know?

Bartender: Well, it just seems like that's where this whole thing has been heading. If you are oriented toward the receiver or receivers of your communication, you'll know that they perceive things differently from the way you do; you'll know that everybody else uses symbols differently from you because meanings are in people; and you'll try to understand what your receivers' past experiences have been in order to reduce distortion. Once you've done all that you'll be able to communicate better.

Louie: Very good!

Bartender: Actually, feedback—including metacommunication—is a part of receiver orientation, too. And all that stuff about keeping messages brief, and repetition, and everything is really just a concession to the perceptual and symbolic limitations that limit communication.

John: Right. Receiver orientation really sums up the whole thing. If everyone else were receiver oriented in his or her communication, we wouldn't have nearly the distortion that we normally have.

Louie: Like the man said, "Communicate unto others as you would have them communicate unto you."

John: Right, Lou. And you know that old saying, "Consider the source."

Louie: Yeah.

John: Well, it's more important to consider the receiver.

Bartender: It's last call. You guys want another pitcher?

John: Now *that's* what I call receiver orientation.

Louie: I'll drink to that.

Curtain

SUMMARY

In this dialogue, we have discussed many concepts we feel are *basic* to human communication. The following is a very brief summary of the points the authors consider *most basic*.

ACT I

1. Everyone perceives realities differently because of his or her past experiences.
2. Everyone holds different values because of his or her past experiences.
3. The different perceptions and the different values that people have are *legitimately* different, because peoples' past experiences are largely not under their control.

ACT II

1. Just as reality is always perceived differently by different persons, symbols (words, gestures, anything that represents reality) are perceived differently by different persons.
2. The meanings that people have for symbols are in persons, not in the symbols themselves or in dictionaries. Every person has a unique meaning for every symbol. No two persons can agree that a given symbol "stands for" an identical thing, because of differing past experiences—both with the symbols and with whatever realities the symbols represent.
3. We *can* communicate, although only imperfectly, because we have had similar, although not identical, past experiences with symbols and with what the symbols stand for. But it is important to remember that only to the extent that we *have had* overlap in past experiences, will we have overlap in meanings for symbols.
4. Much overlap that we share in the meanings we have for symbols is a result of most users of a language having shared the past experience of learning a *standardized usage* for symbols in that language.

ACT III

1. Selective perception, selective recall, leveling, sharpening, and assimilation are all processes that can increase distortion during

communication. All these processes have their origins in the past experiences of communicators.

2. The effects of these processes can be partially overcome by the availability of, and attention to, feedback and metacommunication.

3. Other things to remember about reducing communication distortion are:

    a. Keep messages as brief as possible. If you have a lot of information to communicate, break it down into smaller messages.

    b. The fewer persons who pass a message along from source to receiver, the less the information in the message will be distorted.

    c. The greater the similarity or the familiarity of the communicators, the less the distortion.

    d. The more repetition—to a point—of information, the less distortion.

    e. The more the receiver is familiar with the topic, the less distortion—but watch out for assimilation.

    f. The better organized the message, the less distortion.

4. All communicators are well-advised to maintain a receiver orientation.

QUESTIONS FOR DISCUSSION

1. What is true beauty?

2. Discuss the concepts of *agreed-upon reality* and *absolute reality*, relating them to events that occur in the environment around a person and the person's perceptions of those events.

3. Explain how the past experience of learning a *standardized usage* allows people to broaden their meanings for symbols and thereby to gain information through future experiences with those symbols.

4. How can feedback and metacommunication help to overcome the effects of selective perception and recall, leveling, sharpening, and assimilation?

5. What is meant by a *receiver orientation*?

In "Human Communication: The Basic Proposition," Berlo introduced the concept of *information* and discussed its fundamental differences from physical matter-energy. Meanings cannot be transmitted between persons. Only messages with physical reality can be transferred across the physical realities of space and time. Students of extrasensory perception have attempted to show that messages can be transmitted without apparent physical means, but to this date, at least, their attempts have not been successful enough to impress thoughtful persons that they are correct.

Wayne Cowart stresses the physical nature of the message in his article on information and communication and suggests that information is not transmitted directly in the physical message. The concept of *information* provides one way of thinking about *meaning*. The amount of information a person receives from a message depends upon the information he already possesses, just as the meaning a person assigns to a message depends upon the meanings and beliefs within the person before he receives the message. There are many situations where information and meaning seem to vary, independently of each other, and the exact relationship between them is not yet clearly understood.

4

iNfORMATiON ANd COMMUNiCATiON: wHAT CAN WE lEARN AbOUT pEOplE fROM COMMUNiCATiON MAChiNES

R. Wayne Cowart

Science is a process of making and testing guesses about how the world works. Whatever our interests, the structure of an atom, the way in which a plant makes food through photosynthesis, or the organization of human communication processes, we make progress by first clearly stating our best guesses about how a certain part of nature is organized and then testing our guesses against whatever relevant facts we can find. Though people often think science is mostly a matter of discovering and collecting facts, this is not the case. Facts are often useful only insofar as they help us to decide between different ideas about the organization of nature. The core of science is much more the development of these larger ideas or theories (sophisticated guesses) than the mere collection of facts.

The purpose of this article is to present some ideas developed in the study of machine communication which may be helpful in our thinking about human communication. Communication in machines is far better understood than communication between persons. Among the scientists and engineers who deal with communication machines, the ideas outlined below have proven their practical value time and time again in the nearly thirty years since they were developed. But for those of us who are primarily interested in human communication these ideas serve a different purpose. For us they are hints and suggestions about the way in which human communication might work. These ideas help us to form our guesses so that we can

Wayne Cowart is instructor in linguistics at Queens College, City University of New York, and is a doctoral student in psycholinguistics at the Graduate Center, CUNY. His article was prepared especially for this book.

better organize and understand the information we have about this process. They take their place in our study alongside ideas from disciplines like linguistics, psychology, animal communication, and others. Just as it is easier to appreciate a complicated sculpture if we look at it from several angles, we hope that by looking at human communication from different angles it will be easier to see the nature of this mysterious process. But before we begin we had best consider an important question: *Can ideas about machine communication be relevant to the study of human communication?* We might object that human beings are obviously much more complicated than machines, even those machines that communicate. We could also point out that misguided analogies between machines or natural processes and various human processes have often led to error in the past.

The fault with the first objection, that people are complicated, is that it is exactly this complexity of human beings that makes analogies to machines useful. Human beings are much too complex and subtle for us to comprehend all at once. Scientific study of human beings can best succeed where small parts of the subject are studied in isolation. It is true that we shall never completely understand what a person is until we can see how all the psychological and biological parts fit together and interact with each other. But it is also true that we shall never be able to achieve that overall understanding until we have some grasp of the more crucial parts. Once we isolate an organ or an ability in humans that we want to study, similarities between our subject and some familiar machine may often be helpful.

Machines are much simpler and easier to understand, yet they often employ principles that are similar to those that underlie human biology or the human mind. The lens of the eye is different from the lens of a telescope in many respects, but it was not until people could build telescopes that they began to understand certain basic facts about how the eye works. Your nervous system is different from the circuits and wires of a computer in countless ways, and yet our understanding of the nervous system has been greatly advanced by knowledge that has come from the development of modern computers. It is precisely because machines are much simpler than people that we can hope to understand human communication a little better through an understanding of communication machines.

It is true, of course, that too much simplicity can also get us into trouble. A lot of dumb things have been said about people by constructing analogies with clocks, steam engines, telephones, or computers, to name only a few. Sometimes this kind of error can be thoroughly evil. Not long after Darwin's theory of evolution gained some acceptance there were those who tried to justify cruel and un-democratic social policies by arguing that the victims were being dis-advantaged by some all-powerful natural force, like natural selection, not by the greed or arrogance of those who benefited. We can avoid this kind of mistake only if we keep clearly in mind that we are using our knowledge of machines merely to help us make guesses about people. Once we derive these guesses they have to be tested just as do other guesses. They are no more guaranteed to be right than are other theories. If we are indeed careful in this way, our use of analogies can be a valuable aid to our understanding.

The first problem to attack is the critical notion of information. What is it that seems to get moved around in communication? One word that is often used in this connection is "message."

Is Communication About Messages?

We can define a *message* as an organized string of physical signals that moves between two communicators. By such a definition the actual sounds that go from the mouth of the speaker to the ear of the hearer, the ink on this page, and the electrical impulses that travel over a telegraph wire are all messages. Perhaps because messages, defined in these terms, are so obviously a crucial part of communication, people sometimes say that communication is a process of exchanging messages, in a way that suggests this is somehow the key to the process. Yet it is fairly easy to show that moving messages from place to place is not always the sort of thing we'd want to call communication.

Certainly most of the events we ordinarily call communication involve some sort of message. But notice that the amount of information a person gets out of communication is not something we can predict by looking at the messages that are exchanged. Consider the following:

> Some scientists believe that a new Ice Age will someday envelop North America and that the cooling period could begin within a few decades.

If you've never seen this statement before you may well be sur-prised, intrigued, or possibly disturbed. Yet if you have seen it be-fore it may have no impact on you at all. From simple observations like this we can see that the amount of information a message carries is not simply a function of the message itself. Indeed it is clear that the information associated with the message cannot be *in* the message at all because that would require the message to have the same amount of information at all times and places, and this clearly is not the case. Many messages are informative only once. After that you may receive them thousands of times more without their having the least value for you.

The amount of information a message carries differs from person to person. How much of this sentence do you feel you understand:

> Mathematically entropy is a function of a summation over the probability of each symbol in a system times the probability of each symbol expressed as a logarithm to the base of 2 where the product of the summation is multiplied by a constant.

Unless you are an advanced student of communication theory it probably means very little to you. Yet to those who have an interest in such things this statement may well carry more information and excitement than a prediction of a new Ice Age. So again, information cannot really be part of the message itself, because then we would expect always the same amount, no matter who was receiving.

The information associated with a message seems to be a very slippery quantity. It changes even while the message remains fixed. It appears to have more to do with the relation between message and receiver than with the inherent properties of the message itself. Whatever communication is about, there is much more to it than just sending messages. Precisely because the accomplishments of a communication system cannot be measured by counting messages, there came a time in the 1940s when the designers and builders of communication machines were badly in need of a way to measure how much work a particular machine could do. Just as the designer of a railroad locomotive must be able to predict how much of a load the locomotive will pull in order to design it well, so the communication engineer needs to have some way of knowing how much information a machine will transmit or receive in order to be sure that it does not have either too much or too little capacity for a particular purpose. By the end of the 1940s two theoreticians, Claude Shannon and Norbert Wiener, had developed a body of ideas that provided the needed means of analyzing and understanding communication machines. Though this theory (usually called *information theory*) was originally intended to solve a relatively narrow range of engineering problems, it was immediately apparent that much more had been accomplished. It turned out that the measurement of information had important connections with fundamental ideas in physics, chemistry, biology, and psychology.

Information and Uncertainty

In order to understand the way in which information can be measured we must first agree on certain basic facts about a communication system. A simple, old-fashioned telegraph system can serve as our model, since it has all the essential parts but few of the complexities of modern equipment. What are those essential parts: there is a written message to be transmitted; there is a telegrapher who can translate letters into dots and dashes according to a prearranged code; there is a sending key, wire, and somewhere a receiving key; and there is another telegrapher who translates dots and dashes back into letters. We might diagram the system this way:

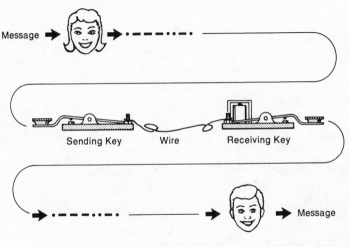

Figure 4.1

Notice that the actual machinery plays a relatively modest role in this system. The keys and wire could easily be replaced by flashing lights or a loud horn if the receiver isn't too far away. The point is that there must be some way of getting a message across some distance. Exactly which way is used is unimportant for our purposes. What is critical is that the spoken or written signals that people ordinarily use in communicating with each other will not travel over the channel we choose. There is simply no way for the telegraph key, the flashing light, or the horn to speak or write English directly in the form that people can understand. In other words what we need to focus on is what's going on in the telegrapher's head. If we were to list the critical parts of this system that are inside the telegrapher we would have to include three things: an alphabet, the set of possible signals (dot and dash), and a set of rules (a code) for relating each letter in the alphabet to a particular combination of dots and dashes. In order to keep things uncomplicated, let's assume that the alphabet being used here includes only eight letters. The following code will serve to translate the letters into dots and dashes:

ALPHABET	CODE
C	. . .
G	. . -
I	. - .
M	. - -
N	- . .
O	- . -
S	- - .
V	- - -

Figure 4.2

Limited as it is this will still allow us to send a variety of abbreviated messages:

GOV IS MISSING   (The Governor is missing)

COG COMING MON   (The cog (you ordered) is coming Monday)

IM GOING MON   (I'm going Monday)

Now we're ready to consider the problem of measuring the information moving over this system. How might we go about it?

The basic problem here and in any communication system is that the receiver is full of uncertainty. When the system is set up and a code is agreed upon the receiver knows roughly the range of messages that can come to him over this channel. Yet at any one moment he never knows exactly which message it will be. From this viewpoint, *the purpose of a communication system is always to reduce the uncertainty the receiver has about which message will come at a given moment.* Notice that if the receiving telegrapher wanted to take the time, he could construct all of the possible messages of a certain length that he would ever receive before he gets anything off the wire. Simply by trying out all the possible combinations of letters up to a certain length he could write out a list of all the possible messages of that length. So in a very real sense the receiver already has all the possible messages when the system is set up. Thus, the problem is not so much to send a message, as to *select* one of the messages the receiver already has available to him. The purpose of the electrical signals on the wire is not actually to carry the message to the receiver, but to point out the one message that the sender intends.

In many respects this may seem a very strange way of looking at the situation. We ordinarily think of messages as things that are somehow new to us, somehow brought into our heads from outside. Yet, if we apply this view of communication to people it says that the sentences we speak or write serve basically as pointers. Their effectiveness depends upon the listener, in some sense, knowing what messages the speaker *might* send in advance. The messages themselves serve only to indicate which one of the possible messages the speaker intends at a given moment. It seems to say that if two persons are to communicate with each other they must first have roughly matched sets of ideas, which they will communicate about simply by indicating various ideas in succession. Yet, there are also reasons to believe that, as bizarre as it may seem, this is a more accurate view than the more common one.[1] Indeed at simpler levels it is quite obvious that this view is consistent with the facts of human communication. If we think of words as representatives of individual ideas (a very crude approximation to the truth) then it is clear that a word will never have the intended meaning for a person until he or she has the idea that goes with that word. That is to say, in order to understand the word when it appears in a message, the idea that goes with it must already be inside the receiver's head waiting to be selected and put into combination with other ideas also represented by the same message. If it were not already in the receiver's head, how would it get there? As we have seen, sentence meanings can't be *in* the physical signals unless we can explain how they can be different for different persons or different for the same person on different occasions. Word meanings also can't be in the physical signals. Consider this: the French word "chien" and the English word "dog" mean the same thing. If Frenchmen and Englishmen have essentially the same thoughts when they use these words, and the meanings are actually in the physical signals, why can't anyone who understands English also understand French? At the still simpler levels of the sounds or letters that make up a word it is even clearer that this selection model of the communication process is appropriate. The question is whether it is appropriate at the highest levels of human intelligence and communication. This certainly seems less likely because of the apparent creativity and unpredictability of human thinking and communication. Still, there is reason to believe that these ideas will someday be helpful in thinking about those processes as well.

Measuring Information

But let's return to the problem of measuring the information on our simplified telegraph system and see how this notion of selecting messages will work for us. Obviously there is a very basic sense in which the electrical impulses on the wire are merely selecting things which the receiver already has, the letters of the alphabet. Clearly our telegraph system is going to work only if both the telegraphers are using the same alphabet. If three dots means C to one and A to the other, nothing is going to come out right. So in the actual case of sending signals over the wire, the combination of dots and dashes will serve to point to the various letters of the alphabet, one at a time. Whenever something comes down the wire that has the effect of reducing the receiver's uncertainty about which letter is intended, we can say that some information has been transmitted. Now notice that in the code of Figure 4.2, half of the strings of dots and dashes begin with a dot and half with a dash. Thus, whenever a string of signals starts off with a dot we know that the letter being selected has to be among the first four: C, G, I, or M. If the next signal after the dot is also a dot, we can eliminate I and M because we know that the signal strings which select them both have a dash in the second position. Now we have received only two dots, and our uncertainty is narrowed down to C and G. If the third signal is a dot, the telegrapher will know that C has been selected and he will write it down. If a dash comes over, he writes down G. Then the next string of signals starts and the process is repeated until the whole message has been selected.

This example shows the basic unit of communication at work. The unit is the **bit**, and we say that a bit of information has been relayed whenever the receiver's uncertainty has been cut in half. Notice that this is exactly what happens every time our telegrapher receives a dot or a dash in this code. Each time he gets a signal he can eliminate half of the remaining letters from consideration. Thus, each dot or dash in our telegraph system conveys one bit of information.

But notice that the bit is not defined in terms of the dots and dashes. The bit, and thus the flow of information, is defined by the effect a given signal has on the receiver. In more realistic situations the actual measurement of the information moving on a channel gets more complicated because receivers can often guess which signal is coming next before they receive it. Suppose, for instance, that the receiving telegrapher gets just this much of a message:

COG COMIN...

What might the next letter be? The telegrapher can of course guess that the next letter is probably going to be G. It doesn't have to be but the odds are that it will be. So when the next sequence of signals starts out with a dot we can't really say that it cuts the receiver's uncertainty in half, because it has already been reduced by his guess. Some uncertainty has been eliminated by the dot, but it is not half. Likewise when the second signal also turns out to be a dot, we can't really say that half the receiver's doubt has been eliminated, because out of the remaining choices the telegrapher knew beforehand that the next letter could not be an M and was very unlikely to be an I.

If this guessing process goes far enough, we reach a point where sending dots and dashes over the wire conveys no information at all. Suppose a telegrapher begins transmitting the text of the Declaration of Independence. As soon as a receiving telegrapher recognizes the text, "When in the course of human events...," he could look up a copy of the full text without receiving anything more over the wire. The only purpose served by all the thousands of dots and dashes to come after those first few would be to indicate just how much of the text was to be transmitted. The average value of each dot and dash in terms of information transmitted would be near to zero bits. Another way to put it is to say that when the telegrapher is sending the Declaration of Independence, he is exercising no choice. The entire long sequence of dots and dashes he sends is dictated by the text, which the receiver already knows. As long as he sticks to the text he has no choice about what to send. *As long as he has no choice, he transmits no information.*

Let's review what we've said about measuring information. We have defined the transmission of information as some action in a communication system that reduces the receiver's uncertainty about which of a set of possible messages is intended. The basic unit for measuring information is the bit, which is the amount of information required to reduce the receiver's uncertainty by half about which message or part of a message has been chosen in a particular situation. The transmission of information requires that the receiver know what the possible messages are in advance, and that the sender have some freedom of choice in selecting messages. The most important observation, though, is simply that we can in principle measure information, that slippery quantity which we found appearing in and disappearing from the messages we considered earlier. We have seen that information is a real quantity, even if it is not much like the quantities we are used to dealing with. In one way we have measured the relationship that must exist between receiver and message in order for a message to convey information. In fact, now that we've said this much about information we may go on to make some other observations which make it look even more unusual.

The Properties of Information

There are certain laws that apply to most quantities we know that restrict the things we can do with them. If you have a pile of bricks, you can keep it or give it away but not both. If you give away what you've got you'll always increase the amount of bricks that are not yours, and decrease those that are yours. If you choose to give your bricks away, anybody can receive them.

Information is not like this. Information can be given away and kept at the same time. The telegrapher in our example doesn't suddenly forget the message he sends as soon as it's sent. If the requirements for communication are met, the end result will be that the amount of information the sender conveys to the receiver will exist in two places instead of one. The sender will have given away information without losing any. Indeed he can keep on giving it away as long as there are new receivers to receive it; and never does he lose any information. There are, however, restrictions. Not everyone will be able to receive from every sender. Just as a telegrapher who has a different alphabet will not be able to receive from the telegrapher in our example, so communication will always require that sender and receiver be set up to use the same signals, codes, etc. They must either directly or indirectly agree in advance or there will be no communication. This also means that an attempt at communication can always turn out to be a dud. If the person at the receiving end in communication isn't prepared to receive my message, I can go on sending forever without ever communicating any information. But if I take one of the bricks from my pile and throw it away, there will always be one more brick in the world outside my pile.

Perhaps the most basic and important property of information is simply that it can be created and destroyed. This fact has enormous implications for our understanding of human behavior, but to see exactly why this is true we would have to go well beyond the scope of this article.

The Minimal Communication System

Before we turn our attention especially to how all this relates to people, let's summarize the way communication is organized when machines are involved. We can start with the message that a customer might hand a telegrapher for transmission. In order for the message to be transmitted, there is just one condition that must be satisfied: the message must be written in an alphabet for which the telegrapher has a code. It doesn't matter what language the message is in and it doesn't matter whether the telegrapher can understand it as long as it uses only the letters covered by his code. Therefore, the first critical part of the simplified communication system is the alphabet in which messages are written. The reason that the alphabet is critical is that the rules the telegrapher uses for translating the message into a signal on the wire refer to just this alphabet. These rules are the second critical part of the system. The third critical part is the set of signals into which the message is translated. All of these parts are inside the telegrapher's head. The actual translation of the message into electrical signals on the wire is a simple, mechanical process which is really less basic to the whole system than the process by which the telegrapher translates the message into the dot-dash code. As we noted before, many different machines could be substituted for the telegraph key and wire, but none of these would work satisfactorily if it weren't for the alphabet, the dots and dashes, and the rules that link these two. Still none of this does us any good unless all of it is matched at the other end of our system. Unless the receiving telegrapher can pick up the dots and dashes, use the same rules, and come up with the same message we start with, we haven't got an adequate system.

All of this is summarized in Figure 3. This diagram represents the minimal components of a communication system: a transmitter that has a set of symbols (an alphabet), a set of signals (dots and dashes), and a set of rules relating symbols to signals. Matched to the transmitter at the other end of the channel (the wire) is a receiver which has all the same critical parts as the transmitter. Any system that satisfies the requirements summarized by this diagram will serve the purpose of communication no matter what sort of machine is used to carry the signals back and forth between the two ends.

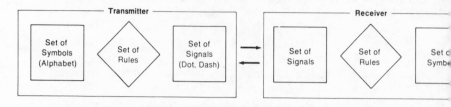

Figure 4.3   The Minimal Communication System

Human Communication in the Light of Machine Communication

Now let's consider some of the ways that these ideas about machine communication may be relevant to the study of human communication. As we do this, there are two kinds of questions to keep in mind: Do the ideas about machine communication seem to be consistent in important ways with what we already know about human communication? Do these ideas about machine communication suggest new ideas about human communication that might not come to us if we approach the subject from some other perspective? In other words, if there seem to be interesting similarities between machine communication and human communication, we then want to see whether our knowledge of machine communication will help us to form new and interesting guesses (theories) about human communication.

It is easy to see that there are a number of ways in which human communication and machine communication seem to be similarly organized. Like communication machines, people must rely on physical signals to carry their messages. Ideas can't float from brain to brain by themselves any more than telegraph messages can float from New York to London on their own. All types of messages must be translated into some physical signal in communication. And just as rules make the translation between message and signal possible in machines, so too in human communication there appears to be a highly complex set of rules relating sound to meaning. Modern linguists have shown that by far the most economical way to describe how human languages make the connection between sound and meaning is to use a set of rules.[2] At the most basic level there is clearly a complex set of rules for relating the sounds of speech to the units of sound that make up the lowest level of language. This aspect of human communication is much too complicated to deal with here. The general point is that there is a very complex relation between the actual sounds that come out of people's mouths in speech and the phonetic units, like [p], [t], [k], [a], [o], etc., out of which words are made. For instance, the actual sounds that represent the phonetic unit [d] are very different in the word "deal" than in the word "duty." There appears to be a highly sophisticated decoder in the human hearing system which translates this widely varying set of sound signals into the limited set of units used to build up a language. The essential middle element in this decoder is apparently describable as a set of rules.

At a more complex level of language there are rules which enable people to relate the strings of words they hear when someone speaks a sentence to the meaning of that sentence. Though we are no more aware of the operation of these rules than we are aware of the rules used by the sound decoder mentioned above, it is clear that we could not use language as we do if there were not such a set of rules. For instance, one of the things this set of rules does is discover some of the cases where different sentences mean the same thing. It is this particular set of rules that tell English-speaking people that "The student read the book" and "The book was read by the student" are nearly identical in meaning despite the considerable difference in the surface form of these sentences.

In language we do not so much send messages from one person to another as we select messages which the receiver already knows how to construct. If we think of sentences as strings of sound units or as strings of words, this idea is clearly appropriate. The receiver is always familiar with a certain number of words, and with relatively rare exceptions the messages received are constructed out of those words. In this sense, the sounds you hear in a message select a certain group of words out of your vocabulary and indicate how the speaker wants you to arrange them. From this string of words you then attempt to reconstruct the thought the speaker had in mind when he formed that sentence. Beyond this point you must use much general knowledge of (beliefs about) the situation in which the sentence is spoken, knowledge about the personality of the speaker, and your knowledge about the nature of the subject, in order to reconstruct the thought. Some of the knowledge you will use deals specifically with the decoding of messages and some is knowledge dealing with general problem-solving. It remains very difficult to see how the total meaning of a sentence or of a complete message could be said to be selected out of a set of possibilities since for every human being there is literally an infinite number of possibilities. Yet it may well be that these ideas, together with an understanding of the power and productivity of rules, will prove most useful in further exploration of this remarkable human capacity for communication.

Overall it does seem that there are important parallels between the way machines communicate and the way that people communicate. The system which people use appears to be much more complicated since there seem to be many levels through which a sentence must go in order to be understood. At one time or another a message is expressed as a series of sounds, a series of phonetic units, a series of words, and so forth. There also appear to be a number of "undiscovered" levels between, above, and below those we know of now. Yet each of those levels seems to be linked to the levels above and below it in the system by a set of rules and, at least at the more basic levels, each level consists of a definite number of units, whether sounds or words or something else.

It will be a very long time before anyone knows just which of the ideas originating in the study of communication machines are truly helpful in understanding human communication and which of them are misleading. In the meantime, the study of communication machines surely provides us with one of the most sophisticated and provocative ways of looking at the process of human communication.

QUESTIONS FOR DISCUSSION

1. People are not machines, so why can the study of machine communication help us to understand human communication?
2. Give several examples that have not been given in the readings which illustrate why information cannot be in the message.
3. How is information related to uncertainty?
4. List as many ways as you can in which information differs from matter-energy.
5. What does Cowart suggest are the minimum components necessary to form a communication system? Remove any one of these components and attempt to describe how communication might occur without it.

NOTES

1. For those familiar with generative linguistic theory, it may be easier to see how the listener can know all possible messages in advance. To do this the listener does not need to have an actual list of the possibilities. He needs to know only what elements the messages are composed of and what the rules are for combining these into complex structures. In this sense every English-speaking person in principle knows in advance all the sentences which he can understand because he can construct all those sentences by combining the words he knows according to the rules of sentence formation that he also knows.

2. Indeed, a remarkably powerful account of the underlying structure of sentences, the relations between different types of sentence, the notion of ambiguity, and other aspects of meaning and structure can be constructed using only the two basic types of rules. One type of rule is an instruction to rewrite an element as something else. In other words, change X into Y. With only a handful of such rules we can generate simple sentences:

Rule 1. Sentence - - - ➤ *Noun Phrase + Verb Phrase*
Rule 2. Noun Phrase - - ➤ [the man, Mary, my dog. . . .]
Rule 3. Verb Phrase - - - ➤ *Verb + Noun Phrase*
Rule 4. Verb - - - ➤   [loves, likes, hates . . .]

To use the rules, we simply start with the first one and do what it says, rewrite "Sentence" as a noun phrase plus a verb phrase. Then we rewrite each of these two elements in turn according to the rules that apply to them. Where there are several elements within brackets to the right of the arrow we choose only one on each use of the rule.

Sentence

Step 1	Noun Phrase + Verb Phrase	(by Rule 1)
Step 2	Noun Phrase + Verb + Noun Phrase	(by Rule 3)
Step 3	Mary + loves + my dog	(by Rules 2 and 4)

The other kind of rule rearranges a string of elements, sometimes adding or deleting elements as it does so. One can write a rudimentary description of English passives using this type of rule:

Rule 5. *Noun Phrase*   *Verb*   *Noun Phrase*

I   II   III

III (be)   II+ed   by I

The rule says that we should take the second noun phrase in a sentence and move it to the front, add a form of "be" behind it, follow that with the verb from the original sentence, add the past tense ending "-ed" to the verb, and follow that with the first noun phrase preceded by "by." Using this rule we can take sentences generated by Rules 1-4 and change them into passives. For instance, with Rules 1-4 we can construct "Mary loves my dog," and with Rule 5 we can turn this into the passive sentence "My dog is loved by Mary."

In the two previous articles, Bender and Hocking, and Cowart, discussed the relationship between *information, meaning,* and *communication* and introduced many other concepts that are used in the study of human communication. In "Modelling the Communication Process," Berlo continues the discussion of these topics and introduces the concepts of *process* and *system* and related notions such as *feedback.* Notice that *feedback* is commonly used in two different ways. Bender and Hocking used it to refer to one person's *response* to another person's message. Berlo discusses feedback as the existence of a link or *channel* between the receiver of a message and the source of the message, which complements the channel from source to receiver. "Modelling the Communication Process" discusses past attempts to model communication, the minimum conditions in order for communication to occur, and the basic effects that communication has on information.

5

modelling the communication process

David K. Berlo

The second essay, *Human Communication: The Basic Proposition*, introduced the notions of matter-energy transfer, information transfer, and communication—and attempted to delineate the differences between these three kinds of processes. It should be recognized that the second essay simply provided an overview of the distinctive characteristics of a communication process. It was not intended as a definitive discussion, but only as a beginning. We shall frequently return to that basic distinction in an attempt to clarify what is meant by communication.

This essay is intended to elicit additional meaning for *communication* by providing a model for a communication transaction. In such a model we need to explain further some basic concepts involved in communication study. Let's look at some of these. If communication is viewed as the transfer of symbolic information, we need to specify what is meant by *symbolic* and by *information*. The concept of information has to do with patterning of discriminable units of matter-energy. One cannot have meaning for pattern unless there are alternatives; i.e., if units of matter-energy can be grouped in one and only one way, with no alternative, we do not talk about the patterning of that matter-energy. To state it differently, a constant is not perceived to have pattern; or, to say it one more way, there is no meaning without contrast.

Given the possibility of two or more patterns, there is *uncertainty* as to which pattern will occur. This concept of uncertainty is central to

This essay was originally part of the reading material in an introductory communication course at Michigan State University. It appears in published form for the first time in this book.

an understanding of human communication. Finally, we refer to information and communication *processes* as well as transfer. The concept of *process* is central to communication. In turn, process implies *system*. As we shall see, it is not meaningful to talk about human communication out of the context of system. Communication is always imbedded in systems and system relationships.

In summary, then, we shall attempt to model a communication transaction in a way that will give us insight into the nature of human communication. That modelling requires that we acquire meaning for the following concepts: *symbol, information, uncertainty, process,* and *system*.

In modelling a process, we may enumerate the components or elements in the system and the structural relationships among those components, or we may specify the activities or functions of those components, or both. As Deutch points out,[1] modelling serves several purposes. A **model** helps organize data, helps provide a conceptual frame to talk about something. It also can serve to generate thinking and hypotheses about the system. Third, it can provide as well as lead to actual predictions about the way in which the system operates. Finally, by providing sufficiently precise statements about the structure and function of the system, it can dictate how to measure various states of the system.

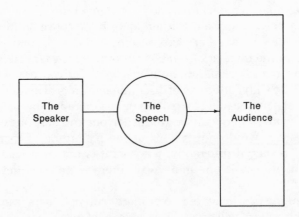

Figure 5.1   A Diagram of Communication According to Aristotle's Model

Figures 5.1 to 5.4 have been added to the original text by the editor

Attempts to model communication transactions should be guided by all four of those objectives. At present, however, most communication models have been restricted to naming the components in the system. A few have attempted to make preliminary statements about how communication works; however, most have not.

Aristotle provided one of the first communication models in the *Rhetoric* when he said that we have to look at three communication ingredients: the speaker, the speech, and the audience. (See Figure 5.1.) He argued that each of these elements is necessary to communication and that we can organize our study of the process under the three headings of 1. the person who speaks, 2. the speech that he produces, and 3. the person who listens.[2]

Little (or no) progress was made in constructing communication models for the next two thousand years. As witness, we can look at the two contemporary models which have had the most influence on thought. In 1948, Lasswell described communication by asking five questions:[3]

1. Who?
2. Says what?
3. In which channel?
4. To whom?
5. With what effect?

In Aristotle's day, there were no print media nor electronic media; therefore, his "who?" was the speaker. His "what?" and "which channel?" was the speech, and his "whom?" was the listener. As for effect, Aristotle discussed several; however, Aristotle believed that the primary goal of communication was persuasion, an attempt to sway other men to the speaker's point of view. Rhetoric, in fact, was defined as the search for "all the available means of persuasion."[4]

The other contemporary communication model of major influence was introduced in 1949 by Shannon and Weaver. (See Figure 5.2.) All discussions since 1949 have used the Shannon-Weaver model as a base, even though it was not a model of communication at all but only of information processing. Shannon, a mathematician, and Weaver, an electrical engineer, developed a model that was used to measure the correspondence of speech patterns when they were at various points in an electronic transmission system (i.e., the telephone system). Their model was not concerned with the *reference* of information, but only with the *fidelity* of the information. By fidelity, they meant a correspondence in pattern between input and output.[5]

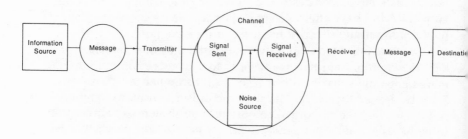

Figure 5.2   Shannon and Weaver's Model of Information
               Transfer
               Adapted from C. Shannon and W. Weaver. *The Mathe-
               matical Theory of Communication* (Urbana, Illinois: Uni-
               versity of Illinois Press, 1949).

Shannon and Weaver[6] said that the ingredients in communication include a source, a transmitter, a signal, a receiver, and a destination. If we translate the source into the speaker, the signal into the speech, and the destination into the listener, we again have the Aristotelian model, plus two added ingredients: a transmitter, which sends the source's message, and a receiver, which catches the message for the destination.

None of these three models explicitly attempts to talk about how communication works, i.e., none provides propositions about the process or function of communication. They are consistent, however, in the implicit assumption of the *directionality* of the transaction. One would infer that for Aristotle communication starts with the speaker, for Shannon-Weaver it starts with the source, for Lasswell it starts with the "who?" This kind of *source orientation* is antagonistic to the concept of system, which will be discussed below.

The three models also are in agreement in viewing the relationship between source and destination as one of dependence on the part of the destination. One gets the impression that communication involves something that one person does to another, and that the doer is free to do most anything he pleases. The listener is dependent on the speaker, but not vice versa, and so on. This assumption of *dependence* rather than interdependence of communication participants is also antagonistic to the concept of system.

The third consistency among models is the implicit assumption that *whatever is of significance* in communication *is carried by the message* that is transferred, i.e., that the "speech" or "signal" or "what?" conveys significance. This causes no problem in the Shannon-Weaver model if one recognizes that it is a model only of information process, not communication process; however, it is a significant problem in the Aristotelian and Lasswellian formulations. Their position is inconsistent with current thinking about the nature of information, the relationship between information and uncertainty, the notion of a symbol as pattern which refers to something at another systems level, and it is inconsistent with the concept of relativity of meaning.

These three points have characterized most thinking about human communication. In general (and, I believe, in error), most people seem to believe that:

Communication *begins* when someone speaks—or writes—or draws.

Communication is something that some people *do* to other people, usually, getting the other people to comply with what they're told.

Communication involves the *conveyance* (or movement or transfer or flow) *of ideas*; the message carries the meaning.

If we are to change those beliefs, we need to understand the concepts of *process, system,* and *information-symbol-uncertainty.*

The Concept of Process

The phrase "In the beginning was the Word" may be appropriate as a theological proposition; however, as a worldly statement, it leads to serious misconception of communication. For one thing, words come after experience, not before. For another, the notion of beginning—and end—are antagonistic to the concept of process.

If we are to accept a view of the world that separates activities into things and actions (and their verbal accompaniments, nouns and verbs), and if we talk about *A* causing *B*, and things as having a beginning, a middle and an end, we are not using the vocabulary of a process orientation. When we say that the relationship between *A* and *B* either is coordinate, subordinate-superordinate, or irrelevant, we are not using the syntax of a process orientation.

If such statements are not processual, what is? At least one dictionary defines *process* as "any phenomenon which shows continuous change in time," or "any continuous operation or treatment." Five hundred years before the birth of Christ, Heraclitus pointed out the implications of process when he stated that a man can never step in the same river twice: the man is different, so is the river, and so is the context. Thomas Wolfe's novel of the 1930s, *You Can't Go Home Again*, makes the same point. To say it differently, the only permanence is change.

If we accept the concept of *process*, we view events and relationships as dynamic, ongoing, ever-changing, continuous. When we label something as a process, we also mean that it does not have *a* beginning, *an* end, a fixed sequence of events. It is not static, at rest. It is moving. The ingredients within a process interact; each affects all of the others.

The concept of process is inextricably woven into the contemporary view of science and physical reality. In fact, the development of a process viewpoint in the physical sciences brought about one of the twentieth-century revolutions. If we analyze the work of physical scientists up to and including Isaac Newton, we do not find a comprehensive analysis of process. It was believed that the world could be divided into "things" and "processes." It was believed also that things *existed*, that they were static entities, that their existence was independent of the existence or operations of other "things."

The crisis and revolution in scientific philosophy brought about by the work of Einstein, Russell, Whitehead, and others denied both of these beliefs in two ways. First, the concept of relativity suggested that any given object or event could only be analyzed or described in light of other events that were related to it, other operations involved in observing it. Second, the availability of more powerful observational techniques led to the demonstration that something as static or stable as a table or a chair could be looked on as a constantly changing phenomenon, acting upon and being acted upon by all other objects in its environment, changing as the person who observes it changes. The traditional division between things and things was questioned. The traditional distinction between things and processes was broken. An entirely different way of looking at the world had to be developed—a process view of reality.

Communication theory reflects a process point of view. A communication theorist rejects the argument that nature consists of events or ingredients that are separate from all other events. He argues that you cannot talk about *the* beginning or *the* end of communication or say that a particular idea came from one specific source, that communication occurs in only one way, and so on.

The basis for the concept of process is the belief that the structure of physical reality cannot be *discovered* by man; it must be *created* by man. In "constructing" reality, the theorist chooses to organize his perceptions in one way or another. He may choose to say that we can call certain things "elements" or "ingredients." In doing this he realizes that he has not discovered anything—he has created a set of tools which may or may not be useful in analyzing or describing the world. He recognizes that certain things may precede others, but that in many cases the order of precedence will vary from situation to situation. This is not to say that we can place no order on events. The dynamic of process does not deny order; it does deny the "reality" of any fixed order.

When we try to talk or write about a process, such as communication, we face at least two problems. First, we must arrest the dynamic of the process, in the same way that we arrest motion when we take a still picture with a camera. We can make useful observations from photographs, but we err if we forget that the picture is not a complete reproduction of the objects photographed. The relationships among elements are obliterated; the fluidity of motion, the dynamics, are arrested. The picture is a representation of the event. It is not the event. As Hayakawa put it, the word is not the thing, it is merely a map that we can use to guide us in exploring the territories of the world.

A second problem in describing a process derives from the necessity for the use of language. Language itself, as used by people over time, is a process. It, too, is changing, ongoing; however, the process quality of language is lost when we write it. Marks on paper are a *recording* of language, a picture of language. They are fixed, permanent, static.

In using language to describe a process, we must choose certain words; we must freeze the physical world in a certain way. Furthermore, we must put some words first, others last. Western books go from left to right, from top to bottom. All languages go from "front" to "back," "beginning" to "end," even though we are aware that the process we are describing may not have a left and right, a top and bottom, a beginning and an end.

This static left-to-rightness, beginning-to-endness, has contributed to many of our models of communication. It contributes to "who says what to whom with what effect," as well as "source creates message for destination," and so forth. To some extent, the characteristics of language make such statements inevitable. To that extent, we must be wary of the ways in which we interpret linguistic reports of any process, including communication processes. However, the limitations in our view of communication are attributable to more than a lack of understanding of process. They are attributable to a lack of understanding of the concept of system.

The Concept of System

The idea of *system* is one of the more exciting concepts of the twentieth century. Today, we take the concept for granted and talk about it casually. For example, we refer to our high-fidelity systems. We talk about getting through the system, or playing it, or beating it, or giving in to it—or even destroying it. We've learned to talk about weapons systems, social systems, the human body as a system. We study systems of playing bridge, or roulette, or dating.

The term *system* is used with high frequency; however, the depth of meaning we have for it or our understanding of its implications is often less than adequate. For example, those who argue that the best way to rehabilitate prisoners to live in society is to remove them from that society until they are ready to return, don't understand the concept of system. Neither do those who talk about mental disturbance as something some people "have," as they would have a broken leg, or a leg of lamb. Those who pollute the air, the land, or the water don't understand the notion of system—or they care not whether they destroy it.

What do we mean by *system*? A thorough answer to that question lies beyond the scope of this essay. Whole books are devoted to the subject. For our purposes, we'll sketch only some of the simpler requirements for the use of the term so that we can relate *system* to *communication*.

Let's take an example with which most of us are familiar: the hi-fi system. Why do we call it a system? For one thing, we are able to specify what is part of it and what is external to it. We can isolate and name a set of matter-energy units which have something in common, and we can specify the boundaries of the set of units. That is one requirement for the term system—the delineation of a set of units and some specification of the boundary of the set.

When we describe a system, we are enumerating the *components* of the set of units. We can talk about speakers, tape decks, amplifiers, tuners, phonographs, and so forth. We can talk about the relationships among those components. The set of components and the relationships among them are referred to as the *structure* of the system.

What does the hi-fi system do? What is its function? It processes information. Given inputs of patterned matter-energy (e.g., a record, a tape, electronic stimuli from the air), it processes that information and produces an output which is audible to the human ear. Quality in such a system is indexed by such things as ability to detect information of various kinds and the distortion which the processing imposes on that information. Evaluation of the system involves an assessment of quality relative to costs and the ability of a second system (the human organism) to process the information it produces.

As a beginning, then, we can specify a **system** as a set of units which can be distinguished from the environment, the set of units having both structure and function. The functioning of the system occurs over time; therefore, we can say that a system has a history, a future, and is evolving.

There are at least three additional concepts implied in the notion of system. The first is interdependency. In our hi-fi set, we don't talk about the effects the tuner has on the speaker, nor do we say that the phonograph causes certain responses in the amplifier. The traditional deterministic notions of cause and effect are subordinated in discussing a system. They are replaced by the idea of changes in the state of the system over time, and the relationship of interdependency among all components of the system. The *dependency* concept of cause-effect is replaced by the *interdependency* notion of change of state. When we say that each component of a system affects each other, we have inhibited the idea that some components do things to others. We have inhibited the idea of *directionality* of effect. Each component affects the other, change is *multi-directional*.

In a traditional cause-effect frame, we talk about actions producing actions (e.g., stimuli producing responses), or action-reaction relationships. The systems frame substitutes the notion of interaction for action-reaction. How does that substitution occur? By a concept that suggests two-way flow of matter-energy rather than one-way flow: the concept of **feedback**. When we talk about feedback loops within a system, we mean that there not only is a path from A to B, but there is one from B to A as well. Feedback implies reciprocity, interdependence.

The term *system* now can be used to refer to a set of components, the structural relationships among those components, and the functions or processes which occur. Components of a system are interdependent, and are linked through reciprocal loops, one of which is referred to as a feedback loop.

One final concept remains. We talked about a hi-fi system and its components: speaker, tuner, amplifier, and so forth. Any of these components itself could be considered a system; i.e., we could talk about the amplifier system. At the same time we could talk about the relationship between the hi-fi system, matter-energy produced for it to process (e.g., a recording), and an individual listening to the output of the hi-fi. Those three units (producer, hi-fi, consumer) also could be viewed as a system in which the hi-fi is a component. What we call a system and what we call a component or sub-system are determined by the level of our interest. Systems vary in complexity as we move from level to level. There is no correct level at which to study a system. The choice of level is determined by the purposes of our concern. It is important to realize that there are levels and to be sure that we do not confuse levels as we analyze systems.[7]

In summary, then, systems have interdependent components (at a given level of complexity). The interdependence is produced through feedback loops among the components. These components have both a structure and a function. Their matter-energy characteristics and the relationships among those characteristics (structure) can be described, as can the process of the system; i.e., the changes in state over time (function).

Now we are ready for a basic proposition. When we say that we are studying the process of communication, we are implying that we are studying (1) functions which communication serves (2) over time. We should specify (3) the level of complexity of the system in which communication is imbedded and (4) the nature of the feedback loops which permit the interdependence of components. Communication then, at a minimum, involves the *systematic* transfer of symbolic information. As we have defined it, communication doesn't occur external to some concept of system, and it is not meaningful to study or discuss it without doing so within the context of system. The functions which communication serve are separable and varied. The levels of complexity of systems in which communication occurs also are separable and varied. However:

> The goal of communication study is an understanding of the functions of symbolic information transfer in structured systems of varying complexity—over time.

The models of Aristotle, Shannon-Weaver, and Lasswell do not predispose one to think in terms of such concepts as process, system, interdependency, feedback loop, structure-function, level, and others. These models, and most which have followed,[8] are undirectional and deterministic. Even if feedback is included as a concept, it is used to refer to a *reaction*—and an interpretation of that reaction—

rather than as a *link* which makes the flow of information nondirectional. These communication models fail to make clear that the concept of process implies the idea of a circle; given feedback loops, we can't talk about the beginning and the end. It does make sense to talk about a chicken as a device an egg uses to reproduce itself.

Some models of the past twenty years have suggested more of a systems approach. Gerbner,[9] though basically following the Shannon-Weaver direction, emphasized the necessity of inputs for the communication source and the perceptual problems of the source. He also emphasized the idea of a transaction between source and receiver. Fearing[10] presented a very simple model; however, it was significant in its emphasis on interpendence and on the dynamic of process. It also related communication to uncertainty, an emphasis we shall return to later.

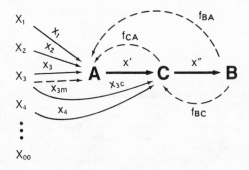

The messages C transmits to B (x") represent his selections from both messages to him from A's (x') and C's selections and abstractions from Xs in his own sensory field (x₃c, x₄), which may or may not be Xs in A's field. Feedback not only moves from B to A (fBA) and from B to C (fBC) but also from C to A (fCA). Clearly, in the mass communication situation, a large number of Cs receive from a very large number of As and transmit to a vastly larger number of Bs, who simultaneously receive from other Cs.

Figure 5.3   The Westley and MacLean Model of the Essential Elements of the Communication Process
From B. Westley and M. MacLean, "A Conceptual Model for Communications Research," *Journalism Quarterly* (Winter 1957), 31-38.

One of the most sophisticated of models is that of Westley and MacLean.[11] Among other things, they emphasized the importance of feedback, placed communication in the frame of an external environ-

ment, made clear that communication is an alternative to direct experience, and distinguished various communicator roles—implying the
continuity of process. Many of these system concepts were also incor-
porated in the model produced by Wendell Johnson.[12]

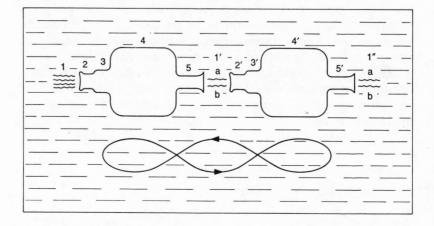

Key: *Stage 1, event, or source of stimulation, external to the sensory end
organs of the speaker; Stage 2, sensory stimulation; Stage 3, preverbal
neurophysiological state; Stage 4, transformation of preverbal into symbolic
forms; Stage 5, verbal formulations in "final draft" for overt expression;
Stage 1', transformation of verbal formulations into (a) air waves and
(b) light waves, which serve as sources of stimulation for the listener (who
may be either the speaker himself or another person); Stages 2' through 1"
correspond, in the listener, to Stages 2 through 1'. The arrowed loops
represent the functional interrelationships of the stages in the process as
a whole.*

Figure 5.4   Wendell Johnson's Model of Communication
               From the *Quarterly Journal of Speech* (December 1955),
               419-429.

I am not arguing that communication cannot be viewed outside
the concept of system, and certainly not that it has not been so viewed.
I am suggesting, however, that it is not fruitful to talk about communication other than as it occurs within a system frame, and that our
understanding of communication principles and our creation of new
principles will not occur unless we do impose the system concept on
our inquiry.

A further implication of a systems orientation bears mention. It is the notion that, in a system, the whole is greater than the sum of its parts; i.e., the patterning of parts is added to the system but is not present if one views components individually. A lack of understanding of this proposition typifies models of communication which look at individual components; e.g., in Borden's discussion of human communication, he says that "we ultimately have to consider the communicative behavior of various individuals."[13] Such a position can be contrasted with the sophisticated view of Ackoff, who is discouraged that "in an era that is so systems-oriented ... an era in which we are becoming increasingly more interested in wholes than in their parts ... human behavior is still conceived, observed, analyzed, experimented on and otherwise treated in a piecemeal way."[14] If we are to impose the concept of system on our view of communication, how shall it be done? An answer to that question requires a somewhat clearer explication of what we mean by symbolic information, or, to be more specific, a symbolic informational system.

Symbolic Information

Earlier, we said that the concept of information implies the imposition of pattern on matter-energy. Perhaps a brief review of that idea will be usefully redundant. To impose a pattern, matter-energy must be divisible into discriminable units; i.e., until the stream of sound producible by man can be perceived as discriminable units of speech, no oral communication will be possible—nor will the information transfer called "song" be possible.

Information is pattern. For there to be information, there must be the possibility of variability, the possibility of alternatives. This is difficult to learn for those who have been taught that one should say of what is, that it is. Why? Because the notion of information implies that nothing "is" except in terms relative to its "is not." Until the beginning of this century, man's philosophy was primarily based on notions of matter and energy. Now, it needs to be based as well, and even primarily, on notions of pattern and information. Relativity theory posits that everything is relative. We all have experienced this. For example, when flying, or riding in a train, one can't tell whether his vehicle is moving or a vehicle he observes is moving, or both, unless he relates both vehicles to a third reference point (e.g., the horizon, physical objects like buildings, and so forth). Movement is relative, of course; however, so is being.

Watzlawick and his colleagues say it well:

Every child learns at school that movement is something relative, which can only be perceived in relation to a point of reference. What is not realized by everyone is that this same principle holds for virtually every perception, and, therefore, for man's experience of reality. Sensory and brain research have proved conclusively that only relationships and patterns of relationships can be perceived, and these are the essence of experience. Thus when, by an ingenious device, eye movement is made impossible so that the same image continues to be perceived by the same areas of the retina, clear visual perception is no longer possible.[15]

Information, then, involves the imposition of pattern on previously undifferentiated matter-energy. It is the source of power to control, the source of meaningfulness. It is inferred from the occurrence of certain events and the nonoccurence of others. The man often accused of disloyalty when he provides the response, "Compared to what?" to the question, "Do you love your wife?" actually is just a sophisticated student of information. There is no meaning in the concept of loving one's wife unless there is contrast between that and either (a) loving someone else, or (b) having other feelings toward one's wife.

Man gathers information by imposing structure on his perceptions. He processes information by processing pattern. Yet, we don't want to call all information processes communication processes. Why not? For one thing, if we place no limits on the kinds of events we shall label "communication," we have imposed no structure on human behavior and, therefore, we can create no information about communication. One definition of a *definition* is that it excludes. Secondly, there are many kinds of information processes that seem separable from communication. . . . Colin Cherry made some of the distinctions we need when he said, "An observer looking down a microscope or reading instruments is not to be equated with a listener on a telephone receiving spoken messages. Mother Nature does not communicate to us. . . . A communication channel should be distinguished from a channel of observation."[16]

A communication channel should be distinguished from a channel of observation. Agreed, but on what criterion? Both involve transfer of matter-energy. Both involve the patterning of that matter-energy; i.e., involve information. The distinction is that communication involves the use of a **symbol system**; i.e., the patterned matter-energy is used, not for itself, but *by convention*, to substitute for some other set of matter-energy. When we are communicating, we are not simply transferring pattern. We are transferring patterns that are linked (through learning) to a state of affairs, i.e., to some component or state of another system. We are transferring patterns that are themselves interdependent, that have a structure of their own, with components. We are transferring patterns that can be treated at various levels, patterns whose structure and function change over time. In short, we are transferring patterns that are elements in the system we refer to as a *language* .... We shall use the term **language** to refer to a system whose components are used to represent matter-energy units outside the system. That is what is meant when we say that communication is *about* something, that communication is information with reference. The elements in a language are called *symbols*.

The *minimum condition*, then, *for the use of the word* **communication** is a situation in which the matter-energy units that are transferred from X to Y are imbedded in a system that has the properties of language for both X and Y.

The term *language* has a broader referent than just English, or French, or analogous languages. Potentially, any set of matter-energy units can be used to construct a language. What are the prerequisites? 1. Pattern must be imposed on the matter-energy. 2. Users of the units must learn the relationships between these units and the referents these units shall be used to replace. 3. The set of units (symbols) shall evolve into a system; i.e., become interdependent, functional, and so forth. As man imposes pattern on matter-energy, he acquires power to control. As he establishes referent for those patterns, he increases his capacity to transfer information, and to control the nature of that information.[17]

This criterion allows us to sort most matter-energy situations into "yes" and "no" categories vis à vis communication; however, neither it nor any other criterion will provide a sorting procedure for which perfect agreement is possible. There are shaded areas, situations which could be argued to be communication or just information. For example, we probably could get agreement that the inference the forest rangers made as to the presence of fire, given smoke, was not communication. We undoubtedly would agree that when the rangers began to speak, in English, with Dick and Jane, it was communication. But what about the Indian who said, "You called?" If you argue that the puffs of smoke had, by convention, been used to represent or stand for particular Indian humans, and if you argue that those puffs were part of a symbol system, then communication. If not, no, just information. I would suggest that, though it is fun to argue about such situations, the resolution of the argument is of little importance to our understanding of communication processes. As Gerbner often puts it, we have to make up our minds as to whether we are trying to put up fences around the perimeter of the farm, so everyone can know whether or not he has crossed over the line—or whether we are trying to locate the house and barn so everyone can tell where the action is. I prefer the latter position. The criterion for "what is communication" is not intended to legislate each and every situation, but to *provide a focus for inquiry and discussion.*

It should be noticed that the criterion for labelling a situation as communication does *not* invoke such typical concepts as mutual awareness, intent, feedback, and so forth. These are all important variables; however, the imposition of them as minimal criteria would eliminate from the focus of communication study much of the data in which we are interested. In particular, a great deal of what we do in consuming the mass media seems encompassed only if we go to the minimal notion of transfer of symbolic information. The viewer of a TV program often has no intent with respect to the producer—or even any awareness of his existence. As Cherry points out, "The reading of a newspaper represents a unilateral, non-cooperative link." I doubt the intensity of Plato's intentions for me when he wrote *The Republic*, and I bear none for him. He gets no feedback from me, nor I from him. Yet, I think we want to call such situations communication situations.

If the minimal criterion doesn't imply social intent on the part of X or Y, or even awareness, it does impose one significant restriction on the X and Y components. They must both be language-users. The necessity for X and Y to be language-users does require us to attend to the characteristics of X and Y. Communication involves the analysis of the messages that are transferred; however, it also requires the analysis of the characteristics of those who send and receive them. Communication transfer is analogous to the concept of *potential*. That potential is in the user. Only when the pattern in the matter-energy and the pattern in the user interact does communication occur. Ackoff points up the central variable in that interaction:

> To improve communication processes we must understand *why* individuals choose to communicate in the way they do. We cannot start our analysis with messages that humans have produced; we must begin with the process by which they are produced. This is a matter of *choice*. Choice must be an integral part of any complete model of communication.[19]

Cherry says it a little differently, introducing the notion of doubt, and relating doubt to choice, first from the consumer's point of view, and then from the producer's.

Information can be received only when there is doubt; and doubt implies the existence of alternatives—where choice, selection or discrimination is called for.[20]

To set up communication, the signals must have at least some surprise value, some degree of unexpectedness, or it is a waste of time to transmit them.[21]

Users of language use it as a tool. Communication serves various functions for humans. The way in which people define a communication situation affects the way in which communication will occur in that situation. But what is the organizing concept for these various functions? Ignoring man's intentions, what are the consequents of communication?

The Effects of Communication

There are two different contexts in which communication consequents can be discussed: decision-making, and human motivation. In my opinion, the two contexts are theoretically identical; however, the terminology in each differs from that in the other. Let us first look at the consequents of communication in a decision-making context. We can delineate three components of a decision-process as follows:

1. The set of alternatives, i.e., acts within the environmental space that have occurred or could occur.
2. The set of criteria that can be used as a basis for that decision, i.e., policy propositions.
3. A set of statements about the efficiency of each alternative in meeting the policy objective, i.e., how well will a given alternative satisfy a policy objective.

Each of these three components can be associated with a kind of information space. For each information space, we can generate all possible events, and attach a probability to each event.[22] Given that we do that conceptually, we can talk about the amount of structure, predictability, information, and so forth.

If there is more than one alternative (i.e., if no alternative has a probability of 1), there is uncertainty with respect to alternatives. Similarly, if there is more than one criterion (i.e., if no criterion has a probability of 1), there is uncertainty with respect to criteria. When we talk about that level of uncertainty from the observer's point of view, we call it *uncertainty*. When we talk about it from the decision-maker's point of view, we call it *choice*. When we talk about it from the point of view of the recipient of the decision, we call it *doubt*. All three terms are referring to the same general concept: **uncertainty**.

Information generally, and symbolic information in particular, serves to affect the level of uncertainty among one or more of these dimensions. Any alteration in the number of elements or the probability attached to these involves information.

If we change the context from decision-making to a concern with human motivation, we again can talk about three aspects:

1. the set of perceptions of the possible activities that could occur; i.e., an assessment of the environment.
2. the set of values that the person holds; i.e., the set of needs, wants, desires, goals, etc.
3. the set of statements about the efficiency of each environmental act in meeting the person's values.

Again, each of these sets can generate a probability for each element. A person can estimate or perceive the probability of each environmental event. He can attach relative weights (i.e., probabilities) to his values. He can place estimates as to the relative merits of each environmental state in meeting his values. Again, information spaces can be generated, and the concepts of structure, predictability, and information can be introduced.

Though these two situational frames differ, they seem conceptually equivalent. In each, man behaves in ways which imply (a) an assessment of the state of the physical environment, (b) an assessment of his own internal states, with respect to his evaluative criteria, and (c) an assessment of the relationship between his internal states and the external world. In each case, if there is uncertainty, there is a potential for information.

Whether we are talking about decision-making or motivated behavior, we can talk about a kind of information that is contained within each of the three component categories.

1. If the information refers to the set of alternative acts that are available (decision-making) or to the state of the external environment (motivation), we can call it *environmental* information, i.e., statements that describe the environment.
2. If the information refers to the criteria for decision-choice, (decision-making) or the values that the person holds (motivation), we can call it *motivational* information, i.e., statements that describe the objectives of the participant.

3. If the information refers to the efficiency of an alternative in meeting a policy objective (decision-making) or the efficiency of an environmental state in meeting a participant's values, we can call it *instructional* information, i.e., statements that dictate the selection of alternatives.

These three categories can be looked upon as ways of describing the consequences of communication—independent of the ways in which messages are intended to be used.

Whether or not man intends communication to serve any particular function, all communication can be viewed as relevant to the concept of uncertainty.[23] Any transfer of symbolic information can be said to have one of the following effects on the uncertainty level of those involved in the transfer: it will increase uncertainty, reduce uncertainty, maintain and reinforce existing levels of uncertainty, or—in the case of a novel situation—explicate the level of uncertainty by generating an information space. All communication then affects the level of uncertainty in its participants.

Given that the patterning of the message is received by both participants, it will affect uncertainty within both participants; therefore, basically, communication is not directional. A message influences both its producer and its receiver—both are consumers.

The influence of communication upon uncertainty can involve influence on one or more of the three dimensions we have referred to. If the message influences uncertainty levels solely about the external environment, we shall call it environmental information. If it influences uncertainty about the criteria which the participant uses to make decisions or the values which he holds, we shall call it motivational information. Finally, if it influences uncertainty in the relationships which the participant has between his values and the external environment, we shall call it instructional information.

SUMMARY

In short, then, the necessary and sufficient condition for our use of the word *communication* shall be the transfer of symbolic information, i.e., the production and consumption of matter-energy units which are imbedded in a symbol system we call language. No characteristic of the communicators is imposed on these conditions, other than the restriction that each communicator must be a user of that language. A definition of communication does not require a stipulation of intent, awareness, and so forth.

Second, the transfer of symbolic information implies the concept of uncertainty in that "information" cannot be used as a concept unless there is the possibility of both occurrence and non-occurrence of an event. Given some level of uncertainty (within a message, a participant, the relationship between message and participant, the relationship between participant and participant . . . or any other level of system), any message-unit affects uncertainty in one of four ways:

1. It increases uncertainty, or
2. It reduces uncertainty, or
3. It reinforces existing levels of uncertainty, or
4. It generates an information space, specifying the level of uncertainty.

Finally, for human participants, whether or not communication is intended to perform any function, it can be considered to influence uncertainty on one or more of the following three dimensions:

1. Uncertainty about the environment (i.e., the number of possible alternatives, and the probability of each). We call this dimension: *environmental information*.
2. Uncertainty about the internal criteria of the participant (either his criteria for decision-making, or his values). We call this dimension: *motivational information*.
3. Uncertainty about the relationship between the participant's values or criteria, and the external environment. We call this dimension: *instructional information*.

That is the consequent of communication.

QUESTIONS FOR DISCUSSION

1. How do the elements that Berlo lists as components of a communication system compare with the essential parts listed by Cowart? Discuss why there might be differences in two such lists.
2. Berlo says it is an error to believe that communication begins when someone speaks. Why does he make this statement? Do you think it would be useful to distinguish between *communication* as a process, and *a particular human interaction* (like saying hello to someone) which involves communication?

3. It is difficult to point to the beginning or the end of communication viewed as a process, since many variables affect any communication interaction long before it takes place, and many effects of that interaction can occur long after the interaction has ended. List as many variables as you can that might affect a communication interaction before that interaction begins. List some effects of communication that might occur long after a particular conversation has ended.

4. What is a process? Without copying what Berlo says, write a brief essay (a page or two) explaining your meaning for *process*.

5. What problems can arise in trying to talk or write about a process? (Your experience from Question 4 should help you here.)

6. Explain your meaning for *system*. How is the concept of *system* different from the concept of *process*?

7. What does Berlo mean by the term *language*? How does his use of *language* compare with the way you would usually use the term?

8. Should a definition of *communication* try to state exactly which events are and are not to be included in the category *communication*? What other approach to defining *communication* does Berlo suggest? Do you agree with him?

9. Without looking at Berlo's definition, write your own definition of *communication*. Think about the situations that would be included and excluded as *communication*, given your definition, and revise your definition until you are satisfied with it. Now compare your definition with that of Berlo. What have you included that he has not? Has he included anything that you have not? Which definition (yours or his) is the right one? Under what conditions is your definition more useful than Berlo's? When is his definition more useful?

10. Discuss the relationship between *choice*, *doubt*, and *uncertainty*. Why are these concepts important in the study of human communication?

NOTES

1. Karl W. Deutsch, "On Communication Models in the Social Sciences," *Public Opinion Quarterly* 16 (Fall 1952), p. 537

2. W. Rhys Roberts "Rhetorica," in *The Works of Aristotle*, XI, W.D. Ross, ed. (New York: Oxford University Press, 1946), p. 14

3. Harold D. Lasswell "The Structure and Function of Communications in Society," in Lyman Bryson, ed. *The Communication of Ideas*, (New York: Harper and Brothers, 1948).

4. Roberts, "Rhetorica," p.6.

5. Similarly, "Fidelity" in a high fidelity recording system is concerned with the pattern of sound reproduction, not with the significance or reference of those sounds.

6. Claude Shannon and Warren Weaver, *The Mathematical Theory of Communication* (Urbana, Ill.: University of Illinois Press, 1949), p.5.

7. An example of such confusion would be a person who made a decision to purchase a hi-fi system solely on the basis of its system characteristics, i.e., without listening to music being processed through it. It's not what is in the hi-fi that one should pay for, but what is in the hi-fi that one hears.

8. Cf. such models as those of Jurgen Ruesch and Gregory Bateson, *Communication: The Social Matrix of Psychiatry* (New York: W.W. Norton, 1951); Wilbur Schramm, "How Communication Works," in *The Process and Effects of Mass Communication* (Urbana, Ill.: University of Illinois Press, 1954), pp. 2-36; Robert D. Hay, *Written Communications For Business Administrators* (New York: Holt, Rinehart and Winston, 1965); J. Harold Janis, *Writing and Communicating in Business* (New York: Macmillan, 1964).

9. George Gerbner, "Toward a General Model of Communication," *Audio-Visual Communication Review*, 4 (Summer 1956), pp.171-99.

10. Franklin Fearing, "Toward a Psychological Theory of Human Communication," *Journal of Personality*, 22 (September 1953), pp.71-88.

11. Bruce H. Westley, and Malcolm S. MacLean, "A Conceptual Model for Communications Research," *Audio-Visual Communication Review*, 3 (Winter 1955), pp.3-12.

12. Wendell Johnson, "The Fateful Process of Mr. A Talking to Mr. B," *Harvard Business Review*, 31 (January-February 1953), pp.49-56.

13. George A. Borden, Richard B. Gregg, and Theodore G. Grove, *Speech Behavior and Human Interaction* (Prentice-Hall, Englewood Cliffs, New Jersey, 1969), p.4.

14. Russell L. Ackoff, *Choice, Communication and Conflict: A System's Approach to the Study of Human Behavior* (Management Science Center, University of Pennsylvania, Philadelphia, 1967), p. 1.

15. Paul Watzlawick, Janet Helmick Beavin, and Don D. Jackson, *Pragmatics of Human Communication* (New York: W. W. Norton, 1967), p. 27.

16. Colin Cherry, *On Human Communication* (New York: Science Editions, 1961), p.217.

17. In this light, it would be interesting to analyze the decision processes of a television producer, theatre director, or news editor. Each makes decisions altering matter-energy states. The question is, how many of these decisions are simply matter-energy changes? How many alter information? How many involve a language that is meaningful to consumers of his medium?
18. Cherry, *On Human Communication*, p.17.
19. Ackoff, *Choice, Communication*, p.12. I am indebted to Ackoff for stimulating much of the ensuing discussion of the dimensionality of communication outcomes.
20. Cherry, *On Human Communication*, p.170.
21. Ibid., p. 14.
22. This is an example of the importance of the concept of *level*. These elements and probabilities may be discussed from the individual's point of view, from an observer's point of view, and so forth.
23. Hopefully, the reader is struggling with the apparently strong relationship between the concept of uncertainty and the concept of information. The struggle requires time during which the concepts age and mature.

TWO

primary channels in interpersonal communication

the perception and decoding of patterned sound

Communication involves far more than talking and hearing. The exchange of mutually understood symbols is best understood as an interacting process. But before we can understand that process as a whole we must study some of the parts or subsystems that go into the formation of the process. On one level of analysis the verbal channel, speaking and hearing, is the most common form of communication. Later articles will discuss other forms and channels such as nonverbal communication, but the following two articles will concentrate on the perception of sound and the assignment of meaning to sound patterns.

"The Sense of Hearing" discusses the perception of sound waves—patterned and unpatterned matter-energy—by human beings.

6

THE SENSE OF HEARING

Craig Stark

"If a tree falls in the forest where no one hears it, does it make any sound?" is an antique conundrum beloved by instructors in freshman philosophy. The answer, of course, depends on how we define "sound." If by "sound" we mean the alternating waves of compression and rarefaction of air particles which a woodsman, if present, would hear, the answer is clearly yes. If, however, we mean an aural sensation produced by the stimuli picked up by the ear, then the answer is no. Since both definitions are equally useful, though for different purposes, there is no real philosophical problem.

Let us complicate our question, however, by supposing that a forester leaves a battery-operated tape recorder running in the woods and later returns to find that he can now reproduce in his living room, at some later time, the "sound" of the falling tree. Most of us would now argue that whether or nor he could hear the "real sound" of the tree would depend on the fidelity of his recorder and component system. But that is only half an answer, for one could still ask how clearly his aural sensations correlated with the sound waves coming from the loudspeakers. Questions such as this are the concern of psychoacoustics, a science which in the last century has made some rather startling discoveries about the relation between the sea of sound that surrounds us and our perception of it. And not until we can bridge the gap between the subjectivity of the trained, knowledgeable ear and the quantitative objectivity of the engineer's measurements can we really know what we mean when we talk about high-fidelity music reproduction. (See Figure 6.2.)

Craig Stark is a contributing editor of *Stereo Review*. Copyright © 1969 Ziff-Davis Publishing Company. Reprinted by permission of *Stereo Review* Magazine.

The human ear is an extraordinary instrument. On the one hand, its sensitivity is so great that, to use the analogy of the noted physicist Alexander Wood, it will respond to a level of energy comparable to a 50 watt light bulb viewed at a distance of 3,000 miles. On the other hand, if one were to set a tape recorder's VU meter to read "0" at this threshold of audibility, the ear would not overload (yielding a sensation of pain rather than one of sound) until an approximate reading of +130 VU (one "Volume Unit" = one decibel). (See Figure 6.1.) This represents a voltage ratio of more than 3,000,000 to 1. Fortunately for the realistic reproduction of music and speech, these extreme limits of the ear's sensitivity are not involved (see Figure 6.3).

But if the sensitivity range of the ear exceeds the capabilities of home audio equipment, its frequency response certainly does not, as the well-known Fletcher-Munson curves (Figure 6.4) attest. Every ardent audiophile knows that if he turns the volume down to a level his wife and the neighbors can tolerate, the music begins to sound "thin" and lacking in the deep bass register, where the ear is much less sensitive. This is the justification, of course, for the fact that almost all amplifiers and receivers have "loudness" controls designed to boost the low frequencies automatically at low listening levels. I, for one, have always found this type of compensation worse than useless—particularly if it cannot be switched off—for the amount of bass boost needed depends on the *perceived* loudness of the music (and the individual's possible deviation from the "normal" Fletcher-Munson response curve), yet the amount of bass boost supplied is determined only by the position of the volume-control knob. The specific setting of the volume control for a given loudness is determined by a number of factors, including the output of the phono cartridge, the sensitivity of the power amplifiers, the efficiency of the speakers, and so forth. With this many variables at work simultaneously, exact loudness compensation is almost impossible with one simple control.

But although the ear has a frequency-response curve much inferior to that of most high-fidelity components, if given enough sound pressure, it is capable of responding to frequencies ranging from approximately 20 to 20,000 Hz. The upper frequency limit tends to vary considerably with the individual, generally being highest in young children and tending to decline (particulary among men) with age.

More important implications about the relation between *what* we hear and *how* we hear arise when we consider the low frequencies, for when sound with a frequency much under 20 Hz is produced, the ear does not perceive a tone, but rather a series of separate pulses. Waveforms with a repetition rate greater than 20 Hz (or 1/20 of a

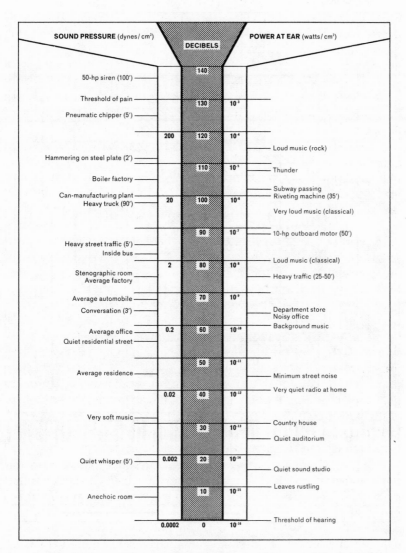

Figure 6.1   Relative Loudness Levels of Common Sounds

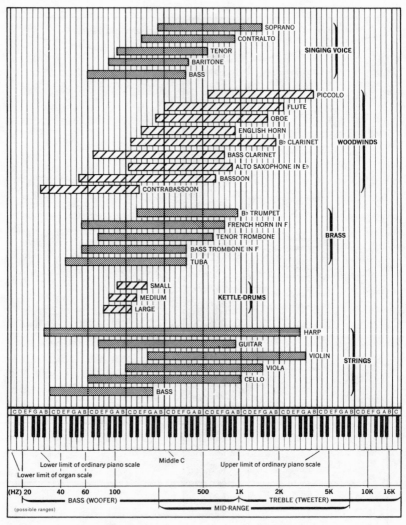

(Ranges of fundamental components of tones for the principal instruments and voices)

Figure 6.2   The Frequencies of Music

second, or 50 milliseconds, whichever you prefer) will be heard as a continuous tone. While experimental results vary somewhat according to the test conditions and the individual ear, it is well documented that sonic events lasting less than 50 milliseconds (50 ms) do not completely overcome the "inertia" of the hearing process. This affects both the perceived intensity of the sound and the ability to recognize a specific tone. Thus, a pure 2,000 Hz tone, if turned on for a period of only 4 milliseconds (ms), will not be heard as a specific pitch, but rather as a click. Down in this area where short tones are heard as clicks, a loud signal only 10 ms long will seem just as long as a weaker signal that lasts, say, 35 ms. This seems to occur because the ear responds to their equal total energy content.

As we investigate the subject we find that there are many areas where the "obvious" relationship between the objective sound waves and the subjective perception of music does not exist. For example, Carl Seashore and other acousticians have reduced the objective measurable physical variables of sound to four: duration, amplitude (or intensity), frequency, and waveform. On the face of it these should correspond to the subjective sensations of time, loudness, pitch, and timbre. But here also our perceptions have no linear or direct correspondence to the objective sonic circumstance. This has important implications for high-fidelity reproduction. For example, even the subjective perception of the pitch of a pure tone depends not only on its frequency, but to some degree on its loudness. Research has shown that for low-frequency tones the pitch goes down as the intensity increases; and for high-frequency tones the pitch increases with intensity. At moderate listening levels, two pure tones of 168 and 318 Hz sound very discordant, but Harvey Fletcher (best known for his research with Wilden A. Munson) showed that if they are played loud enough, the ear hears them as a pure octave: 150 and 300 Hz.

Fortunately, the kind of distuning that takes place with pure tones does not so greatly affect our perception of the complex waveforms produced by musical instruments. As every audiophile knows, musical notes contain not only the "fundamental" frequency, but many harmonics or overtones as well, and the overtone structure establishes the timbre of the sound. A harmonic, sometimes called a "partial," is any whole-number multiple of the fundamental frequency, though it is sometimes mistakenly identified with the overtones that occur at successively higher octaves. Since an octave represents a 2:1 frequency ratio, the second harmonic *is* exactly one octave higher than the fundamental, but beyond this point the harmonic and octave sequence diverge. If an organist, for example, played a very low C (approximately 32 Hz) an overtone could, in theory, at least, appear nine octaves higher (16,384 Hz), but this would be the 512th harmonic! Practically speaking, of course, instruments are not likely to generate many overtones as high as that, but the importance of the number and relative strength of differing instrumental harmonics can hardly be overstated. (See Figure 6.5.) The highest fundamental tones produced by a piano or a piccolo, for example, are less than 5,000 Hz, but switching in a scratch filter or turning down the treble control so that high-frequency response is lowered by even 3 dB at 10,000 Hz distinctly alters the perceived character of the instrument.

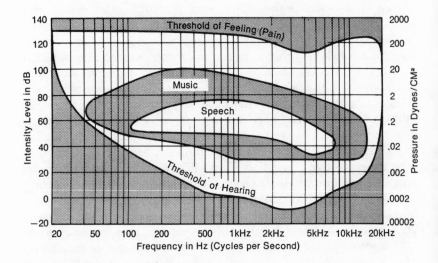

Averaged and approximate intensity and frequency ranges of speech and music are shown in relation to the upper and lower extremes that can be handled by the human hearing apparatus. The upper limit is the threshold of pain; the lower limit is the threshold of hearing.

Figure 6.3

The sounds we hear even in a live musical performance are not all produced by the instruments, for the ear itself is a source of both harmonic and intermodulation distortion. The latter occurs when two (or more) tones of different frequencies are sounded simultaneously and totally new tones representing the sum and difference frequencies are created. As early as the eighteenth century the Italian violinist Giuseppe Tartini (known today primarily as the composer of the

"Devil's Trill" Sonata) noticed that when he played two notes together he could distinctly hear a third tone, much lower than either. Thus, if he simultaneously played a B of 480 Hz and a G of 384 Hz, he could detect another G (96 Hz), two octaves below. The phantom sounds produced by such difference frequencies have been known ever since as "Tartini tones," though he was by no means the only one to discover them. About the same time the German organist W. A. Sorge found that if he played a musical fifth consisting of a C (32 Hz) and a G (48 Hz), he could induce the ear to perceive a C at 16 Hz, and this principle has been used by organ builders ever since, because it would take a rather costly 32 foot pipe to produce the lowest C (16 Hz) in the bass register of the pipe organ.

Curiously, the difference frequency between two tones is much more audible than the sum frequency. But its subjective existence can be proved by any audiophile who can borrow a pair of audio oscillators and whose speakers have wide-range tweeters. Using a 1,000 Hz tone as a reference, plug one generator into each channel and adjust both for equal output from the speakers at normal listening level. Then shift the frequency of one generator to about 23 kHz and the other to about 24 kHz without changing the level settings. When either generator is operating by itself, nothing will be heard, for both frequencies are beyond the range of human hearing. (Your dog may get up and leave the room in disgust however.) But when both generators are working through their respective speakers, assuming that your tweeters are good enough and you are standing at the right spot, you should hear a distinct 1,000 Hz tone. Larry Klein, the technical editor of this magazine, has suggested that one of the minor factors responsible for the differences between what we hear at a live performance and from a home music system may be just this loss of the beating together of the supra-audible harmonics which are present during the live experience but are lost through deficiencies of the recording process.

Along this same line, it has been suggested by researcher Charles J. Hirsch that the pleasurable richness we associate with consonant sounds and the unpleasant roughness we call dissonance is as much a subjective creation of the ear as it is an objective configuration of sound waves. Consider, for example, the following experiment. Feed into one stereo channel a tone of about middle C (261 Hz) from an audio generator set to provide a comfortable volume. Then adjust another generator to provide a 330 Hz signal at about the same volume through the other channel. With slight adjustment of one of the generators this will produce a pleasing, if somewhat musically dull, consonant major third (C-E). If the speakers are now replaced by a pair of stereo earphones, however, the harmonious blending of the sound will be entirely lost, and one will hear the two tones completely independently. Similarly, if one of the generators is adjusted to give a terrible dissonance (C-C#) when heard through the speakers, the two tones will not sound at all dissonant when they are heard isolated from each other by the separate earphones.

Hirsch carried his experiment even further by having a cellist record the same musical selection in two different keys (kept in synchronism by a metronome) on the two tracks of a stereo recorder. When mixed together and played back through a stereo system the result was a predictable cacophony. Reproduced through stereo headphones, however, the two renditions were heard in isolation.

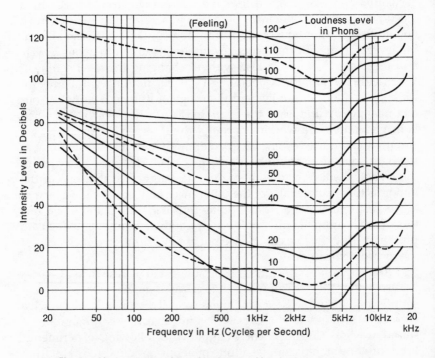

Fletcher-Munson curves show what the actual levels of test tones must be for them to be heard as having the same loudness. The curves at 10, 50, and 110 dB, derived from the later studies of Robinson and Dadson, are included for comparison.

Figure 6.4

"Listeners describe the effect as if there were a wall in the middle of their heads that separates the two sounds," Hirsch reported. He then concluded that "the ears have largely independent effects on the brain, and that the brain does not combine tones, transmitted simultaneously but separately by the two ears, to produce harmony. Harmony, which includes consonance and dissonance . . . requires that the simultaneous component tones be combined in one ear . . . ."

In the performance of music, however, even highly trained listeners exhibit a degree of tolerance for slight differences in pitch or intonation that would be easily detected under test conditions in a laboratory. If two steady tones were sounded through our loudspeakers, one at 297 Hz and the other at 293.665 Hz, we would all hear the 3 to 4 Hz beat between them. Yet in listening to a violin and piano sonata we do not. The perfect musical fifth to which the A and the D strings of the violin are tuned represents a frequency ratio of 3:2, a fact which has been known since the time of the Greek philosopher Pythagoras in the sixth century B.C.. But to construct a piano that could modulate from one key to another while maintaining a Pythagorean or "just intonation" scale would require at least thirty separate intervals within the octave, an obvious impossibility. Thus, the octave on the piano is divided into twelve "equally tempered" semitones. While the violin and piano are in perfect unison at A (440 Hz), the dynamic life of the music itself disguises from our consciousness their slight discord at the D in the same octave.

The question of the slight indeterminacy of pitch perception during a musical performance brings us back to our discussion of how we hear the sound waves within that first 1/20 of a second (50 ms) that it takes for the ear to respond fully. In audio terminology we are accustomed to speaking of very short bursts of sound as "transients," but we generally associate them only with staccato passages or percussion instruments. This is an error, however, for every note in music (or every sound in speech) has a dynamic life of its own from the time of its onset to the time of its decay into inaudibility.

The importance of the onset transients of even the most smoothly-spoken orators or of legato passages in music can be dramatized very simply by playing a tape recording backwards, thus causing the initial transient to appear at the end of the sound. Owners of full or half-track stereo recorders can perform such an experiment very easily by turning a played tape over and threading it up again. Even with the much more prevalent quarter-track recorders one can achieve the same result, however, by playing through a tape and twisting it between the capstan and the take-up reel so that it is

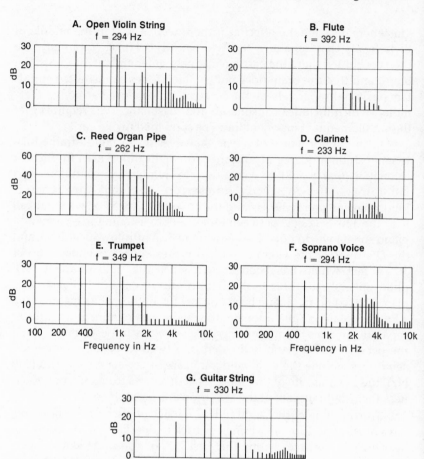

Distribution and relative strengths of overtones (harmonics) for various instruments and soprano voice. Fundamentals (f) are given above each graph. Note that though all fundamental frequencies fall in the same octave, the frequencies and intensities of the overtones vary widely, giving each instrument a characteristic timbre.

Figure 6.5

wound with the oxide side facing outwards. Then turn it over and play it through again, this time with the backing rather than the oxide in contact with the recorder heads. There will be some loss of volume and of the high frequencies, but the startling effect of the transients will still be audible.

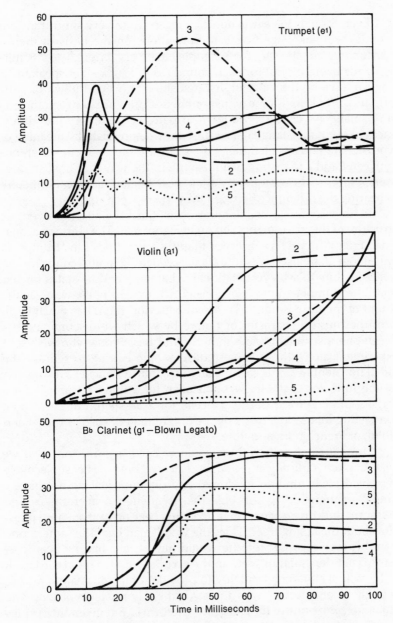

In the first tenth of a second, transients occur that provide a substantial part of the characteristic timbre of an instrument. Relative strengths of the fundamental (1) and harmonics (2, 3, 4, 5) are plotted against elapsed time.

Figure 6.6

Even though the ear is not fully receptive to very short transient sounds, we make significant interpretations on the basis of them. Consonants in speech, for example, are very brief, 5 to 15 milliseconds being typical for such sounds as *p*, *t*, or *k*. Yet speakers of English have no difficulty in distinguishing between the words *part*, *tart*, and *cart* although the actual phonetic difference between them is very small. As children we learn to perceive such very fine differences in our native language because they distinguish the meaning of words. The Japanese language does not use the phonetic difference between *l* and *r* to distinguish meaning in the way that English does (*rung*, *lung*), and consequently a Japanese person has great difficulty in hearing the difference between these two speech sounds.

In this context, consider the onset times versus the overtone structure of the instruments shown in Figure 6.6. The German acoustician Fritz Winckel has observed that the onset time of the trumpet is only about 20 milliseconds, but it takes 200 to 300 milliseconds for the tone of a flute to achieve a stationary character, and he states further that "the trumpet sound is especially rich in overtones, whereas the sound of the flute is not." Transient behavior, then, has much to do with the musical character of timbre by which we discriminate between one instrument and another. And for anyone who wishes to experiment along these lines, judicious tape editing to remove the initial transient in a musical tone should confirm Winckel's results: "A tuning fork, for example, was mistaken for a flute, a trumpet for a cornet, an oboe for a clarinet, a cello for a bassoon; but even more contrasting tone colors could not be differentiated, such as cornet and violin, or French horn and flute."

More anomalies than these could be cited to show that *what* we hear is often radically affected by *how* we hear. The subjectively perceived pitch, timbre, loudness, and duration just do not have a simple relationship to the objective frequency, waveform, sound pressure, and time. How then does this bear on our opening question about the falling tree? Does the woodsman hear the same sound from his tape recorder that he would have heard had he been present? That depends, in part, on the accuracy of his tape recorder. It is the task of stereo high fidelity to provide sonic information precise enough to enable our ears to make their normal distortions and (mis)interpretations of the musical waveforms. But given the strange ways in which our ears actually operate, it is little wonder that we promptly run into contradictions whenever objective theory encounters subjective practice and our ears deny what our measurements tell us.

QUESTIONS FOR DISCUSSION

1. How exact is the relationship between *sound waves* and *perceived sound*? Give examples to support your answer.
2. How are very short bursts of sound (lasting for less than 50 milliseconds) perceived? Why are they perceived in this way?
3. "Fletcher-Munson curves" state the relationship between the actual loudness of a sound and its perceived loudness for a given pitch (frequency) for the average person. How do these curves relate to a music lover's desire to turn up the stereo to loud levels?
4. A poor stereo system may disguise some of the discordant sounds in a performance while a high fidelity stereo system will reproduce the discords clearly enough for you to hear. Why spend more money for a better system if one of its major effects will be to enable you to hear discords that a less expensive system might hide in its distortion?
5. How does the perception of two discordant sounds through both ears differ from the perception of the same two sounds when one is heard in each ear?

Stark discussed the perception of sound and the relationship of the perceptions to musical sounds. In "The Speech Code," Liberman discusses the assignment of meaning to spoken sound. He argues that speech is a form of communication that has fundamental differences from other forms such as written communication.

Information involves patterned matter-energy. How does this patterned matter-energy become patterned in such a way that a human being can understand it and assign meaning to it? "The Speech Code" gives part of the answer.

7

tHE speech code

Alvin M. Liberman

Speech is such an easy and convenient thing that most people are misled into thinking it must also be very simple. If it were really very simple, of course, there would not be very much to say about it. In fact, however, speech is one of the most complicated and intricate skills that we ever acquire, and there is a great deal that can be said about it. We can talk about the sentences we speak, or about the meanings they have, or about the purposes they serve. But even if we ignore all those complicated aspects of speech, there is still much left to say that is interesting about the way we speak and the way we hear speech.

How do we make the vowels and consonants of our language? This question is far more complex than it seems. Speech is very special. It bears a special relation to language. It uses a special set of sounds. It is processed by a special part of the nervous system. It is perceived in a special mode.

Now most people do not realize that speech is so special. The common assumption is that the sounds of speech are like the letters of an alphabet. As I hope to show, that assumption is entirely wrong. I would like, nevertheless, to discuss this erroneous view, because it is important to see just where the mistake lies.

Let us consider, then, what it means to represent language alphabetically. Suppose we wish to communicate a simple word—for

Alvin M. Liberman is professor of psychology at The University of Connecticut and adjunct professor of linguistics at Yale. "The Speech Code," by Alvin M. Liberman, from *Communication, Language, and Meaning: Psychological Perspectives*, edited by George A. Miller, © 1973 by Basic Books, Inc., publishers, New York.

example, *bag*. To do that in writing, we must first appreciate that the word comprises three phonetic elements or segments: the first segment is the consonant we call "b," the second is the vowel "ae," and the third is the consonant "g." To write the word, we have only to select the appropriate letters of the alphabet, one for each of the three phonetic segments, and set them down in the proper order. Thus we have the simplest possible relationship between the phonetic message and its written form: for each unit of the message there is a unit letter.

Nor is there anything special about the optical shapes that we use as letters. Indeed, the selection of letter shapes is a matter of perfectly arbitrary convention. If, like most speakers of English, the writer is accustomed to using a Roman alphabet, then he would certainly choose from among the optical shapes in that particular set. But he could as well communicate the word with letters of the Cyrillic alphabet, or, indeed, he might, if he wished, invent a new one. Any alphabet, old or new, need meet only two requirements: there must be a letter for every phonetic segment, and the letters must be easy to identify. But since we can identify indefinitely many optical shapes, we can have indefinitely many alphabets.

If speech were like alphabetic writing, then to say the same word, "bag," the speaker would select three sounds, appropriate for the three phonetic segments, and utter them in proper sequence. To carry the analogy with writing further, we should suppose that selecting the sounds would be a matter of social convention. It is commonly assumed, however, that there are very many of these sounds, and that each community of speakers chooses, quite arbitrarily, the particular set it wishes to use.

My point is that speech is not at all like that. Speech is not an arbitrary alphabet on the language. Rather speech is linked to language by way of a complex and especially efficient code. As a result of research on speech, most of which has been done in the last twenty years, we now know something about the characteristics of the speech code, and we are able to say in what ways and in how far it is special. Later I will summarize some of those research findings. But first I would remind you that, even without doing any research on the speech signal, we can find much evidence that the sounds of speech have a special relation to language. At the very least, they are privileged and uniquely efficient vehicles for the communication of linguistic information. To see that this is so we should continue our comparison of speech and writing, but now, instead of supposing that these two ways of communicating language are similar, we should consider in what quite obvious ways they are different.

The ability to speak and to perceive speech is universal; with the exception of people who are deaf or brain injured, everyone does it. Reading, on the other hand, is quite rare. Many languages do not have a written form, and even in literate societies there are, among those who speak and listen, many who cannot read and write.

Speech comes first in the history of the race, writing comes second. Indeed, writing is a comparatively recent development. Speech is a product of natural evolution, or so we should suppose if only because it is something that every human being does. Writing, on the other hand, is quite clearly an invention. Moreover, the easiest way of writing—that is, by an alphabet—is so far removed from man's biological base that it has been invented only once in all history.

Consider, too, that language survives blindness but not deafness. Children who are born blind develop language in a perfectly normal way. Being unable to see the world they talk about is, of course, a terrible handicap, but it does no harm to language. Nor is their language development impaired in any essential way by their inability to read. On the other hand, children who are born deaf suffer a severe linguistic disability. Now it is easy enough to understand why a deaf child should not learn to speak. Being unable to hear, he cannot properly control and correct the sounds he makes. It is, however, much less obvious why deaf children who do not acquire speech cannot easily be taught to read or write. If speech and writing are but equivalent representations of language, why is the spoken form prerequisite to the written? Why is it, in fact, so very difficult to substitute the optical shapes of an alphabet for the acoustical shapes of speech?

Putting all these readily available facts together, we might conclude that there is something special about speech. But first we must ask whether the obvious priority of speech over writing is owing to factors that are, from our point of view, trivial. Are there explanations for the superiority of speech that have nothing to do with man's capacity for language or its relation to speech? Let us consider the trivial reasons that might be advanced.

One might argue, first, that the superiority of speech can be explained by supposing that the ear is a better organ than the eye. But such an argument runs contrary to fact. By almost any standard we can think of, the eye is a wider and deeper channel of information transmission than the ear.

If we cannot argue that speech is better than print because the ear is the better organ, then we might try the argument that speech sounds are the better signal. Perhaps these acoustic signals are, by comparison with print, particularly clear or simple. Suppose that is so, and imagine then what would happen if we were to try to build two analogous machines: one to perceive speech, the other to perceive print. It would not be required of these machines that they understand the message, only that they respond differentially to the phonetic elements. If speech were the better signal, then the speech perceiver should be the easier to build. But the experience of engineers has run directly contrary to that expectation. Engineers have succeeded fairly well in building machines that read print, but they have had almost no success in building machines to perceive speech. It is important to emphasize that the failure in the case of speech is not for want of trying; some of the best engineers in the world have given their best efforts to the solution of this problem. The difference in difficulty is owing to the fact that the advantages of clarity and simplicity lie with print, not speech. Print presents the engineer with a very clean signal that bears a straightforward relation to the message it conveys. Speech, on the contrary, is a very murky signal and is related to the rest of language in a very complicated way, as we shall see shortly. For now it is enough merely to point to a most interesting fact: for machines, print is easy to perceive but speech is very hard, while for us human beings, it is just exactly the other way around.

Knowing that the speech signal is neither clear nor simple, let us now try the argument that the advantage of speech lies in the fact that it is sound, and that sound is the best vehicle for language because it always attracts attention. We don't have to be looking at sound in order to hear it, and we don't have earlids with which to shut it out. But if the advantage of speech over writing lay in this, then we might expect to find many sets of sounds that would work equally well. Though there are many different alphabets, and though none is as easy for human beings as speech, they are all equally good. It is the more interesting, therefore, to note that the situation in speech is very different: there is only one set of sounds—those of speech—that will work well. We know that this is so because of what happens when people try to substitute nonspeech sounds for speech. Consider the familiar dots and dashes of the Morse telegraphic code. After years of practice people can perceive these signals at rates hardly one-tenth those at which they easily perceive speech. Less familiar, perhaps, are the attempts to contrive nonspeech substitutes for speech in connection with the development of reading machines for the blind.

These are devices that transform print into sound. But if you know the history of the attempt to build such devices, you know that the first one was constructed more than fifty years ago. You must then also know that in the many machines that have been developed since that time, many sound alphabets have been tried, yet none has ever been found that is better than the sounds of Morse, and Morse is less than one-tenth as good as speech.

Of course, we should have known all along that sound alphabets could not possibly be substituted for speech. Consider that in the case of speech we can perceive at rates that require us to take in as many as twenty-five or even thirty phonetic elements per second. If each of these elements were represented in speech as they are in the nonspeech alphabets, there would be a unit sound for each phonetic element. But surely twenty-five or thirty such sounds per second would merge into a tone or buzz. The ear does not, and indeed cannot, separate individual acoustic events that occur at that rate; rather it integrates or merges them to form a unitary sensation, just as it integrates the individual pressure pulses of a tone and converts the signal into what we describe subjectively as pitch. Speech somehow evades this limitation. We should suppose, therefore, that speech is not a sound alphabet.

These facts suggest that the sounds of speech are somehow special. They are uniquely efficient and natural carriers of linguistic information. This is not for trivial reasons. Rather, we must look to the possibility that speech is, in some interesting way, uniquely well matched to language and to man. But the match cannot be a simple one; that is, speech cannot be a sound alphabet on the language. With that as background, let us now look at speech and try to find out what it is.

We should begin with the production of speech and, for that purpose, return to the example we used before—the word *bag*. If speech were like writing, then we should select three articulatory gestures, one for each of the phonetic segments, and string them end to end. But that is not what we do. The first segment of *bag*—the "b"—is made by closing the lips and then opening them. The second segment, "ae," is made by putting the tongue into a particular position. Now it is clear enough that we do not make these gestures in tandem, first one and then the other; rather we do both at the same time. That is, we put the tongue into position for the vowel "ae" at the same time that we close and open the lips for the consonant "b." The next segment, "g," requires that we close the vocal tract by putting the back of the tongue up against the roof of the mouth. Many component parts of that gesture can be also overlapped in time with movements characteristic of the vowel. In this way we organize the phonetic segments into syllables, like *bag*, which is to say that we overlap the segments that constitute the syllable and transmit them at the same time.

Notice how very efficient this procedure is, especially by contrast with writing. In writing we must make the movements for one gesture and then the movements for the next. The rate at which we transmit the segments of the message is limited by the rate at which we can move our muscles. In speech we are, of course, also limited by the rate at which we move our muscles, but in speech we move muscles for several successive phonetic segments all at once.

From a physiological point of view, the kind of efficiency we achieve in speech is not easy to arrange. It requires, in fact, a great deal of organization and coordination. Not only are the articulatory movements made with great speed and accuracy, but, as we have seen, they are organized and overlapped in very complex ways. It is of considerable interest that such organization and coordination is not found in the vocalizations of animals other than man. Our closest primate relatives vocalize, but recent evidence indicates that they produce only variants of a single vowel-like sound, one approximating the neutral vowel "uh." There is no evidence that they can co-articulate in such a way as to produce consonant-vowel syllables of the kind that are found in every language of the world. Yet this complex co-articulation is so easy for us human beings that one-year-old infants do it quite expertly in their spontaneous babbling. We should suppose that the ability and tendency to speak in this way is a part of our biological nature.

Let us turn our attention now from production to perception and see that there is also great efficiency in the way language can be listened to. Because the phonetic segments are, as we saw, overlapped and shingled into syllabic packages, we can perceive speech faster than we could if there were a unit sound for each phonetic segment. Earlier I said that if speech were an alphabet on the phonetic structure—that is, if each phonetic segment were represented by a unit sound—then the sounds of speech would merge into an unanalyzable buzz at the relatively low rates of speaking. We have seen, however, that the phonetic segments are organized in such a way that an entire syllable is transmitted as a whole in one burst of sound. As a consequence, the limit on the rate at which we can perceive speech is set, not by the number of phonetic segments, but by the number of syllables.

I cannot emphasize too strongly, however, that the gain in listening efficiency is achieved at a considerable cost: in order to transmit several phonetic segments at the same time, there has to be a very complex relation between those segments and the sound that conveys them. Let us see in what way this is so. We have noted that in the production of speech the component elements of a syllable are put onto more or less independent muscles and overlapped in time. From the standpoint of muscular control, this is a very complex situation. But the result in sound is even more complex. The additional complication arises because there are fewer independent dimensions of the sound signals than there are muscles of articulation. Consequently, the simultaneously active muscles, representing successive segments of the message, affect exactly the same part of the sound. We find then that the same piece of sound is, at every instant, transmitting information simultaneously about more than one segment of the phonetic message. Indeed, a single aspect of the sound will sometimes carry information about three successive phonetic segments, all at the same time.

The relation between sound and phonetic message is now complicated in two important respects. First, there is no simple correspondence between the segments of the sound signal and the segments of the message, either in the number of segments or in their structure. Therefore, the sound signal requires very complex processing before we can know how many phonetic segments are encoded into it. Second, the part of the sound that carries information about a particular segment, say "b," will necessarily be very different depending on what other segments come next. This requires further complex processing if we are to discover the identity of the segments. In both these respects, the sounds of speech are different from the letters of an alphabet. In the case of an alphabet there is a simple, one-to-one correspondence in segmentation—one letter for each phonetic segment—and the letter shape is the same regardless of the phonetic context. To borrow a distinction from cryptanalysis, we might say that a written alphabet is a simple substitution cipher, but that the sounds of speech are a form of very complex code. Yet, as we know, human beings perceive the complex code more readily than the simple cipher. We should suspect that this is so because human beings have physiological devices that are specifically designed to decode these complex sounds and recover the phonetic message.

There is now a great deal of evidence that we human beings do, in fact, possess a special speech decoder. We don't know yet exactly how this decoder works, but we know what it has to do, and we have indirect, but very strong, evidence for its existence.

First of all, the speech decoder must decode. It must recover the phonetic message from an acoustic signal into which it has been complexly encoded. In the case of our example, "bag," it must determine that there are three phonetic segments. From the standpoint of an engineer or cryptanalyst this is a very difficult thing to do, because the three segments have been merged into just one burst of sound. The decoder must also cope with the fact that the part of the sound that carries information about the consonant "b," for example, is vastly different for every context in which that consonant appears. The fact that we nevertheless hear the consonant "b," both in "bag" and in "boog," indicates that the speech decoder is somehow able to hear through the physical variations and perceive the consonant in its canonical form.

But decoding is not all that our special speech processing device must do. When one examines the speech sound he finds that the important linguistic information, carried largely by so-called formants, often constitutes only a relatively small part of the total sound energy. The important information does not stand out clearly, as in the case of printed letters. If we human beings nevertheless hear speech well, it is because our speech processor is somehow able to extract and attend to the very indistinct parts of the signal that carry the linguistic information.

Thus, we might suppose that we have a special speech device simply because the successful perception of speech implies that a special decoding has been accomplished, and also that the essential parts of the signal have been separated from the unessential parts. But there is other, more direct evidence for the existence of such a special device.

If the physiological device for perceiving speech were special— that is, different, in some important respect, from the device that perceives nonspeech—then we might expect that speech would be heard in a special way. Let me describe one bit of evidence that fits that expectation. Consider, first, what we have recently discovered about the acoustic cues on the basis of which we distinguish speech sounds. The primary cue that enables us to tell "ba" from "ga," for example, is in the movement of a band of acoustic energy at the beginning of each syllable. In the case of "ba," this band moves upward on the frequency scale, but in the case of "ga" it moves downward. Now a band of acoustic energy that moves up in frequency would be heard normally as a pitch that rises—that is, as an up-going glissando—and a band that moves down, as a pitch that falls—a down-going glissando. By dealing with synthesized speech we are able to remove these bands from a speech context and listen to them in isolation. We then hear exactly what we might expect: a rising pitch in the case of the band taken from "ba," and a falling pitch for the band from "ga." But when we listen to exactly these same bands in their normal speech patterns, we cannot hear anything like pitch glides, no matter how hard we try. What we hear then is not an auditory event, like a rising or falling pitch, but speech. We hear "ba" or "ga." This is to say simply that "ba" and "ga" cannot be heard in auditory terms. We should suppose that this is so because our perception of these sounds is accomplished by a processor that is specialized to deal with speech. As a consequence there is, in the perception of sound, not only an auditory mode, but also, and quite separately, a mode in which we hear speech.

There are other research results that point even more directly to the existence of a special speech processor, but I will describe only one. Suppose we present a stop-consonant—vowel syllable—say "ba"—to one ear and a different nonsense syllable—say "ga"—to the other. If we do this many times, using all pairs of "ba," "da," "ga," "pa," "ta," and "ka," we find that most people hear better the non-sense syllables presented to the right ear. If we now do the same experiment, but instead of nonsense syllables, we present simple musical patterns, we get the opposite effect—that is, our listeners hear better the patterns presented to the left ear. Now we know that each ear is connected to both sides of the brain, but we also know that the connection is stronger to the opposite side. That is, the connection between the right ear and left brain is stronger that the connection between right ear and right brain. The right-ear advantage for speech and the left-ear advantage for music indicate, then, that these two kinds of signals want to be processed on opposite sides of the brain, speech on the left, and music on the right. Of couse, it has long been known that higher-level language functions tend to be localized on the left side of the brain. What these newer experiments teach us is that phonetic perception is there, too. This reinforces the view that the lowest level of speech perception is an integral part of language. But it is more relevant to emphasize that perception of speech sounds is carried out in one part of the brain and perception of nonspeech in another. Surely this supports the assumption that speech and nonspeech sounds are perceived by different devices.

If the production and perception of speech are special, then we are left with at least one more important question: Is speech unique to man, and, if so, then in what sense? Nonhuman primates produce only a single vowel—the neutral "uh"—and no consonants. More important, they show no evidence of the highly coordinated overlap-

ping of articulatory components that occurs in the prelinguistic babbling of human infants. How, then, do nonhuman primates hear
speech? Unfortunately, we don't know. But if all that I have been
arguing is correct, we should have to suppose that they cannot hear
speech as we do, even at the lowest phonetic level. This is not to say
that animals should be deaf to speech, or that they should fail to
discriminate speech sounds, but only that their perception of speech
should be different from ours. Recall that though the primary acoustic
difference between "ba" and "ga" is in the direction of movement of a
band of sound, we humans hear not pitch glides, but unanalyzable
linguistic events we call "ba" and "ga." I would guess that if we could
get inside the monkey's head we might discover that, lacking our
speech-sound processor, he hears not "ba" and "ga" but pitch glides.

Is this to say that speech is, in every sense, unique to man? Not
necessarily. To suppose that speech production and perception occur
only in man is to make a statement about behavior, not about underlying mechanisms. It is possible, indeed likely, that the special devices
that enable us to produce and perceive speech are special only in the
particular end they achieve. The basic principles they represent may
be very similar to those that produce other highly specialized behaviors
in animals other than man. As an example, recall that the speech
processor must be able to attend to the linguistically important parts of
the speech signal, even though those parts often constitute a relatively
small part of the total acoustic stream. Now we know that many
animals have devices that are specialized to respond to particular
patterned aspects of the animal's environment. There is, for example,
the bug detector of the frog. Investigators have found that the frog has
a perceptual device that responds specifically to objects that move
across its visual field at particular rates. Thus, the frog is made sensitive to an aspect of the environment that is of particular importance to
him as a source of food. Somewhat similar, though surely still more
complicated, mechanisms may be put together in different ways to
make us human beings particularly sensitive to the linguistically significant parts of the speech signal, an aspect of our environment that is
as important to us as flying bugs are to a hungry frog. Of course, such
a speech detector is only the first step in the processing of the speech
signal, since it will succeed only in paying attention to those sound
patterns that have linguistic significance. A device to decode the
signal and recover the message is still necessary. But when we understand how that decoder works, we may again discover that the underlying principles are not entirely new, but are rather old ones turned to
new purposes. If that proves to be so, we shall have discovered that

what is unique about man is not that he alone possesses these interesting physiological mechanisms, but that only he is able to use them in vocal communication.

SUMMARY

There is evidence all around us to show that the sounds of speech are uniquely natural and efficient carriers of linguistic information. We might then expect to find that the speech signal is special in some interesting sense. When we do research on speech that expectation is confirmed. We discover that the sounds of speech do not bear a simple alphabetic relation to the phonetic message they convey, but are rather a complex and special code. The essence of the code is that information about two or more successive phonetic segments is carried simultaneously on the same piece of sound. This makes for rapid transmission of information, but at the cost of a complex relation between the sounds and the message. Speech is nevertheless easy to perceive because we human beings have ready access to physiological devices that are specialized to decode the sound and recover the linguistic message. In this sense speech is a special system of communication; it is well matched to man and forms a significant part of his unique capacity for language.

QUESTIONS FOR DISCUSSION

1. List the most important similarities and the most important differences between speaking and writing.
2. Deaf children cannot learn to speak so easily as children who can hear. Does deafness also affect a child's ability to read and write? Why should this be so? What does it imply about the relative importance of written and spoken communication?
3. The superiority of speech over written communication might be due to the superiority of the ear over the eye, the superiority of speech signals over print signals, or to the superiority of sound over light for carrying patterned matter-energy. Why does Liberman reject each of these possibilities?
4. We must move muscles to speak, just as we move muscles to write. Why is speaking more efficient if we cannot move our speaking muscles much faster than our writing muscles?
5. (a) Which side of the brain (left or right) contains the higher language functions?

(b)   Liberman suggests that our right ear possesses an advantage over the left ear for processing speech sounds. How does this relate to your answer to 5 (a) above?

6.   A *special speech decoder*, which is separate from the normal human apparatus for perceiving sound, is a possible explanation for our ability to deal far more efficiently with spoken than with written patterns. What evidence suggests the existence of such a device?

THREE

PRIMARY CHANNELS in INTERPERSONAL COMMUNICATION

NONVERBAL COMMUNICATION

There is little question that words, particularly spoken words, are an important channel of communication. As Liberman says: "The sounds of speech are uniquely natural and efficient carriers of linguistic information." But speech sounds are by no means the only channel. The inflections and intonations given to the sounds and the facial expressions that accompany them are another important channel. Albert Mehrabian introduces some nonverbal channels of communication in "Communication Without Words."

8

COMMUNICATION WITHOUT WORDS

Albert Mehrabian

Suppose you are sitting in my office listening to me describe some research I have done on communication. I tell you that feelings are communicated less by the words a person uses than by certain nonverbal means—that, for example, the verbal part of a spoken message has considerably less effect on whether a listener feels liked or disliked than a speaker's facial expression or tone of voice.

So far so good. But suppose I add, "In fact, we've worked out a formula that shows exactly how much each of these components contributes to the effect of the message as a whole. It goes like this: Total Impact = .07 verbal + .38 vocal + .55 facial."

What would you say to *that*? Perhaps you would smile good-naturedly and say, with some feeling, "Baloney!" Or perhaps you would frown and remark acidly, "Isn't science grand." My own response to the first answer would probably be to smile back: the facial part of your message, at least, was positive (55 percent of the total). The second answer might make me uncomfortable: only the verbal part was positive (seven percent).

The point here is not only that my reactions would lend credence to the formula but that most listeners would have mixed feelings about my statement. People like to see science march on, but they tend to resent its intrusion into an "art" like the communication of feelings, just as they find analytical and quantitative approaches to the study of personality cold, mechanistic, and unacceptable.

Albert Mehrabian is associate professor of psychology at the University of California, Los Angeles. Reprinted from *Psychology Today* Magazine, September 1968. Copyright © 1968 Ziff-Davis Publishing Company.

The psychologist himself is sometimes plagued by the feeling that he is trying to put a rainbow into a bottle. Fascinated by a complicated and emotionally rich human situation, he begins to study it, only to find in the course of his research that he has destroyed part of the mystique that originally intrigued and involved him. But despite a certain nostalgia for earlier, more intuitive approaches, one must acknowledge that concrete experimental data have added a great deal to our understanding of how feelings are communicated. In fact, as I hope to show, analytical and intuitive findings do not so much conflict as complement each other.

It is indeed difficult to know what another person really feels. He says one thing and does another; he seems to mean something but we have an uneasy feeling it isn't true. The early psychoanalysts, facing this problem of inconsistencies and ambiguities in a person's communications, attempted to resolve it through the concepts of the conscious and the unconscious. They assumed that contradictory messages meant a conflict between superficial, deceitful, or erroneous feelings on the one hand and true attitudes and feelings on the other. Their role, then, was to help the client separate the wheat from the chaff.

The question was, how could this be done? Some analysts insisted that inferring the client's unconscious wishes was a completely intuitive process. Others thought that some nonverbal behavior, such as posture, position, and movement, could be used in a more objective way to discover the client's feelings. A favorite technique of Frieda Fromm-Reichmann, for example, was to imitate a client's posture herself in order to obtain some feeling for what he was experiencing.

Thus began the gradual shift away from the idea that communication is primarily verbal, and that the verbal message includes distortions or ambiguities due to unobservable motives that only experts can discover.

Language, though, can be used to communicate almost anything. By comparison, nonverbal behavior is very limited in range. Usually, it is used to communicate feelings, likings, and preferences, and it customarily reinforces or contradicts the feelings that are communicated verbally. Less often, it adds a new dimension of sorts to a verbal message, as when a salesman describes his product to a client and simultaneously conveys, nonverbally, the impression that he likes the client.

A great many forms of nonverbal behavior can communicate feelings: touching, facial expression, tone of voice, spatial distance from the addressee, relaxation of posture, rate of speech, number of errors in speech. Some of these are generally recognized as informative. Untrained adults and children easily infer that they are liked or disliked from certain facial expressions, from whether (and how) someone touches them, and from a speaker's tone of voice. Other behavior, such as posture, has a more subtle effect. A listener may sense how someone feels about him from the way the person sits while talking to him, but he may have trouble identifying precisely what his impression comes from.

Correct intuitive judgments of the feelings or attitudes of others are especially difficult when different degrees of feeling, or contradictory kinds of feeling, are expressed simultaneously through different forms of behavior. As I have pointed out, there is a distinction between verbal and vocal information (vocal information being what is lost when speech is written down—intonation, tone, stress, length and frequency of pauses, and so on), and the two kinds of information do not always communicate the same feeling. This distinction, which has been recognized for some time, has shed new light on certain types of communication. Sarcasm, for example, can be defined as a message in which the information transmitted vocally contradicts the information transmitted verbally. Usually the verbal information is positive and the vocal is negative, as in "Isn't science grand."

Through the use of an electronic filter, it is possible to measure the degree of liking communicated vocally. What the filter does is eliminate the higher frequencies of recorded speech, so that words are unintelligible but most vocal qualities remain. (For women's speech, we eliminate frequencies higher than about 200 cycles per second; for men, frequencies over about 100 cycles per second.) When people are asked to judge the degree of liking conveyed by the filtered speech, they perform the task rather easily and with a significant amount of agreement.

This method allows us to find out, in a given message, just how inconsistent the information communicated in words and the information communicated vocally really are. We ask one group to judge the amount of liking conveyed by a transcription of what was said, the verbal part of the message. A second group judges the vocal component, and a third group judges the impact of the complete recorded message. In one study of this sort we found that, when the verbal and vocal components of a message agree (both positive or both negative), the message as a whole is judged a little more positive or a little more negative than either component by itself. But when vocal information contradicts verbal, vocal wins out. If someone calls you "honey" in a nasty tone of voice, you are likely to feel disliked; it is also possible to say "I hate you" in a way that conveys exactly the opposite feeling.

Besides the verbal and vocal characteristics of speech, there are other, more subtle, signals of meaning in a spoken message. For example, everyone makes mistakes when he talks—unnecessary repetitions, stutterings, the omission of parts of words, incomplete sentences, "ums" and "ahs." In a number of studies of speech errors, George Mahl of Yale University has found that errors become more frequent as the speaker's discomfort or anxiety increases. It might be interesting to apply this index in an attempt to detect deceit (though on some occasions it might be risky: confidence men are notoriously smooth talkers).

Timing is also highly informative. How long does a speaker allow silent periods to last, and how long does he wait before he answers his partner? How long do his utterances tend to be? How often does he interrupt his partner, or wait an inappropriately long time before speaking? Joseph Matarazzo and his colleagues at the University of Oregon have found that each of these speech habits is stable from person to person, and each tells something about the speaker's personality and about his feelings toward and status in relation to his partner.

Utterance duration, for example, is a very stable quality in a person's speech; about 30 seconds long on the average. But when someone talks to a partner whose status is higher than his own, the more the high-status person nods his head the longer the speaker's utterances become. If the high-status person changes his own customary speech pattern toward longer or shorter utterances, the lower-status person will change his own speech in the same direction. If the high-status person often interrupts the speaker, or creates long silences, the speaker is likely to become quite uncomfortable. These are things that can be observed outside the laboratory as well as under experimental conditions. If you have an employee who makes you uneasy and seems not to respect you, watch him the next time you talk to him—perhaps he is failing to follow the customary low-status pattern.

Immediacy or directness is another good source of information about feelings. We use more distant forms of communication when the act of communicating is undesirable or uncomfortable. For example, some people would rather transmit discontent with an employee's work through a third party than do it themselves, and some find it easier to communicate negative feelings in writing than by telephone or face to face.

Distance can show a negative attitude toward the message itself, as well as toward the act of delivering it. Certain forms of speech are more distant than others, and they show fewer positive feelings for the subject referred to. A speaker might say, "Those people need help," which is more distant than, "These people need help," which is in turn even more distant than, "These people need our help." Or he might say, "Sam and I have been having dinner," which has less immediacy than, "Sam and I are having dinner."

Facial expression, touching, gestures, self-manipulation (such as scratching), changes in body position, and head movements—all these express a person's positive and negative attitudes, both at the moment and in general, and many reflect status relationships as well. Movements of the limbs and head, for example, not only indicate one's attitude toward a specific set of circumstances but relate to how dominant, and how anxious, one generally tends to be in social situations. Gross changes in body position, such as shifting in the chair, may show negative feelings toward the person one is talking to. They may also be cues: "It's your turn to talk," or, "I'm about to get out of here, so finish what you're saying."

Posture is used to indicate both liking and status. The more a person leans toward his addressee, the more positively he feels about him. Relaxation of posture is a good indicator of both attitude and status, and one that we have been able to measure quite precisely. Three categories have been established for relaxation in a seated position: least relaxation is indicated by muscular tension in the hands and rigidity of posture; moderate relaxation is indicated by a forward lean of about 20 degrees and a sideways lean of less than 10 degrees, a curved back, and, for women, an open arm position; and extreme relaxation is indicated by a reclining angle greater than 20 degrees and a sideways lean greater than 10 degrees.

Our findings suggest that a speaker relaxes either very little or a great deal when he dislikes the person he is talking to, and to a moderate degree when he likes his companion. It seems that extreme tension occurs with threatening addressees, and extreme relaxation with nonthreatening, disliked addressees. In particular, men tend to become tense when talking to other men whom they dislike; on the other hand, women talking to men *or* women and men talking to women show dislike through extreme relaxation. As for status, people relax most with a low-status addressee, second-most with a peer, and least with someone of higher status than their own. Body orientation also shows status: in both sexes, it is least direct toward women with low status and most direct toward disliked men of high status. In part, body orientation seems to be determined by whether one regards one's partner as threatening.

The more you like a person, the more time you are likely to spend looking into his eyes as you talk to him. Standing close to your partner and facing him directly (which makes eye contact easier) also indicate positive feelings. And you are likely to stand or sit closer to your peers than you do to addressees whose status is either lower or higher than yours.

What I have said so far has been based on research studies performed, for the most part, with college students from the middle and upper-middle classes. One interesting question about communication, however, concerns young children from lower socioeconomic levels. Are these children, as some have suggested, more responsive to implicit channels of communication than middle- and upper-class children?

Morton Wiener and his colleagues at Clark University had a group of middle- and lower-class children play learning games in which the reward for learning was praise. The child's responsiveness to the verbal and vocal parts of the praise-reward was measured by how much he learned. Praise came in two forms: the objective words "right" and "correct," and the more affective or evaluative words, "good" and "fine." All four words were spoken sometimes in a positive tone of voice and sometimes neutrally.

Positive intonation proved to have a dramatic effect on the learning rate of the lower-class group. They learned much faster when the vocal part of the message was positive than when it was neutral. Positive intonation affected the middle-class group as well, but not nearly as much.

If children of lower socioeconomic groups are more responsive to facial expression, posture, and touch as well as to vocal communication, that fact could have interesting applications to elementary education. For example, teachers could be explicitly trained to be aware of, and to use, the forms of praise (nonverbal or verbal) that would be likely to have the greatest effect on their particular students.

Another application of experimental data on communication is to the interpretation and treatment of schizophrenia. The literature on schizophrenia has for some time emphasized that parents of schizophrenic children give off contradictory signals simultaneously. Perhaps the parent tells the child in words that he loves him, but his posture conveys a negative attitude. According to the "double-bind" theory of schizophrenia, the child who perceives simultaneous contradictory feelings in his parent does not know how to react: should he respond to the positive part of the message, or to the negative? If he is frequently placed in this paralyzing situation, he may learn to respond with contradictory communications of his own. The boy who sends a birthday card to his mother and signs it "Napoleon" says that he likes his mother and yet denies that he is the one who likes her.

In an attempt to determine whether parents of disturbed children really do emit more inconsistent messages about their feelings than other parents do, my colleagues and I have compared what these parents communicate verbally and vocally with what they show through posture. We interviewed parents of moderately and quite severely disturbed children, in the presence of the child, about the child's problem. The interview was video-recorded without the parents' knowledge, so that we could analyze their behavior later on. Our measurements supplied both the amount of inconsistency between the parents' verbal-vocal and postural communications, and the total amount of liking that the parents communicated.

According to the double-bind theory, the parents of the more disturbed children should have behaved more inconsistently than the parents of the less disturbed children. This was not confirmed: there was no significant difference between the two groups. However, the *total amount* of positive feeling communicated by parents of the more disturbed children was less than that communicated by the other group.

This suggests that (1) negative communications toward disturbed children occur because the child is a problem and therefore elicits them, or (2) the negative attitude precedes the child's disturbance. It may also be that both factors operate together, in a vicious circle.

If so, one way to break the cycle is for the therapist to create situations in which the parent can have better feelings toward the child. A more positive attitude from the parent may make the child more responsive to his directives, and the spiral may begin to move up instead of down. In our own work with disturbed children, this kind of procedure has been used to good effect.

If one puts one's mind to it, one can think of a great many other applications for the findings I have described, though not all of them concern serious problems. Politicians, for example, are careful to maintain eye contact with the television camera when they speak, but they are not always careful about how they sit when they debate another candidate of, presumably, equal status.

Public relations men might find a use for some of the subtler signals of feeling. So might Don Juans. And so might ordinary people, who could try watching other people's signals and changing their own, for fun at a party or in a spirit of experimentation at home. I trust that does not strike you as a cold, manipulative suggestion, indicating dislike for the human race. I assure you that, if you had more than a transcription of words to judge from (seven percent of total message), it would not.

QUESTIONS FOR DISCUSSION

1. Which is broader in the range of events it can communicate about: Language or nonverbal communication?
2. What type of information is communicated most readily through nonverbal channels?
3. Do parents of disturbed children give more inconsistent messages than parents of normal children? What difference is there in the behavior of the two sets of parents?

Verbal communication and nonverbal communication differ in several ways, one of which is the relative size of the common meaning a patterned, matter-energy event has for two persons. While verbal symbols usually have some degree of common meaning between any two speakers of the same language, this is often not true of nonverbal patterns of matter-energy. If a girl at a party folds her arms and sits in a rigid position, one might assume she is sexually unresponsive, while she may be physically cold and trying to get warm. People assign meanings to nonverbal patterns of matter-energy, just as they do to words, but there is little or no guarantee that the nonverbal patterns have any common meaning between any two persons. When no common meaning exists, the patterned matter-energy does not meet the requirements of a language, and the transfer of the matter-energy is not nonverbal *communication* but nonverbal *behavior*.

In assigning meaning to *nonverbal behavior* one person is making inferences or guesses about what these behaviors indicate concerning the other person's internal states, with no agreement between them that the behaviors will indicate anything at all. In *nonverbal communication*, there is at least some agreement on the meaning the behaviors will have. The girl with folded arms is an example of nonverbal *behavior*. Certain inflections and facial expressions have the common meaning that qualifies them as nonverbal *communication*. In our culture, raised eyebrows are usually nonverbal *communication*, because we have high confidence that others will interpret them in the same way we do. With nonverbal *behavior*, such confidence often is not warranted. This does not mean that inferences made from nonverbal behaviors are always wrong. It means that the source of our confidence in nonverbal communication is different from the source of our confidence about meanings assigned to nonverbal behavior.

9

A Language within Language

Albert Mehrabian

In describing what his girl friend did, John could say, "Mike was dancing with her," "She was dancing with Mike," or, "They were dancing together." These three statements show increasing degrees of John's acceptance of what his girl friend did.

Bob could describe his activity to his wife as follows: "Alice and I danced," "She and I danced," "I danced with her," "She danced with me," or, "I had to dance with her," depending, perhaps, on his feelings about liking Alice or about his wife's reaction—the last statement being, of course, the most cautious.

Talking about a party you attended, you say, "The food was pretty good," "They had a good time," "They were having a good time," "We had a good time," or "I had a good time." All these are different ways of making a positive statement about the party; however, when analyzed in some detail, they show interesting differences in feeling.

The previous reading emphasized the role of silent messages in social interaction. In cultures like our own, these constant companions of what we say constitute an important way of conveying feelings and evaluations, the expression of which would otherwise sometimes be unacceptable. Increased focus on the nonverbal modes may help to overcome the handicapping reliance on words in communication, at least as communication skills are formally taught, and may contribute to a better understanding of the significance of various gestures, postures, and expressions. Let us now note the numerous and frequently overlooked subleties of speech itself that are part of the expression of feelings, evaluations, and preferences [2, 7, 11].

Distance in Time and Place

The stylistic differences of the sentences selected to express a certain idea can be used to infer (1) feelings toward the thing being described, (2) feelings toward the listener, or (3) feelings about the act of saying certain things to a certain listener [15]. Here again, we shall use the important concept of immediacy in making inferences about positive-negative feelings revealed in any of these three cases. Notice the difference in each of the following pairs: "Here they are," "There they are"; "These people need help," "Those people need help"; "I can't understand this man," "I can't understand that man"; "I am showing Liz my collection of etchings," "I have been showing Liz my collection of etchings." In each example, the first sentence of the pair is the more immediate one. This is due to the particular use of demonstrative pronouns ("this" or "these" versus "that" or "those"), adjectives ("here," "there"), or verb tense (present versus past).

There are many situations in which either an immediate or nonimmediate form can effectively be used to communicate the verbal message, and thus the particular usage becomes significant [14]. For instance, in talking about a minority group, the speaker who says, "Those people need help" is putting the group further away from himself in this very subtle verbal form than when he says, "These people need help." Consider another example: As a woman enters a crowded room, two men exclaim simultaneously. One says, "Here's Kathy"; the other says, "There's Kathy." It turns out that the first is her current favored escort; the second used to be.

When the form of demonstrative pronoun or tense used is incongruous with the time or place of the actual event, it suggests some special feelings of the speaker [12]. For example, a person says, "I don't understand those people," about some people in the room with him. His demonstrative "those" is incongruous for the situation, which is here and now. In another example, John is showing Mary his cherished collection of plants when his wife, Tina, joins them. When he says, "I am showing Mary the plants," he places the entire activity in the present tense and doubtless is easy in his own mind about the activity. This is closer in time to the actual activity than if he were to say, "I have been showing Mary the plants" or "I showed Mary the plants." If John uses one of the less immediate forms, he may be revealing his awareness of Tina's jealousy of Mary's attentiveness to him or, even though Tina does not mind what she considers to be an innocent relationship, he may feel some edge of uneasiness about his own interest in Mary.

These kinds of nonimmediacy involve putting something at a physical distance through the use of demonstrative pronouns or at a temporal distance through the use of past tenses. But nonimmediacy can be indicated in other ways, one of which is mention of the more unpleasant, or less pleasant, things later in a sequence [12]. Such ordering can occur when we describe different parts of an event or situation. We might refer to a couple we know as "John and Marge," to another couple as "Jane and Jack," and yet another couple as "the Browns." In the first case, chances are that John is the more important, better-known, or better-liked member of the pair. In the second case, Jane may be the more important or better-liked member. In the last case, perhaps neither one of the pair is well known to the speaker, or there is a certain formality and social distance in the relationship with these people.

In describing a day's activities I could say, "We went to the bank, shopped, and visited some friends"; or I could say, "We visited some friends, shopped, and also went to the bank." Assuming that neither one of these orders corresponds to the actual sequence of events, it is safe to infer that the first item mentioned is probably the more important or the more preferred part of the day's activities. In some situations, we may have the necessary information to be able to consider the actual sequence of events and the way in which it is recited in a description. If an event that actually occurred first in the sequence is mentioned last, perhaps the speaker does not like it as well as he does the other items and has delayed mentioning it quite unintentionally. Even stronger negative feelings are implied when he leaves out an item entirely.

In the psychotherapy situation, when we mention something first it is not because we like it more but rather because it is easiest for us to mention that particular problem to a stranger. Thus, another value of the order in which things are mentioned is that it shows how easily certain things can be described to someone else. The general rule for making such interpretations is that nonimmediacy can be due to discomfort about saying a particular thing to a particular listener.

There is a related way in which nonimmediacy comes into play in speech. Hesitant and halting speech with errors, incomplete sentences, and repetition of words indicates anxiety and negative feelings [5, 6, 7]. One would tend to make more errors when talking about a distressing subject than a pleasant one. *Note*: "How did it go at the dentist's?" "Well, uh (pause) it went fine"; "Did you cook dinner?" "I, I thought . . . uh, we could go out tonight." This is reminiscent of Freud's [3] discussion of slips of the tongue—a special kind of error, which, in his view, reveals conflicts in the speaker and negative feelings to aspects of the current situation. What, indeed, is the function of halting and faltering speech? Halting speech delays the completion of a statement. Errors associated with such speech make the descriptions less effective, more difficult to understand, and generally inhibit the communication process. In this sense, the errors serve to delay what a person has to say and lead us to infer that he has at least some reservations about saying it.

The Form of Reference

We can show a less positive feeling toward something by putting it at a distance; by avoiding any mention of it; or, as in the following examples, by referring to it in ambiguous ways [9]. This ambiguity makes it more difficult for our listeners to understand what exactly our statement refers to and reflects our unwillingness to express a certain idea in a certain situation.

One important source of ambiguity of reference is the *overinclusive* statement. Let us say that a friend has recommended a certain restaurant; and, to your chagrin, you have tried it. You have put off mentioning anything about it to him (already, one kind of nonimmediacy), but he asks you, "How did you like your dinner at One-Eyed Joe's?" You say, "It was a pleasant evening" instead of "It was a pleasant dinner." You use the more inclusive term "evening" which involves a broader set of events, thus making an ambiguous positive remark. With this kind of overinclusive statement the involvement with a particular event is minimized since the stated relation includes many parts in addition to the specific referent in question (for example, "evening" includes other events apart from "dinner").

There are two ways of making such overinclusive statements: (1) placing the referent within a more comprehensive category and (2) including oneself within a larger group of people. If I am asked, "How do you like Wanda?" and answer, "I like the Smiths," I have not specifically referred to Wanda in my answer but rather have referred to her and her husband, the Smiths, thereby minimizing involvement. It could be that I have reservations about Wanda or that I am unwilling to say what I feel about her to the person who asked me the question. On the other hand, I could have answered, "We like Wanda," implying that my friends and I like her. Using an inclusive "we" instead of "I" in the statement dilutes the relation with Wanda, which is again indicative of less positive feelings.

The use of "we" instead of "I" is a familiar rhetorical device. If a speaker uses both "I" and "we," we can infer which of his statements he feels more strongly about and which are token statements to placate or gratify his listeners. When a speaker feels strongly about the accuracy of some statement or wishes to be identified with a certain proposition, he is more likely to start that sentence with "I." But when he feels less confident about something and does not want to be held responsible for it, he may use the pronoun "we." *Note:* "I believe that the national economy will respond favorably to increase in money supply" versus "We believe . . ." The "we" may refer to the speaker and his wife, to many Americans, or to some economists; it is not altogether clear to the listeners that this is the speaker's particular stand on the issue . . .

Another way, perhaps more extreme, of diluting the relationship between self and the referent is to make a statement that touches only tangentially on the person or the issue being considered. A question like, "What do you think of their marriage?" may be answered with remarks such as, "My wife thinks it's great" or, "Don't you think it's great?" rather than, "I think it's great." In the first two instances, the speaker is implying that not he but someone else thinks the marriage is exceptionally suitable. We may infer that he has some reservations about the soundness of this marriage—or perhaps is simply not particularly interested. Quite frequently, the negative significance of such answers is overlooked, but experimental findings have consistently shown that this kind of nonimmediacy is a powerful indicator of a speaker's negative feelings about what he is discussing. The difference between, "I lost control of the car" and the more nonimmediate form, "The car went out of control," can be similarly interpreted. It is evident that the person making the latter statement is unwilling to accept responsibility for the accident.

Elaborate and adept applications of such tangential references to oneself are very common in public speeches and debates when the speaker feels that a remark may be controversial or that it is only weakly supported by facts and reasoning. Common examples are: "You would expect," "You'd think," "It would seem to be," "It would be expected," all of which serve as substitutes for "I think" or "I expect." Similar hedging also occurs frequently in scientific writings, in which it is especially important to emphasize the tentative quality of one's ideas.

The complement of tangential reference to self occurs when a subject of distaste is described in such a way that it is unclear who or what is being described. A mother, in referring to her son's fiancée, could say, "our daughter-to-be," "our son's fiancée," "his fiancée," "his lady friend," "his friend," "she," or "that thing"—showing increasing nonimmediacy and dislike of the girl. Similarly, across the generation gap, a shaven and shorn solid citizen may refer to his hirsute son as "that hippie," while the youth may reciprocate with "that reactionary" or "that uptight square" (if he uses printable epithets).

An interesting variant of the overinclusive statement is *negation*. Following a brief encounter with someone whom we do not really care to meet again, we say, "Why don't we get together sometime?" instead of, "Let's get together." If we are enthusiastic about meeting this person again, we actually suggest a time and place for the next meeting. Our negative feelings toward a listener or our feeling that the listener will feel negative about complying with a request can also become evident in examples such as this: "Why don't you type this one first and then go back to what you were doing." In this instance, the executive may use this particular form to request his secretary to change her priorities because he is aware that she will be inconvenienced and will have a negative reaction to his request.

More generally, the "why don't you" statement is likely to occur when the speaker doubts that his request or suggestion will be complied with, either because he feels that his request may sound imposing or demanding, as in the case of the employer, or because he shares little mutual feeling of goodwill with the listener, as in our first example.

Another kind of negation that reveals one's reservations is illustrated by, "How did you like the movie?" answered with, "It wasn't bad." This answer conveys a feeling different from that indicated by "It was fine." We can understand the difference in terms of the overinclusive quality of "not bad" relative to "fine." The former includes "fine" as well as "so-so," and more than likely the feeling was indeed "so-so." Other examples are "We're not exactly buddies" and, "The movie is not the best I've seen."

Think back to the times when you have answered a question in just this way or made such a statement. You probably used this kind of negation because you did not really care for the experience you were describing but, as a matter of politeness or caution, preferred not to express your strong feelings to your listener.

The exact opposite of the overinclusive statement is yet another source of information about feelings. "I dig being with her, for an evening" shows how, in addition to using overinclusive reference, a speaker can also minimize his relation to a referent by using *overspecific* statements. In this case, the "digging" is restricted to an evening, rather than left unqualified. Overspecification arises when we refer to a part of the referent in a context that requires a more complete statement: "How did you like my new production?" is answered with, "I liked the acting" instead of simply, "I liked it." In saying, "I liked (or enjoyed) the acting," the speaker has managed to pick out the one part of the production that he liked best or, which is more likely to be the case, disliked least. An astute and straightforward producer at this point might say, "What was the matter with the rest of it?" More than likely, however, he will simply go on with a discussion of the acting and will fail to consider possible weaknesses in his play that are implied by the remark.

Someone asks you about the ball game he had suggested you go to: "How was the game?" You say, "It was a nice day, and it was fun to be outdoors." These references to the weather and to the outdoors touch only in part on the game and reveal less positive or possibly negative evaluation of the game by you.

Just as overspecificity shows negative feelings when it involves the referent, the same kind of implication is made when it involves the speaker [8]. After an accident, I could say, "My car slid out of control and struck her" instead of, "I struck her with my car." In the first statement something associated with me, "my car," is the implied agent responsible for this action; in the second, "I," the actor, am the responsible agent. Someone says, "The thoughts that come to my mind are . . . " instead of, "I think . . . ," thus implying that only a part of him, "his thoughts," should be held responsible for what he is to say. A more straightforward example of overspecificity is, "His hands touched her hair" instead of, "He touched her hair."

In all these cases, a part of the person speaking (his hand, his thoughts) or something that belongs to or is associated with the speaker (his car) is the ostensible actor and the responsible agent in a situation. Thus, we can infer that the speaker does not feel very comfortable about a statement he is going to make, since he is unwilling to assume full responsibility. Indeed, an entire set of nonimmediate statements can be analyzed directly in terms of the desire to minimize responsibility.

Responsibility

As he brings his date back home, a young man says, "I would like to see you again," instead of the less conditional, "I want to see you again." In this case, he probably uses the less immediate conditional form because he does not want to seem too forward with a girl he has taken out for the first time or lay himself on the line to be rejected. In other words, he has trouble expressing his enthusiasm about the girl, not because he does not like her, but because there are social sanctions against it or because of the possibility of being turned down.

Usually, the conditional is used when the speaker does not like what he is going to say [10]. *Note:* "You'd think they would do something to improve the quality of service here" instead of, "I think they ought to improve the quality of service here." Of course, this example involves at least two kinds of nonimmediacy. One is the use of "you" instead of "I," and the other is the use of the conditional. Here the speaker is trying to avoid seeming domineering or authoritarian to his addressee. Alternatively, the addressee in this case may be connected with the management of the place being criticized, and the speaker may be uncomfortable about being directly critical. Whatever the reason for making such conditional statements, it is obvious that the speaker is trying to imply a lack of familiarity and a weaker relationship with the object being discussed.

When an author sends his manuscript to a publisher and receives the following kind of initial response, he has some reason to wonder whether his manuscript will be accepted. "The manuscript seems very interesting and apparently does a very good job of portraying youth in our society. Our readers are now giving your manuscript a closer look, and I will be getting in touch with you about it." The words "seems" and "apparently" may indicate that the editor has some reserve about the manuscript. In this case, even though the editor is making a number of positive statements, the author probably should not take the letter as an enthusiastic reception of his manuscript.

In a similar minimizing of responsibility, a speaker makes no direct reference to himself: "It is evident that. . . ," "It is obvious that . . . ," or "Most people realize that she's an intolerable bitch." The implication here is that others are responsible for the view being expressed and that the speaker merely shares that view. This device is likely to be used by a speaker who does not wish to be held answerable for what he is going to say and is especially concerned about possible disagreement from his listener. By protecting himself from rebuff in this way, he hints at the quality of his relationship with the listener: They are not likely to agree on this and perhaps many other matters. Experimental findings have consistently shown that people tend to dislike others who hold different opinions and attitudes, that is, those they would disagree with frequently [1, 13]. So in this instance, the implication of expected disagreement of the listener is indicative of negative feelings toward him.

Of course, another way to avoid responsibility for what we say is to qualify our statements. Common forms are, "I feel. . . ," "I think . . . ," "It seems to me. . . ," or, "It is possible that she's pregnant." With such qualification, the speaker shows his reluctance to make the particular statement as a matter of established fact and again highlights his awareness of possible disagreement from his listeners. This device is also used in gossip. By prefacing a scandalous thought with, "I think. . ." or, "They say . . . ," the speaker technically avoids responsibility for the truth or falsehood of his statement, yet he still gets the pleasure of saying it.

In some situations, the nonimmediacy and associated negative feeling of the speaker is evident in statements that very obviously seek to minimize his responsibility [4]. A girl who is asked for a date by someone whom she does not like says, "I have to go with someone else," instead of the more straightforward, "I prefer (or want) to go with someone else." The nonimmediacy in, "I have to" reflects her difficulty in being frank with him.

In departing from a friend's house, we could use the more immediate forms, "I am leaving now" or, "I want to leave now" instead of nonimmediate forms such as, "I should leave now," "I have to leave now," or, "I really should leave now." The second set of statements implies that we are leaving, not because we want to, but because of some extraneous circumstances that force us to do so. In other words, something other than our own desires is responsible for the fact that we must leave. This kind of nonimmediacy is used if the relationship with the listener is more formal, less straightforward, and generally one in which feelings cannot be clearly and directly expressed without fear of hurting others.

People tend to attribute responsibility to some external agent in their statement for departing, especially because the act of departure increases nonimmediacy. If we leave a party at 11:00 P.M. instead of 2:00 A.M. or if we are first rather than last to leave, this departure time indicates something about how much we are enjoying the party. So, when we do leave at a time that we think is too early and might lead the host to think we did not enjoy the party (which is actually the case), a statement such as, "We've got to get back" helps to save face for the host and provides an easy out for the guest.

When a couple is going to get married, and they tell their friends, "We have to get married," it doesn't take much psychological training for friends to wonder about possible reservations and negative feelings of the engaged couple toward the marriage. But when someone says, "I can't come because I have to see a friend off at the airport," the negative affect is less likely to be detected without knowledge of speech immediacy. We know that he could have said, "I can't come because I am going to see a friend off at the airport."

Another way in which responsibility for an action or a statement is minimized is through the use of the passive rather than the active form. I could say, "The results of my experiments have led me to this conclusion" instead of "I conclude this from my experiments." I would be more likely to use the passive form if I were not quite sure about the results or how they should be interpreted. The use of the passive form in this case implies that anybody else, just like myself, could have been led to the same conclusion, and that I should not be held responsible for making the particular interpretation. However, if I were to use the active form, I would not provide myself with this "out."

Examples so far in this section show how avoiding responsibility is generally indicative of negative feelings about the contents of one's communication. There are other times, however, when the sharing of responsibility with the listener, a form of *mutuality*, can be informative about the relation between speaker and listener. *Note:* "Remember what we decided about the office?" instead of, "Remember what I suggested about the office?" In the first case, the decision is a mutual one involving the speaker and the listener, whereas in the second the decision is a unilateral one. It involves the speaker alone and implies his separation from the listener, at least in terms of their contribution to this activity [8].

When such expressions occur frequently in a relationship, they can serve as clues about how two people, who are closely involved in either a social or working relationship, feel toward each other. The statements implying mutuality are likely to arise in more positive relationships, since they indicate a more intense involvement of the pair in the activity in which they are engaged. Let us say that two persons are having lunch and a third person joins them. At this point, one of the two says, "John and I have been discussing your project" instead of, "I have been telling John about your project." Either one of these two statements could be quite legitimate in the situation, but the former implies equality of status between John and the speaker and a more intimate feeling.

This concept allows us to interpret, "I was dancing with her" or, "She was dancing with me" differently from, "We were dancing." The first statement implies that she really was not participating much, possibly because she does not like the speaker. The second statement implies that the speaker does not like her or that he does not want to let his listener know that he likes her. The last statement shows no reservations about dancing with this particular person or the act of mentioning it to someone else.

Guarded Expressions of Liking

So far most of our discussion has focused on how nonimmediacy reflects negative feelings. On some occasions, a more nonimmediate statement is used because the speaker feels uncomfortable about saying what he wants to say to his listener. This idea can be turned to one's advantage. In a number of social situations, it may seem too forward to make strong statements of liking or interest to a stranger or a casual acquaintance, but a more nonimmediate statement of liking would be socially acceptable.

A man sees an interesting girl in the hallway of the office building where he works and wishes to get to know her. The first chance he gets, he says, "That's a nice dress you have on." In this instance, the less immediate remark ("I like you" would be immediate) serves as an indirect way of conveying his liking. The nonimmediacy of the remark reflects his uneasiness, not because he dislikes her, but because he feels uncomfortable about this initial contact with a stranger.

Other examples: "I heard that you have a marvelous wine cellar" or, "Someone told me that you grow prize-winning camellias." The speaker desires to somehow compliment his listener but feels that he cannot do so in a very direct and obvious way. So he selects something related to the listener to compliment, because the more indirect statement involving greater nonimmediacy happens to be more socially appropriate. The nonimmediacy of his statement still shows that the speaker feels uncomfortable in the situation, which is indeed why this kind of statement is more acceptable in formal relationships or contacts with a stranger.

Relations of Verbal and Nonverbal Immediacy

Our analyses of speech here and of actions in Chapter 1 [of *Silent Messages*] have been based on the same basic metaphor: People seek out and get involved with things they like and they try to minimize their relationship or, if possible, entirely avoid contact with things they dislike or fear. We have examined the many special devices that are available in speech to reflect a speaker's negative feelings. At this point, let us consider some analogues of these speech nonimmediacy forms in silent messages.

For example, the times at which various participants at major political negotiations arrive for a specific meeting can be important cues, provided the persons whose behaviors are under scrutiny have some prepared remarks for that session. Thus, if one of the participants comes with some prepared remarks of a hopeful quality, but makes his entrance late (relative to other sessions), this provides some grounds for questioning the sincerity of the remarks. His delay shows a reluctance to make those remarks. On the other hand, if he delivers some prepared, negative remarks, his delay would constitute a positive sign and show his reluctance to seem antagonistic. In either case, the delay can also be a function of the importance of the remarks (he was busy up to the last minute preparing them) or a variety of other factors. This is of course true, but suppose we make these observations repeatedly over a large number of instances, say weekly meetings. In this case, the extraneous and unsystematic effect of some of these factors (for example, he was delayed in traffic) is washed out in the averaging process, and the underlying attitudes tend to become evident from the nonverbal or the verbal behavior of the participants. This is exactly what is done in any experiment where such ideas are tested. We do not rely on a single incident to make a judgment, so most of our experiments employ large numbers of subjects to test the immediacy ideas.

In a somewhat different context, Freud's [3] discussion of forgetting provides another point of similarity between verbal and nonverbal forms of nonimmediacy. The verbal analogues of forgetting are the speech errors and other obstructions that delay the expression of an idea [5, 6, 7]. As in the case of forgetting, such phenomena make it possible for the speaker or the actor to put off or avoid saying something that is unpleasant. Freud [3] did not interpret forgetting or slips specifically in terms of immediacy. Nevertheless, his analyses always implied that the unconscious conflicts which led to these errors or even more serious symptoms were motivated by negative feelings. In the case of forgetting, the negative feelings were toward the forgotten object. Thus, when we forget to mail a letter we have written, this helps delay contact with the intended receiver of the letter and shows reservations of the writer about the contents of his letter or toward the person who would receive it.

I have frequently and painfully been reminded of the validity of this idea when I have belatedly come across an unpleasant chore which I had forgotten to get done on time. It seems much easier to forget an unpleasant or time-consuming chore than a pleasant one.

After hearing a lecture on immediacy, a student asked if the immediacy concept could help explain why her boy friend was invariably about half an hour late for their dates. She said that this was very annoying for her but that otherwise the relationship was perfect. I suggested that this was a way for him to express some negative feelings that he was otherwise unable to convey. As we discussed her problem, it became apparent that he had a great deal of trouble refusing her requests. It also became apparent that he was especially late to their dates when these also involved her parents, so that on such occasions his tardiness was especially embarrassing to her. She concluded that most of the time she had gotten her way in the relationship. The possibility of marriage, which was also her idea initially, was highlighted by those evenings spent with her parents and accounted for his greater tardiness when the parents were involved. Considering his inability to refuse her requests, the boy was resisting in the only way that he knew how—on the most important issue that would affect the rest of his life.

TABLE I

Definitions of Immediacy Categories with Examples
of Context and Speech Immediacy

Category	Immediate/ Nonimmediate Context	Immediate/ Nonimmediate Speech
Distance: spatial distance between communicator and object of communication.	A man standing on the edge of a pool comments to a friend standing beside him./A man standing on the patio some distance from a pool comments . . .	"Go ahead and jump into this pool."/"Go ahead and jump into that pool."
Time: temporal distance between communicator and object.	Question asked of communicator: "Do you think about X?"/"Have you been thinking about X?"	"I think about X."/"I used to think about X."
Order of occurrence: order of interaction with the object in an interaction sequence.	Question asked of communicator: "Did you visit X and Y?"/"Did you visit Y and X?"	"I visited X and Y."/"I visited Y and X."

Category	Immediate/ Nonimmediate Context	Immediate/ Nonimmediate Speech
Duration: duration of interaction or duration (e.g., length) of communication about interaction.	A is asked to write a long letter about B./A is asked to write a short letter about B.	A writes a long letter about B./A writes a short letter about B.
Activity-passivity: willingness vs. an obligatory quality of communicator-object interaction.	X stopped to help someone fix a flat tire./X had to stop to help someone fix . . .	X says, "I stopped to help someone fix a flat tire."/"I had to stop to help . . ."
Mutuality-unilaterality: degree of reciprocity of communicator-object interaction.	Question asked of communicator: "Have you and X met each other?"/"Have you met X?"	"X and I met yesterday."/"I met X yesterday."
Probability: degree of certainty of communicator-object interaction.	Question asked of communicator: "Are you taking physical education courses?"/"Could you take physical education courses?"	"I am taking physical education courses."/"I could take physical . . ."
Communicator participation₁: the totality vs. only a part, aspect or acquaintance of the communicator interacts with the object.	Question asked of communicator: "Are you going to the store?"/"Is your friend going to the store?"	"I am going to the store."/"My friend is going to the store."
Communicator participation₂: the communicator interacts individually with the object vs. being part of a group of people who interact with the object.	Question asked of communicator: "Did you go to the beach last summer?"/"Did you people go to the beach last summer?"	"I went to the beach last summer."/"We went to the beach last summer."

Category	Immediate/ Nonimmediate Context	Immediate/ Nonimmediate Speech
Object participation$_1$: the totality vs. only a part, aspect or acquaintance of the object interacts with the communicator.	X is asked to write a letter and describe Y's personality. /X . . . describe some of Y's habits.	In his letter, X describes Y's personality. / In his letter, X describes some of Y's habits.
Object participation$_2$: the object interacts individually with the communicator vs. being part of a group of people who interact with the communicator.	A and B are talking about C, and A asks, "Do you see C near the pool?"/"Do you see the people near the pool?"	B says, "I see C near the pool."/"I see the people near the pool."
Communicator-object participation: the presence vs. the absence of participation of the communicator (or object) in the interaction.	Question asked of communicator: "How are you and B doing at school?"/"How are you doing at school?"	"B and I are doing well at school."/"I am doing well at school."

From A. Mehrabian, The effect of context on judgments of speaker attitude. *Journal of Personality*, 1968, 36, pp. 21-32. Copyright 1968 Duke University Press. Reproduced by permission.

Immediacy and Context

More accurate estimates of the speaker's feelings can be made provided knowledge of the context in which he makes those statements is available. When a psychotherapist listens to his patient list a series of problems in an initial interview, he has no knowledge of the sequence in which these problems occurred. Therefore, he can rely only on the sequence in which they are given to infer the corresponding ease with which his patient can discuss these (that is, the less negative quality of the problems mentioned earlier in the series). However, in case the therapist has an independent source of information, such as a relative of the person whom he is interviewing, then he is in an even better position to estimate the patient's feelings from the sequence in which he relates his problems. So, if the problems occurred in the sequence A, B, C and are described in the sequence C, A, B, he knows that the patient feels less negatively about C than about A.

In applying immediacy analyses, the person doing the analysis can himself create the context within which he can make a more accurate interpretation. This is done with a careful selection of the wording of the question. If I ask you, "How did you like the movie?" and you say, "I like it," there is a striking tense shift in your answer. It shows your desire to bring this experience closer to yourself than the context allows and leads me to infer that you really like the movie. On the other hand, if I ask, "How do you like my tie?" and, as you stand in front of me, you answer, "I like that one better than your other ties," then despite the immediate context, your statement implies nonimmediacy and a desire to place this object farther away. Table 1 illustrates the different categories of immediacy and provides all possible combinations of immediate or nonimmediate context with immediate and nonimmediate speech. In the first example, a man standing on the edge of a pool comments, "Go ahead and jump into this pool," which is congruent with the immediacy of the context. Or he could say, "Go ahead and jump into that pool," which would be nonimmediate and would show negative feelings. On the other hand, another man standing on the patio some distance from the pool could say, "Go ahead and jump into this pool," which shows a more positive feeling than if he were to say, "Go ahead and jump into that pool," for which statement the nonimmediacy is congruent with the context.

The finer points illustrated in Table 1 can be useful when a very cautious scrutiny of the material is required. Most everyday situations provide obvious and blatantly nonimmediate forms that can be readily interpreted. So we'll close with the following instance: "One would think that those people could do something to help themselves!" Such a statement made in reference to minority groups reveals an underlying prejudicial attitude, which may not be evident from a casual perusal of the meaning of the words but is readily detected from the excessive nonimmediacy of the style.

QUESTIONS FOR DISCUSSION

1. What does Mehrabian mean by *immediacy*?
2. List the ways in which immediacy can be expressed, giving a brief example of each.
3. One of the uses of nonimmediacy is to avoid responsibility for the implications of a statement. What other uses are made of nonimmediate forms of expression?

4. Examine the table. For each category (the first column) choose another context (the second column) and give an example of immediate and nonimmediate messages for that context (the third column).

References

1. Byrne, D., "Attitudes and Attraction." In L. Berkowitz, ed., *Advances in Experimental Social Psychology*, 4 (New York: Academic Press, 1969), 35-89.
2. Davitz, J. R., *The language of emotion* (New York: Academic Press, 1969).
3. Freud, S., "The Psychopathology of Everyday Life." In *The Basic Writings of Sigmund Freud* (New York: Random House, 1938. First German edition, 1904).
4. Gottlieb, R., Wiener, M., and Mehrabian, A., "Immediacy, Discomfort-Relief Quotient, and Content in Verbalizations about Positive and Negative Experiences." *Journal of Personality and Social Psychology*, 7 (1967) 266-274.
5. Kasl, S. V., and Mahl, G. F., "The Relationship of Disturbances and Hesitations in Spontaneous Speech to Anxiety," *Journal of Personality and Social Psychology*, 1 (1965) 425-433.
6. Mahl, G. F., "Measuring the Patient's Anxiety During Interviews from 'Expressive' Aspects of his Speech," *Transactions of the New York Academy of Sciences*, 21 (1959) 249-257.
7. Mahl, G. F., and Schulze, G., "Psychological Research in the Extralinguistic Area." In T. A. Sebeok, A. S. Hayes, and M. C. Bateson, eds. *Approaches to Semiotics* (The Hague: Mouton, 1964), 51-124.
8. Mehrabian, A., "Attitudes in Relation to the Forms of Communicator-Object Relationship in Spoken Communications," *Journal of Personality*, 34 (1966) 80-93. (a)
9. Mehrabian, A., "Immediacy: An Indicator of Attitudes in Linguistic Communication," *Journal of Personality*, 34 (1966), 26-34. (b)
10. Mehrabian, A., "Attitudes Inferred from Neutral Verbal Communications," *Journal of Consulting Psychology*, 31 (1967), 414-417. (c)
11. Mehrabian, A., "Substitute for Apology: Manipulation of Cognitions to Reduce Negative Attitude Toward Self," *Psychological Reports*, 20 (1967), 687-692.(d)
12. Mehrabian, A., "The Effect of Context on Judgments of Speaker Attitude," *Journal of Personality*, 36 (1968), 21-32.(c)
13. Mehrabian, A., and Ksionzky, S., "Anticipated Compatibility as a Function of Attitude or Status Similarity," *Journal of Personality*, 39 (1971), 225-241.

14. Mehrabian, A., and Wiener, M., "Nonimmediacy Between Communicator and Object of Communication in a Verbal Message: Application to the Inference of Attitudes," *Journal of Consulting Psychology, 30* (1966), 420-425.

15. Wiener, M., and Mehrabian, A., *"Language Within Language: Immediacy, a Channel in Verbal Communication"* (New York: Appleton-Century-Crofts, 1968).

Mehrabian says that facial expressions account for fifty-five percent of the affective meanings assigned to individual words. Suggesting that "the head and face are perhaps man's richest sign system," Randall Harrison discusses the use of the human face in interpersonal communication. Raised eyebrows and wrinkled brows are some of the more obvious uses of the human face during communication. Harrison discusses these and other expressions but emphasizes that they are only a few of many nonverbal uses of the human face.

10

tHE HUMAN fACE

Randall P. Harrison

> *She had a pretty face.*
> *He raised his eyebrows and smiled.*
> *"I'm Bill."*
> *She nodded. "Hi. I'm Xan."*

The head and face are perhaps man's richest sign system. In Western
culture, the head is frequently used in art to represent the whole man;
it is seen as the locus of his personality, his intelligence, his soul. The
face is central in most communication situations. In fact, we speak of
"face-to-face" communication. Or, the face is used symbolically, as in
"face the music," or tragically, "losing face." The head is the locus of
most of the primary sense receptors: eyes, ears, nose, mouth—seeing,
hearing, smelling, tasting. By looking at a person's head we know
whether he is awake or asleep, listening, smelling, tasting, hearing.
Vocalizations come out of the mouth. Facial expressions play across
the features. And we tend to read a man's physiognomy for his
history—his genetic heritage, his time on this earth, and the way that
time has marked his character. This chapter examines areas of performance code in the head and face: (a) appearance cues, (b) facial
expressions, (c) eye behavior, and (d) head nods and movements.

Randall P. Harrison is professor of communication at Michigan State University. From
Beyond Words: An Introduction to Nonverbal Communication by Randall P. Harrison, © 1974,
pp. 114-127. Reprinted by permission of Prentice-Hall, Inc.

Appearance Cues

As with the voice, the head and face present some cues which are enduring, some which are semifixed or situation-specific, and some which are momentary or fleeting. The enduring cues reveal demographic data: the individual's age, sex, race, possibly ethnic and national origins, possibly status or occupation. The cues include: baldness, gray hair, wrinkles, muscle tone and fat deposits, pigmentation of the skin, color of the eyes, the shape and configuration of features. The semifixed markers are less permanent. But they are likely to remain constant during one interaction. Cues include the length of hair and the way it is styled, the degree to which the individual is shaved or not shaved, the way eyebrows are plucked, how clean the individual is. The semifixed markers are likely to signal the individual's concepts about beauty, his reference groups, his self-perceived or desired status. They may indicate his definition of a communication situation: for formal groups he is combed and shaved and scrubbed; for informal gatherings he is less meticulous. Finally, the momentary markers are the fleeting facial expression: the raised eyebrow, the curled lip, the snort, the lowered eyes. They signal emotions. They are likely to be read for interest or boredom, for belief or skepticism, for signs of acceptance or rejection.

Enduring Markers

Because they are difficult to change, the enduring markers make relatively inefficient codes for the producer, but effective codes for the observer. The producer has three options: (1) he can choose to reveal the marker; (2) he can conceal the marker; or (3) he can mask the marker, changing it into a different cue. Some people are proud of their gray hair, their dark skin, their crow's feet, their kinky hair, their unique features. They display these cues and capitalize on them. Jimmy Durante, for example, made a fortune being shot in profile so that you couldn't miss his prominent proboscis.

Some of the enduring markers may be concealed, perhaps with an article of costume, an artifact. The middle-aged lady may wear a scarf, or a high-necked dress, to conceal the unflattering neck wrinkles. Or, like Bing Crosby and Frank Sinatra in their later years, the aging gentleman may take to wearing a hat to conceal the balding pate. Similarly, the aging star may take to wearing dark glasses to help conceal the telltale bags under the eyes.

The masking or changing of an enduring cue is more radical. It may involve an artifact. The girl with stringy hair puts on a wig of flowing locks. The balding man covers up with a toupée. The young lady changes the color of her eyes with contact lenses. But it may require major effort, and even pain: plastic surgery, capping the teeth or replacing them with dentures, dyeing the hair, face lifts, hair transplants, tanning or bleaching the skin, straightening the hair.

Because the enduring markers are so hard to change, they may be important signs for the observer. They are likely to absorb great uncertainty about the other person's age, sex, and background. They tend to be reliable.

They may quickly provide information that would be hard to ask for. In the formation stage of interaction, they may play an important role in decisions. Most people find it easiest to interact with people like themselves. It takes less effort. There are fewer unpleasant surprises. It is usually more rewarding. If given a choice, they will often choose to interact with others who are like themselves, in age, in sex, in social status. On the other hand, man sometimes seeks variety. He is attracted to people of beauty, of status, of unique and interesting background. Again, the appearance markers may provide good predictors about the potential rewards and costs of interaction.

Face Reading

The "reading of the face" is an ancient and venerable art, comparable to reading tea leaves, or the palm, or bumps on the head. A legend in the Talmud tells of "the science of physiognomy" in the time of Moses. According to the story, a famous king sent his court painter to capture the likeness of Moses so that his wise men could analyze this famous face and explain to the king what made Moses so great. The king could then cultivate these same qualities in himself. But when the painter returned with the likeness, and the physiognomers studied it, they told the king: "There must be some mistake in this likeness, for we have analyzed it and it represents the worst possible set of characteristics that could be collected in one man's face; each feature reveals some conflicting and terrible flaw of character."

Enraged, the king sent a messenger back to Moses to compare the likeness, thinking, of course, that the painter had badly botched the job. But when Moses heard of the incident, he responded, "Ah no, that is precisely the source of my greatness; I had all the worst possible passions a man could know—and it is out of mastering these conflicting forces that I emerged such a wise and great man."

This story, interestingly enough, has also been told about Socrates and Alexander the Great and perhaps many other great ancients.

In the early days of psychology, a good deal of effort was spent on sweeping away some of the "old wives' tales" that populated folklore. And, of course, notions about being able to read man's character or fate from his facial features was an early target of investigation. For the most part, research did not reveal any systematic relationship between a man's physiognomy and his character, talent, intelligence, or fate. A man with a low forehead was not necessarily low in intelligence. Close-set eyes did not reveal a "criminal type," and so on. What was surprising about many of these studies, however, was that judges frequently agreed about these cues and their meaning. In other words, you might have a man with a low forehead who was demonstrably a very intelligent individual. But show his picture to a group of judges and they would tend to agree that, yes, this person was not very bright.

This then became a very interesting problem for social psychologists. Why do people have these stereotypes? Are there culturally induced notions about beauty, or ideal types? And what effect do these stereotypes have on individuals? If, for instance, people always look at you and expect that you will be stupid, you may have to be very bright indeed to escape these expectations. Or vice versa. For example, Robert Rosenthal at Harvard recently did a study in which he told teachers that certain students—randomly selected— were going to be "late bloomers" and evince a sudden spurt in IQ during the following year. Rather startlingly, many of these children—given their teacher's expectations—did evidence significant increases in objectively measured IQ during the school year.[1] I have a very bright Ph. D. friend who has a low forehead and a face that would look well on a boxer. I've always thought his appearance was quite an advantage; people are constantly underestimating him—and then he pounces on them when they least expect it.

While the research literature has continued to fail to find any relationship between facial types and character, fate, and the like, the idea is very persistent. And, in some cases, very elaborate theories have been advanced as to why there should be a relationship. The Hungarian psychologist Lipot Szondi, for example, developed a theory of "genotropism" that argued that men are driven to their fates by latent hereditary factors. Further, he argued that these recessive genes would show up in facial features and that you could look at a young man or woman and predict quite well what would happen to this individual later in life. Finally, he contended that people would be attracted to others who had similar latent qualities. Thus, you could, as he did, take photographs of individuals who were known to suffer from various mental disorders or sexual perversions. When shown to someone else, to a judge, the choices made would reveal the judge's own deepseated proclivities. The projective test that Szondi developed is still being used today, although usually now divorced from his original theory.

Recently, a California lawyer has revived many of the ancient physiognomy predictions in a system called "personology." From years of watching people in the courtroom, the attorney argues that he can make good predictions about an individual just from physiognomic cues alone. While this topic continues to arouse speculation and is an amusing party game activity, the research continues to suggest that the inferences people make can be very misleading. From basic features of the face we may be able to tell something of the individual's genetic heritage. We may be able to read from broken noses and cauliflowered ears some of the experiences that have marked his life. And we may be able to make some judgments about his current vitality, his capacity for interaction. But beyond that, the inference process becomes very complex, blending with many cultural stereotypes which may do considerable injustice to the individual human being.

Facial Expressions

Just as there has been long controversy over what facial features reveal, so there has been a continuing controversy over what facial expressions reveal. More precisely, researchers have asked: (a) Are certain facial movements related to specific emotions; (b) and, if so, can the average person accurately judge what those facial affects are? Over the past one hundred years, most of the research has focused on the expression of emotion. But recently, investigators have also begun to look at other functions of facial expression. Does, for instance, facial expression serve to regulate interaction? Can facial expressions punctuate conversations or express other meanings?

Affect Displays

An early pioneer was Charles Darwin. After his historic treatise on the evolution of the species, Darwin wrote a book entitled, *The Expression of the Emotions of Man and Animals*.[2] A surprisingly good, scientific endeavor, the book represents Darwin's attempt to systematically explore facial expressions. He asked how they differed—and were similar—among men and animals, and among different peoples, around the world. In general, Darwin argued that human facial expressions have their roots in animal behavior; many of the expressions seen in man arose for very practical purposes in lower animals. He thus expected that facial expressions of emotion would be the same around the world. While some of Darwin's notions have not stood the test of time, a surprising number of his predictions have worked out and many are still being explored today, a century after Darwin wrote his original book.[3]

European psychologists tended to follow Darwin's lead, but most American psychologists—until very recently—tended to disagree with the father of evolution. The early American findings seemed to indicate that there were few reliable cues in facial affect displays. Further, judges of facial expression seemed to be very poor at discerning what the expressor was really feeling. Among the researchers who did find some regularity, a division grew up between those who thought there were several categories of facially expressed emotion and those who thought that there were a few major dimensions. One early study, for example, found that judges were fairly reliable if you used a few major categories along a continuum: happiness, surprise, fear, anger, suffering, and disgust.[4] Other researchers, however, argued that these expressions could be arranged in a three-dimensional space, with dimensions such as: "pleasant-to-unpleasant" (i.e., happy, smiling faces to sad, crying faces); "attention-to-rejection" (i.e., faces with eyes, mouth, and nostrils open and receptive to stimuli as opposed to faces in which eyes, mouth, and nose appeared to be closed tight as if warding off unpleasant stimuli); and "tension-to-sleep" (i.e., faces that appeared alert, excited, and agitated as opposed to those that appeared relaxed and sleepy).

While the battle still continues between the category approach and the dimensional approach, much of the recent research on facial affect display has been stimulated by a theory of emotion developed by Silvan Tomkins.[5] He argues that the face is a key site of emotion. When an emotion is aroused in an individual, one of the first things that happens is that a neural program fires messages to the face, which, in turn, cause the contraction and relaxation of certain facial muscles. According to Tomkins's theory, the feedback you get from feeling your muscles contract is one of the cues that tells you what emotion you are feeling. Finally, this theory argues that there are unique facial configurations associated with each of the primary affects. The basic emotions identified by Tomkins are (a) interest-excitement, (b) enjoyment-joy, (c) surprise-startle, (d) distress-anguish, (e) shame-humiliation, (f) contempt-disgust, (g) anger-rage, and (h) fear-terror. In each pair, the first is less intense. For each of these affects, with the exception of happiness, there should be one or more unique configurations in each area of the face: brows, eyes, and mouth. Happiness displays itself primarily in the eyes and lower face.

In Tomkins's scheme, the positive emotions center around enjoyment-joy and interest-excitement. Surprise and startle are what Tomkins calls "re-setting" affects and are not in themselves either positive or negative. Finally, the other affects, such as anguish, disgust, fear, and anger, can be classified as negative emotions. Empirical research has been particularly successful in discriminating cues for surprise, happiness, sadness, disgust, fear, and anger. Increasingly, these basic expressions of emotion have been found around the world, just as Darwin predicted.[6] Figure 10.1 shows a selection of the key cues, in a simplified and somewhat exaggerated form.

Partials, Blends, and Micros

The full display of an emotion results in muscle movements in all three areas of the face (with the noted exception of happiness, which is reflected primarily in the eyes and mouth). Man can also display *partials*, however. These are expressions in which only one portion of the face is activated. Surprise might, for example, be shown only in a raised brow, or only in a widening of the eyes. In addition, some expressions are *blends*, where one affect, such as happiness, is showing in the mouth, and another affect, such as surprise, is showing in the brow or eye. Finally, some affect displays flit across the features at very fast speeds, for as little as a fifth of a second. These are called micromomentary facial expressions, or *microfacials*. They are almost impossible for the untrained observer to see with the naked eye. They are, however, very evident in slow motion pictures of the face in action. They show up even when the performer is trying to conceal his feelings—and thinks he has been totally successful. The occurrence of partials, blends, and micros explains, in part, why researchers have had such difficulty in studying the face. It also helps account for the enormous individual differences among people in their ability to recognize and identify facial affect displays.

Display Rules

While recent research indicates that men in all cultures have similar affect displays, people do differ in what they will show in different communication contexts. Figure 10.2 shows a model of affect display

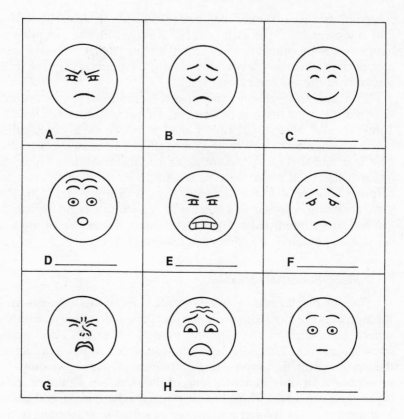

Can you match the above sketches with the correct affects?
(1) happy, (2) sad, (3) surprise, (4) fear, (5) anger, (6) disgust.

Answers: A-5, B-2, C-1, D-3, E-5, F-2, G-6, H-4, I-3.

Figure 10.1   Cues of the Primary Affects

that points to the panhuman and the cultural ingredients of facial expressions.

The various affects may be elicited by a variety of stimuli. And depending on learning, different events may trigger joy, fear, surprise, and so forth. In our culture, for example, the sight of an insect or reptile might stimulate disgust or fear. In another culture, however, the same creature might be an edible delicacy. It might elicit pure joy. If the stimulus is eliciting the same emotion, then the neural program should be the same. This neural message to the face is filtered, however, through one's culturally learned *display rules*. As we grow up, we learn what is appropriate to feel and hence to show. Within a culture, it may be appropriate to *intensify* certain emotional displays. We may not feel much joy at receiving a particular present, but we may intensify what pleasure we do feel, because it is the socially appropriate response. The gift giver expects us to be pleased—and we try to show that we are. On the other hand, there may be occasions when we *deintensify*. It may, for example, be impolite to show how much glee we feel at beating a competitor. We deintensify our display and only evince mild pleasure. In the middle range, we may *neutralize* expressions, bringing whatever we feel back to an unexpressive "poker face." Finally, some affect displays may require *masking*. The young warrior may be feeling fear but he learns to mask this unwelcome emotion with another, such as anger.

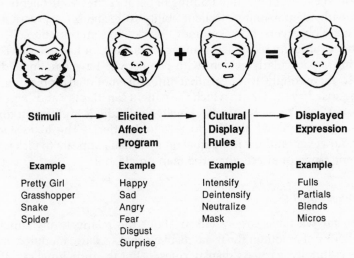

Stimuli	→	Elicited Affect Program	→	Cultural Display Rules	→	Displayed Expression

Example	Example	Example	Example
Pretty Girl	Happy	Intensify	Fulls
Grasshopper	Sad	Deintensify	Partials
Snake	Angry	Neutralize	Blends
Spider	Fear	Mask	Micros
	Disgust		
	Surprise		

Different stimuli in different cultures may elicit different affects as a result of learning, but the affect program, once elicited, should be panhuman. Cultures also differ, however, in the "display rules" they impose on expressions.

Figure 10.2   Affects and Their Display

Affect Recognition

The affect displays tend to be important social signals. They help reduce our uncertainties about an important dimension of interaction. We receive early warning when anger is building. We get reassuring messages when our partner is happy. It helps us make important predictions about what will happen next. Similarly, it provides information which is not always easy to get in other ways. We may pick up affect cues from tone of voice, or body posture. But the movements of the face are easily accessible and uniquely reliable. At the same time, it takes skill to interpret facial expressions. It requires seeing the affect display in the first place. Then it requires a complex inference process. It is necessary to decide when the affect is felt, and when it is being simulated without feeling. It is necessary to pick up "false notes" that might indicate masking, or neutralizing, or shifts in intensity.

Some people appear to be very good at recognizing even brief facial affect displays. It is a very useful skill in some professional roles: bank loan officers, psychiatrists, nurses, police officers. Some people in these roles, either through training or because they were talented to begin with, demonstrate excellent ability to recognize expressions. Even good observers, however, may "block" on some emotion. They may have difficulty recognizing anger, or disgust, or happiness. This blocking is particularly evident with people who have emotional disorders. Increasingly, it appears that different emotional problems may be diagnosed by the way in which the patient can identify and express, on request, the primary affects. Finally, individuals in different toxic states show impaired abilities to recognize affect. The toxic states differ, however, and the individual on marijuana appears to pick up a different range of affects than the man on alcohol.

Other Facial Signs

So far we have largely talked about the relatively involuntary expressions of emotion, the facial displays that well up, modified only by the culturally learned "display rules." But the individual can also create an apparent expression of emotion, even when no affect is present. And the face can be used to produce other signs.

The "put-on" expression of emotion may be done either (a) with the expectation (or hope) that the receiver will take it for a felt affect, or (b) with the open indication that it is an act. An example of the first would be a young lad who puts on an angry face hoping to scare off a bully. (As indicated before, if such an expression covers up some other emotion, such as fear, it is called "masking." If no other emotion is present, it does not "mask" another affect; it simulates one which is not there.)

Just as some people are good at catching expressions of emotion generally, some individuals are very adept at ferreting out simulated as opposed to felt affects. Among the cues that people may use are inconsistencies in (a) partials, (b) blends, and (c) timing. The person who is simulating an affect display, may, for example, get part of the expression but not all of it. He may smile with his lips, but his eyes may be "icy cold," as the detective novels like to say. Second, the individual attempting simulation may get part of the affect he wants—but blend in another affect expression. He may smile in apparent pleasure, but his brows may knit in concern. Finally, the timing of the expression may be off. The person wants to display pleasure— and he does. But the reaction is a bit delayed, a beat off. It becomes apparent that the expression was not automatic; the individual had to think about the expression he wanted to display and then produce it. Similarly, the put-on expression may not last as long as it should. We sometimes see someone who appears to be happy in interaction. But the instant he turns his back, the signs of pleasure disappear. There are no lingering, slowly dissolving remnants of the earlier state. It is rather as if a mask has been dropped. We have been witnessing a "social smile"—rather than a felt affect.

Sometimes, of course, an individual puts on a face with no attempt at deception. He is, for example, reenacting an emotion felt earlier. He says, "So that made me feel just terrible"—and he re-creates his sad expression. Or, an individual may be imitating the affect display of someone else: "She looked like the cat that ate a canary"—followed by a broad grin. Some are very good at mimicking the expressions of others. They can visually re-create images of their own joy, or excitement, or horror. They spice their conversations or enliven their speeches with appropriate facial gestures. And we tend to think of these individuals as "vivacious," "expressive," and "dymanic"— rather than as "deadpan" or "boring."

While the expressions of emotion, felt or simulated, provide the basic vocabulary of facial communication, the human face can telegraph a wide spectrum of subtle but telling statements. An individual may look serious or kidding, concerned or indifferent, seductive or hostile. The communicator may indicate that he is believing or skeptical, accepting or unaccepting, sincere or insincere. These cues may, in turn, have an impact on the relationship, on the ongoing communication system.

In another area of regulation, certain facial expressions may be linked to particular phases of a communication system. Evidence now suggests, for example, that the eyebrow "flash," the rapid raising and lowering of the brow, may be a universal form of greeting.[7] Finally, the head and face may be used as a pointer or indicator. In some cultures, for example, it is impolite to point with one's finger. Rather, pointing is done with the lips or with a head movement. A similar "pointer" is simply the way the head is turned, and the way gaze is directed.

Eye Behavior

The eye is poetically referred to as "the window to the soul." As a chief sensory receptor, which is easily observable by another, it can reveal much. It is likely to signal what interests. It also may indicate what is being rejected. In interaction, it appears to signal major shifts in the pattern of communication. Like a traffic signal, it helps regulate the communication system.

At a physiological level, the eye dilates in darkness. The organ operates automatically to open its lens and receive more light. But dilation can also be caused by psychological factors. The presentation of interesting objects, even in normal light, will cause the eye to dilate. Both extremely pleasant stimuli, such as beautiful women or handsome men, and very unpleasant stimuli, such as spiders or snakes, may cause the eye to dilate. This fact has been used by researchers in the mass media. They have exposed viewers to ads and other messages. Then, with an eye camera, measurements are taken of eye movement and pupil dilation.[8]

Normally, dilation would not be under the control of the producer. He cannot easily use it as a sign for communication. There are, however, ancient drugs, such as belladonna, which have been used for centuries by women who wish to make their pupils larger and their eyes more alluring. Similarly, photographers have retouched photographs, widening the pupil, to make the woman more attractive. The observer who sees such a retouched photograph or an individual with drug-widened eyes usually knows something is different. Observers vary in their response, but typically, the actual cue is one of awareness. The observer cannot pinpoint what it is that makes the individual different.

Also at a basic physiological level, the eyes dilate during problem solving. And they tend to move either right or left. People can, in fact, be classified as "right-lookers" or "left-lookers." The average individual makes about 75 percent of his movements in one direction or the other. This "right-looking" and "left-looking," in turn, appears to be related to activities in the two cerebral hemispheres. Right-looking is related to left hemisphere activity, and left-looking is related to right hemisphere activity. The left hemisphere tends to be strong on verbal and digital processing, while the right hemisphere excels in the nonverbal, in analogic, and spatial problem solving. You may be able to sort the "verbals" from the "nonverbals" by asking questions that the individual works "in his head."

From basic physiological findings, predictions have been made about eye behavior in social interaction. Perhaps, for example, gaze will increase toward individuals we like. And conversely, perhaps gaze will decrease toward those we dislike. Also at a fundamental information-processing level, perhaps eyes will be averted to avoid feedback. When the person doesn't want more information, or wants to think, he may close off incoming stimuli. These predictions do tend to be borne out, although eye behavior in interaction turns out to be a complex and intricate pattern, a choreographed exchange that depends on the mutual activity of both partners.

In the formation of a communication system, eye contact is a crucial key. We try to "catch the eye" of the waiter so we can engage him in our service. At other times we are careful not to "catch the eye." As we walk down the street, we let our eyes rove with what Erving Goffman has called "civil inattention." We pass over the eyes of other people and don't pause with a look of recognition. Goffman points out that we usually exchange glances until we are about eight feet from the other person.[9] Then we set ourselves on a noncollision course, and lower our eyes, a sort of "dimming of the lights."

In conversation, the speaker is likely to catch the listener's attention. But then, before launching into a long utterance, the speaker will drop his eyes. He will make periodic checks, to see if his listener is still there—and still a listener. But he will avoid eye contact at pauses when, for example, he is trying to think of how to complete his thought. When he is finished, however, he will return his gaze to the listener and prepare to give up the floor.

During an interaction, the participants look at each other between 25 to 75 percent of the time. This mutual looking tends to increase when the participants like each other, and when they are deeply involved in their discussion. As expected, eye contact can drop when touchy subjects are brought up. And people tend to have less eye contact when they are very close to each other physically. Moving across cultures, distinct differences can be seen in what is appropriate eye behavior. The British apparently "stare" more than we do. Meanwhile, in many cultures, it is polite to avert the eyes when conversing with a superior. The American's demand to "look me in the eye" is very dissonant to the foreigner who has been taught to communicate respect by doing just the opposite. The degree of eye contact may, in turn, follow a cultural pattern that prescribes touch—no touch, interpersonal spacing, and the way people orient their bodies (e.g., standing face to face versus shoulder to shoulder).[10]

Head Nods

The vertical head nod for affirmation, and the head shake for negation, were long thought to be human universals. Theories were developed about the origin of the gesture in man's repertoire. One suggested that the infant uses an up and down movement in searching for his mother's breast, and a sidewise movement to get rid of the nipple when he is through feeding. There are, however, cultures that do not exhibit this same pattern of up and down movements to signal "yes."

Within our own culture, the head nod is seen as agreement, support, affirmation. Meanwhile, the head shake is seen as disagreement. Within the communication context, the head nod becomes a powerful reinforcer. When one participant nods, the other tends to increase whatever it is he's doing. In conversation, a series of slow head nods is likely to keep the speaker going indefinitely. Meanwhile, a series of fast head nods typically indicates that the listener now wants to speak. He wants the speaker to hurry up. He agrees. He knows. He is preparing to interrupt.

Beyond that, the pattern of the head nods becomes an intricate gestural dance, apparently related to events in the linguistic band, and to the behaviors of the other participant. While the pattern is elaborate, most people in the culture know it thoroughly. And if head nods are completely inhibited, interaction will slow down. It may terminate. Or the other participant may ask: "What's wrong?"

SUMMARY

Man produces many cues: cues of general facial appearance, cues of expression, cues of eye behavior, and cues of head movements. Some of these cues are enduring, difficult for the producer to change, but perhaps particularly informative for the observer. Some cues are semifixed, perhaps linked to a particular communication situation. And some are momentary—fleeting but telling cues in interaction. Some of these cues are used to encode content, such as the re-creation of an earlier expression, or the imitation of another's facial display. But many of these cues are in the area of regulation. They reveal inner emotional states. They reveal attempts to hide feelings, or fabricate feelings which are not felt.

The communicator may find these cues of the head and face particularly informative, in assessing the state of the interaction, what the other communicator is feeling, about himself, about his fellow communicators, about the communication situation. The communicator may find that his own facial cues can enliven, punctuate, regulate. He may be able to telegraph his own intentions and read the intentions of others. He may be able to assess the impact his messages are having. And he may increase their impact with his own facial cues.

QUESTIONS FOR DISCUSSION

1. Examine facial expressions in news photos, ads, illustrations, and on television. What affects are being displayed? What are they being used to communicate?
2. If people are asked to judge a person's character and intelligence from the person's facial features, do they tend to agree or disagree about these two characteristics? How do these judgments compare with the person's character and intelligence? Why do you think this happens?
3. What is the category approach to facial emotion? Contrast it with the dimension approach. How are they different?
4. Harrison lists several steps that a person must go through in order to interpret someone's facial expressions. Describe each of these and discuss the complexities and potential problems involved in each.
5. What part of the face is most involved in signaling the beginning, end, and various in-between stages of a particular communication interaction? Why might this be so?

NOTES

1. Robert Rosenthal and L. Jackson, *Pygmalion in the Classroom* (New York: Holt, Rinehart and Winston, 1968).
2. Charles Darwin, *The Expression of the Emotions in Man and Animals* (Chicago: The University of Chicago Press, 1965).
3. Paul Ekman, *Darwin and Facial Expression: A Century of Research in Review* (New York: Academic Press, 1973).
4. Paul Ekman, Wallace V. Friesen, and Phoebe Ellsworth, *Emotion in the Human Face: Guidelines for Research and an Integration of Findings* (New

York: Pergamon Press, 1972). See also C. E. Izard, *The Face of Emotion* (New York: Appleton-Century-Crofts, 1971).

5. Silvan S. Tomkins, *Affect, Imagery, Consciousness* (New York: Springer, Vol. 1, 1962, Vol. 2, 1963).

6. Paul Ekman, "Universals and Cultural Differences in Facial Expressions of Emotion," in J. Cole, ed. *Nebraska Symposium on Motivation*, 1971 (Lincoln, Nebraska: University of Nebraska Press, 1972), pp. 207-283.

7. I. Eibl-Eibesfeldt, "Similarities and Differences Between Cultures in Expressive Movements," in Robert A. Hinde, ed. *Non-verbal Communication* (New York: Cambridge University Press, 1972), pp. 297-314.

8. E. H. Hess, "Attitude and Pupil Size," *Scientific American*, 212 (April 1965), pp. 46-54.

9. Erving Goffman, *Behavior in Public Places* (New York: Free Press, 1963), p. 84.

10. O. Michael Watson, *Proxemic Behavior: A Cross-Cultural Study* (The Hague: Mouton, 1970).

FOUR

COGNITIVE PROCESSES AFFECTING HUMAN COMMUNICATION

CATEGORIES AND LANGUAGE

The previous articles contain a common assumption: that one particular eye gaze which signals the beginning of an interaction is somehow similar to all other such eye gazes which signal the same meaning; that one consonant sound "b" is similar to any other consonant sound "b"; that a 480 Hz B struck on one piano at one time is very similar to any other 480 Hz B played on any other piano at any other time.

The process view of reality states that the world which is open to our perception is continuous. It is not broken up into discrete units for us to perceive. But our perceptual processes operate in such a way that they impose a structure on our perceptions. They separate the continuous field into discrete objects and events so that our internal information processing systems may handle the continuous flow more readily. Some of these objects and events are perceived as members of the same *category* due to similarities perceived to exist between the events. The rules a person uses to determine which events possess these similarities and which do not, in order to place the events in categories, are equivalent to the meaning the person has for the category. If we could specify all of these rules we could specify meaning. People apparently use these rules to recognize quite different members of a class or category from the infinite ways of subdividing the continuous experience available to them at any one moment. The next article continues with the discussion of how patterned matter-energy becomes patterned in such a way that people can understand it.

11

AN INTRODUCTION TO CATEGORIZING

Jerome S. Bruner
Jacqueline J. Goodnow
George A. Austin

We begin with what seems a paradox. The world of experience of any normal man is composed of a tremendous array of discriminably different objects, events, people, impressions. There are estimated to be more than 7 million discriminable colors alone, and in the course of a week or two we come in contact with a fair proportion of them. No two people we see have an identical appearance and even objects that we judge to be the same object over a period of time change appearance from moment to moment with alterations in light or in the position of the viewer. All of these differences we are capable of seeing, for human beings have an exquisite capacity for making distinctions.

But were we to utilize fully our capacity for registering the differences in things and to respond to each event encountered as unique, we would soon be overwhelmed by the complexity of our environment. Consider only the linguistic task of acquiring a vocabulary fully adequate to cope with the world of color differences! The resolution of this seeming paradox—the existence of discrimination capacities which, if fully used, would make us slaves to the particular—is achieved by man's capacity to categorize. To categorize is to render discriminably different things equivalent, to group the objects and events and people around us into classes, and to respond to them in terms of their class membership rather than their uniqueness. Our refined discriminative activity is reserved only for those segments of

Jerome S. Bruner is Watts professor of psychology, Oxford University. From *A Study of Thinking* by Jerome S. Bruner, Jacqueline J. Goodnow, and George A. Austin, copyright © 1956, John Wiley and Sons, Inc. Reprinted by permission of John Wiley and Sons, Inc.

the environment with which we are specially concerned. For the rest, we respond by rather crude forms of categorial placement. In place of a color lexicon of 7 million items, people in our society get along with a dozen or so commonly used color names. It suffices to note that the book on the desk has a "blue" cover. If the task calls for finer discrimination, we may narrow the category and note that it is in the class of things called "medium blue." It is rare indeed that we are ever called upon to place the book in a category of colors comprising *only* the unique hue-brightness-saturation combination it presents.

The process of categorizing involves, if you will, an act of invention. This hodgepodge of objects is comprised in the category "chairs," that assortment of diverse numbers is all grouped together as "powers of 2," these structures are "houses" but those others are "garages." What is unique about categories of this kind is that once they are mastered they can be used without further learning. We need not learn *de novo* that the stimulus configuration before us is another house. If we have learned the class "house" as a concept, new exemplars can readily be recognized. The category becomes a tool for further use. The learning and utilization of categories represents one of the most elementary and general forms of cognition by which man adjusts to his environment. . . .

The Invention of Categories

To one raised in Western culture, things that are treated as if they were equivalent seem not like man-made classes but like the products of nature. To be sure, the defining criteria in terms of which equivalence classes are formed exist in nature as potentially discriminable. Rocks have properties that permit us to classify them as rocks, and some human beings have the features that permit us to categorize them as handsome. But there exists a near infinitude of ways of grouping events in terms of discriminable properties, and we avail ourselves of only a few of these.

Our intellectual history is marked by a heritage of naive realism. For Newton, science was a voyage of discovery on an uncharted sea. The objective of the voyage was to discover the islands of truth. The truths existed in nature. Contemporary science has been hard put to shake the yoke of this dogma. Science and common-sense inquiry alike do not discover the ways in which events are grouped in the world; they invent ways of grouping. The test of the invention is the predictive benefits that result from the use of invented categories. The revolution of modern physics is as much as anything a revolution against naturalistic realism in the name of a new nominalism. Do such categories as tomatoes, lions, snobs, atoms, and mammalia exist? Insofar as they have been invented and found applicable to instances of nature, they do. They exist as inventions, not as discoveries. See Burma and Mayr (1949) for an enlightening discussion of the "reality" of the species concept in systematic zoology [*Evolution*, III, 4, 369-373].

Stevens (1936, p. 93) sums up the contemporary nominalism in these terms: "Nowadays we concede that the purpose of science is to invent workable descriptions of the universe. Workable by whom? By us. We invent logical systems such as logic and mathematics whose terms are used to denote discriminable aspects of nature and with these systems we formulate descriptions of the world as we see it and according to our convenience. We work in this fashion because there is no other way for us to work." Because the study of these acts of invention is within the competence of the psychologist, Stevens calls psychology "the propadeutic science."

The recognition of the constructive or invented status of categories changes drastically the nature of the equivalence problem as a topic for psychological research. The study of equivalence becomes, essentially, a study of coding and recoding processes employed by organisms who have past histories and present requirements to be met. The implicit assumption that psychological equivalence was somehow determined by the "similarity" or "distinctive similarity" of environmental events is replaced by the view that psychological equivalence is only limited by and not determined by stimulus similarity. The number of ways in which an array of events can be differentiated into classes will vary with the ability of an organism to abstract features which some of the events share and others do not. The features available on which to base such categorial differentiation, taken singly and in combination, are very numerous indeed. As Klüver (1933) so well put it more than two decades ago, the stimulus similarity that serves as a basis for grouping is a selected or abstracted similarity. There is an act of rendering similar by a coding operation rather than a forcing of equivalence on the organism by the nature of stimulation.

Two consequences immediately become apparent. One may ask first what are the preconditions—situational and in the past history of the organism—that lead to one kind of grouping rather than another. The characteristic forms of coding, if you will, now become a dependent variable worthy of study in their own right. It now becomes a matter of interest to inquire what affects the formation of equivalence classes or systems of equivalence coding. The second consequence is that one is now more tempted to ask about systematic individual and cultural difference in categorizing behavior. Insofar as each individual's milieu and each culture has its own vicissitudes and problems, might one not expect that this would reflect itself in the characteristic ways in which members of a culture will group the events of their physical and social environment? And, moreover, since different cultures have different languages, and since these languages code or categorize the world into different classes, might it not be reasonable to expect some conformance between the categories normally employed by speakers and those contained in the language they use? . . .

The Achievements of Categorizing

What does the act of rendering things equivalent achieve for the organism? It is a good preliminary question, like the functional query of the biologist: "What is accomplished by digestion?" The answer provides only a prolegomenon to further inquiry, for if we reply, "Digestion serves to convert external substances into assimilable materials that can then enter into the metabolic process," the next question is bound to be, "How is this accomplished?" But the functional question is clearly important, for unless it is fruitfully posed, the later question about "how" must surely miscarry. So long as the nervous system was conceived of as something that cooled the humors, it served little purpose to ask how this was accomplished

A first achievement of categorizing has already been discussed. By categorizing as equivalent discriminably different events, the organism *reduces the complexity of its environment*. It is reasonably clear "how" this is accomplished. It involves the abstraction and use of defining properties in terms of which groupings can be made and much will be said of these things later.

A second achievement has also been mentioned: Categorizing is the *means by which the objects of the world about us are identified*. The act of identifying some thing or some event is an act of "placing" it in a class. Identification implies that we are able to say either, "There is thingamabob again" or, "There is another thingamabob." While these identifications may vary in the richness of their elaboration, they are never absent. A certain sound may be heard simply as "that sound which comes from outdoors late at night." Or it may be heard as "those porcupines chewing on that old tree stump." When an event cannot be thus categorized and identified, we experience terror in the face of the uncanny. And indeed, "the uncanny" is itself a category, even if only a residual one.

A third achievement, a consequence of the first, is that the establishment of a category based on a set of defining attributes *reduces the
necessity of constant learning*. For the abstraction of defining properties
makes possible future acts of categorizing without benefit of further
learning. We do not have to be taught *de novo* at each encounter that
the object before us is or is not a tree. If it exhibits the appropriate
defining properties, it "is" a tree. It is in this crucial aspect, as we
mentioned earlier, that categorizing differs from the learning of fiat
classes. Learning by rote that a miscellany of objects all go by the
nonsense name BLIX has no extrapolative value to new members of the
class.

A fourth achievement inherent in the act of categorizing is the
direction it provides for instrumental activity. To know by virture of discriminable defining attributes and without need for further direct test
that a man is "honest" or that a substance is "poison" is to know *in
advance* about appropriate and inappropriate actions to be taken. Such
direction is even provided when we come up against an object or event
which we cannot place with finality. To the degree the new object has
discriminable properties and these properties have been found in the
past to be relevant to certain categories, we can make a start on the
problem by a procedure of "categorial bracketing." The object appears
to be animate; what does it do if it is poked? It stands on two legs like a
man; does it speak? Much of problem-solving involves such repeated
regrouping of an object until a pragmatically appropriate grouping has
been found. In short, such successive categorizing is a principal form
of instrumental activity.

A fifth achievement of categorizing is the opportunity it permits
for *ordering and relating classes of events*. For we operate, as noted
before, with category *systems*—classes of events that are related to each
other in various kinds of superordinate systems. We map and give
meaning to our world by relating classes of events rather than by
relating individual events. "Matches," the child learns, will "cause" a
set of events called "fires." The meaning of each class of things placed
in quotation marks—matches, causes, and fires—is given by the im-
beddedness of each class in such relationship maps. The moment an
object is placed in a category, we have opened up a whole vista of
possibilities for "going beyond" the category by virtue of the superordinate and causal relationships linking this category to others.

In speaking of achievements we have not, perhaps, placed
enough stress on the anticipatory and exploratory nature of much of
our categorizing. In the case of most categorizing, we attempt to find
those defining signs that are as *sure* as possible as *early* as possible to

give identity to an event. At the barest level of necessity, this is essential to life. We cannot test the edibility of food by eating it and checking the consequence. We must learn ways of anticipating ultimate consequences by the use of prior signs. In simpler organisms than man, one often finds that there is a built-in mechanism for response to such anticipatory signs. The greylag gosling, observed by Tinbergen (1948), responds with a flight reaction to a hawk-like silhouette drawn on a wire across its pen. The young of the black-headed gull responds to a red spot on the side of its mother's bill with a "begging response" for food and the mother responds to the open bill of the young by inserting food. Lashley's description (1938) of the response of cyclostoma to anticipatory danger signs by the mobilization of stinging nettles provides an example at an even simpler phyletic level. Anticipatory categorizing, then, provides "lead time" for adjusting one's response to objects with which one must cope.

It is this future-oriented aspect of categorizing behavior in all organisms that impresses us most. It is not simply that organisms code the events of their environment into equivalence classes, but that they utilize cues for doing so that allow an opportunity for prior adjustment to the event identified. We are especially impressed with the anticipatory nature of categorizing when we consider the phenomenon of the "empty category."

This is the process whereby defining attributes are combined to create fictive categories: classes of objects that have not been encountered or are clearly of a nature contrary to expectancy. The empty category is a means whereby we go beyond the conventional groupings we impose on the segments of nature we have encountered. It is a way of going beyond the range of events one encounters to the sphere of the possible or even, in the phrase of the philosopher Nelson Goodman (1947), to the "counterfactual conditional"—events that could be but which are contrary to experience. This surely is one of the principal functions of categorizing.

Two cases may be given to illustrate the uses of such categories in the cognitive economy of man. One is the class of creatures known as centaurs, half man, half horse. The other is the class of "female Presidents of the United States, past, present, and future." The first example illustrates the use of the empty category as the currency of art, fantasy, and dream; perhaps it is a vehicle for exploring the ambiguous interstices of experience. The second example of an empty category is from the sphere of problem-solving and thinking. Hypotheses in problem-solving often take the form of creating new categories by the combining of potential defining attributes. The physicist says, "Consider the possibility of a nuclear particle whose orbit is a spiral." Indeed, the neutrino in nuclear physics was postulated first as an empty category on logical grounds, and only when appropriate measures became available was it "found." So too Neptune. Working from data on the perturbation of Uranus, Bessel reached the conclusion that a trans-Uranian planet must exist. Adams and LeVerrier computed possible orbits for the as yet undiscovered planet. It was only then that the planet was "found" by observation at the Berlin Observatory in 1846, twenty-three years after Bessel's conclusion.

On The Validation of Categorizing

Categorizing an event as a member of a class and thereby giving it identity involves, as we have said, an act of inference. Whether one is deciding what the blob was that appeared for a few milliseconds in a tachistoscope or what species of bird it is that we have our binoculars trained on or what Pueblo period this potsherd belongs to, the basic task is not only to make an inference but to make the "right" inference. Is the blob a face, the bird a scissor-tailed flycatcher, the potsherd from Pueblo II? How can we be sure? Let it be clear that we are not asking philosophical questions. We want to know, simply, how people make sure (or make sur*er*) that they have placed an event in its proper identity niche.

There appear to be four general procedures by which people reassure themselves that their categorizations are "valid." The first is *by recourse to an ultimate criterion*; the second is *test by consistency*; the third, *test by consensus*; and the fourth, *test by affective congruence*. Consider each in turn.

Recourse to an Ultimate Criterion

A simple, functional category provides an example. By means of such defining properties as color, size, and shape, mushrooms are divisible into a class of edible mushrooms and a class of inedible ones. A mushroom fancier, out in the woods picking mushrooms, must decide whether a particular mushroom is or is not edible. To the extent that the defining properties are not masked, he is able to make a preliminary categorization: he calls it inedible. If you should ask him how he can be sure, he would doubtless tell you that the way to be absolutely sure is to eat it. If it makes you sick or kills you, then his categorization was "right" or "valid."

The example chosen is perhaps too simple. For there are many categories where it is difficult to specify *the* ultimate criterion against which to check the adequacy of the defining attributes. But the simplification will serve us for the while.

When recourse to an ultimate criterion for defining a category is of grave consequence, the culture may take it upon itself to invent labels or signs by which examplars of the category can be spotted in sufficient time for appropriate avoidance. The custom of putting a red skull and crossbones on bottles of poison, the use of red color on dangerous industrial machinery, stop signs at dangerous intersections—all of these are examples of the artificial creation of anticipatory defining attributes that in effect save one an encounter with a dangerous ultimate criterion.

Test by Consistency

Perhaps the simplest example one can give of such testing is the perception of speech. One is "surer" that one identified a word correctly if the word fits the context of what has gone before. Since the categorization of events usually takes place in a context which imposes constraints on what a particular event can be, there is more often than not the possibility of validation by consistency.

Some listeners to the famous Orson Welles broadcast of *The War of the Worlds*, faced with the choice of deciding whether the Martian invasion was "real" or "theatrical," used a consistency criterion determined by the set of beliefs that had already been established in their past lives. "We have found that many of the persons who did not even try to check the broadcast had preexisting mental sets that made the stimulus so understandable to them that they immediately accepted it as true. Highly religious people who believed that God willed and controlled the destinies of man were already furnished with a particular standard of judgment that would make an invasion of our planet and a destruction of its members an 'act of God.' This was particularly true if the religious frame of reference was of the eschatological variety providing the individual with definite attitudes or beliefs regarding the end of the world. Other people we found had been so influenced by the recent war scare that they believed an attack by a foreign power was imminent and an invasion—whether it was due to the Japanese, Hitler, or Martians—was not unlikely" (Cantril, 1940, p. 191).

Validation by consistency is perhaps nowhere better illustrated than in modern taxonomic research. At the lowest level, so-called alpha taxonomy, one seeks to differentiate as many species as possible in terms of whatever defining properties are visible. Such a technique leads to vast multiplication of categories. There are now about a third of a million species of plants, and each year about 5,000 are added. There are about 2 million species and subspecies of animals, and it is estimated that new ones are being added at the rate of 10,000 per year. Some estimates of the number of insect species run as high as 3 million (Silvestri, 1929), and given new radiological methods of producing mutations, the possible number of virus types seems almost unlimited. As far as identification is concerned, the modern taxonomist readily agrees (Mayr, 1952) that species are not "discovered" but "invented." The principal problem of "validation" at this level is to establish the "existence" of a category, which means, essentially, that other investigators can distinguish the same grouping if they follow directions for finding it.

It is at the next level of taxonomy, beta taxonomy, that the criterion of consistency becomes critical, for now the task is to order the bewildering array of species into a *system* of classification. Whether or not one's grouping of a series of species into genera and then into a phylum is "valid" or not depends upon whether the properties of the grouped species are consistent with one's conception of evolution. The correctness of the grouping "elasmobranchs" as distinguished from "teleostean fishes" depends upon whether the defining morphological properties of the two classes fit a consistent pattern of development as formulated in evolutionary theory. Teleostean fishes are more "evolved" or "higher than" sharks because of the consistent differences in skeletal system, renal system, circulatory system, etc. What makes the classification valid is that it is explicable in terms of a more general theory about the changes in morphology and physiology that characterize the evolution of animal life. If one would seek to establish the validity of considering a certain group of animals as constituting a phylum, the test would be by consistency with the requirements of the theory governing classification not only of this new phylum but of phyla generally.

Test by Consensus

Such categories as "good citizen" or "decent person" are often in effect consensually validated. Because the defining properties are vague and disjunctive, there is often uncertainty about the status of instances. In consequence, to validate our categorization of a man as a "decent fellow" we may turn to the categorizations made by people with whose values we identify—what a number of sociologists call a *reference group* (cf. Merton and Kitt, 1950). Under other circumstances, we may turn simply to those individuals who happen to be in the immediate vicinity when a categorial decision must be made. We see two men fighting on the street: "Who started it?" we ask a man on the edge of the crowd that has collected, in an attempt to categorize the guilty member. In deciding whether the Welles broadcast was "real" or a play, many victims were determined in their categorization by the fact that others were treating the broadcast as "news" rather than "entertainment."

Where the placement process has marked consequences for the society and when the criteria to be used are ambiguous in nature, virtually every culture has devised a process whereby an official decision can be provided. In our own society, the courts and the judicial process provide this means. Whether or not a man is a felon is decided by specialists in such matters, working with the guide of official definitions embodied in a legal code. Due process of law involves a careful inspection of the degree to which an individual and his acts "fit" the defining properties of a thief or an embezzler. We also create official definitions of a more positive type. Working with a highly ambiguous set of standards, the French Academy makes the decision whether or not a given Frenchman is "an immortal"; or a special body weighs the scientific products of a man and decides whether he should be "starred" in *American Men of Science* or be entitled to the distinction of wearing the initials "F.R.S." after his name. Establishment of consensus by official action is effective to the degree that people will give precedence to the official decisions made. If validation by either direct test, consistency, or unofficial concensus is given precedence, then official methods of categorizing may be at odds with what generally prevails as categorization in a society.

Test by Affective Congruence

While this is a special case of test by consistency, it merits treatment on its own. It is best described as an act of categorizing or identifying an event that carries with it a feeling of subjective certainty or even necessity. Such subjective certainty may also characterize an act whose validation rests on other forms of validating test. But we refer here to the pure case: the unjustifiable intuitive leap buttressed by a sense of conviction. One infers the existence of God, for example, from the overwhelming beauty of a mountain scene: "Such beauty could be produced neither by man nor by the random force of nature." God's presence is thereafter inferred from the experience of beauty.

There is buttressing both by consistency and by consensus, but what provides the basic validating criterion is the affective component in the act of categorizing.

Such acts, because they are particularly inaccessible to disproof, are of special interest to the student of nonrational behavior. What seems especially interesting about acts of categorization of this sort is that they seem to be inaccessible in proportion to the strength of certain inner need systems whose fulfillment they serve. "The more basic the confirmation of a hypothesis is to the carrying out of goal striving activity, the greater will be its strength. It will be more readily aroused, more easily confirmed, less readily infirmed," (Bruner, 1951, p. 127). In its most extreme pathological form, validation by affective congruence makes it possible for the paranoid to construct a pseudo-environment in which the random noises about him are categorized as words being spoken against him. At the level of normal functioning, it permits the acceptance of such unknowable absolutes as God, the Dignity of Man, or Hell.

Learning to Categorize

Much of our concern . . . [is] with the "attainment of concepts," the behavior involved in using the discriminable attributes of objects and events as a basis of anticipating their significant identity. We can take as a paradigm the behavior of a young gourmet who is determined to gather his own mushrooms in the conviction that the wild varieties are far more worthy of his cooking skills than the cultivated types available in the market. His first aim is to discriminate between edible and nonedible mushrooms. If he were really starting from scratch, he would have two sources of information. On the one hand, he would be able to note the characteristics of each mushroom or toadstool he picked. He could note its color, shape, size, habitat, stalk height, etc. He would also know whether each mushroom, fully described as we have noted, made him ill or not when eaten. For the sake of the inquiry, we endow our man with considerable enthusiasm and sufficient sense so that he eats only a small enough portion of each mushroom to allow him to determine edibility without being killed by the adventure. His task is to determine which discriminable attributes of the mushrooms he tries out lead with maximum certainty to the inference that the type is edible.

Note that our man already knows of the existence of the two classes of mushroom in terms of the ultimate criterion of edibility. He is seeking defining attributes that will distinguish exemplars of these two classes. In this sense, we speak of his task as one of concept *attainment*, rather than concept *formation*. If his task were that of attempting to sort mushrooms into some meaningful set of classes, *any* meaningful set of classes in the interest of ordering their diversity, then we might more properly refer to the task as concept formation. Concept formation is essentially the first step en route to attainment. In the case of mushrooms, the formation of the hypothesis that *some* mushrooms are edible and *others* are not is the act of forming a concept. *Attainment refers to the process of finding predictive defining attributes that distinguish exemplars from nonexemplars of the class one seeks to discriminate.*

QUESTIONS FOR DISCUSSION

1. Why is categorizing necessary for human beings? What functions does it serve? What would happen if people did not (or could not) group events into categories?

2. The objective of science is "to discover the islands of truth" which exist in nature. What is wrong with this viewpoint? Relate your answer to the concept of process.

3. What is "the equivalence problem"? Why is it important and why is it a problem?

4. Discuss the importance of the "empty category." Give some examples of your own use of empty categories.

5. Bruner, Goodnow, and Austin list procedures people use to check on the validity or correctness of their categorizations. Describe each of these procedures in such a way that the differences between them are clear.

6. Distinguish between the *formation* of a concept and the *attainment* of a concept. Give an example not used in the article.

References

1. Bruner, J. S., Postman, L., and Rodrigues, J., "Expectation and the Perception of Color," *American Journal of Psychology, 64*, (1951) 216-227.

2. Cantril, H., *The Invasion from Mars*. (Princeton: Princeton University Press, 1940.)

3. Goodman, N., "The Problem of Counterfactual Conditionals," *Journal of Philosophy, 44*, (1947), 113-128.

4. Klüver, H., *Behavior Mechanisms in Monkeys* (Chicago: University of Chicago Press, 1933).

5. Lashley, K. S., "Experimental Analysis of Instinctive Behavior," *Psychological Review,* 45 (1938), 445-472.

6. Mayr, E., "Concepts of Classification and Nomenclature in Higher Organisms and Microorganisms," *Annals of the New York Academy of Sciences,* 56, (1952), 394-397.

7. Merton, R. K., and Kitt, A. S., "Contributions to the Theory of Reference Group Behavior," in R. K. Merton, and P. F. Lazarsfeld, eds. *Continuities in Social Research.* (Glencoe, Illinois Free Press, 1950) pp. 40-105.

8. Silvestri, F., "The Relation of Taxonomy to Other Branches of Entomology," *Fourth International Congress of Entomology,* 2, (1929), 52-54.

9. Stevens, S. S., "Psychology: The Propaedeutic Science," *Philosophy of Science,* 3 (1936), 90-103.

10. Tinbergen, N., "Social Releasers and the Experimental Method Required for Their Study," *Wilson Bulletin, 60,* (1948), 6-51.

A language is composed of words and rules for putting the words together. A word is the name of a category, a symbol that represents the category. The following article discusses limitations of names for categories. Berlo, Cowart, and authors of other readings have suggested that it is not possible to transmit meaning since symbols can only elicit meanings that are already present in another individual. Weinberg reemphasizes the distinction between internal and external realities which leads to the view that "meanings are in people."

12

SOME LiMiTATiONS Of LANGUAGE

Harry L. Weinberg

Irving J. Lee often likened language to a tool, perhaps man's most important one, more useful than fire, the wheel, or atomic energy. It is most likely that none of these, most certainly not the latter, could ever have been put to use by a non-symbol-using creature. But, like any tool, language has its limitations. There are certain things we cannot do with it, and the attempt to make it do what it cannot do often leads to trouble.

In expanding upon this, Lee compared language with a fish net. The very small fish escape from the web; the very large ones cannot be encircled. In the case of language, the small fry are the infinite details of the material world; no matter how fine we weave the mesh, an infinity escape. We can never describe completely even the simplest bit of matter. We can never exhaust what could be said about a single grain of sand. For convenience, and by utter necessity, we concentrate on a large number (though relatively few) of the characteristics of grains of sand, noting those similarities important to us at the moment and neglecting differences which seem to make no difference for our generalizations. In this way we come to talk about "properties" of sand. These are the fish—descriptions and inferences—for which the net of language is most suited.

But there is something very peculiar about the catch: it is nonexistent. It is as though the fish had slipped from their skins and what we

The late Harry L. Weinberg was professor of speech at Temple University. This article is from "Some Limitations of Language," *Levels of Knowing and Existence* by Harry L. Weinberg (Harper and Row, Publishers, 1959) pp. 34-47. Copyright © 1959, by Harry L. Weinberg. Reprinted by permission of Blanche Weinberg.

have left is lifeless and unchanging, a dull and hazy replica of the ones that got away. For words are *about things*: they are *not* the things themselves. The world of things is constantly changing; it "is" bright, hard, soft, green, rosy, acrid, black, burnt, rubbery, loud, sharp, velvety, bitter, hot, freezing, silent, flowing, massive, ephemeral, wispy, granitic. Or rather, these are the names we use for the way it seems to us. Above all, it appears "real"; it is not words. Whatever we call a thing, whatever we say it is, it is not. For whatever we *say* is words, and words are words and not things. The words are maps, and the map is not the territory. The map is static; the territory constantly flows. Words are always about the past or the unborn future, never about the living present. The present is ever too quick for them; by the time the words are out, it is gone. When we forget this, we tend to act as if words were things, and because they are so much more easily manipulated and molded to our desires, there is the danger of building maps that fit no known territory and the greater danger of not caring whether or not they do. We then tend more and more to live in the past and the future and we lose the present, the sense of nowness, the feeling of the immediacy, mystery, and flow of the sensory world; we drift into the gray, dead world of words.

The Queerness of Thingness: What Is Red Like, "Really"?

The nonverbal quality of the sensory world—the world of thingness—is the large fish which escapes the net of language. If you were asked to describe the color "red" to a man blind from birth, you would very quickly discover that this is an absolute impossibility. No matter what you said, you could never convey to him the sensation you experience when you see a color called red. The same observation applies to smells, tastes, sounds—any sensory perceptions. They are literally unspeakable, as are all feelings and emotions. During his lectures, Alfred Korzybski would ask the members of the audience to pinch themselves, to concentrate on the feeling, and then try to describe the pain. It does no good to say sharp, dull, or prickly, for then you have to describe these words, *ad infinitum*. Incidentally, it might interest the reader to know that it is quite difficult to get some people, especially the more sophisticated intellectuals, to perform this little experiment. It is silly, childish, and obvious. They "know" words are not things. But to really know it on all levels of abstraction, one must actually do and experience this nonverbal act. If not, then one is acting as if his words were the actual sensations.

All that words—descriptions and labels—can do is evoke sensations and feelings which the reader or listener has already experienced. They can never transmit new experience. If one has never experienced what is described, one is absolutely incapable of experiencing it through description alone. No woman can make me feel what it is like to give birth to a child. I may infer it is similar to a bad case of cramps, but I will never know, no matter what she says. Since I know that a toothache differs in "quality" from a headache, and that a burn does not feel like bruised skin, it is a reasonable inference on my part that birth pains are different in some respects from anything I have ever experienced or ever will.

This poses an interesting question. If you feel a pain in your jaw and say, "I have a toothache," have you made an inferential or factual statement? Certainly it has been made after observation, but what about verification by accepted standards? What is the accepted standard for sensations, feelings, emotions? It can only be the person experiencing them. Only you can feel your pain and the experience itself represents the verification. Your statement is a factual one for you and inferential for everyone else. We can only guess that you are reporting the "truth" about your feelings.

The limitations of language go even further. I have no way of knowing what "red" looks like even to another sighted person. He cannot tell me; I cannot check. I can only infer that what he experiences is similar to what I experience. It cannot be identical because our nervous systems are different, and an experience is a product of both what is "out there" and the way the organism reacts to it. But in order to get on with the business of living together and reaching some kind of agreement, we are forced to assume a similarity in response. The danger lies in our forgetting that this similarity is only a convenient inference. There may be important differences in what different people perceive in the "same" situation or in what one individual perceives at different moments. Hundreds of experiments designed by psychologists, physiologists, and others demonstrate this dependence of perception upon both the structure of the stimulus and the structure and state of the responding organ.

Let us take a simple example. Eat a lump of sugar and concentrate on the taste. Then take another and another. After a few lumps, the sweetness changes. It may become cloying or its sweetness may be diminished. What has happened? Has the sugar changed its taste? If you say no, you have become satiated, but the sweetness of the sugar is the same, why do you assume that the first taste of sugar is the "real" taste, and that after six lumps it is less "real"?

Or place a piece of red paper on a gray background. Place another piece of the same paper on a bright green background. Compare the two and you will find that the pieces of red paper look different. Which is the "real" color? It won't do to say that the real color is that of the red paper by itself. It is never by itself; there is always a background. Which is the right background? One is as arbitrary as the other.

We could go on and on with this. How about the color-blind man who presumably sees only a shade of gray when he looks at your red sheet? Who is seeing the correct, the "real" color? If you say you are because your range of color perception is greater than his, consider these facts: The majority of people cannot see ultraviolet light. If we filter out light in the range of the visible spectrum, red to violet, in an ultraviolet lamp, the average person would see nothing and would say that the lamp is not lit. However, it has been discovered that a few people do see a fraction of the ultraviolet range. This means that they see a color they cannot describe to us if we are one of the majority who cannot see ultraviolet light, and we cannot imagine what the color is like. It is no good to say it is like violet; that would be like saying green must be like yellow because it follows it in the spectrum. If you have seen yellow but never green, you cannot imagine, on the basis of yellow, what green is like.

Now, since there is, normally, ultraviolet light in daylight, it will be reflected from the "red" sheet of paper, so that the person who can see ultraviolet light will see a different shade of "red," that is, red and ultraviolet. Which is the "real" color of "red," his or ours?

We met this problem before when we tried to find the "real" height of the table, which upon analysis we found to be a meaningless, unanswerable question. A similar solution can be found in this case by tracing the sequence of events. Light waves (shower of particles?), reflected from the paper to our eyes, are electromagnetic waves and have no color. These waves hit our eyes and give rise to a series of complex psychophysical responses, resulting in the sensation red, gray, or some other color. Two things should be noted here. First, the electromagnetic (light) waves have no qualities (no color, sounds, smells) and their existence is inferred. Second, when a response is aroused in an organism, that response is in terms of some sensation like red, gray, and so forth. The particular quality of the response depends upon the structure and condition of the organ and the organism. Given a different organism, a different sensation arises in response to the "same" electromagnetic waves. Thus, the light *waves* produce this sensation of *light* in the organism, but one is not the other.

Incidentally, by distinguishing between sound waves and sound, we can speedily dispatch that old riddle concerning the tree that falls in the forest when no one is about. Does it make a sound? The answer is no! We infer that the tree produces sound waves, a reasonable inference based on past factual data on falling objects. But sound is sensation produced in and by an organism as a result of being stimulated by sound waves (which are not sound) and until such an organism is present, the tree makes no sound. If a man is present when the tree falls, it is a factual statement for him to say, "I hear a sound," provided he is not deaf. But any statement I make about his hearing it is purely inferential.

What Is a Quality: To-Me-Ness

In asking what is the "real" color of a piece of paper, we imply that color is *in* the paper, that it exists independently of the responding organism. But since the color, or any quality for that matter, is a product of both the observer and the observed, in order to make language fit these facts as discovered by science, we must change the question to, "What color does it appear to me at this moment?" In this way, the structure of the language fits the structure of reality. By adding "to me at this time," we imply in our language a universe characterized by constant change, one whose qualities are given it, projected upon it, by a responding organism. By omitting these words, we imply a simple, absolute, static world where the organism is simply a mirror, largely a distorting one, of an ideal world whose qualities are independent of and unchanged by the observer.

This may not matter much when talking about color, taste, or sound, but when we are evaluating the realm of the social it makes quite a difference whether one says "Johnny is bad" or "Johnny appears bad to me now." If he *is* bad, he has badness in him; it is a part of him, and he is always bad in everything he does and will appear that way to every "normal" observer. When we add "to me, now," we imply there is a possibility that he may not appear that way to everyone else. We are more prepared to consider other evaluations of his behavior, on the possibility that they may be more accurate than our own. Actually, if I tell you Johnny is bad, I tell you very little about him other than that I probably dislike him if I dislike those I label bad. If I say that he appears bad to me, I invite the obvious questions, "What kind of behavior do you call bad? What did Johnny do?" If I then describe what he did, we might discover that you do not consider such behavior bad; rather, to you, it may show that Johnny is independent and self-reliant. To Mr. X, this behavior may mean Johnny is trying to hide his insecurity and lack of parental affection. Who is right? All may be partly right and partly wrong, but at least the situation can be discussed on a much more objective, descriptive level. The probability of agreement and of more appropriate behavior with respect to Johnny is much greater. When we say *and mean*, "It appears this way to me," we invite checking, discussion, reevaluation. When we say, "It is," we cut off further investigation. It is the contention of the general semanticist that the constant, conscious use of the "to me" will help make proper evaluation more likely, for language structure influences thought, behavior, and feelings. Constant talking in absolute terms produces a feeling of the "rightness" of such patterns of evaluation, and this emotional barrier is most difficult to crack in attempting to change behavior. It stifles questioning the appropriateness of patterns of evaluation and talking both by the speaker himself and by others, and is one of the foundation stones in man's grimmest prison— prejudice.

Cracking the Language Barrier: Phatic Communion

Because feelings, sensations, and emotions cannot be transmitted by language, but only evoked in the listener, and because of our great need to find out how others feel and to communicate our own feelings to them, we spend much time trying to crack this sound barrier. A writer uses hundreds of examples, descriptions, image-evoking words, hoping they will be similar enough to past experiences of the reader to provoke his memory and recreate a similar nonverbal reaction in him. For this reason it may take an entire novel or play to make a simple point. One of the themes of the play *Death Takes a Holiday* is that love is stronger than the fear of death. Why doesn't the author simply make the statement and call it quits? Obviously because it doesn't work; we don't "feel" this by reading one sentence. It takes the writer with his shotgun loaded with pellets of description to wing the emotions of the reader.

Another technique we use in our attempt to overcome this linguistic barrier, interestingly enough, involves the use of nonsymbolic language, the language of sound as such. This is the language of lovers and infants and animals, and we all use it in addition to symbolic language. Bronislaw Malinowski called it "phatic communion."

When Fido growls and bares his teeth, he is letting us and other animals know that he is angry. When the baby howls and bares his gums, he communicates to us his unhappiness. And Fido and the baby are equally adept at reading our feelings by the tone of our voice totally apart from the verbal meanings of the words used. All of us gather our impressions of a person's sincerity, for example, by the inflections of his voice, not by any protestation by him.

Not only do sounds serve to convey expressions of feelings, but also the general musculature of the body plays a part in this type of communication. The good poker player "reads" the faces (the tiny movements of the muscles around the eyes and mouth) of the other players to see if they are bluffing or suppressing excitement. Indeed, there is evidence to suggest that the very young infant is frighteningly adept at picking up the "true" feelings of his mother toward him, which she herself may have repressed. Thus, if she unconsciously rejects him and, feeling guilty, talks fondly or rather, uses fond language, he will feel this rejection by "reading" the inflections in her voice and the tensions in her muscles.

When Sense Is Nonsense

Much social talk is in the same category. It is our attempt to escape the desperate loneliness that is, in a sense, our lot. No one can know how we feel, what we see; nor we, they. Each is a solitude. No logic or analysis or theorizing is nearly as effective in softening this aloneness as phatic communion. Misevaluation enters when we expect them to. It has been stated that a bore is a man who, when you greet him with, "How are you?" tells you. You are not really asking about his health but saying, "Let's be friends." If you are fixing a flat tire on a hot day and a passerby asks, "Got a flat?", he is asking you to be friendly. If you take his words literally, you are likely to become angry and say, "Any damn fool can see I have."

It is often a temptation to snicker or feel very superior to the logically absurd "itsy bitsy boo" talk of lovers. But if we remember that it is the sound, not the literal meaning that conveys the affection in this case, then any attempt to talk "sense" in this kind of situation is itself a form of nonsense. Consequently the general semanticist does not demand that we talk sense all the time. All he asks is that we distinguish between situations that call for big talk and those that do better with small talk, and not confuse the two or try to pass off one as the other. Small talk is the oil in social machinery. Big talk—logic, theorizing, factual statements—will help solve the problems; small talk eases the way.

Most commonly both types of communication occur simultaneously and in varying degrees, which serves to complicate mutual understanding and gives the lie to the assertion that facts speak for themselves. Meaning occurs on all levels of abstraction, and differs in character at each level. At the feeling level it is a diffuse, deep, primitive, alogical meaning expressed in the scream of anguish, the coo of affection, the snarl of hatred, the *tra la la* of the poet.

QUESTIONS FOR DISCUSSION

1. It seems obvious that "the word is not the thing" so why does Weinberg suggest that pinching oneself and trying to describe the feeling is necessary? What is the difference between cognitively knowing that something is true and experientially knowing it to be true?
2. Why might the statement "I have a toothache" be an inference rather than an observation?
3. What is *phatic communication*? Is phatic communication *communication* by Berlo's definition of communication? Do you consider phatic communication to be communication? If so, can you reconcile your views with Berlo's discussion of the distinction between an information process and a communication process?

FIVE

COGNiTiVE PROCESSES AFFECTiNG HUMAN COMMUNiCATiON

beliefs and belief systems

Perception is one type of internal cognitive process, a type that forms a representation of the events outside of a person for use by the cognitive processes inside the person. Daryl Bem discusses the concept of *belief* as another type of cognitive event. A belief is an assumption a person makes about anything that is, has been, or might be available to the person's perceptual processes. We can have beliefs about anything of which we are aware, and we usually do. All knowledge that a person has is represented inside of the person in the form of beliefs. One of the major effects of human communication is to change old beliefs and to form new ones.

Bem refers to *opinions, attitudes,* and *values* as well as to beliefs. The term *opinion* is usually used to refer to what a person *says* about his beliefs. Statements are available to everyone who hears them. Beliefs are internal states available only to the individual who possesses them.

Bem uses the term *attitude* to refer to the affective part of a belief—likes and dislikes—or to the belief together with its affective part.

A *value* is an enduring belief about ultimate goals or ways of achieving them. If the belief is temporary it is not a value. A person usually has very few values compared to the total number of his beliefs. Enduring beliefs about ultimate goals are called *terminal values* and beliefs about ways of getting to those goals are called *instrumental values.*

13

COGNitive foundAtioNs
of beliefs

Daryl J. Bem

Certain opinions seem to go together. For example: I support strong
civil rights legislation; I was always a "dove" on Vietnam; I am more
afraid of facism than of communism in our country; I worry less about
the size of our national debt than about the unequal distribution of our
national wealth; I believe that college women should no more be
subjected to curfews than college men; and I think the Black Power
movement is a good thing. On their surface, these diverse opinions do
not seem to follow logically from one another—there are even some
implied inconsistencies among them—and yet, if you knew only one of
my opinions, you could probably guess the others with pretty fair
accuracy. Certain opinions do seem to go together.

Of course, there does seem to be a kind of logic involved here. The
opinions given above all appear to follow more or less from a common
set of underlying values (such as equality, for example). This can be
true of "conservative" opinions as well. For example, my neighbor
says that his major value is individual freedom and that therefore he is
opposed to openhousing laws and to legislation which regulates the
possession of firearms. I may disagree with his opinions, but I can
appreciate the logic involved. Curiously, however, my freedom-
loving neighbor also advocates stiffer penalties for the use of
marijuana, feels that women belong in the home, and believes that
consenting adults who engage in homosexual behavior should get long

Daryl J. Bem is professor of psychology at Stanford University. This article is from
Beliefs, Attitudes, and Human Affairs by Daryl J. Bem. Copyright © 1970 by Wadsworth
Publishing Company, Inc. Reprinted by permission of the publisher, Brooks/Cole
Publishing Company.

prison terms. Here the logic involved is less than clear, yet these opinions too seem strangely predictable. Indeed, my neighbor and I both profess to hold individual freedom as a basic value, and we both claim that our opinions are consistent with our values. Yet we find each other's opinions highly disagreeable.

In short, beliefs, attitudes, and values do seem to be logically connected, but in some instances the logic seems more Freudian than Aristotelian. It is this mixture of logic and psychologic that concerns us. It is this mixture of logic and psychologic that constitutes the cognitive foundations of beliefs and attitudes.

Primitive Beliefs

If a man perceives some relationship between two things or between some thing and a characteristic of it, he is said to hold a belief. For example, he might suppose asteroids and oranges to be round, the dean of women to be square, God to be dead, men to love freedom, himself to dislike spinach, and Republicans to promote progress. Collectively, a man's beliefs compose his understanding of himself and his environment.

Many beliefs are the product of direct experience. If you ask your friends why they believe oranges are round, they will most likely reply that they have seen oranges, felt oranges, and that oranges are, indeed, round. And that would seem to end the matter. You could, of course, ask them why they trust their senses, but that would be impolite.

Consider a more complicated belief. If you ask your friends why they believe that asteroids are round (that is, spherical), the more sophisticated among them might be able to show how such a conclusion is derived from physical principles and astronomical observations. You could press them further by asking them to justify their belief in physical principles and astronomical observations: Whence comes their knowledge of such things? When they answer that question—perhaps by citing the *New York Times*—you can continue to probe: Why do they believe everything they read in the *Times?* If they then refer to previous experience with the accurancy of the *Times* or recall that their teachers always had kind words for its journalistic integrity, challenge the validity of their previous experience or the credibility of their teachers.

What you will discover by such questioning—besides a noticeable decline in the number of your friends—is that every belief can be pushed back until it is seen to rest ultimately upon a basic belief in the credibility of one's own sensory experience or upon a basic belief in the credibility of some external authority. Other beliefs may derive from these basic beliefs, but the basic beliefs themselves are accepted as givens. Accordingly, we shall call them "primitive beliefs."[1]

Zero-Order Beliefs

Our most fundamental primitive beliefs are so taken for granted that we are apt not to notice that we hold them at all; we remain unaware of them until they are called to our attention or are brought into question by some bizarre circumstance in which they appear to be violated. For example, we believe that an object continues to exist even when we are not looking at it; we believe that objects remain the same size and shape as we move away from them even though their visual images change; and, more generally, we believe that our perceptual and conceptual worlds have a degree of orderliness and stability over time. Our faith in the validity of our sensory experience is the most important primitive belief of all.

These are among the first beliefs that a child learns as he interacts with his environment, and in a psychological sense, they are continuously validated by experience. As a result, we are usually unaware of the fact that alternatives to these beliefs *could* exist, and it is precisely for this reason that we remain unaware of the beliefs themselves. Only a very unparochial and intellectual fish is aware that his environment is wet. What else could it be? We shall call primitive beliefs of this fundamental kind "zero-order" beliefs. They are the "nonconscious" axioms upon which our other beliefs are built.[2]

First-Order Beliefs

Because we implicitly hold these zero-order beliefs about the trustworthiness of our senses, particular beliefs that are based upon direct sensory experiences seem to carry their own justification. When a man justifies his belief in the roundness of oranges by citing his experiences with oranges, that in fact usually does end the matter. He does not run through a syllogistic argument of the form:

First Premise: My senses tell me that oranges are round.
Second Premise: My senses tell me true.
Conclusion: Therefore, oranges are round.

There is no such inferential process involved in going from the first premise to the conclusion, as far as the individual himself is concerned, because he takes the second premise for granted: It is a zero-order belief. Accordingly, the first premise ("My senses tell me that oranges are round") is psychologically synonymous with the conclusion ("Oranges are round"). We shall call such conclusions "first-order" beliefs. Unlike zero-order beliefs, an individual is usually aware of his first-order beliefs because he can readily imagine alternatives to them (oranges could be square), but he is usually *not* aware of any inferential process by which they derive from zero-order beliefs. Like zero-order beliefs, then, first-order beliefs are still appropriately called primitive beliefs—that is, beliefs which demand no independent formal or empirical confirmation and which require no justification beyond a brief citation of direct experience.

Primitive Beliefs Based on External Authority

We not only experience our world directly; we are told about it as well. It is in this way that notions about such intangibles as God, absent grandmothers, and threatened tooth decay first enter a child's system of beliefs. And to the child, such beliefs may seem as direct, as palpable, and as assuredly valid as any beliefs based on direct sensory encounter. When mommy says that not brushing after every meal causes tooth decay, that is synonymous with the *fact* that not brushing after every meal causes tooth decay. Such a belief is a primitive first-order belief for the child because the intervening premise, "Mommy says only true things," is nonconscious; the possibility that mommy sometimes says false things is not a conceivable alternative. First-order beliefs based upon a zero-order belief in the credibility of an external authority, then, are functionally no different from first-order beliefs based upon an axiomatic belief in the credibility of our senses. As sources of information, mommy and our senses are equally reliable. Our implicit faiths in them are zero-order beliefs.

This emphasis upon the innocence of childhood should not obscure the fact that we all hold primitive beliefs. It is an epistemological and psychological necessity, not a flaw of intellect or a surplus of naïvetè. We all share the fundamental zero-order beliefs about our senses, and most of us hold similar sorts of first-order beliefs. For example, we rarely question beliefs such as, "This woman is my mother" and "I am a human being." Most of us even treat arbitrary social-linguistic conventions like, "This is my left hand" and "Today is Tuesday" as if they were physical bits of knowledge handed down by some authority who "really knows." Finally, most religious and quasi-religious beliefs are first-order beliefs based upon an unquestioned zero-order faith in some internal or external source of knowledge. The child who sings, "Jesus loves me—this I know, /For the Bible tells me so" is actually being less evasive about the metaphysical—and hence nonconfirmable—nature of his belief than our founding fathers were when they presumed to interpret reality for King George III: "We hold these truths to be self-evident . . . . "

Generalizations and Stereotypes

Very few of our primitive beliefs rest directly upon a single experience. Most of them are abstractions or generalizations from several experiences over time. Thus an individual may believe life in the city to be hectic, John to be generous, freedom to be wonderful, and modern art to be hard to understand. Each such belief arises out of several separate situations, but because the individual still relates such beliefs to direct experience, they are properly classified as primitive beliefs. As far as the individual is concerned, they still spring directly from a source whose credibility is axiomatic and self-evident: his senses.

But life in the city is not always hectic; John has been stingy on occasion; freedom is sometimes not so wonderful; and modern art is frequently comprehensible. Generalizations, in short, are not always true for all instances beyond the set of experiences upon which they are based. And when an individual treats such generalizations as if they were universally true, we usually call them stereotypes. For a number of reasons, most of us have learned to regard stereotypes as undesirable. Sometimes, for example, stereotypes are based upon no valid experience at all but are picked up as hearsay or are formed to rationalize our prejudices. Then, too, stereotypes are frequently used to justify shabby treatment of individuals on the basis of assumed group characteristics which neither they nor the group, in fact possess.

But it is important to realize that the process by which most stereotypes arise is not itself evil or pathological. Generalizing from a limited set of experiences and treating individuals as members of a group are not only common cognitive acts but necessary ones. They are "thinking devices" which enable us to avoid conceptual chaos by "packaging" our world into a manageable number of categories. It is simply not possible to deal with every situation or person as if it or he were unique, and the formation of "working stereotypes" is inevitable until further experiences either refine or discredit them. For example, many freshmen from rural areas of the country spend the first few weeks of college thinking all New Yorkers are Jews and all Jews are New Yorkers. There is not necessarily any malice or ill will behind such a stereotype; the freshman has simply not yet seen the distinguishing characteristics of Jews and New Yorkers uncorrelated—if there are such characteristics. But when his "obviously-New-York-Jewish" roommate turns out to be a Christian Scientist from New Jersey named Murphy, and the Texan with cowboy boots allows as how his father is a rabbi in Houston, the freshman soon begins to sort his social environment into more finely differentiated categories. I suspect that most of our stereotypes are of this benign variety and that we learn to discard the irrelevant characteristics from our social categories as our experiences broaden and multiply.

The most important word here, however, is "broaden." The new experiences must be the kind which does, in fact, separate the relevant characteristics from the irrelevant ones, not the kind which serves to reinforce the stereotypes. For example, it is often suggested that increased contact between ethnic groups will automatically cause the disappearance of stereotypes. But nobody has more interracial contact than black ghetto residents and white policemen. Yet these interracial contacts are not particularly noted for producing spectacular interracial tolerance. The point, of course, is that the white policemen deal primarily with the criminal element within the ghetto and that the black residents see precisely those whites in the ghetto who are cast in authoritarian roles. Such contacts only reinforce the stereotypes on both sides because the racial identification continues to be coupled with the irrelevant characteristics.

The worst failure of such contacts is not that they occur in hostile situations (although that certainly doesn't help) but that the participants are not of equal status (Allport, 1954). Thus, we see similar kinds of stereotypes being maintained on both sides even in the more benign encounters between black ghetto residents and white shop owners or welfare agency employees, where, again, the equal-status requirement is not fulfilled. It is when this requirement is satisfied that the participants are most likely to see each other as sharing common beliefs, attributes, and goals, rather than perceiving each other as participants in the old stereotyped roles.

The kind of vicarious interracial contact supplied by the mass media must operate on this same principle of equal-status representation if it too is to be helpful in eliminating stereotypes. In 1968, after years of pressure from civil rights organizations, the mass media finally began to observe this principle by regularly featuring black faces in other than "Negro" roles. Thus, although television commercials may continue to offend our sensibilities for other reasons, they actually do help Americans lose their stereotypes—if only by demonstrating that any odors black Americans may have are the familiar kinds which can be cured by Dial or Listerine.

But if some stereotypes are vulnerable to new experiences, many others can be remarkably impervious to evidence against them. Even repeated disconfirmations of a stereotype can often fail to alter it because the individual treats them as exceptions. Thus, he notes that there is Sidney Poitier or Supreme Court Justice Thurgood Marshall—but then there are "all the rest of them." And some stereotypes are even more cleverly insulated from reality than this because the individual sees to it that there is no way even for exceptions to occur. He simply never bothers to check the stereotype against an independent criterion. For instance, many people claim they can "spot a homosexual a mile away." They can do no such thing, of course. What they can do is recognize a man who displays slightly effeminate gestures, and when they do, they proclaim that they have "spotted another homosexual," thereby reinforcing their stereotype. But since they decline to ascertain the sexual preferences of the "spotted" individual, their reasoning is purely circular. They thus mistakenly classify as homosexual large numbers of nonhomosexual individuals who display effeminate gestures. The man who lays claim to such "homosexual radar" might be mildly unhappy to learn that he is misclassifying these individuals, but it is a safe bet that he would be considerably more agitated to learn that he is failing to detect all those homosexuals who are so inconsiderate as to mingle in our midst without an identifying "swish." But he is safe: Since evidence plays no valid role in the maintenance of such a stereotype, it is effectively insulated against either kind of disconfirmation, and he will never know.

Stereotypes, then, are overgeneralized beliefs based on too limited a set of experiences. Whether stereotypes are evil or benign in their consequences, they are like other first-order primitive beliefs in that they appear to the individual to be self-evident; they appear to demand no justification beyond a citation either of direct experience or of some external authority whose credibility is taken for granted, whose credibility, in other words, is a zero-order primitive belief. All of us rely upon sterotypes to some extent for "packaging" our perceptual and conceptual worlds.

Higher-Order Beliefs

The Vertical Structure of Beliefs

Although we all hold primitive beliefs throughout our lives, we learn as we leave childhood behind us to regard our sensory experiences as potentially fallible and similarly learn to be more cautious in believing external authorities. We begin, in short, to insert an explicit and conscious premise about an authority's credibility between his word and our belief:[3]

> The Surgeon General says that smoking causes cancer.
> The Surgeon General is a trustworthy expert.
> Therefore, smoking causes cancer.

In such cases, we no longer treat the first premise as synonymous with the conclusion because the second premise is no longer a nonconscious zero-order belief. We are, for example, explicitly aware of the possibility that the Surgeon General might be in error. Accordingly, the conclusion "Smoking causes cancer" is not a primitive belief but rather a derived, or higher-order, belief. It has a "vertical structure" of beliefs underneath it, beliefs which "generate" it as the product of quasi-logical inference.

We also learn to derive higher-order beliefs by reasoning inductively from our experiences:

> My aunt contracted cancer.
> She died soon after.
> Therefore, cancer can cause death.

And finally, we can derive beliefs of a still higher order by building upon premises which are themselves conclusions of prior syllogisms. For example, we can use as premises the conclusions to the two syllogisms above:

> Smoking causes cancer .
> Cancer can cause death.
> Therefore, smokers die younger than nonsmokers.

Note that it is possible for two men to hold the same surface belief but to have different vertical structures of belief. For example, the Surgeon General believes that smokers die younger on the average than nonsmokers, but so also does the man who believes that:

Smoking is a sin.
The wages of sin is death.
Therefore, smokers die younger than nonsmokers.

But the Surgeon General's belief is a higher-order belief based upon a long chain of careful syllogistic reasoning, whereas, for this man, the same conclusion, or surface belief, is only a second-order belief (based on two first-order primitive beliefs).

When a belief has a deep vertical structure, it is said to be highly elaborated or differentiated; to the extent that it has little or no syllogistic reasoning underneath it, it is said to be unelaborated or undifferentiated. A primitive belief is, by definition, completely undifferentiated.

The Horizontal Structure of Beliefs

We might expect higher-order beliefs to be quite vulnerable to disconfirmation because any one of the underlying premises could be destroyed. Thus, a higher-order belief would appear to be only as strong as its weakest link. This would be true if most higher-order beliefs were not also bolstered by "horizontal" structures as well. That is, a particular higher-order belief is often the conclusion to more than one syllogistic chain of reasoning. For example, the Surgeon General believes that:

Smoking causes cancer.	Smokers drink more heavily than non-smokers.	Statistics show smokers die younger than nonsmokers.
Cancer can cause death.	Heavy drinking can lead to early death.	These statistics are reliable.
Therefore, smokers die younger.	Therefore, smokers die younger.	Therefore, smokers die younger.

If a man derives his belief that "smokers die younger" from all three lines of reasoning, then his belief will only be partially weakened if one of the syllogisms is faulty or one of the premises turns out to be false. It seems likely that most of our higher-order beliefs rest not upon a single syllogistic pillar but upon many. They have broad horizontal as well as deep vertical structures.

In the course of time, the vertical and horizontal structures of a higher-order belief can change without disturbing the belief itself. We believe as we did before, but our reasons for believing have altered. For example, all the evidence upon which we once based our trust in the *New York Times* may have faded from memory until now our devotion is a blind article of faith, a zero-order belief. Alternatively, additional support may have been obtained for beliefs that were once primitive beliefs or otherwise lacking in respectable justification.

The Centrality of Beliefs

A belief which has both a broad horizontal and a deep vertical structure is still not necessarily a very important or central belief in an individual's belief system. For example, my belief that asteroids are spherical is based on several different kinds of evidence, and some of the chains of reasoning behind the belief are quite lengthy. My belief therefore has a broad horizontal and a deep vertical structure; it is broadly based and highly differentiated. But if my belief in round asteroids were to be changed somehow, few of my other beliefs would have to be changed as a consequence. In terms of our syllogistic model, many syllogisms lead up to my belief in round asteroids, but few syllogisms depart from it; it appears as a conclusion to many syllogisms but enters as a premise into a very few. This is what is meant by saying that the belief is not very central in my belief system.

Highly differentiated and broadly based beliefs are not necessarily central; the opposite is also true. For example, primitive beliefs are, by definition, completely undifferentiated; they have neither vertical nor horizontal support. And yet many of our primitive beliefs are very central in our belief systems. In fact, our primitive zero-order belief in the general credibility of our senses is the most central belief of all; nearly all of our other beliefs rest upon it, and to lose our faith in it is to lose our sanity. Also, as noted earlier, most of our religious and philosophical beliefs are primitive first-order beliefs upon which many of our other beliefs are built. They, too, are central.

Beliefs, then, differ from one another in the degree to which they are differentiated (vertical structure), in the extent to which they are broadly based (horizontal structure), and in their underlying importance to other beliefs (centrality). These are some of the major factors that contribute to the complexity and richness of our cognitive belief systems.

Logic Versus Psychologic

Underlying the syllogistic description of beliefs presented in this chapter is the notion that individuals do not merely subscribe to random collections of beliefs but rather they maintain coherent systems of beliefs which are internally consistent. This central theme has been the basis for a number of recent psychological theories, called "cognitive consistency" theories. But it is appropriate to point out that to say that a man is consistent is not necessarily to say that he is logical or rational. Thus, even though we have employed the syllogism as a convenient way of representing the structure of beliefs, many of the examples have shown that we are not dealing with strict deductive logic but rather with a kind of psychologic.

First of all, an inductive generalization based upon experience is often faulty—as our discussion of stereotypes has indicated. Second, even when the logic itself is impeccably deductive, the conclusions to syllogisms can be wrong if any one of the underlying premises is false. Third, there are often inconsistencies between different higher-order beliefs even though the internal reasoning behind each separate belief is consistent within its own vertical structure. That is, one line of reasoning leads to one conclusion; a second line leads to a contradictory conclusion. Finally, one's attitudes and "ulterior motives" can distort the reasoning process so that the logic itself is subtly illogical. When I mention this final point in class, my students are quick to provide their parents' favorite syllogism as an example:

> **Most heroin addicts started on marijuana.**
> **You kids are experimenting with marijuana.**
> **Therefore, you will become heroin addicts.**

As my students suggest in rebuttal, most heroin addicts started on mother's milk. Therefore . . . .

QUESTIONS FOR DISCUSSION

1. How does the article on categorizing by Bruner, Goodnow, and Austin, relate to Bem's discussion of the belief that oranges are round? What categories are involved in the belief?
2. What is the fundamental difference between a zero-order belief and a first-order belief?
3. Compare Weinberg's discussion of the statement, "I have a toothache" with Bem's discussion of primitive beliefs. What relationship do you see?
4. What essential feature sets stereotypes apart from other generalized beliefs?

5. Do you see any relationship between Bem's discussion of a *working stereotype* and Bruner, Goodnow, and Austin's discussion of categorizing? Discuss.
6. What characteristics set higher order beliefs apart from primitive beliefs?
7. When is a belief *differentiated*?
8. Discuss the difference between *vertical structure* and *horizontal structure* of beliefs.
9. How does the *centrality* of a belief differ from vertical structure and horizontal structure?

References

1. Allport, G. W., *The Nature of Prejudice* (Reading, Mass.: Addison-Wesley, 1954).
2. Jones, E. E., and Gerard, H. B., *Foundations of Social Psychology* (New York: Wiley, 1967).
3. Rokeach, M., *Beliefs, Attitudes, and Values* (San Francisco: Jossey-Bass, 1968).

NOTES

1. I have borrowed and slightly modified the concept of a primitive belief from Rokeach (1968).
2. I have chosen the word "nonconscious" to characterize the kind of unawareness described here. In this book, the term "unconscious" is reserved for beliefs or attitudes that we "repress" or keep out of awareness because we find them too painful to admit to ourselves.
3. I have borrowed the idea of using syllogisms to characterize beliefs and attitudes from Jones and Gerard (1967). They are not, of course, responsible for the modifications I have introduced.

A most important set of beliefs that influences the effects of human communication is the beliefs that each person in a communication interaction holds about himself or herself. This set of beliefs is called the *self-concept* or the *attitude-toward-self*. The *self-image* corresponds to the cognitive or knowledge part of these beliefs, while *self-esteem* corresponds to the liking or affective part.

Consider a person who believes that he does not know so much as those around him. The effect of the statement, "Don't you know how a carburetor works?" might lead the person to feel ashamed and result in resentment toward the questioner for exposing a raw nerve. Someone else who feels confident in his general knowledge of the world might respond simply, "No, I don't" without feeling that he should possess such knowledge. The effects of communication on people are tied to their self-concept.

14

SElf-iMAGE
ANd SElf-ESTEEM

Michael Argyle

People categorize each other in a number of ways, in order to know how to behave towards them. When a person is constantly categorized and treated in a particular way, he acquires a *self-image*. Depending on how far others treat him with approval and respect he will acquire some degree of *self-esteem*.

People have a need for a distinct and consistent self-image and a need for self-esteem. This may result in attempts to elicit responses from others which provide confirmation of these images and attitudes towards the self. These "self" phenomena are so central to social interaction that they need a special chapter, although the same principles are involved as for other forms of social motivation. It is necessary to introduce concepts which some psychologists may regard as woolly and subjective for two reasons. In the first place some aspects of social performance appear to be controlled by cognitive constructs of this kind; for example, when a person sees that he is not being treated in accordance with his self-image he engages in "self-presentation" to correct this state of affairs. Secondly, the self-image, or identity, is one of the central and stable features of personality, and a person cannot be fully understood unless the contents and structure of his self-image are known.

Michael Argyle is reader in social psychology at Oxford and is a Fellow of Wolfson College. From Michael Argyle, *The Psychology of Interpersonel Behavior* by Michael Argyle (Second Edition, 1972) pp. 150-169. Copyright © Michael Argyle, 1967, 1972. Reprinted by permission of the publisher.

The Dimensions of Self and Their Measurement

The self-image, or "ego-identity," refers to how a person consciously perceives himself. The central core usually consists of his name, his bodily feelings, body-image, sex, and age. For a man the job will also be central—unless he is suffering from job alienation. For a woman her family and her husband's job may also be central. The core will contain other qualities that may be particularly salient, such as social class, religion, particular achievements of note, or anything that makes a person different from others.

One method of finding the contents of a person's self-image is the Twenty Statements test: subjects are asked to give twenty answers to the question "Who am I?" The first half of the answers are usually roles—sex, social class, job, and so forth, and the rest consist of personality traits or evaluations—happy, good, intelligent, and so forth (Kuhn and McPartland, 1954). A person may play a number of different roles; he may be a lecturer, a father, and a member of various committees and clubs. He plays these roles in a characteristic style; the way he sees himself in these roles is a part of his ego-identity. He may perceive himself vaguely or clearly. The more he has discussed his personal problems with others the more clearly he is likely to see himself. During psychotherapy, the therapist may provide the concepts which the patient can use to talk about himself. Some aspects of the self-image are more important to a person than others: it is more upsetting if these are challenged.

Another method of assessing the self-image is by seven-point scales such as the "Semantic Differential"; subjects are asked to describe "the kind of person I actually am" along a series of seven-point scales such as:

strong - - - - - - - weak
kind - - - - - - - cruel (Osgood *et al.,* 1957)

The answers are affected by the tendency to give a favorable impression, although that does not necessarily matter since it is important to know how favorably a person views himself. A method which is free from this difficulty is the so-called Q-sort in which subjects are asked to place a series of statements on cards in order, with the cards which apply most to themselves at the top. If all the cards have equally desirable (or undesirable) descriptive phrases on them, a purely descriptive and nonevaluative account of the ego-identity can be obtained.

The body image is an important part of the self-image, especially for girls and young women. Males are most pleased with their bodies when they are large—females are most pleased when their bodies are small, but with large busts (Jourard and Secord, 1955). Clearly there is a cultural ideal of the size and shape that bodies should be.

How far does a person's self-image correspond with the way he is seen by others? As will be seen, people present a somewhat improved, idealized and censored version of themselves for public inspection, and may come to believe it themselves. On the other hand reality in the form of others' reactions prevents the self-image from getting too far out of line. It is no good thinking you are the King of France if no one else shares this view. However, some people succeed in insulating themselves from the views of others so that they are simply unaware of how they are regarded.

The *ego-ideal* is the kind of person one would most like to be; it is a personal goal to be striven for, and it may also be the image that is presented to others. It may be based on particular individuals who are taken as admired models, and who may be parents, teachers, film stars, or characters from literature. It may consist of a fusion of desired characteristics drawn from various sources. The ego-ideal may be remote and unattainable, or it may be just a little better than the self-image in certain respects. The gap between the two can be assessed by means of the measures described already. The semantic differential can be filled in to describe "the kind of person I actually am" and "the kind of person I would most like to be." The average discrepancy between scale scores is then worked out thus:

(ego-ideal) (self)

X   X

kind - - - - - - - cruel

A number of studies have found that neurotics have greater self/ego-ideal conflict than normals, and that the discrepancy gets smaller during psychotherapy—though this is mainly because of changes in self-ratings. However there are some groups of people, by no means well adjusted, who show very little conflict—because they perceive themselves so inaccurately (Wylie, 1961).

When there is much conflict, it contributes to low self-esteem. It may also lead to efforts to attain the ego-ideal: when there is actually movement in this direction there is said to be "self-realization." There may be efforts to actually change the personality, i.e., some aspects of behavior, in some way; or there may be efforts to persuade others to categorize one differently, by better self presentation. A curious feature of the ideal-ego is that a person who attains it does not necessarily rest on his laurels enjoying the self-esteem, but may revise his goals upwards—like a high-jumper who moves the bar upwards a notch. This revision upwards does not usually produce dissatisfaction with the self, but rather the reverse; when a goal has become part of the ideal-self there seems to be gratification just from having this goal, the ego-ideal is part of the self-image, and one may travel hopefully even though one never arrives.

Self-esteem is the extent to which a person approves of and accepts himself, and regards himself as praiseworthy, either absolutely or in comparison with others. Like ego-identity, self-esteem has a stable core, together with a series of peripheral esteems based on different role relationships. One complication about self-esteem is that some people develop an exaggerated self-regard in compensation for basic feelings of inferiority. In these cases it is difficult to decide whether they "really" have high or low self-esteem—it would depend on whether this is measured by direct or indirect measures.

A measure of self-esteem can be obtained from self ego-ideal discrepancies, but a better measure is the direct rating of self on evaluative scales (e.g., good-bad). Rosenberg (1965) constructed an attitude scale for measuring self-esteem that was found to agree well with free self descriptions, and in the case of hospital patients with ratings by nurses. It is also possible to find out the basic, unconscious degree of self acceptance. The method is to ask the subject to make ratings of samples of recorded speech, handwriting, and so forth including specimens from the subject himself. It is found that subjects often give very favorable self-evaluations, and a number give very unfavorable judgments, but few give neutral ratings (Huntley, 1940).

Dimensions of the Self

We have just descibed one kind of conflict between ego-identity and ego-ideal. There may also be conflicts within each of these. As has been seen, the ego-identity contains a series of subidentities referring to relations with particular groups; the same is true of the ego-ideal. A child may admire saints and soldiers, poets and financiers, but eventually he has to decide which is the direction in which he really wants to go. The degree of integration or diffusion of ego-identity is an important aspect of personality. At one extreme are the completely dedicated, single-minded fanatics; at the other are those adolescents who do not yet know "who they are or where they are going. The more integrated the self-image, the more consistent a person's behavior will be: one effect of the self-image on behavior is the suppression of behavior that is out of line. This "consistency" may take various forms, depending on whether the self-image is based on the attributes of some person, on a set of ethical or ideological rules of conduct, or on an occupational or social-class role. Another aspect of the self-image is the extent to which a person sees himself as unique and different from others. The child in the family, a soldier in the Army, a member of a crowd—they may simply see themselves as members of a group, not differing notably from the others. Most adolescents try to separate themselves from the corporate family identity by joining a group outside the family; this is still a shared identity, but it gives them a new status in society. Or they can engage in eccentric, deviant or delinquent behavior to show their separate identity. Adolescent drug-takers, isolated old people, and others feel apart from other people and do not share the common goals and norms of the surrounding society. Probably the normal condition is a combination of unique and shared elements, such as taking a role in a group where all members share common ways of behavior, but recognize and accept the individual contributions and idiosyncrasies of each person (Ziller, 1964). There are probably wide variations in the extent to which uniqueness is stressed. It seems to be a strong tendency among middle-class intellectuals, but is less strong for working-class youth, who cling to group identities such as "skinhead."

The Origins of the Self

The Reactions of Others

The main origin of self-image and self-esteem is probably the reactions of others—we come to see ourselves as other categorize us. This has been called the theory of the "looking-glass self"—to see ourselves we look to see how we are reflected in the reactions of others. Many studies have found that self-ratings correlate with ratings by others, though the self-ratings are more favorable (Wylie, 1961). There is experimental evidence that others' reactions affect self-ratings. In one experiment subjects were asked to read poems; some were evaluated favorably, others unfavorably, by a supposed speech expert. Self-ratings on ability to read poems and on related scales shifted accordingly (Videbeck, 1960). If parents tell a child he is clever, or treat him as if he is untrustworthy, these attributes may become part of the ego-identity. The whole pattern of reaction is important here, the spoken and the unspoken. A group of students once played a joke on a rather dull, unattractive female student, by treating her as if she was tremendously attractive and popular. "Before the year was over, she had developed an easy manner and a confident assumption that she was popular" (Guthrie, 1938).

Adults and teachers do not hesitate to give full descriptive feedback to children, but amongst older people there is something of a taboo on such direct verbal feedback, especially in its negative aspects. It is reported that those who go on leadership training courses ask to be told point-blank how others perceive them (Bennis *et al.*, 1964), and it has been suggested that it would be helpful to provide people with rather more of such information than is currently regarded as polite. On the other hand, it can be very traumatic to find this out, and it should be done with tact, or indirectly by subtle cues, hints, and nonverbal reactions. The effect is greater when the critic is regarded as an expert or if his opinion is valued for some other reason. Parents are a most important source of both self-image and self-esteem for children; those who are rejected come to reject themselves and have low self-esteem in later life. The writer has formulated this as a process of *introjection*, whereby children adopt the perceptions, attitudes and reactions to themselves of parents and others (Argyle, 1964a).

Comparison with Others

Self-perceptions may include objective properties such as "tall"; these only become meaningful in comparison with others. An important source of the self-image is the comparison of oneself with brothers, sisters, friends, or others who are constantly present and are sufficiently similar to invite comparison. If other families in the neighborhood are wealthier, a child will regard himself as "poor"; if his brothers and sisters are cleverer, he will see himself as not clever, and so on. It is possible to change a child's self-image completely, and quite rapidly, by sending him to a different school, where the other children are, for example, more athletic, or of a lower social class. People compare their abilities or fortunes with others who are similar: a tennis-player does not compare himself either with Wimbledon champions or with hopeless beginners, manual workers do not compare their wages with those of the managing director or of Indian peasants. Subjects in experiments are most interested to know about those who are slightly better than themselves (Latané, 1966), as if they were trying to do better by small installments. In a study of a large number of adolescents in New York State, Rosenberg (1965) found that those with the highest self-esteem tended to be of higher social class, to have done better at school, and to have been leaders in clubs—all of which could be bases for favorable comparisons of self and others.

Roles Played

Medical students come to see themselves as "doctors" during their training—31 percent in the first year, 83 percent in the fourth year. Most medical students see themselves as doctors when dealing with patients. The third source of the self-image is simply the roles a person has played in the past, or is playing in the present. A child plays at many parts, and the adolescent crisis of identity which commonly occurs in Western society is brought about by the need to choose which of these parts to emphasize. Adults often see themselves primarily in terms of the job they do, although roles of particular importance or excitement in their past may be even more salient. Roles provide an easy solution to the problem of ego-identity—there is a clear public identity to adopt. There are individual differences in role performance, and a person may come to see himself as an *intelligent* juvenile delinquent, i.e. as combining a role and a trait. Goffman (1956) suggested that in order to perform a role effectively, the newcomer has to put on a mask to act the part; however when he has acted the part for long enough and others have accepted the performance this becomes a real part of his personality and is no longer a mask.

Identification with Models

Children identify with a succession of people—parents, teachers and other models, i.e., they admire these models and want to be like them. The ego-ideal is mainly based on a fusion of these models. However it has been found in a number of experiments that identification also modifies the self-image, i.e., people feel that they *already* resemble the model. A very important part of the self is mainly acquired through identification—the sex-role. If a child has plenty of contact and a warm relationship with the same sex parent it will come to behave in a male (or female) way, and feel male (or female) accordingly (Mussen and Distler, 1964).

The Adolescent Identity Crisis

Children play at roles, adolescents experiment with them--during student life it is possible to try out a number of roles and identities without commitment. However, pressures to commit oneself build up, and somewhere between the ages of sixteen and twenty-four there is often an identity crisis when a young person is forced to make up his mind which of all these bits and pieces of identity to hang on to, which to suppress (Erikson, 1956). The basis of this is partly the necessity of adopting one job rather than another, to choose a particular spouse, to make some decision about political and religious attitudes, and to choose a style of life. At this stage the choice is helped by the existence of alternative models to identify with, and of a number of "social types" in the community. A young person in England might consider becoming a scientist or a teacher but would be unlikely to contemplate becoming a witch-doctor or a gangster. To have formed an ego-identity is to have "a feeling of being at home in one's body, a sense of knowing where one is going, and an inner assurance of anticipated recognition from those who count" (Erikson 1956).

The course of identity formation does not always run smoothly, and a number of intermediate and temporarily unsuccessful states of the identity are commonly found in young people. (1) A conflict between two or more alternative identities which cannot be reconciled, such as wishing to be both a clergyman and a whiskey distiller; if the two cannot be combined (e.g. making sacramental wine, or being a Benedictine monk), one is usually chosen and the other relegated to week-ends or holidays. (2) A state of "moratorium" in which decisions about identity are postponed. After going to university (which itself provides such a moratorium) some students travel to remote and exotic lands to "find out who they are." (3) Forming a prestigeful identity, which cannot really be sustained, and required continual confirmation from others. (4) There are various pathological conditions—forming a totally unrealistic identity as in paranoia, and forming no identity at all as in schizophrenia.

The Need for Self-Esteem

We have seen that there are forces in the personality to achieve a *unified* identity, and that this is controlled by outside forces to keep it *realistic*. There is a third force—to produce a *favorable* self-image which provides sufficient self-esteem. We have seen that self-ratings are usually somewhat more generous than ratings given by others. However, the self-image depends on the reactions of others; this is why such a lot of effort is put into self-presentation, the manipulation of others' perceptions. What happens if others' evaluations are *more* favorable than self-evaluation? Experiments show that this is found to be uncomfortable—but is not so unpleasant as the opposite situation (Deutsch and Solomon, 1959).

The need for self-esteem is limited by reality; otherwise behavior becomes absurd and preposterous, and there is continual lack of confirmation by others. This happens in the case of paranoia. In fact people vary widely in their feelings of esteem, from conceit to inferiority. Both extremes usually reflect failure to perceive accurately the present responses of others, and can be regarded as failures of adjustment. A mythical psychotherapist is said to have told a patient who suffered from feelings of inferiority, "But you really are inferior." The real reason that people feel inferior is usually that they have been unduly rejected by their parents, or have chosen too elevated a comparison group.

It is quite possible to select prestigeful items out of the long list of self-attributes and roles once played, and such items often become a favorite item of conversation. However, the total self-esteem is greatly affected by the ego-ideal. Thus self-esteem depends jointly on a person's position in a series of evaluative dimensions, and upon the value placed on each of these dimensions. Values depend on the group, so self-esteem depends on whether the group values a person's attributes—but a group will have been joined because it does value them.

Conditions Under Which the Self is Activated

The self is not at work all the time; people are not continually trying to discover, sustain, or present a self-image. For example, when at home rather than at work, in the audience rather than on the stage, the self-system is not very active.

Most people feel self-conscious when appearing in front of an audience, and some people feel very anxious. It has been found that these effects are greater when the audience is large, and fails to give positive responses. The performer is the center of attention for a number of people and his performance will be assessed, so that there is the danger that he will receive disapproving reactions, and self-esteem (rather than self-image) may be damaged.

When someone addresses any kind of audience it is no good his speaking in the informal "familial" style—he won't be heard properly; it is inevitable that he must put on some kind of "performance." Once he does so he is accepting a certain definition of the situation and presenting a certain face. He is someone who is able to perform before this audience and is worth attending to. It is this implicit claim which creates the risk of loss of face. We shall discuss later the social skills of dealing with audiences, including how stage fright can be reduced.

There are many social situations where other people can be regarded as a kind of audience and where one's performances may be assessed. Argyle and Williams (1969) asked subjects, "To what extent did you feel mainly the observer or the observed? after they had been in different situations.

It was found that they felt more observed when:

being interviewed, rather than interviewing
with an older person
a female with males

Individuals differ in the extent to which they see themselves as observers of others or being observed by others. It is found that some people consistently see themselves as observed, particularly males who are insecure and dependent. It is interesting to find that females feel observed, especially by males. Human females wear more colorful and interesting clothes and take more trouble about their appearance. On the other hand males appear to put on a performance in the fields of physical and verbal prowess.

The self can be activated in a number of other ways. A person may be different from everyone else present, for example, by wearing different clothes or by being the only female or the only Negro present. Conversely "de-individuation" can be brought about by dressing everyone up in white laboratory coats or other uniforms; this produces a loss of individual responsibility, and people even forget who said what (Singer *et al.*, 1965). Self-awareness is brought about by "self-confrontation" as when looking in a mirror, or watching a videotape recording of oneself. The latter has a stronger appeal because the watcher is not able to control the visible performance, but is aware that he is seeing (and hearing) himself as others see him. Self-awareness is produced by "penetration" of territory or privacy—being discovered with too few clothes on, or when one has not been able to arrange one's appearance, or when awkward private facts are disclosed.

There are individual differences in self-consciousness. Some people suffer from *audience anxiety*, that is, feel nervous when appearing in public or being the center of attention. Another variable is

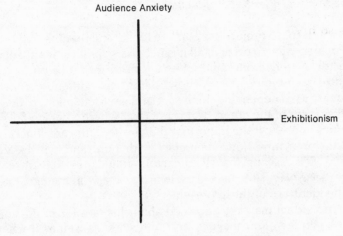

Figure 14   (From Paivio, 1965)

exhibitionism, which is the desire to appear in public and be seen. It is found that these two dimensions are independent (see Figure 14), so that some people both desire to be seen and are made anxious by it; such people are found to make a large number of speech errors when speaking in public (Paivio, 1965).

Those who have low self-esteem are shy, easily embarrassed, eager to be approved of, and are easily influenced by social pressures; they are clearly taking the observed role. Insecure people, i.e., those who have not formed a stable self-image, are very sensitive to the reactions of others, since they are still seeking information which will affect their self-image. Those who have achieved an integrated identity are no longer so bothered about the reactions of others, and are not upset if others mistake their identity, or react negatively to them (Marcia, 1966).

The Effects of the Self-Image on Behavior

Certain aspects of behavior during social encounters can be looked at as consequences of the participants having self-images. They present themselves in a certain way, adopt a particular 'face,' and try to get others to accept this picture of themselves. Various strategies are adopted to do so; if unsuccessful there will be embarrassment and a breakdown of interaction.

The Motivation for Self-Presentation

People want to project a self-image for several reasons. To begin with, for interaction to occur at all it is necessary for the participants to be able to categorize one another—they need guidance on how to respond to each other. It was shown before that different styles of behavior are used depending on the social class, occupation, nationality, and so forth of the other. If it is not clear where a person falls on such dimensions, or if the important things about him are concealed, people do not know how to interact with him, and will be very perplexed. It is essential that all interactors should present themselves clearly in *some* way. It is necessary to arrive at a working agreement about the identities of those present.

An individual may be concerned about his face for professional purposes. Butlers, lord mayors, and film stars, as well as teachers, psychotherapists, and salesmen, all need to project a certain image of professional competence. There is a good reason for this: clients are more likely to respond in the desired way if they have confidence in the expertise of the practitioner. There is widespread evidence that pupils learn more if they think their teachers are good, and that patients in psychotherapy recover faster if they believe that the therapist can cure them. Another reason a person may need confirmation of his self-image or self-esteem is that he may be "insecure", i.e., be in constant need of reassurance from others that he is what he hopes he is. If the self-image has not been firmly established in the past, more time has to be spent looking in the mirror of others' reactions in the present. Adolescents, who have only just formed a tentative self-image, are particularly sensitive to the reactions of others, and are "insecure" in this sense. People who have changed their social class, their job, or their nationality are often in a similar position.

Goffman (1956) observed that undertakers, salesmen, waiters, and other professional and service workers engage in a lot of deception and impression manipulation which is often in their client's interests. The stage is set in the "front regions" of premises, and may involve collusion between team-members. Members of the public are kept out of the back regions, which are dirtier and less impressive, and where behavior is more vulgar and informal. Goffman maintains that a similar degree of deception occurs in many other nonprofessional situations, such as a family receiving guests.

How do people project an identity? The most obvious way would be simply to tell the others present, but it is not socially acceptable to do this except with intimate friends and relations; in England particularly, only the most modest of claims is acceptable. Verbal self presentation appears to be acceptable provided that it is very indirect; if such messages are too direct they can easily become ridiculous, as in "name-dropping." Stephen Potter has given a satirical account of indirect ways of claiming a prestigeful identity in his book *One-Upmanship* (1952). For example:

Layman: Thank you, Doctor. I was coming home rather late last night from the House of Commons . . . .

M.D.-Man: Thank you . . . now if you'll just let me put these . . . hair brushes and things off the bed for you . . . that's right . . .

Layman: I was coming home rather late. Army Act, really . . .

M.D.-Man: Now just undo the top button of your shirt or whatever it is you're wearing . . .

Layman: I say I was coming . . .

M.D.-Man: Now if you've got some hot water—really hot—and a clean towel.

Layman: Yes, just outside. The Postmaster-General . . .

M.D.-Man: Open your mouth, please.

This is another case where nonverbal communication is more effective than verbal. Nonverbal signals here act as "gestures" which symbolize aspects of the self which cannot easily be displayed in the course of interaction. Personality traits can be displayed by acting, e.g., in a clearly "intelligent" manner. Clothes can be used to signal personality traits. Gibbins (1969) found that English grammar school girls were agreed as to what kind of girl would wear various kinds of clothes, whether she would be promiscuous, go to church, drink, and so forth; the clothes they preferred themselves had images which resembled both their actual self and their ideal-self. Roles like occupation, class, and so forth, are difficult to communicate. Appropriate clothes, appropriate accent, and style of behavior, are the usual methods; professional people can create impressive offices or other settings for this purpose. A working-class person who has adopted a middle-class identity will strive to adopt the appropriate ways of behaving, including the way he speaks and the way he votes. If a young person comes to look on himself as a juvenile delinquent, and as one who is alienated from society, he will be more likely to act out this part by further law-breaking. Part of the success of Chinese thought reform is due to bringing about a different self-perception of the "students" as a result of a lengthy process of confession-writing.

Deception and Concealment

Another feature of self presentation is concealment: people are careful not to reveal aspects of themselves which are likely to lead to disapproval. Jourard (1964) surveyed large numbers of students, using a questionnaire asking how much they had revealed about themselves to other people. This varied greatly with content: more was revealed about opinions and attitudes than about sexual behavior or money for instance. People will reveal more to people whom they can trust not to reject them—to their mothers, close friends, people who are similar to themselves, and (we may add) to psychiatrists and clergymen. Another case of concealment is the cautious, ritualized, and conventional behavior which people display on first meeting strangers. Disclosure is a risk, as there is a danger of the other person disapproving. Jourard has found that if an interviewer makes some self-disclosures, the other is more likely to do the same.

As we saw above, Goffman (1956) believes that social behavior involves a lot of deliberate deception, in that impressions are created for others. Jourard (1964) and others have argued that behavior *ought* to be authentic.

I shall not discuss the moral issue here but shall list the main forms of deception, and consider their consequences. (1) The self presented is partly bogus, and nearer the ideal self than the actual self. We shall see below that this can lead to embarrassment if the deception is unmasked. On the other hand this is part of the process of moving towards the ideal self—being accepted as a somewhat different kind of person; people can help each other to move towards their ideal self and there will be consistency pressures to bring behavior outside the interaction situation into line. (2) Discreditable episodes or features of the self are concealed. In any group of people who know each other well, there is collaboration in the process of forgetting unfortunate events. Similarly, if someone has a low opinion of a colleague it is probable that the most constructive line of action involves some concealment of these opinions. (3) Concealment is often practiced by homosexuals, ex-convicts and others for whom interaction might otherwise be impossible. (4) Deception by undertakers and waiters is not so much about the self but about other features of the professional performance. Sometimes this is to the performer's advantage—as for salesmen and waiters, sometimes it is to the client's advantage—as for undertakers and doctors.

Embarrassment

Embarrassment is a form of social anxiety which is suddenly precipitated by events during interaction; the victim loses poise, blushes, stutters, fumbles, sweats, avoids eye contact, and in more severe cases flees from the situation and (mainly in the Far East) commits suicide. Embarrassment is contagious; it spreads rapidly to the others present. Once a person has lost control this makes the situation worse, as he is now ashamed also of his lack of poise. He is temporarily incapable of interacting.

Goffman (1955) offered a theory of embarrassment: people commonly present a self which is partly bogus; if this image is discredited in the course of interaction, embarrassment ensues. For example, a person's job, qualifications, or social origins may turn out to be less impressive than had been suggested. This theory can be checked against the 1,000 instances of embarrassment collected by Gross and Stone (1964). About a third of these cases involved discrediting of self-presentation, but the rest could not really be classified in this way, and two other sources of embarrassment need to be considered.

A second source of embarrassment is "rule-breaking." Garfinkel (1963) has carried out some intriguing "demonstrations" in which investigators behaved in their own homes like lodgers, treated other customers in shops as salesmen, or flagrantly broke the rules of games—such as by moving the opponent's pieces. This produced embarrassment, consternation, and anger. Rule-breaking may involve mistaking the role of others, disagreeing over the nature of the situation, breaking the basic rules of interaction, or simply offending against arbitrary cultural conventions. Rule-breaking causes consternation because it is unexpected, it breaks the smooth flow of interaction, and because others may not know how to deal with it.

Accidents are a third source of embarrassment—tripping over the carpet, uncontrollable mirth or drunkenness, forgetting someone's name, social gaffes like talking about an apparently harmless matter which unexpectedly upsets someone, e.g., about his college when he has just been sent down, or his grandmother who has just died. Gross and Stone report an extraordinary case of a man at a banquet who got the tablecloth caught in his trouser zip fastener, and pulled everything off the table when he rose to speak. Such episodes are more embarrassing at formal occasions since one is to some extent putting on a performance and implicitly making claims of competence.

Can embarrassment be avoided? Some people are able to remain poised when embarrassing incidents occur; they "keep their cool" and prevent the situation from disintegrating. Adolescents often tease and insult one another, perhaps as a kind of training in dealing with embarrassment. Some of the possible causes of embarrassment can be avoided by presenting a face which cannot be invalidated, and it is less likely to happen to those who are not dependent on external confirmation of their self-image and self-esteem. Breakdown of interaction may still occur, however, as a result of accidental errors, as in social gaffes. Rules of etiquette and skills of tact help to avoid such breakdowns. An example of etiquette is the rule not to send invitations too long before the event, because it is difficult to refuse them. An example of tact is knocking on doors or coughing when a couple may be making love on the other side. Embarrassment can perhaps be controlled by understanding its causes. There is really no need to be disturbed by accidents committed in good faith and without hostile intention—it is more useful to put things right.

When a person is embarrassed, the others present usually want to prevent the collapse of social interaction, and will help in various ways. To begin with, they will try to prevent loss of face by being tactful in the ways described. They may pretend that nothing has happened, make excuses for the offender—he was only joking, was off form and so forth, or in some other way "rescue the situation." Finally, if face is irrevocably lost they may help the injured party to rehabilitate himself in the group in a new guise (Goffman, 1955; Gross and Stone, 1964).

Disconfirmation of Self-Image

When A's face has been disbelieved or discredited there are various strategies open to him. One is simply to ignore what has happened or to laugh it off as unimportant. It would be expected from the analysis given in earlier chapters that a person who had failed to project an image would try alternative ways of doing so. If he is rattled he may fall back on less subtle techniques of the kind, "Look here, young man, I've written more books about this subject than you've read"; "Do you realize that I. . . ," and so forth. This may succeed in modifying the other's perceptions, but it will almost certainly cause embarrassment and make the speaker look ridiculous. A milder technique might be, "Well, as a matter of fact I have taken some interest in that subject. . . ."

What very often happens is that A forms a lower opinion of a person or group that does not treat him properly, and he goes off to present himself to someone else. It has been found that salesgirls in shops preserve their image of competence in the face of customers whom they can't please by categorizing them as "nasty," or in some similar way (Lombard, 1955). If a low opinion is formed of B, it doesn't matter whether B confirms the girl's self-image of competence or not. A number of experiments show that people withdraw from groups who do not react to them in the desired way, and that they prefer the company and friendship of those who confirm their self-image (Secord and Backman, 1965).

Sometimes a person is still keen to belong to a group even though it does not accept his self-image or does not treat him with enough respect. When it is mainly esteem which has been withheld by the group, it is possible to alter behavior in a way that will produce the desired response from others. It is found that insecure people are more affected by social influences and pressures of all kinds. In small social groups, for example, one of the main causes of conformity is the avoidance of being rejected, as deviates tend to be. Those who conform most are those who feel inferior, lack self-confidence, and are dependent on others (Krech, Crutchfield, and Ballachey, 1962). People may embark on all kinds of self-improvement, either apparent or real, in response to negative reactions from others, including the modification of styles of interaction as in operant verbal conditioning.

The remaining responses can really be regarded as "defense mechanisms," whose main object is the avoidance of anxiety, while no realistic adjustment of self-image or behavior is involved. One of these is self-deception in its various forms. A person may distort the reactions of others in a favorable direction, or simply not perceive them at all. The extreme of this is psychotic withdrawal from the difficulties of interpersonal relations into a private world of fantasies which cannot be disturbed by outside events.

QUESTIONS FOR DISCUSSION

1. Clearly distinguish between *self-concept, self-image, self-esteem, ego ideal,* and *self consciousness.*
2. How do people come to form a self-concept? Discuss the major forces Argyle suggests affect beliefs about the self. Which influences are the most important?
3. What are the major factors that influence self-esteem?
4. Is a person always influenced by his self-concept or are some situations more likely to activate the self-concept than others? What are they?

5.   What functions does the self-concept serve for the individual?
6.   How does the self-concept relate to embarrassment?

References

1.   Argyle, M., and Williams, M., "Observer or Observed? A Reversible Perspective in Person Perception," *Sociometry*, 32 (1969), pp. 396-412.
2.   Bennis, W.G., *et al.*, *Interpersonal Dynamics* (Homewood, Ill.: Dorsey Press, 1964).
3.   Deutch, M., and Solomon, L., "Reactions to Evaluations by Others as Influenced by Self-Evaluations," *Sociometry*, 22 (1959), pp. 93-111.
4.   Erikson, E.H., "The problem of ego identity," *American Journal of Psychoanalysis*, 4 (1956), pp. 56-121.
5.   Garfinkel, H., "Trust and Stable Actions," in Harvey, O.J., *Motivation and Social Interaction* (New York: Ronald Press, 1963).
6.   Gibbins, K., "Communication Aspects of Women's Clothes and Their Relation to Fashionability," *British Journal of Social and Clinical Psychology*, 8 (1969), pp. 301-12.
7.   Goffman, E., "On Face-Work: An Analysis of Ritual Clements in Social Interaction," *Psychiatry*, 18 (1955), pp. 213-31.
8.   Goffman, E., *The Presentation of Self in Everyday Life* (Edinburgh University Press, 1956).
9.   Gross, E., and Stone, G.P., "Embarrassment and the Analysis of Role Requirements," *American Journal of Sociology*, 70 (1964), pp. 1-15.
10. Guthrie, E.R., *The Psychology of Human Conflict* (New York: Harper, 1938).
11. Huntley, C.W., "Judgements of Self Based Upon Records of Expressive Behaviour," *Journal of Abnormal Social Psychology*, 35 (1940), pp. 398-427.
12. Jourard, S.M., *The Transparent Self*, (Princeton, N.J: Van Nostrand, 1964).
13. Jourard, S.M., and Secord, P.F., "Body-Cathexis and Personality," *British Journal of Psychology*, 46 (1955), pp. 130-38.
14. Krech, D., Crutchfield, R.S., and Ballachey, E.L., *Individual in Society*, (New York: McGraw-Hill, 1962).
15. Kuhn, M.H., and McPartland, T.S., "An Empirical Investigation of Self-Attitudes," *American Sociological Review*, 19 (1954), pp.68-76.
16. Latané, B., ed., "Studies in Social Comparison," *Journal of Experimental Social Psychology*, Supplement 1. (1966).
17. Lombard, G.G.F., *Behavior in a Selling Group*, (Harvard University Press, 1955).
18. Marcia, J.E., "Development and Validation of Ego-Identity Status," *Journal of Personality and Social Psychology*, 3 (1966), pp. 551-58.
19. Mussen, P., and Distler, L., "Child-Rearing Antecedents of Masculine Identification in Kindergarten Boys," *Child. Develop.*, 31 (1964), pp.89-100.
20. Osgood, C.E., Suci, G.J., and Tannenbaum, P.H., *The Measurement of Meaning*, (University of Illinois Press, 1957).

21. Paivio, A., "Personality and Audience Influence," *Progress in Experimental Personality Research*, 2 (1965), pp. 127-73.

22. Potter, S., *One-Upmanship* (Hart-Davis, 1952; New York: Holt, Rinehart and Winston, 1971).

23. Rosenberg, M., *Society and the Adolescent Self-image*, (Princeton University Press, 1965).

24. Secord, P.F., and Backman, C.W., *Social Psychology* (New York: McGraw-Hill, 1964).

25. Singer, J.E., Brush, C.A., and Lublin, S.C., "Some Aspects of Deindividuation: Identification and Conformity," *Journal of Experimental Social Psychology*, 1 (1965), pp. 356-78.

26. Videbeck, R., "Self-Conception and the Reactions of Others," *Sociometry*, 23 (1960), pp. 351-59.

27. Wylie, R.C., *The Self Concept*, (University of Nebraska Press 1961).

28. Ziller, R.C., "Individuation and Socialization," *Human Relations*, 17 (1964), pp. 341-60.

Dominic Infante discusses some of the ways in which the results of persuasion research can be applied to interpersonal communication situations. He emphasizes the internal cognitive events that occur during persuasion and the necessity for understanding these processes in order to improve one's persuasive abilities. Occasionally, people mistakenly assume that persuasion research has produced tools for persuading others that are far more powerful than they actually are in their current state of development, and that persuading another person is somehow immoral. Successful persuasion is not easy; and like any development in society (cars and airplanes, for example) persuasion has the capacity to be used for good or evil ends. People attempt to persuade each other in most activities throughout any given day. Thus it is a process we should be informed about.

This article discusses the concepts of *cognitive structure, hierarchical arrangement, ego involvement,* and *assimilation* and *contrast affects. Cognitive structure* refers to the way in which the human mind seems to be organized. A hierarchy implies an ordering on some basis. For example, people who work in an organization can be ordered on a hierarchy of importance and status. Infante suggests that the beliefs in a person's cognitive structure are ordered in a hierarchy of importance to the person. *Ego involvement* occurs when a person's self-concept or ego becomes tied to an idea or event. This often happens when a person expends considerable time and energy on a project and feels that anything that is said about, or happens to, the project is said about or happens to him personally. *Assimilation affects* and *contrast affects* commonly occur when a person is asked to judge the position of a statement relative to his belief. If the statement is close to his belief, the person often tends to perceive it as closer than it actually is. This is an assimilation affect. If the statement is relatively far away from what the person believes, he will often perceive it as further from his own position than it actually is. This is a contrast affect.

15

COGNITIVE bEhAVIORS ANd INTERPERSONAL COMMUNICATION

Dominic A. Infante

Children learn at an early age that they can influence the behavior of others. As he matures the child realizes that whether he obtains a desired response from another person depends upon something more than simply expressing his wishes. A general principle which the child learns is that what one says and how one says it make a difference. To further complicate life, the child learns that all people do not respond in the same way to a given message. Asking mother for something in one way may produce the desired response while asking father in the same way may result in no response. What works with father may cause big sister to say, "You little brat!" This awareness of social reality may not have bothered us much when we were children because we soon learned that it is possible to manage in such a complex world. All one has to do is learn the different ways of talking with different people. The task was not that difficult since simply observing the behavior of others created an image of their thinking and their likes and dislikes. Once acquired, the various images provided a reasonably sound basis for decisions regarding what to say and how to say it.

As children grow up they encounter a diversity of people and situations which often make the social problems encountered in early home life seem like "two-plus-two" compared with calculus. However, the principle has not really changed. The better one understands the other's thinking, the better are the chances of a satisfying communication experience. In attempting to understand why people be-

Dominic A. Infante is associate professor in the Division of Rhetoric and Communication of the School of Speech at Kent State University. Mr. Infante's paper was prepared especially for this book.

have as they do the child discovers a number of principles that seem to explain types of behaviors and categories of people, and which also provide direction for what to say and how to say it, e.g., "I should wait until dad shows the signs that he is in a good mood before asking him to fix my bicycle." This is all a part of social learning, a process that never really ends. The longer we live the more we learn about people. Our satisfaction in interpersonal relations is dependent upon becoming ever more understanding of why people behave as they do.

It would be presumptuous of me to tell you that you need to adapt what you say to the **cognitive characteristics** (ways of thinking) of your receiver. You have known this from early childhood. Further, you have developed a wealth of sophisticated principles regarding the most intelligent ways of communicating with people who seem to possess particular cognitive characteristics. For example, young men usually develop a wide variety of tactics for courting what they perceive as different types of females, depending upon different situations. A young man might see an attractive female at a party who appears a bit aloof, uninterested, and unapproachable. His reaction might be, "I've seen this before and I know how to handle it." Guided by his image of her probable cognitive behavior and of the situation, he moves toward her with shoulders back and chin up, touches her lightly on the arm and says, without breaking eye contact, "It looks like you and I both have concluded that this party is a drag." After a few ritualistic remarks he says, while beginning to move confidently toward the door, "Let's split; I know a place that's just right for you."

Now I am not sure what this chapter will do for your love life. It just might be that you have this dimension of your communication behavior organized pretty well into a science. However, I am confident that although you have discovered many principles of human cognitive behavior that have direct application to your interpersonal communication behavior, you should discover some in this chapter that are, if not new, at least presented in a way that will stimulate new insights. Such insights should help you better understand why others behave as they do and should provide you with some new interpersonal strategies for influencing behavior.

Researchers in a number of disciplines have conducted a good deal of exploration which has focused on discovering the nature of attitudes and how attitudes change. **Attitude** will be considered here as the degree of favorableness that an individual feels regarding an attitude object, that is, how much he likes the object.[1] An *attitude object* is anything about which we have such feelings as: good or bad, right or wrong, valuable or worthless, fair or unfair, attractive or unattractive, desirable or undesirable. In other words, attitude is conceived in terms of how favorably an individual *evaluates* an attitude object. The research on attitude and attitude change has isolated a number of cognitive behaviors that appear to be important with reference to how we evaluate an attitude object and how we can be influenced to change an attitude. A **cognitive behavior** is, in a sense, a way in which our minds operate. Probably no two minds work in the same way. However, there seems to be some uniformity in: (1) the ways in which we organize new beliefs, (2) the ways that we rearrange and change old beliefs, (3) the ways in which changes in parts of the cognitive system lead to changes in other parts, and (4) the effects that certain variables have on cognitive processes.

The research that I am referring to has been applied to what has been termed "persuasion theory" by the communication discipline,[2] or "attitude and attitude change theory" by social psychology.[3] The focus of this research has been mainly on a one-to-many or speaker-audience situation. Although some of the research has investigated important factors in social influence when one person talks with another, the main goal of attitude research has not been on explaining interpersonal communication behavior. Most of the theory and research used to conceptualize interpersonal communication has been from the area of humanistic psychology.[4] However, persuasion or attitude change is often an important dimension of interpersonal communication. Some of the cognitive behaviors that have been used for explaining persuasion in a one-to-many situation also have applicability in conceptualizing some of the things that happen in the interpersonal communication arena. This chapter will focus on cognitive behaviors that are important in the rather interesting interpersonal situation in which two persons attempt to influence each other. We shall maintain that each cognitive behavior can be used to help in the understanding of some aspects of interpersonal communication and also can be used to provide direction regarding "what to say and how to say it."

Before we discuss some of the cognitive behaviors that have implications for interpersonal communication, it is necessary to establish a framework that can be used for presenting each cognitive behavior. Such a framework is presented in the following section.

The Organization of Cognitive Structure

We shall describe an individual's **cognitive structure** in this section with little emphasis on the changes (or cognitive behaviors) that occur within a cognitive structure. The cognitive behaviors will be saved for the later sections where they will be explained and related to interpersonal communication.

The organization of cognitive structure presented here is similar in some ways to the conceptualizations of other writers.[5] The basic pattern of an individual's cognitive structure is a *hierarchical* arrangement with the less important, less organized components at the lowest level and the more important, more organized components at the highest level.

An adult's cognitive structure contains a mass of attitude objects numbering at least in the thousands. Recall that an attitude object is anything that the individual has learned to evaluate in a favorable or unfavorable manner. Some attitude objects are people or particular behaviors of people, while others are events, organizations, policies (past, present, and proposed), animals, inanimate objects, extrasensory objects (e.g., god, devil, a curse).

The attitude objects in our universe of experience differ along a number of dimensions. *Specificity* is a meaningful way to differentiate attitude objects. In terms of events, for example, hunger in your house, town, state, country, and so forth, proceeds from the more specific to the more general. *Importance* is used to give meaning to attitude objects. Using inanimate objects as an example, your notebook, a stereo album, and a college diploma may respectively represent increasing levels of importance to you. Attitude objects differ in terms of our *personal involvement* with them. With policies, for instance, you might have little interest, concern, or involvement with legalized gambling, while you may feel very involved regarding legalized abortions. We also use a *time orientation* for attitude objects. We recognize that some attitude objects span time (e.g., heroin addiction) while others are more meaningful if placed in a time context (e.g., prohibition of liquor, all volunteer army, manned exploration of Mars, are recognized respectively as past, present, and future orientations). We differentiate attitude objects in terms of their *degree of favorableness*. Attitude toward an object could span from extremely favorable to extremely unfavorable. Also, we are aware that attitude objects differ in terms of what we *associate* with the objects. If you just learn of a new proposal, you may only associate one or two things with it, while you may associate twenty-five things with legalized marijuana. Finally, *concrete-abstract* distinctions among attitude objects are meaningful. For example, a situation of being verbally abused because you had long hair would be a more concrete attitude object when compared to "the generation gap" which would be a more abstract attitude object.

Next, we shall specify the structure that is common to each of the attitudes in a cognitive structure. An attitude object has meaning because of the characteristics, attributes, consequences, values, and so forth, that we associate with the object. There are at least three ways in which we perceive each thing associated with a given attitude object: (1) we have a feeling of how *desirable* the characteristic, consequence, and so forth, is; (2) we have a perception of the *importance* of the characteristic to ourselves and to liked and disliked persons; (3) we have a belief as to the *likelihood* that the characteristic will be (or has been) produced by the attitude object.

We shall use these ideas to conceptualize the way one person's attitude structure might appear for legalized abortions. Suppose that Betty associates five consequences with the attitude object: (1) less mental anguish with reference to unwanted pregnancies, (2) a control for overpopulation, (3) fewer women harmed by illegal abortionists, (4) the state's sanctioning of the termination of human life, and (5) a decline in sexual morals. Betty feels that the first three consequences are quite desirable, the fourth is extremely undesirable, and the fifth is slightly undesirable. She also feels that the first three and the fifth are only of slight importance to her and to valued others while the fourth is extremely important both to her and to valued others. Further, Betty believes that the first three consequences are quite likely to occur because of legalized abortions, the fourth is extremely likely and the fifth is extremely unlikely.

Affective-cognitive consistency theory maintains that Betty's attitude is controlled by her perceptions of what is associated with the attitude object.[6] Betty's attitude toward the object (her degree of favorableness felt toward the object) should be consistent with the feelings she has about the consequences she believes to be related to the object. Her perceptions of what is or is not related to the object represent what we shall call the cognitive components of attitude. If Betty's attitude toward legalized abortions is related to her feelings about the consequences related to the object, then we can examine the attitude structure we described above and make a prediction about Betty's attitude toward legalized abortion. Betty's perceptions of the first three consequences indicate that she has some favorable feelings toward legalized abortion. These three consequences are perceived as quite desirable, slightly important, and quite likely to happen. But her perceptions of the fourth consequence (extremely undesirable, important, and likely) indicate a large source of unfavorable feeling toward the policy. Although she perceives the fifth consequence as undesirable, it does not add much to the unfavorable feeling toward the policy, for it is believed to be extremely unlikely. Considering all of this information, our prediction would be that Betty has a quite unfavorable attitude toward legalized abortion (but not extremely unfavorable since there is some favorable feeling). A large body of research suggests that our prediction would be reasonably accurate.[7] There are techniques for measuring all of the perceptions that we discussed in this example and formulas for combining the perceptions into a score which indicates how favorably an individual like Betty will evaluate an attitude object.[8]

Although we said that we would only describe cognitive structure in this section, the prediction of attitude which we just made involved introducing a cognitive behavior. That is, the affective-cognitive consistency principle which we used to predict Betty's attitude is a conception of something that happens in our minds, a cognitive change or cognitive behavior. The principle claims that we try to maintain a tolerable level of consistency between an attitude and the characteristics we believe are related to the attitude object. We did not predict a favorable attitude in the example because such an attitude would have been inconsistent with the perceptions of the fourth consequence which was seen as important, likely, and extremely undesirable. The affective-cognitive consistency tendency was introduced here because it is utilized in this paper as the fundamental behavior that occurs in an individual's cognitive structure. The more specific cognitive behaviors, which will be introduced in the following sections and applied to interpersonal communication, are all based on the notion that our cognitive systems tend toward affective-cognitive consistency.

Values are the final elements which we shall consider as part of one's cognitive structure. A value is a belief about a desired end state of behavior or a belief about means for achieving such a goal. Values guide the individual's behavior, direct the individual as to what should be associated with an attitude object, influence whether a person changes an attitude, and provide a basis for judging things. According to Rokeach,[9] *instrumental values* are beliefs regarding modes of conduct, the means that we prefer in proceeding through life, e.g., honesty, being helpful, working hard, being daring. *Terminal values* refer to end-states of existence, e.g., freedom, equality, social recognition. While instrumental values are means, terminal values are ends. How many values do we have? Rokeach says that we probably operate with a few dozen instrumental values and around eighteen or so terminal values.[10]

A value can be thought of as a superordinate term which we invent to give meaning to a group of attitudes. We perceive some of our attitudes as related. Attitudes that "go together" represent a cluster or group of attitudes. A **superordinate term** is a "name" for the cluster that captures the essence of what is in the cluster. For example, imagine that Jerry has a very favorable attitude toward each of the following attitude objects: radical speakers on campus, professors saying what they wish in class, students expressing any position on any issue, X-rated movies, pornography shops, radical newspapers, radical organizations, burning the flag in protest, and so forth. Jerry perceives that these attitudes are somehow related, that they have some higher meaning. The higher meaning which Jerry perceives is that these attitudes indicate that "freedom of expression" is very important to him. "Freedom of expression" is a superordinate for Jerry as it organizes and gives meaning to a group of specific objects. Such a superordinate is a belief and it may be considered a value.

At the beginning of this section we said that the basic pattern of organization in a cognitive structure is a hierarchical arrangement with the less important, less organized components at the lowest level of the hierarchy and the most important, most organized components at the highest level. Since we have described the components of cognitive structure and their specific organizational patterns, we can now proceed to specify the overall organization of cognitive structure.

The highest level in the cognitive structure hierarchy consists of one or more groups of attitudes. Each group of attitudes represents a value that is perceived as extremely important. Imagine that Jerry believes his "freedom of expression" is one of his most important values. This value and the attitudes which comprise it would occupy the highest level in Jerry's cognitive structure (along with other values that he has which are about equal in importance to the freedom of expression value). The next highest level of cognitive structure contains groups of attitudes which represent values that are perceived as important, but not so important as the values at the first level. This principle holds throughout the remainder of the hierarchy: the higher the group of attitudes, the more important the value. The lowest level of cognitive structure contains all of the attitudes that the individual does not perceive as related to values. The attitude objects are perceived as low in importance, and attitudes toward these objects are easily changed since they are relatively isolated and unconnected to the rest of the cognitive system.

An important point to remember is that all attitudes, whether at the top or bottom of the hierarchy, have a common structure. That is, we associate characteristics, consequences, and so forth with each attitude object, and we have at least three perceptions for each characteristic of an attitude object: *desirability, importance* to self and valued others, and the *likelihood* that the characteristic is produced by the attitude object.

We shall use the ideas developed in this section as a framework for presenting the cognitive behaviors that are discussed in the following sections. We shall consider five cognitive behaviors in terms of their relationship to interpersonal communication.

Cognitive Behavior

Cognitive Change to Affect Change

In the previous section the affective-cognitive consistency princi-ple was used to explain how favorably a given attitude object is evaluated. Consider the situation in which an individual is stimulated by another person to change some of his perceptions about what is related to an attitude object. If the *original* perceptions are consistent with the attitude, then a *change* in the perceptions will represent new perceptions that will be inconsistent with the attitude. To restore consistency the person could change the attitude so that it is consistent with the new perceptions.

For example, let us imagine that you have an extremely favorable attitude toward legalized marijuana and you believe that it is very likely that such a policy will result in four important and desirable consequences, one of which might be "less paranoia in young adults." Further, you believe that it is very unlikely that three important unde-sirable consequences (one of them might be higher rate of chromosome damage) will be caused by legalized marijuana. These perceptions, you will recall, are the cognitive components of attitude. A close friend tells you that she is not going to support legalized marijuana anymore because she has learned of convincing evidence that three bad con-sequences will happen if marijuana is legalized. Suppose that you partially accept your friend's arguments. You change your percep-tions of the three undesirable consequences from extremely improba-ble to slightly probable. If this happens, then the new perceptions of slightly probable bad things would be inconsistent with your ex-tremely favorable attitude toward legalized marijuana. To restore consistency in this example you would probably change your attitude, not all the way to extremely unfavorable, but to slightly favorable or perhaps near neutral.

This principle, that cognitive changes lead to attitude change, also applies when a person is the attitude object. Consider your friend who tried to influence your attitude about legalized marijuana. You have a very favorable attitude toward her and perceive that she has, say, seven important desirable attributes (friendly, kind, helpful, honest, intelligent, attractive, loyal), and you believe that she has only a few unimportant bad attributes (she is untidy and fears snakes). Imagine that you listen to her arguments and reject them. There would be no changes in perceptions of consequences, hence your attitude toward legalized marijuana would not change. However, your friend is also an attitude object and because of her arguments you conclude that she is gullible (an undesirable attribute) for believing such reports and is more conservative (another bad thing according to your values, let us say) than you previously believed. This leads you to change your perception of her intelligence (one of the original desirable attributes) so that you perceive a lower probability that she is intelligent. These three cognitive changes about your friend (more gullible, more conservative, less intelligent) would be inconsistent with your extremely favorable attitude toward her. The changes would lead to a less favorable attitude. Since you still perceive that she has six important desirable attributes, your attitude would not change greatly, but it would change.

This cognitive behavior therefore involves attitude toward an object controlled by desirability, importance, and likelihood perceptions of the characteristics which we associate with the attitude object. If these controlling perceptions change, then the attitude changes to be consistent with the new perceptions. Attitude change from extremely favorable to extremely unfavorable probably is relatively rare. A change from extremely favorable to quite favorable would be more typical in interpersonal influence and, although slight, could be an important change as it could significantly modify our interpersonal relations (in the case of attitude change toward a close friend).

Recent research has revealed another cognitive behavior that is closely related to what we have been discussing. It appears that a favorable attitude toward an object is controlled by perceptions of the *likely, desirable characteristics* associated with the object, while an unfavorable attitude is controlled mainly by perceptions of *likely, undesirable characteristics*.[11] That is, what is perceived as *likely* to be related to the attitude object, best explains attitude. What is perceived as *unlikely* does not seem to be very important to us in terms of how we decide to evaluate an attitude object. Research has discovered that arguments which claimed that something was likely persuaded people more than arguments about unlikely things. Also, people perceived the speaker's character less favorably when he presented arguments that claimed low likelihood. [12]

These results are somewhat parallel to Clark's research on positives and negatives in language. [13] Clark discovered that positives (e.g., *is, can, will*) in language are easier to understand when compared to negatives (e.g., *no, not, never*). Negatives in sentences result in the receiver having to use more cognitive operations to achieve understanding, hence more time is involved and a greater chance of misunderstanding. An argument that claims high likelihood would be a positive in Clark's terms while a claim that something is unlikely would be a negative. Norman Vincent Peale has praised the power of positive thinking. It may be that there is also a potency in positive speaking. You might experiment with your own messages in interpersonal communication and observe whether people respond differently when you use all positives (claims that something is related to an attitude object) as compared with the use of negatives (claims that something is not related or will not happen).

Affect Change to Cognitive Change

The second cognitive behavior is, in a way, the reverse of the previous one. At times our attitude toward an object changes, but the change is not due to someone influencing the perceptions of the things that we had associated with the attitude object. This occurs more often than we might suppose. If we have a traumatic experience with the attitude object, this could change even an extremely favorable attitude. An unusually pleasant experience could change an unfavorable attitude. Affective-cognitive consistency theory predicts that when an attitude changes because of a single strong experience, we later turn to the original cognitive components of the attitude and change them so that they are consistent with the new attitude. Thus, while the previous section dealt with the cognitive behavior of cognitive change to affect change, we shall focus in this section on the cognitive behavior of affect change to cognitive change and how it is relevant to interpersonal communication.

The prospect of receiving social approval or social disapproval from people that we value can exert a powerful influence on our interpersonal behaviors. Either type of reaction from others can be strong enough to stimulate affect to cognitive change. When a singular experience causes attitude to change, the person should then turn to the original cognitive components and realign them with the new attitude. For example, let us imagine that you have arrived recently on campus as a freshman from a small town. You have a conservative background and one of your attitudes is that you have an unfavorable attitude toward Senator Edward Kennedy. You have recently entered a circle of friends. They seem more liberal than your high school friends. However, you really like these people and want to be accepted. You have never mentioned your feelings about Kennedy to your new friends, and his name enters a conversation for the first time one evening when the conversation moves to politics. One individual says, "I sure hope Teddy changes his mind about running for president in '76; the country needs him and he would do a great job." Several other persons in the group voice extremely enthusiastic support for this position. One person asserts, "He won't get the redneck vote; but they are a minority anyway." Someone turns to you and says, "How do you feel about Teddy? Do people in your part of the country see what this man could do for the country?"

One possible reaction to this event is that you could enter a state of disbelief and quietly exit to search for new friends. However, given the circumstances created, a different reaction is likely. You would begin talking, but you probably would not express feelings about Kennedy that you would say if you were in your home town. In fact, you probably would avoid the first question and speak to the second question initially. You might say in moderate terms that some people in your home town have a few reservations about Kennedy. Finally, you would deal with the first question. You might say, "Well, I really haven't thought about the matter that much. From what I've seen he seems like he might be OK." Such a statement is not exactly raving enthusiasm, but it certainly is a distance from your unfavorable attitude. Now if you really do like this group of people and want to be accepted, then what you just said should stimulate at least a twinge of affective-cognitive inconsistency. That is, you said that he seems OK, which probably indicates a slightly favorable attitude. You do not believe that you lied; however, you previously had an extremely unfavorable attitude. The attitude was controlled by perceptions that it is likely that Kennedy has important bad characteristics and unlikely that he has good characteristics. Given these circumstances you could deal with the inconsistency in at least one of three ways. You could change your likelihood perceptions so that the good characteristics are perceived as more likely to be true for Kennedy and the bad characteristics perceived as less likely. Second, you might change your feelings about the desirability of the bad characteristics without changing the likelihood perceptions, e.g., "These things are not so bad." Third, you might change the importance of the bad characteristics, e.g., "So what, these things do not matter." Or, of course, some combination of these inconsistency reduction techniques could be employed.

One easy way to observe this cognitive behavior in interpersonal communication is to induce a person to eat some food which he says he has never tried but "just knows" that he would not like the food. Now, the individual might react to the first taste by saying that he was right, he did not like it. That would be a case of affective-cognitive consistency. The problem is that it would blow the experiment. Try another dish. If you get lucky, the person will say, "Well, that's not so bad." When this happens you have an affect to cognitive change taking place across the table from you. Ask a few questions and you should see it unfold. If he felt unfavorably toward the food before tasting it, he must have believed that the food had bad attributes and that good attributes were unlikely. Ask the person about these attributes before he tastes the food. Then, if you get the desired favorable response to the food, ask again about the attributes. You should see the person change the desirable attributes from unlikely to likely (e.g., "I didn't think that it would smell so good or be so tender") and the undesirable attributes from likely to unlikely (e.g., "I guess it really doesn't leave a sour taste in your mouth").

The Socratic Effect

Consider the classic syllogism: All men are mortal (major premise), Socrates is a man (minor premise), therefore, Socrates is mortal (conclusion). Let us suppose that you believe it is highly probable that all three statements are true, but you receive a message that argues persuasively that the minor premise is not true. If you changed your belief in the probability that the minor premise is true, would that be the total extent of your change? Or, would you change your beliefs in the probability that the major premise and conclusion are true, even though the message did not mention these premises? McGuire discovered that people make changes in beliefs that are logically related to the belief argued in a message even when the logically related beliefs are not addressed in the message.[14] He termed this phenomenon "the Socratic effect," inspired apparently by Socrates in Plato's dialogues who was able, through skillful questioning, to cause people to realize belief inconsistencies which then motivated them to change the beliefs toward greater consistency.

I discovered a different form of the Socratic effect.[15] I had people listen to a speech that opposed a guaranteed minimum annual income proposal. The speech argued that some bad consequences would be likely to happen if the proposal were adopted. Almost all of the listeners favored the proposal before hearing the speech and believed that four desirable consequences would be likely and that four undesirable consequences would be unlikely. The results revealed that when people were persuaded by the speech that claimed likely undesirable consequences, they tended to change their beliefs about the desirable consequences so that they were perceived as less likely to result from the proposal. Recall that the speech did not mention these desirable consequences; therefore, these perception changes were a type of Socratic effect. Some listeners rejected the speaker's arguments and moved to even more favorable attitudes toward the proposal. The Socratic effect for these listeners who changed away from the speaker's position was that they changed their beliefs about the unmentioned desirable consequences so that they were perceived as even more likely to happen. Overall, the change in perceptions of the unmentioned desirable consequences was a more accurate predictor of attitude change when compared with change in perceptions of undesirable consequences.

The results of this research suggest that in some communication situations the way that a listener perceives the actual arguments in a message may not explain attitude change so well as changes in perceptions of things not mentioned in the message. The perception changes that best predict attitude change seem to be the perceptions that control attitude. Earlier, we discussed research which discovered that favorable attitudes toward proposals are controlled by perceptions of desirable consequences while unfavorable attitudes are controlled by perceptions of undesirable consequences.[16] When we try to influence another person, should we attack the beliefs that control the person's attitude? That is, if a person likes a proposal should we say, "Those desirable consequences will never happen;" or if the person dislikes a proposal, "You don't have to worry, those undesirable consequences won't happen"? The research cited earlier[17] suggests that arguments that claim high likelihood would be more effective than the arguments in the previous sentence that claimed low likelihood. To change another's attitude, what do you claim will be likely? It appears that you should claim as "likely" the consequences that your receiver believes are unlikely. If you can influence your receiver to perceive that the consequences are likely to be caused by the proposal, then the desirability or undesirability of these consequences will take control of the receiver's attitude. What will happen to the other consequences that you did not mention but the receiver believed to be likely? The

Socratic effect should take care of this as your listener should experience the "pull" of affective-cognitive consistency which will motivate the person to perceive these consequences as less likely.

All of this has an interesting application in interpersonal communication where one person tries to influence another person who is very ego-involved in an issue. A person who is **ego-involved** in a proposal, for example, is extremely enthusiastic about the proposal, devotes considerable mental and perhaps physical activity to the proposal, and is very resistant to attempts to change his or her position on the proposal. We have all probably tried to influence a person who is ego-involved in an issue. Not only is it difficult to persuade such a person, but if we push too hard he becomes more firmly entrenched in his position. A crucial factor for success in this situation depends upon stimulating the ego-involved person to perceive that our position is not really that far removed from his or her position. How might this be accomplished?

Let us suppose that you have a younger brother who has a very favorable ego-involved attitude toward a group that he has recently joined. The group is devoted to saving mankind and womankind by motivating people to abandon such "base" pursuits as smoking, drinking, dancing, and making love. In addition to a concern for the procreation of the human race, you are concerned that your brother will have his bank account ripped off via a vow of poverty and eventually become disillusioned with the whole idea of helping other people. What should you do? Should you directly attack the beliefs that control his favorable attitude toward the group (that the group has desirable characteristics, attributes, goals) and directly charge that the group is a sham? The research suggests that this approach would be a bad choice of tactics. He would probably view such arguments as very removed from his own position. Ego-involvement theory terms this a *constrast effect* (where the message is perceived as more extreme than it actually is). The result would be that your brother probably would become more firmly entrenched in his position.

Instead, let us try a strategy that employs three things: the principle that high likelihood claims are more convincing than low likelihood claims, the idea that a message does not seem so extreme if it begins by agreeing with the receiver, and the Socratic effect. This attempt to change your brother's attitude will probably take some time, as one message usually does not have much impact on an ego-involved attitude.

You might begin by telling your brother that you can see why he might be interested in the group because they do seem to have some desirable goals. Then you could proceed, using neutral language, to speculate as to whether some undesirable attributes might be associated with the group (e.g., some members may be insincere about their beliefs, intending to exploit members) or whether some bad consequences might befall your brother (e.g., loss of freedom).

As time passes you might strengthen your language. However, because he is ego-involved you should not explicitly say that the group is bad. To do so might stimulate a strong defensive reaction. Our tactic should increase the chances that he will perceive your message(s) as not that removed from his own position. This perception (ego-involvement theory calls this an *assimilation effect*) is necessary to influence an ego-involved person. If he develops beliefs that bad things just might be likely to issue from the group, then these beliefs will begin to take control of his attitude. When this happens the Socratic effect will start operating and the desirable attributes of the group will be perceived as less likely. Such changes in cognitive structure will lead to a less favorable attitude. There is no guarantee that this strategy will work. But keep in mind that this situation, attempting to persuade a highly ego-involved individual, is probably the most difficult of all social influence situations.

The Habit-Family Hierarchy and Saliency

The beliefs which we have about an attitude object (e.g., a person, proposal, institution, and so forth) often differ in terms of saliency and this has some interesting implications for our interpersonal communication behavior. Let us consider **belief saliency** as the ease with which we become aware of a particular belief. Suppose that you have twenty beliefs regarding the attitude object "teaching as a career." If someone asked you, "What do you think about teaching as a career?" the question would trigger your awareness of several of the beliefs. How many of the beliefs about teaching will you become aware of? According to the research on the number of things that people typically are able to be aware of at a given time, you probably would think of no more than about five to nine beliefs.[18] Since you have twenty beliefs about teaching and you become aware of, let us say, seven of those beliefs, do the thirteen beliefs that you do not think of affect how you feel at the time about teaching as a career? Could the beliefs that you do not recall be used to change how you feel about the attitude object?

We can answer these questions by utilizing the **habit-family hierarchy** concept as applied to attitude theory.[19] Fishbein says that we learn to associate things with an attitude object. Our beliefs about the things associated with the attitude object are arranged in a hierarchy. The strongest beliefs (highest in perceived probability) are highest in the hierarchy. When asked what we think about an attitude object, we become aware first of the beliefs highest in the hierarchy. In other words, the stronger the belief, the greater the ease with which we become aware of the belief. Thus, belief saliency is a function of belief strength. Attitude toward the object is thought to be controlled almost entirely by the salient or strongest beliefs. Since at a given time it is possible to have up to nine salient beliefs about an attitude object, attitude toward the object at that time will be determined by the nature of those nine or so salient beliefs. Two points are important. First, if a nonsalient belief is moved to the salient level of the hierarchy, attitude toward the object will be affected. Second, if the perceived importance or the perceived likelihood of the belief is influenced, the saliency of the belief will be affected.

With these principles in mind let us return to our example. You become aware of seven beliefs when your friend asks about teaching as a career. Further, the beliefs are all unfavorable with respect to the attitude object: salaries are inadequate, my creativity will be restricted, discipline will be a problem, and so forth. As explained above, salient beliefs control attitude. Therefore, it would be no surprise that the feelings (your attitude) which you experience at the time regarding teaching as a career would be unfavorable. Imagine that you also have some favorable beliefs about teaching, namely, time to develop other abilities, opportunity to help people, job security, and so forth. However, these beliefs are low in your habit-family hierarchy; the perceived likelihood that these good things will happen is not high, and they are not perceived as high in importance. According to the earlier reasoning, all that your friend would have to do to get you to feel more favorably about teaching would be to make you aware of these favorable beliefs. Once these beliefs are salient they will play a part in determining how you will feel about teaching. Since the perceptions of likelihood and importance with relation to these desirable attitudes are not strong, you will only feel a bit more favorably toward teaching. When your friend mentions these favorable beliefs your reaction might be, "OK, I didn't think of those things; however, even if they should turn out to be true, they would not be that important to me. So that doesn't change my feelings much."

By simply making you aware of these beliefs your friend influences your attitude a bit. However, he wants to achieve more influence than this. So, your friend goes on to develop convincing arguments as to how the desirable consequences of teaching would be extremely likely and important to you. If you accept the arguments, then the perceived importance and likelihood of the consequences would increase and you would have moved them higher in the habit-family hierarchy. A Socratic effect could also occur, lowering the perceived importance and likelihood of the undesirable consequences. Since the desirable things moved up in saliency and the undesirable things moved down, you would feel more than just a bit greater favorability toward teaching. In the future, you would become aware of the desirable aspects of teaching more easily; i.e., you would exhibit the new hierarchy.

Let us reverse the example and imagine that you reject your friend's fervent arguments. While you are aware of the desirable consequences, your unfavorable feelings about teaching will be a little less intense. As soon as your friend gives you the opportunity you will return the desirable consequences to their original position—low in the hierarchy—and before long they will have virtually no effect on your attitude.

Even when a belief is very low in a person's habit-family hierarchy, making the belief temporarily salient for the person may affect his or her behavior. A way to observe this is to wait until someone is just about to do something that is generally considered safe. Mention the importance of a remote undesirable aspect of the act, i.e., since it is remote it is probably low in the person's habit-family hierarchy for the act. The chances are that the person will pause, not only long enough to listen to your message, but also long enough to consider whether the undesirable consequence deserves its assigned low position in the hierarchy.

Recent research suggests that the habit-family hierarchy notion is important in communication.[20] We should give more attention to this in interpersonal communication, as salient beliefs probably are major determinants of attitudes and behavior. If we become sensitive to what is salient for another person, we should better understand his or her interpersonal behavior. Also, to make another person aware of beliefs that are low in his or her hierarchy could be an effective tactic to employ in interpersonal influence.

The Motivational Potency of Values

Values were depicted in the earlier discussion on cognitive structure as important beliefs that organize attitudes and provide a framework for making decisions. Research on values suggests several implications as to how values are important in interpersonal communication.[21] We shall examine four possible applications.

Research by Rokeach indicates that if an individual is made aware of an inconsistency between his values and an attitude, the individual will change the attitude and related behavior.[22] One reason why this research is important is that the persuasion achieved was not temporary, but persisted for many months. An example will illustrate Rokeach's general technique.

Imagine that someone asks you to rank a series of eighteen values in terms of importance to you. Then you are asked how sympathetic you are to the civil rights movement. Suppose that you ranked "freedom" first and "equality" eleventh in terms of importance to you. Also, you said that you are in favor of the civil rights movement. Next, the person says to you, "Why do you say that you favor civil rights? You ranked equality eleventh. You ranked freedom first. Does this mean that you are much more interested in your own freedom than the freedom of others? Are you claiming that you favor civil rights because it is the fashionable thing to say?" How would you react to this situation? Would you change your attitude toward civil rights? How you ranked equality? Would you be more easily induced to engage in behavior which could be interpreted as sympathetic to civil rights?

Rokeach found that a situation such as this has some startlingly strong effects on the person who is made aware of value-attitude inconsistencies. When compared to a control group that was not made aware of inconsistencies, subjects who were made aware of value-attitude inconsistencies changed their ranking of equality so that it moved higher in their value hierarchies. This change was present even when the measurement was taken seventeen months after the experiment. Attitudes toward civil rights also became more favorable during this period, while the control group's attitudes did not change. Interestingly, in terms of behavior, the subjects who were made aware of inconsistencies responded more to letters from the NAACP which asked each subject to join the NAACP and submit one dollar. Subjects received the first letter three to five months after the experimental treatment.

This research suggests that causing a person to realize value-attitude inconsistencies is a particularly powerful motivational factor. We can live with some inconsistencies. However, when the inconsistency involves something that we perceive as very important, like a value, our tolerance for inconsistency is exceeded and we tend to feel compelled to make changes that will restore consistency.

Now I am not suggesting that we scurry around asking people to rank order their values and then point out how some of their attitudes are inconsistent with what they say they value. But the principle explicated above is an important one and worth keeping in mind. At times we hear an individual say things that really do not follow from the values that we think the person espouses. For instance, a friend of yours might agree with a court decision to close a movie theater in your neighborhood that shows X-rated films. Your friend has indicated on several occasions in the past that he values freedom of expression. There is an apparent inconsistency between this person's value and attitude toward the specific action of closing a particular theater. If you ask your friend about the inconsistency, you probably will stimulate some concern on his part. It is a good bet that he will try to resolve the inconsistency in some way. There are at least four possible reactions to the inconsistency which you made salient for your friend. If the value is really important, he might change the attitude toward closing the theater. Or he could lower the importance of the freedom of expression value. Or a principle could be discovered that reduces the relevancy of the value to the court's action, e.g., the "moral welfare" of the neighborhood's children supersedes other concerns on the issue. Perhaps the least likely possibility is that he could decide to tolerate the inconsistency.

A relatively direct approach to influencing people in interpersonal communication is to argue that certain values are relevant to your position on some issue. For instance, imagine that you are trying to convince a friend to join you in a venture to operate a summer day camp. You could claim that your proposal would result in you and your friend achieving satisfaction of such values as financial security, independence, helping others, pleasure, happiness, and so forth. If your friend perceives connections between the values and your idea for a summer day camp, his attitude toward the idea should become more favorable, increasing the chance that he would join you in the venture.

Some research that I have conducted indicates that at times one has to say very little in order to use values in influencing people.[23] Specifically, if someone has a favorable attitude toward a proposal that you would like to change to unfavorable, the following seems to be effective. Simply ask the person whether important values (e.g., freedom, happiness, security, and so forth) would be hindered or frustrated because of the proposal. This tactic seems to cause people to become aware of possible undesirable consequences of a proposal that they otherwise would not have realized. This realization causes attitude to become less favorable. The tactic allows you to maintain a very low profile in the influence attempt since it is necessary to say only a sentence or two. However, it is also risky as some people will not always perceive the undesirable consequences. Thus, it is necessary to have good arguments in reserve if this strategy fails.

Values also have applicability in causing people to resist persuasion. There may be times when you know that someone is going to try to influence a friend. Suppose you believe that it would be detrimental to your friend's welfare if he is influenced. How do you induce your friend to resist being influenced?

Research by Nelson suggests that if a listener is stimulated to see how his attitude is related to important values, the attitude will be less likely to change when subjected later to a strong persuasive message.[24] Imagine that you and a friend work in a store that sells stereos. Your friend is going to talk with a district manager who recruits people to sell vacuum cleaners on a door-to-door basis. You think that changing jobs would be a bad move for your friend, and you would like to increase the chance that he will not be influenced when he talks with the district manager. Nelson's research indicates that your friend will be more resistant to influence if you cause him to have salient beliefs as to how the present job results in important values being satisfied. Further, you might alert your friend to the possibility that selling vacuum cleaners could result in the frustration of such values as honesty, satisfaction, imagination, independence, and ambition.

Conclusion

A basic assumption in this paper has been that we may exercise more control over the outcomes of our interpersonal transactions if we are more sensitive to the dynamics of the other person's thinking. This focus should not be considered as unduly emphatic of the social influence dimension of interpersonal communication. Schutz maintains that in addition to interpersonal needs for inclusion and affection, one has a strong interpersonal need for control.[25] Satisfaction of the need for control entails the individual's believing that he achieves a reasonable degree of success in influencing the nature of his social universe. If the need for control is not satisfied, the result is a feeling of social alienation, powerlessness, and helplessness. Such a predispositional state is obviously uncomfortable, emotionally distressing, yet probably unnecessary if we do not forget the basic workable principles of social influence that we began learning when we were young children. At the beginning of this paper we said that the fundamental principle simply involves adapting our messages to the characteristics of the other person. An assumption was that we have been aware of the importance of adapting to the other's thinking. However, a further assumption was that although we have been aware of the matter, our understanding should be enhanced by an explanation of some of the cognitive behaviors uncovered and refined by recent research. The approach was first to present a way of conceptualizing an individual's cognitive structure. We then described five cognitive behaviors that operate within a cognitive structure, and we proceeded to discuss how these behaviors operate in interpersonal communication. An emphasis was placed on how the understanding of each cognitive behavior could enhance attempts to exercise control in interpersonal transactions.

In addition to the five cognitive behaviors presented in this paper, there are others that are important in explaining interpersonal communication behavior. Some of these are: selective perception, perceptual distortion, selective recall, need for consistency and tolerance of inconsistency, rigidity and flexibility in cognitive structures, cognitive complexity, belief centrality, ego involvement, and the functions that attitudes serve for the individual. You will probably encounter many of these constructs in detail in the more advanced courses in communication which are approached from a behavioral science orientation.[26] In the meantime, utilize the cognitive behaviors that were discussed in this paper to help you better understand people in interpersonal communication and to provide direction for adapting your ideas to others.

QUESTIONS FOR DISCUSSION

1. Explain the difference between cognitive to affect change and affect to cognitive change.
2. Select an editorial from a newspaper. What cognitive changes did the writer seem to want to achieve in receivers? What affect changes did the writer seem to want to follow from the cognitive changes?
3. Explain the similarities and differences between beliefs, attitudes, and values.
4. Select an editorial from a newspaper which seems to make use of values in the attempt to influence receivers. Are the arguments about values different from arguments about consequences such as increased taxes and inflation? How?
5. Why do people seem to be persuaded more when arguments claim that consequences are likely as compared to unlikely?

6. Give an example from your interpersonal communication experi-
    ence that could be explained by one or more of the cognitive
    behaviors discussed in this chapter.

NOTES

1. This is a common way to conceptualize an attitude. For a review of other
    conceptions see: William J. McGuire, "The Nature of Attitudes and
    Attitude Change," in Gardner Lindzey and Elliot Aronson, eds. *The
    Handbook of Social Psychology*, Sec. Ed., III (Reading, Mass.: Addison-
    Wesley, 1968), pp. 136-314.
2. For example, see: Gary Cronkhite, *Persuasion: Speech and Behavioral
    Change* (Indianapolis: Bobbs-Merrill, 1969); Erwin P. Bettinghaus, *Persua-
    sive Communication*, Sec. Ed. (New York: Holt, Rinehart and
    Winston, 1973).
3. For instance, see: Charles A. Kiesler, et al., *Attitude Change: A Critical
    Analysis of Theoretical Approaches* (New York: John Wiley, 1969); Harry C.
    Triandis, *Attitude and Attitude Change* (New York: John Wiley, 1971).
4. Two examples are: Kim Giffin and Bobby R. Patton, *Personal Communica-
    tion in Human Relations* (Columbus, Ohio: Charles E. Merrill, 1974); John
    W. Keltner, *Elements of Interpersonal Communication* (Belmont, Cal.:
    Wadsworth, 1973).
5. Cronkhite, pp. 74-91; William J. McGuire, "Theory of the Structure of
    Human Thought," in Robert P. Abelson, et al., eds. *Theories of Cognitive
    Consistency: A Sourcebook* (Chicago: Rand McNally, 1968), pp. 140-162;
    Milton Rokeach, *Beliefs, Attitudes, and Values* (San Francisco: Jossey-Bass,
    1968).
6. Milton J. Rosenberg, "A Structural Theory of Attitude Dynamics," *Public
    Opinion Quarterly*, 24 (1960), pp. 319-340; Rosenberg, "An Analysis of
    Affective-Cognitive Consistency," in eds. Rosenberg et al. *Attitude Or-
    ganization and Change* (New Haven: Yale University Press, 1960), pp.
    15-64.
7. Dominic A. Infante, "Predicting Attitude from Desirability and Likeli-
    hood Ratings of Rhetorical Propositions," *Speech Monographs*, 38 (1971),
    pp. 321-326: Infante, "Cognitive Structure as a Predictor of Post Speech
    Attitude and Attitude Change," *Speech Monographs*, 39 (1972), pp. 55-61;
    Rosenberg, "Cognitive Structure and Attitudinal Affect," *Journal of Ab-
    normal and Social Psychology*, 53 (1956), pp. 367-372.
8. Formulas and measurement techniques can be found in: Infante, "The
    Perceived Importance of Cognitive Structure Components: An Adapta-
    tion of Fishbein's Theory," *Speech Monographs*, 40 (1973), pp. 8-16.
9. Rokeach, *The Nature of Human Values* (New York: The Free Press, 1973),
    pp. 7 ff.
10. Rokeach, "A Theory of Organization and Change within Value-Attitude
    Systems," *Journal of Social Issues*, 24 (1968), pp. 13-33, esp., 18.

11. Infante, "Differential Functions of Desirable and Undesirable Consequences in Predicting Attitude and Attitude Change toward Proposals," *Speech Monographs*, 42 (1975).

12. Infante, "Differential Functions of Desirable and Undesirable Consequences." pp. 115-134.

13. Herbert H. Clark, "The Power of Positive Speaking," *Psychology Today*, 8 (1974), pp. 102, 108, 109, 111.

14. William J. McGuire, "Cognitive Consistency and Attitude Change," *Journal of Abnormal and Social Psychology*, 60 (1960), pp. 345-353.

15. Infante, "The Socratic Effect in Responses to Speeches Opposing a Proposal," *Central States Speech Journal*, 26 (1975).

16. Infante, "Differential Functions of Desirable and Undesirable Consequences." pp. 201-206.

17. Infante, "Differential Functions of Desirable and Undesirable Consequences."

18. G. A. Miller, "The Magic Number Seven, Plus or Minus Two: Some Limits on Our Capacity for Processing Information," *Psychological Review*, 62 (1956), pp. 81-97.

19. Martin Fishbein, "A Behavior Theory Approach to the Relations between Beliefs about an Object and the Attitude toward the Object," in Fishbein, ed. *Readings in Attitude Theory and Measurement* (New York: John Wiley & Sons, 1967), pp. 389-400.

20. Vernon E. Cronen and Richard L. Conville, "Belief Salience, Summation Theory, and the Attitude Construct," *Speech Monographs*, 40 (1973), pp. 17-26.

21. Rokeach, *The Nature of Human Values*.

22. Rokeach, "Long-Range Experimental Modification of Values, Attitudes, and Behavior," *American Psychologist*, 26 (1971), pp. 453-459.

23. Infante, "Persuasion by Superordinate Cues Which Influence the Saliency of Proposal-Value Relationships" (unpublished research report, Department of Communication, Queens College, CUNY, 1975).

24. Carnot E. Nelson, "Anchoring to Accepted Values as a Technique for Immunizing Beliefs Against Persuasion," *Journal of Personality and Social Psychology*, 9 (1968), pp. 329-334.

25. William C. Schutz, *FIRO: A Three Dimensional Theory of Interpersonal Behavior* (New York: Holt, Rinehart and Winston, 1958).

26. An introduction to most of these other concepts can be found in Thomas M. Steinfatt, *Human Communication: An Interpersonal Introduction*, (Indianapolis: Bobbs - Merrill, 1977) chaps. 7-10.

SIX

VARiAblES AffECTiNG THE COMMUNiCATiON SiTUATiON

Many variables affect communication interactions. Some of these variables are direct parts of the communication process such as the words used in a message, while other variables are a part of the situation in which communication occurs. The three readings that follow discuss variables that affect communication mainly through their effect on the situation.

The first reading is on the effect that the *physical distance* between two persons may have on their interactions.

16

REWARds
OTHERS pROVidE:
pROpiNQUiTY

Ellen Berscheid and Elaine Hatfield Walster

Proximity as an Intensifier of Sentiment

A frequently advanced and commonly accepted notion is that propinquity, or proximity, has a strong influence on one's friendship
choices. Stated in its simplest form, the proposition is as follows:
Other things being equal, the closer two individuals are located geographically, the more likely it is that they will be attracted to each other.
Studies demonstrating the impact of proximity of friendship choices
are so numerous that we will mention only a few.

Several investigators have collected data which indicate that students tend to develop stronger friendships with those students who
share their classes, or their dormitory or apartment building, or who sit
near them, than with those who are geographically located only
slightly farther away (Maisonneuve, Palmade, & Fourment, 1952; Willerman & Swanson, 1952; Festinger, 1953; Byrne & Buehler, 1955,
Byrne, 1961). Clerks in a large department store and members of a
bomber crew have been found to develop closer relations with those
who happen to work next to them than with co-workers a few feet
away (Gullahorn, 1952; Kipnis, 1957; Zander & Havelin, 1960).

One of the more interesting studies demonstrating the relationship between proximity and friendship choice was conducted by Festinger, Schachter, and Back (1950). These investigators examined the

Ellen Berscheid is professor of psychology at the University of Minnesota. Elaine
Walster is professor of sociology at the University of Wisconsin. From *Interpersonal
Attraction* by Berscheid and Walster, copyright © 1969, Addison-Wesley Publishing
Company. Reprinted by permission of the publisher.

development of friendships in a new housing project for married students. The housing development studied consisted of small houses arranged in U-shaped courts, such that all except the end houses faced onto a grassy area. The two end houses in each court faced onto the street. Festinger (1951) arrived at the intriguing conclusion that to a great extent architects can determine the social life of the residents of their projects. According to Festinger:

> It is a fair summary to say that the two major factors affecting the friendships which developed were (1) sheer distance between houses and (2) the direction in which a house faced. Friendships developed more frequently between next-door neighbors, less frequently between people whose houses were separated by another house, and so on. As the distance between houses increased, the number of friendships fell off so rapidly that it was rare to find a friendship between persons who lived in houses that were separated by more than four or five other houses. . . .
> There were instances in which the site plan of the project had more profound effects than merely to determine with whom one associated. Indeed, on occasion the arrangements of the houses severely limited the social life of their occupants . . . . In order to have the street appear "lived on," ten of the houses near the street had been turned so that they faced the street rather than the court area as did the other houses. This apparently small change in the direction in which a house faced had a considerable effect on the lives of the people who, by accident, happened to occupy these end houses. They had less than half as many friends in the project as did those whose houses faced the court area. The consistency of this finding left no doubt that the turning of these houses toward the street had made involuntary social isolates out of the persons who lived in them. (L. Festinger, "Architecture and Group Membership," *Journal of Social Issues*, 1 [1951], pp. 156,157.

There were still other architectural features which were found by Festinger, Schachter, and Back to have important effects on the social life of the residents. Any architectural feature which brought an individual into proximity with other residents tended to increase his popularity. It was found, for example, that the positions of the stairways enabled the residents of the apartments near the entrances and exits of the stairways to make more friends than other residents. Similarly, the position of the mailboxes in each building improved the social life of the residents of the apartment near which they were located.

Many of the studies which have demonstrated the potency of proximity upon friendship formation have important social implications. It has been found, for example, that white persons who experience increased contact with Negros become less prejudiced subsequent to that contact. This finding has been secured in such varied settings as in a meat packing plant (Palmore, 1955), a housing project (Deutsch & Collins, 1958), and in a university classroom (Mann, 1959). It is interesting that this finding, that integrated housing may produce increased racial harmony, has been the ammunition with which both integrationists and segregationists have defended their disparate points of view. Deutsch and Collins (1958), for example, concluded on the basis of these data that integrated housing should be encouraged since such integration helps eradicate racial prejudice. Segregationists, however, have concluded that since the evidence suggests that integration would lead to interracial friendships and "race mixing," segregation should be preserved at all costs.

Propinquity also has been found to be an important factor in mate selection. Several studies have demonstrated that there is an inverse relationship between the distance separating potential marriage partners and the number of marriages. One such study was conducted by Bossard (1932) who examined 5,000 marriage licenses in which one or both applicants were residents of Philadelphia. He found that twelve percent of the couples were already living at the same address at the time they applied for their license; one third of them lived within five or less blocks of each other. The percentage of marriages decreased steadily and markedly as the distance between the residences of the engaged couples increased. Corroboration of the importance of propinquity in mate selection comes from Abrams (1943), Kennedy (1943), and Katz and Hill (1958).

All of these data are compatible with the hypothesis that the less physical distance there is between two individuals, the more likely it is that they will become attracted to each other. But since these studies have focused upon friendship formation rather than "enemy formation," their findings do not disconfirm the equally plausible, but contrary, proposition that the less physical distance there is between two individuals, the more likely it is that they will dislike each other.

Evidence that close proximity to another may be likely to produce interpersonal hostility as well as interpersonal attraction comes primarily from police records, rather than from the social scientist's notebook. The Detroit Police Department's 1967 Annual Report, for example, indicated that in the majority of robberies the perpetrator was either related to or acquainted with, the victim. It is somewhat surprising to find that thieves are much more likely to rob an intimate than a stranger. It would seem that if a thief had common sense, he would be careful to steal from someone who could not easily identify him. The evidence, however, indicates that individuals are most likely to victimize those in close proximity. Perhaps those ladies who fear the intrusion of "thieving maniacs" into their homes may be able to take some comfort from the fact that the intruder is likely to be a friend.

Aggravated assault, like thievery, appears also to be directed toward intimates. According to J. Edgar Hoover, "Most aggravated assaults occur within the family unit or among neighbors and acquaintances. The victim and offender relationship as well as the very nature of the attack make this crime similar to murders" (1966,p.9). With respect to homicide, Hoover's statistics reveal that killings within the family make up almost a third of all murders. If one adds to this those which occur between "romantic lovers," the figure is even higher.

It seems logically clear, then, that distance per se does not have the strong consequences for positive attraction which the friendship-formation data suggest. While propinquity may be a necessary condition for attraction, it appears that it also may be a necessary condition for hatred.

Increased Probability of Acquiring Information

What underlies the often obtained relationship between proximity and sentiment? Obviously something is made possible, or more likely, with decreasing distance. It seems apparent that what is made possible is an increased probability of receiving information about another person and an increased probability of receiving rewards or punishments from the other. Sentiments such as liking or disliking, and especially the strong sentiments of love and hate, are not likely to be felt for people about whom we have minimal information and with whom we have had little experience. What proximity appears to allow, and what distance prevents, is an opportunity to obtain information and accumulate experience regarding the rewards or punishments we are likely to receive from the other person.

Can we conclude, then, that if we know the degree of proximity between two people, and do not have knowlede of the content of the information exchange such proximity has made possible, we cannot make a prediction concerning whether a positive sentiment or a negative sentiment will develop? There appear to be a number of factors which may make such a conclusion erroneous: It appears that there is a somewhat greater tendency for proximity to breed attraction than hostility.

Newcomb has advanced the hypothesis that proximity should produce positive rather than negative attraction. He argues that " . . .

when persons interact, the reward-punishment ratio is more often such as to be reinforcing than extinguishing . . . " (1956, p.576). Thus, he reasons that the information which proximity permits is more likely to be favorable than unfavorable and that liking, therefore, will more often result from proximity than disliking. There is little direct evidence to support this proposition. Nevertheless, Newcomb's arguments do seem plausible. Since people are to a great extent dependent upon one another for the satisfaction of their needs, it seems probable that individuals generally take care to reward others as much as possible in interaction with them. In addition, social canons of courtesy often prohibit dealing out punishments to others even when one is so inclined.

Heider's Balance Theory

There is yet another reason why close proximity with another may favor the development of positive rather than negative affect. The prediction that proximity will more often lead to liking than disliking can be derived from a number of the cognitive-consistency theories. It can perhaps be most easily derived from Heider's (1958) balance theory. The basic tenet of Heider's theory is that people strive to make their sentiment relationships harmonious with their perception of the unit relationships existent between objects.

What does Heider mean by the phrase "sentiment relationships"? A "sentiment" is simply a positive or negative attitude toward someone or something. What does Heider mean by the phrase "unit relationships"? Separate entities are said to have a unit relationship when they are perceived as belonging together. The members of a family, for example, are usually perceived of as a unit, as are a person and his clothing, and so on. In his discussion of the conditions which facilitate unit formation, Heider draws upon the principles of perceptual organization which were formulated by the Gestalt psychologists. The Gestaltists discovered that one relationship between objects which is especially likely to lead to unit formation is proximity: Objects which are close together spatially tend to be perceived as a unit. According to Heider's theory, then, if one perceives that a unit relationship with another exists (e.g., the other is in close proximity), this perception should induce a harmonious sentiment relationship (e.g., liking).

To test whether or not unit formation produced by the anticipation of interacting intimately with another would increase attraction, Darley and Berscheid (1967) led college women to expect that they were going to discuss their sexual standards and behavior with another girl, ostensibly participating in the same study. After the expectation of further interaction had been induced, each girl was given two folders. One folder was said to contain personality information about her partner, the girl with whom she would converse and exchange information. The other folder was said to contain information about another girl, who would also participate in the study but whom she would never meet. The personality information contained in both folders was designed to produce as ambiguous a picture as possible of the girl described.

Half of the subjects believed that the girl described in folder A was their "randomly selected" discussion partner; the other half believed that the girl described in folder B was their partner. Subjects were instructed to read through both folders, form a general impression of both girls, and then rate each of them along a number of dimensions, including liking.

The results of this study clearly indicated that the subjects expressed more liking for the girl who had been designated as their discussion partner than they did for the girl who was not.

This study suggests, then, that the factor of proximity, uncontaminated by the specific information which proximity often permits to be exchanged, may produce a feeling of unit formation between two people. This feeling of being in a unit relationship with another may then induce feelings of liking for that other. Knowledge that one will be in close proximity with another may result, then, in an individual's going *into* an interaction situation with increased liking for the other person prior to the actual interaction and prior to actual knowledge of possible rewards which may be obtained in the interaction.

It is interesting that the liking produced by the anticipation of being in close proximity with another may lead a person to voluntarily choose to associate with the other person, even though the original interaction which was anticipated has been canceled. Berscheid, Boye, and Darley (1968) found that even when a subject anticipated interacting with an objectively undesirable person, the attraction induced by the anticipation of close interaction caused subjects to choose voluntarily to interact with that negative person more readily than did people who had not previously anticipated association with him.

In conclusion, then, actual proximity is probably correlated with attraction (or repulsion) because proximity allows one to obtain an increased amount of information about the other person and to experience rewards or punishments from the other. There is some suggestive evidence that proximity in and of itself, apart from any information it may provide about another and apart from any rewards or punishments which the other may administer, may facilitate attraction as a by-product of the individual's desire for cognitive consistency.

QUESTIONS FOR DISCUSSION

1. The people we choose for friends and for marriage partners tend to live or work in close proximity to us. Discuss why this is true and what it implies about the variety of opinions and cultures that tend to be available to any particular person.
2. How does the variety of opinions and cultures that are available to a person affect a person's beliefs?
3. Is the affection we feel for a person likely to be greater the closer that person lives to us?
4. Does proximity tend to produce affection because of the information that people are likely to exchange when they are physically close? Discuss.

References

1. Abrams, R.H., "Residential Propinquity as a Factor in Marriage Selection," *American Sociological Review*, 8, (1943), pp. 288-294.
2. Berscheid, E., Boye, D., and Darley, J.M. "Effects of Forced Association upon Voluntary Choice to Associate," *Journal of Personality and Social Psychology*, 8, (1968), pp. 13-19.
3. Bossard, J.H.S., "Residential Propinquity as a Factor in Mate Selection," *American Journal of Sociology*, 38, (1932) pp. 219-224.
4. Byrne, D., "The Influence of Propinquity and Opportunities for Interaction on Classroom Relationships," *Human Relations*, 14, (1961), pp. 63-70.
5. Byrne, D., and Buehler, J.A., "A Note on the Influence of Propinquity upon Acquaintanceships," *Journal of Abnormal and Social Psychology*, 51, (1955), pp. 147-148.
6. Darley, J.M., and Berscheid, E., "Increased Liking as a Result of the Anticipation of Personal Contact," *Human Relations* 20, (1967), pp. 29-40.
7. Deutsch, M., and Collins, M.E., "The Effect of Public Policy in Housing Projects upon Interracial Attitudes," in eds., Eleanor Maccoby, et al., *Readings in Social Psychology*, Third Ed. (New York: Holt, Rinehart and Winston, 1958), pp. 612-623.
8. Festinger, L., "Architecture and Group Membership," *Journal of Social Issues*, 1, (1951), pp. 152-163.
9. Festinger, L., "Group Attraction and Membership," in eds., D. Cartwright and A. Zander, *Group Dynamics: Research and Theory* (New York: Harper & Row, 1953).

10. Festinger, L., Schachter, S., and Back, K., *Social Pressures in Informal Groups: A Study of Human Factors in Housing* (New York: Harper & Row, 1950).
11. Gullahorn, J., "Distance and Friendship as Factors in the Gross Interaction Matrix," *Sociometry*, 15 (1952), pp. 123-134.
12. Heider, F., *The Psychology of Interpersonal Relations* (New York: Wiley, 1958).
13. Hoover, J.E., "Crime in the United States," *Uniform Crime Reports*, (Washington, D.C.: U.S. Dept. of Justice, August, 1966).
14. Kennedy, R., "Premarital Residential Propinquity," *American Journal of Sociology*, 48, (1943), pp. 580-584.
15. Katz, A.M., and Hill, R., "Residential Propinquity and Marital Selection: A Review of Theory, Method, and Fact," *Journal of Marriage and the Family*, 20, (1958), pp. 327-335.
16. Kipnis, D.M., "Interaction Between Members of Bomber Crews as a Determinant of Sociometric Choice," *Human Relations*, 10, (1957), pp. 263-270.
17. Maisonneuve, J., Palmade, G., and Fourment C., "Selective Choices and Propinquity," *Sociometry*, 15, (1952), pp. 135-140.
18. Mann, J.H., "The Effect of Interracial Contact on Sociometric Choices and Perceptions," *Journal of Social Psychology*, 50, (1959), pp. 143-152.
19. Newcomb, T.M., "The Prediction of Interpersonal Attraction," *American Psychologist*, 11, (1956), pp. 575-586.
20. Palmore, E.B., "The Introduction of Negroes into White Departments," *Human Organization*, 14, (1955), pp. 27-28.
21. Willerman, B., and Swanson, L., "An Ecological Determinant of Differential Amounts of Sociometric Choices Within College Sororities," *Sociometry*, 15, (1952), pp. 326-329.
22. Zander, A., and Havelin, A., "Social Comparison and Interpersonal Attraction," *Human Relations*, 13, (1960), pp. 21-32.

Proximity is one variable that affects whom people will interact with and how the outcomes of that interaction will be experienced. *Familiarity* is another such variable. Its effects are discussed in the following article by David Stang and Rick Crandall. Do you prefer to be around familiar people, places, and things, or are you happier when meeting new people in unfamiliar surroundings? While individuals differ to some extent in their preferences, Stang and Crandall discuss the variables that operate across individuals in influencing the effects of novelty and familiarity.

17

fAMiliARiTy
ANd likiNq

David J. Stang and Rick Crandall

Predicting your preferences is big time business in America. What you like is important in many ways. During elections your preferences are measured with votes. In daily life, your dollars spent on one product instead of another are important consumer "votes." When people stop buying the latest new cars, Detroit must scramble to produce a car they will like enough to buy. On a more personal level, whom you like and who likes you is very important.

Because people are so complex, we often assume that what or whom they like can only be predicted by taking dozens of factors into account. This paper describes some effects of *familiarity*, one simple factor which may often account for preferences. We don't pretend to account for all preferences with such a simple variable as familiarity. But we do want to show the amazing variety of preferences that seem to be influenced by this factor. Perhaps the more you think about this explanation, the more you'll like it!

How familiar something or someone is and whether or not this object is present can have strong effects on your preferences. Common sense and popular folklore speak about this effect. Old sayings like "out of sight, out of mind" and song lyrics like "to know, know, know him is to love, love, love him" imply that familiarity and contact lead to liking. However, we have sayings like "familiarity breeds contempt" and "absence makes the heart grow fonder" and advertising exhorting us to buy products because they are "new." This implies

David J. Stang is an administrative officer for the American Psychological Association. Rick Crandall is assistant professor of psychology at the University of Illinois. Their article was prepared especially for this book.

that familiarity and contact lead to negative feelings and that novel things are liked more than the familiar. A great deal of research has been done to determine the effects of familiarity and contact on preferences. As common sense suggests, the results show that sometimes familiarity leads to liking and sometimes it leads to disliking. Looking at several examples of each effect will help us understand the overall pattern.

Cases Where Familiarity Leads to Liking

Contact between people has often been strongly related to positive interpersonal attraction. It has been found that people are most likely to marry others who live or work near them, even though the number of persons who do live or work nearby is extremely small compared to the number who don't live or work nearby. (Bossard, 1932; Schnepp and Roberts, 1953.) For any single similar finding, there are other explanations. For instance, people are more likely to marry others of similar socioeconomic status and persons who live close to each other are usually of similar socioeconomic status. However, other studies show that contact alone can lead to liking.

Festinger, Schachter, and Back (1950) found that within one residence building, those who happened to live near stairways and mailboxes had more friends within the building than those who lived just a few doors away. In "experiments" where students are randomly assigned seats or dormitory rooms, they are more likely to become friends with those who sit or room near them (Byrne and Buehler, 1955; Segal, 1974).

Interpersonal contact caused by incidental factors like where one lives or works generally leads to increased liking. Of course contact with people does not always lead to friendship. For instance, Festinger (1951) reported that in a housing project where residents felt they had been forced to live, "Many residents . . . had not expected the type of person who lived [there] . . . . There was a surprisingly great amount of hostility expressed toward neighbors in the project (p. 161)." And Hessler, et al. (1971) suggests that when people experience forced social contact, physical and mental stress may be increased.

Other general areas where familiarity usually leads to liking involve attitude change, advertising or elections. Advertisers have long been interested in the ability of repeated ads to create positive attitudes about their products (Strong, 1914). Repetition of an attitude message increases its reception (Cromwell & Kunkel, 1952). And this familiarity often leads to changes in attitude, especially when the messages vary slightly (Wilson and Miller, 1968; McCullough and Ostrom, 1974). Familiarity is also likely to cause attitude change when the source is credible and the argument strong (Weiss, 1969) and when the argument is sufficiently complex that it can't be fully understood in a single exposure. At the end of the paper, other factors will be discussed that can reduce attitude change from repeated messages, particularly in the case of advertisements.

Elections represent another area where familiarity can have dramatic, positive effects. While we do not like to believe that election outcomes are determined by factors so simple as the number of campaign posters or the total minutes of TV commercials, evidence suggests that familiarity has a strong effect on our voting preferences. In several field studies, we have found that candidates for student government who win usually have had the most campaign posters around campus. In a controlled field experiment where poster frequency was experimentally manipulated, "candidates" with the most posters received the most "votes" (Wandersman, Schaffner, and Stang, 1975). It is well-known political wisdom that the incumbent has an advantage partly because he is better known than challengers. The recent election victories of people who are well known outside of politics (such as entertainers) also suggests that the familiarity of a candidate can be an important variable, a fact long recognized by politicians.

Cases Where Novelty Increases Attractiveness

Considerable evidence has shown that people can prefer the novel and unusual to the familiar (Cantor, 1972; Berlyne, 1970). Many factors can affect whether something is liked less as it becomes more familiar, including complexity, the exposure context, and how much the object is liked initially. However, the most obvious factor is general boredom. Many theories suggest that we like things that give us an intermediate level of stimulation (Maddi, 1968). If something is very familiar it may become boring and negative while new things often capture our interest and attention.

It may be true that when we are bored and seeking stimulation, we like new people or things. However, we do not always like things that attract our attention. Novel situations can attract our attention while being threatening or unpleasant. Thus, the amount of attention we pay to something cannot be assumed to measure our liking for it (Harrison, 1968).

An interesting case where novelty seems to play a strong role is in sexual arousal. Novel persons of the opposite sex may be more sexually arousing than familiar persons, but the available evidence is largely anecdotal. If you are married or living with someone, you may remember that your first few days of sexual contact with your "spouse" were much more active than your current level. In sexual fantasies, novel persons or activities are often involved. *Playboy*, *Playgirl* and similar magazines provide a variety of sexual stimuli. Presumably sales would drop if only one person appeared in an issue or if everyone appeared in the same pose or setting.

The role of novelty in sexual behavior may differ for males and females. For male rats, novel females cause more arousal than familiar females, and other novel stimuli in the situation such as flashing lights or tones will also increase sexual activity (Fisher, 1962; Krames, 1970; Zucker and Wade, 1968). Baron, Byrne and Griffitt (1974 pp. 481-482) have reviewed some of the evidence on the effects of novelty on sexual arousal. They suggest that females may show a preference for familiar partners and males for novel partners. Studies of mate-swapping suggest that the husband usually initiates the idea and that "boredom" is often given as a reason. And most individuals report engaging in more sexual acts and having more orgasms at mate-swapping parties than at home, although there are several other good explanations for this.

Cases Where Familiarity Leads Both to Positive and Negative Effects

Laboratory studies, where participants rate pictures of other persons, it is usually found that the more a picture is seen, the more the person is liked (Zajonc, 1968). Exposing individuals to real people during an experiment often increases liking. (Brockner, 1974; Saegert, Swap and Zajonc, 1973.) Unpublished data collected by Matz and Crandall found that people agreed to help those they had previously met more than they agreed to help those they had not seen. Other studies have found that familiarity increases cooperative behavior and decreases aggression in experimental settings (Harrison and McClintock, 1965; Silverman, 1971).

Other laboratory results however, suggest that initial attitudes and the exposure context may also be important. Some evidence has shown that things initially liked are better liked as they become familiar, but that things initially disliked may be disliked more as they become familiar (Brickman, Redfield, Harrison and Crandall, 1972; Tesser and Conlee, in press). Perlman and Oskamp (1971) found that repeatedly exposing pictures of blacks and whites in positive settings (dressed as a clergyman or white -collar worker) resulted in increased liking for the individuals. However, when pictures of the same persons in negative settings (dressed as a prisoner or janitor) were repeatedly exposed, the individuals were liked less. One prediction from some of the findings discussed here is that contact between different ethnic, national or racial groups *can* lead to increased liking and reduced prejudice or discrimination. However, contact often results in diminished liking (Amir, 1969; Salter and Teger, 1972). Amir's (1969) analysis seems correct: when the context of contact is negative, repeated exposure may result in greater dislike. This can be the case when the minority group is of lower status, when the interaction is competitive rather than cooperative or when the social climate does not favor intergroup contact. Data cited earlier from the housing studies support this analysis. The authors strongly favor integration because, historically, "separate" has meant "unequal." However, if contact is to have positive results, special care must be taken that the conditions of contact are favorable to the development of positive attitudes for all parties.

Two related areas where the effects of familiarity have been of great interest are advertising and music. The relevance of familiarity for advertising is obvious and was touched on in the section on attitudes. Generally speaking, exposure to advertisements increases the learning of the message. Advertisers assume that a new ad has appeal. As it becomes more familiar it increases "learning" of the product. Eventually, the ad becomes boring and loses impact. Greenberg and Sutton (1973) discuss some of these processes, and detailed discussions of the general issues can be found in the *Handbook of Communication* (Pool et al., 1973). The time and type of exposure is one important factor (Strong 1914; McClure and Patterson, 1974). For instance, McClure and Patterson concluded that TV news coverage of political campaigns has little effect on voter belief but that TV political ads have a great effect.

The case for popular music seems quite similar to that for ads, elections, and attitude change in general. Feelings about popular music seem to be strongly influenced by familiarity. You may have some initial feelings about a song when you first hear it; however, you are likely to have neutral feelings immediately. As you hear the song again, you may begin to learn the words or melody. Learning more about the song may give you reasons to like it (you agree with the message, like the group, and so forth). If you had a strong initial reaction to the song or associated it with a very pleasant or unpleasant event (such as your last date), increased familiarity might work to intensify your original feelings about the song.

After you have heard the song many times you will probably grow tired of it, and if you are forced to keep listening you may come to dislike it. When the song becomes a golden oldie, you may again enjoy it. We might say that when familiarity breeds contempt, absence makes the heart grow fonder.

Some Possible Effects of Familiarity You May Not Have Considered

It is well known that we tend to like those who are similar to ourselves in interests, values, and backgrounds (Baron, Byrne and Griffitt, 1974). One reason why this may be true is that similar persons are familiar persons. If you are similar to me, I may be able to understand you better since I know lots of things about myself. Feeling that I know more about you may make you more predictable or allow me to relax more. Familiarity may not be a sufficient explanation for the effects of similarity on attraction, but it is beginning to receive attention (Brickman, Meyer and Fredd, in press; Moreland, 1975).

Extreme instances of dissimilarity and unfamiliarity involves those with obvious physical handicaps, speech impediments, or strange behavior. Most persons feel uncomfortable or upset by such "unusual" ones. This may stem largely from unfamiliarity. Once we know more about an unusual type of person, we may become more comfortable and tolerant. Unfortunately, at the moment unusual persons are still shunned or locked away. Thomas Szasz in The Manufacture of Madness (1970) presents a disturbing picture of how abnormal human beings have been locked away, or worse, for the crime of being different. From children's stories about Rudolf the Rednosed Reindeer and the ugly duckling we learn that deviance is punished, and we can see this in society's reactions to deviants such as lepers, witches, "draft dodgers," and "closet queens." Schachter (1951) and recent work on similarity have shown that those with differing opinions can be ignored and rejected if they do not come to agree with the group. Some of the rejection of minority racial and ethnic groups discussed earlier may also be caused by their unfamiliarity. Of course, you and your friends don't demand of each other complete conformity. But if you think about it, you will see that you do have many subtle standards and rules that must be complied with. And standards only tend to change as new codes of behavior become familiar and acceptable.

SUMMARY

Exposure (familiarity) seems to be strongly related to attraction in interpersonal situations, but its effects are fairly complex. We seem to find novelty both interesting and frightening. As persons and things become familiar we like them more, especially if we liked them initially. If we become bored, familiar objects lose some of their appeal, which may be regained after a brief absence. The nature of information received from the stimulus, the exposure context, and our initial attitudes, may have additional effects on our liking for the familiar and the novel.

You may want to consider how you can use exposure to benefit yourself. Exposing yourself (modestly!) to teachers, roommates, and the opposite sex may cause them to like you. Their familiarity with you may also allow you to be judged and liked on your less superficial merits. When dealing with strangers it may also be constructive to remember that if you give the other the benefit of the doubt while you become more familiar with the other, considerable unpleasantness, based on little more than novelty, might be avoided.

QUESTIONS FOR DISCUSSION

1. Under what conditions does *familiarity* lead to liking?
2. When does *novelty* lead to liking?
3. How is familiarity related to proximity?
4. How are your interactions with different persons potentially affected by how familiar you are with them?

References

1. Amir, Y., "Contact Hypothesis in Ethnic Relations," *Psychological Bulletin, 71* (5) (1969), pp.319-341.
2. Baron, R.A., Byrne, D., and Griffitt, W., *Social Psychology* (Boston: Allyn and Bacon, 1974).
3. Berlyne, D.E., "Novelty, Complexity, and Hedonic Value," *Perception and Psychophysics, 8* (1970), pp. 279-286.
4. Bossard, J.H.S., "Residential Propinquity as a Factor in Marriage Selection," *American Journal of Sociology, 38* (1932), pp.219-224.
5. Brickman, P., Meyer, P., and Fredd, S., "Effects of Varying Exposure to Another Person with Familiar or Unfamiliar Thought Processes," *Journal of Experimental Social Psychology* (in press).

6. Brickman, P., et al., "Drive and Predisposition as Factors in the Attitudinal Effects of Mere Exposure," *Journal of Experimental Social Psychology, 8* (1972), pp.31-44.

7. Brockner, J., "The Effects of Repeated Exposure and Attitudinal Similarity on Self-Disclosure and Interpersonal Attraction," unpublished master's thesis, Tufts University, June, 1974.

8. Byrne, D., and Buehler, J.A., "A Note on the Influence of Propinquity upon Acquaintanceship," *Journal of Abnormal and Social Psychology, 51* (1955), pp.147-148.

9. Cantor, G., "Effects of Familiarization on Children's Ratings of Pictures of Whites and Blacks," *Child Development, 43* (1972), pp. 1219-1229.

10. Cromwell, H., and Kunkel, R., "An Experimental Study of the Effects on the Attitude of Listeners of Repeating the Same Oral Propaganda," *Journal of Social Psychology, 35* (1952), pp.175-184.

11. Festinger, L., "Architecture and Group Membership," *Journal of Social Issues, 7* (1951), pp.152-163.

12. Festinger, L., Schachter, S., and Back, K., *Social Pressures in Informal Groups: A Study of a Housing Community* (New York: Harper and Row, 1950).

13. Fisher, A., "Effects of Stimulus Variation on Sexual Satiation in the Male Rat," *Journal of Comparative and Physiological Psychology, 55* (4), (1962), pp.614-620.

14. Greenberg, A., and Sutton, C., "Television Commercial Wearout," *Journal of Advertising Research, 13* (1973), pp.47-54.

15. Harrison, A.A., "Response Competition, Frequency, Exploration Behavior and Liking," *Journal of Personality and Social Psychology, 9* (1968) pp.363-368.

16. Harrison, A.A. and McClintock, C.G., "Previous Experience Within the Dyad and Cooperative Game Behavior," *Journal of Personality and Social Psychology, 1* (1965), pp.671-675.

17. Hessler, R.M., et al., "Demographic Context, Social Interaction, and Perceived Health Status: Excedrin Headache #1," *Journal of Health and Social Behavior, 12* (1971), pp. 191-199.

18. Krames, L., "Sexual Responses of Polygamous Female and Monogamous Male Rats to Novel Partners After Sexual Cessation." Unpublished manuscript, University of Toronto, Erindale College, July, 1970.

19. Maddi, S.R., "Meaning, Novelty, and Affect." *Journal of Personality and Social Psychology, 9* (2, pt.2), (1968), pp.28-29.

20. McClure, R.D. and Patterson, T.E., "Television News and Political Advertising: The Impact of Exposure on Voter Beliefs," *Communication Research, 1* (1974), pp. 3-31.

21. McCullough, J.L., and Ostrom, T.M., "Repetition of Highly Similar Messages and Attitude Change," *Journal of Applied Psychology, 59* (1974), pp.395-397.

22. Moreland, R.L., "Familiarity, Similarity and Interpersonal Attraction." University of Michigan, 1975.

23. Perlman, D., and Oskamp, S., " The Effects of Picture Content and Exposure Frequency on Evaluations of Negroes and Whites," *Journal of Experimental Social Psychology, 7* (1971) pp.503-514.

24. Pool, I., et al., eds. *Handbook of Communication.* (Chicago: Rand McNally, 1973).

25. Saegert, S., Swap, W., and Zajone, R.B., "Exposure, Context, and Interpersonal Attraction," *Journal of Personality and Social Psychology, 25* (1973), pp.234-242.

26. Salter, C.A. and Teger, A.I., "Change in Attitudes Toward Other Nations as a Function of the Type of International Contact." Paper presented at the annual meeting of the Eastern Psychological Association, 1972.

27. Schachter, S., "Deviation, Rejection and Communication," *Journal of Abnormal and Social Psychology, 46* (1951), pp.190-207.

28. Schnepp, G.J. and Roberts, L.A., "Residential Propinquity and Mate Selection on a Parish Basis," *American Journal of Sociology, 58* (1953), pp.45-50.

29. Segal, M.W., "Alphabet and Attraction: An Unobtrusive Measure of the Effect of Propinquity in a Field Setting," *Journal of Personality and Social Psychology, 30* (1974), pp.654-657.

30. Silverman, W., "The Effects of Social Contact, Provocation, and Sex of Opponent upon Instrumental Aggression," *Journal of Experimental Research in Personality, 5* (1971), pp.310-316.

31. Strong, E.K., Jr., "The Effect of Size of Advertisements and Frequency of their Presentation," *Psychological Review, 21* (1914), pp.136-152.

32. Szasz, T., *The Manufacture of Madness* (New York: Harper and Row, 1970).

33. Tesser, A., and Conlee, M.C., "Some Effects of Time and Thought on Attitude Polarization," *Journal of Personality and Social Psychology.* In press.

34. Wandersman, A., Schaffner, P., and Stang, D.J., "An Extension of the Attitudinal Effects of Exposure to Voting Behavior." Unpublished manuscript, 1975.

35. Weiss, R.F., "Repetition of Persuasion," *Psychological Reports, 25* (1969), pp.669-670.

36. Wilson, W., and Miller, H., "Repitition, Order of Presentation and Timing of Arguments as Determinants of Opinion Change," *Journal of Personality and Social Psychology, 9* (1968), pp.184-188.

37. Zajonc, R.B., "Attitudinal Effects of Mere Exposure," *Journal of Personality and Social Psychology, 9* (2, pt. 2) (1968), pp.1-27

38. Zucker, I. and Wade, G., "Sexual Preferences of Male Rats," *Journal of Comparative and Physiological Psychology, 66*(3) (1968), pp.816-819.

The following article was written especially for administrators and businessmen, but its content is relevant to many situations in which the people who are interacting are from different cultural backgrounds. Hall and Whyte try to make us aware of the different interpretations that will be placed on the uses of time, space, and other nonverbal variables by the members of different cultures. Notice that the reference to former President Nixon refers to his vice-presidential trip to Latin America during the 1950s when his car was attacked by a mob.

18

iNTERCULTURAL COMMUNICATION

Edward T. Hall and William Foote Whyte

How can anthropological knowledge help the man of action in dealing with people of another culture? We shall seek to answer that question by examining the process of intercultural communication.

Anthropologists have long claimed that a knowledge of culture is valuable to the administrator. More and more people in business and government are willing to take this claim seriously, but they ask that we put culture to them in terms they can understand and act upon.

When the layman thinks of culture, he is likely to think in terms of (1) the way people dress, (2) the beliefs they hold, and (3) the customs they practice—with an accent upon the esoteric. Without undertaking any comprehensive definition, we can concede that all three are aspects of culture, and yet point out that they do not get us very far, either theoretically or practically.

Dress is misleading, if we assume that differences in dress indicate differences in belief and behavior. If that were the case, then we should expect to find people dressed like ourselves to be thinking and acting like ourselves. While there are still peoples wearing "colorful" apparel quite different from ours, we find in many industrializing societies that the people with whom we deal dress much as we do—and yet think and act quite differently.

Knowledge of beliefs may leave us up in the air because the connections between beliefs and behavior are seldom obvious. In the case of religious beliefs, we may know, for example, that the Moham-

Edward T. Hall is professor of anthropology at Northwestern University.
From *Human Organization* 19, 1, 1960. Reproduced by permission of the Society for Applied Anthropology.

medan must pray to Allah a certain number of times a day and that therefore the working day must provide for praying time. This is important, to be sure, but the point is so obvious that it is unlikely to be overlooked by anyone. The administrator must also grasp the less dramatic aspects of everyday behavior, and here a knowledge of beliefs is a very imperfect guide.

Customs provide more guidance, providing we do not limit ourselves to the esoteric and also search for the pattern of behavior into which a given custom fits. The anthropologist, in dealing with customary behavior, is not content with identifying individual items. To him, these items are not miscellaneous. They have meaning only as they are fitted together into a pattern.

But even assuming that the pattern can be communicated to the administrator, there is still something important lacking. The pattern shows how the people act—when among themselves. The administrator is not directly concerned with that situation. Whatever background information he has, he needs to interpret to himself how the people act *in relation to himself*. He is dealing with a cross-cultural situation. The link between the two cultures is provided by acts of communication between the administrator, representing one culture, and people representing another. If communication is effective, then understanding grows with collaborative action. If communication is faulty, then no book knowledge of culture can assure effective action.

This is not to devalue the knowledge of culture that can be provided by the anthropologist. It is only to suggest that the point of implementation of the knowledge must be in the communication process. Let us therefore examine the process of intercultural communication. By so doing we can accomplish two things: (a) broaden knowledge of ourselves by revealing some of our own unconscious communicative acts; (b) clear away heretofore almost insurmountable obstacles to understanding in the cross-cultural process. We also learn that communication, as it is used here, goes far beyond words and includes many other acts upon which judgments are based of what is transpiring and from which we draw conclusions as to what has occurred in the past.

Culture affects communication in various ways. It determines the time and timing of interpersonal events, the places where it is appropriate to discuss particular topics, the physical distance separating one speaker from another, the tone of voice that is appropriate to the subject matter. Culture, in this sense, delineates the amount and type of physical contact, if any, which convention permits or demands, and the intensity of emotion which goes with it. Culture includes the relationship of *what is said to what is meant*—as when "no" means "maybe" and "tomorrow" means "never." Culture, too, determines whether a given matter—say, a business contract—should be initially discussed between two persons or hacked out in a day-long conference which includes four or five senior officials from each side, with perhaps an assist from the little man who brings in the coffee.

These are important matters which the businessman who hopes to trade abroad ignores at his peril. They are also elusive, for every man takes his own culture for granted. Even a well informed national of another country is hard put to explain why, in his own land, the custom is thus-and-so rather than so-and-thus; as hard put, indeed, as you would probably be if asked what is the "rule" which governs the precise time in a relationship that you begin using another man's first name. One "just knows." In other words , you do not know and cannot explain satisfactorily because you learn this sort of thing unconsciously in your upbringing, in your culture, and you take such knowledge for granted. Yet the impact of culture on communication can be observed and the lessons taught.

Since the most obvious form of communication is by language, we will first consider words, meanings, voice tones, emotions, and physical contact; then take up, in turn, the cultural impact of time, place, and social class relations on business situations in various lands. Finally, we will suggest what the individual administrator may do to increase his effectiveness abroad, and what students of culture may do to advance this application of anthropology.

Beyond Language

Americans are often accused of not being very good at language, or at least not very much interested in learning foreign languages. There is little evidence that any people are inherently "better" at languages than any other, given the opportunity and incentive to learn. The West and Central European who has since childhood been in daily contact with two or three languages learns to speak them all, and frequently to read and write them as well. Under similar conditions, American children do the same. Indeed, a not uncommon sight on the backroads of Western Europe is a mute, red-faced American military family lost on a Sunday drive while the youngest child, barely able to lisp his own English, leans from the window to interpret the directions of some gnarled farmer whose dialect is largely unintelligible to most of his own countrymen.

We should not underestimate the damage our lack of language

facility as a nation has done to our relations all over the world. Obviously, if you cannot speak a man's language, you are terribly handicapped in communicating with him.

But languages can be learned and yet most, if not all, of the disabling errors described in this article could still be made. Vocabulary, grammar, even verbal facility are not enough. Unless a man understands the subtle cues that are implicit in language, tone, gestures, and expression, he will not only consistently misinterpret what is said to him, but he may offend irretrievably without knowing how or why.

Do They Mean What They Say?

Can't you believe what a man says? We all recognize that the basic honesty of the speaker is involved. What we often fail to recognize, however, is that the question involves cultural influences that have nothing to do with the honesty or dependability of the individual.

In the United States we put a premium on direct expression. The "good" American is supposed to say what he means and to mean what he says. If, on important matters, we discover that someone spoke deviously or evasively, we would be inclined to regard him thereafter as unreliable if not out-and-out dishonest.

In some other cultures, the words and their meanings do not have such a direct connection. People may be more concerned with the emotional context of the situation than with the meaning of particular words. This leads them to give an agreeable and pleasant answer to a question when a literal, factual answer might be unpleasant or embarrassing.

This situation is not unknown in our culture, of course. How many times have you muttered your delighted appreciation for a boring evening? We term this simple politeness and understand each other perfectly.

On the other hand, analogous "polite" behavior on a matter of factory production would be incomprehensible. An American businessman would be most unlikely to question another businessman's word if he were technically qualified and said that his plant could produce 1,000 gross of widgets a month. We are "taught" that it is none of our business to inquire too deeply into the details of his production system. This would be prying and might be considered an attempt to steal his operational plans.

Yet this cultural pattern has trapped many an American into believing that when a Japanese manufacturer answered a direct question with the reply that he could produce 1,000 gross of widgets, he meant what he said. If the American had been escorted through the factory and saw quite clearly that its capacity was, at the most, perhaps 500 gross of widgets per month, he would be likely to say to himself:

> Well, this fellow probably has a brother-in-law who has a factory who can make up the difference. He isn't telling the whole story because he's afraid I might try to make a better deal with the brother-in-law. Besides, what business is it of mine, so long as he meets the schedule?

The cables begin to burn after the American returns home and only 500 gross of widgets arrive each month.

What the American did not know was that in Japanese culture one avoids the direct question unless the questioner is absolutely certain that the answer will not embarrass the Japanese businessman in any way whatsoever. In Japan for one to admit being unable to perform a given operation or measure up to a given standard means a bitter loss of face. Given a foreigner who is so stupid, ignorant, or insensitive as to ask an embarrassing question, the Japanese is likely to choose what appears to him the lesser of two evils.

Americans caught in this cross-cultural communications trap are apt to feel doubly deceived because the Japanese manufacturer may well be an established and respected member of the business community.

Excitable People?

Man communicates not by words alone. His tone of voice, his facial expressions, his gestures all contribute to the infinitely varied calculus of meaning. But the confusion of tongues is more than matched by the confusion of gesture and other culture cues. One man's nod is another man's negative. Each culture has its own rich array of meaningful signs, symbols, gestures, emotional connotations, historical references, traditional responses, and—equally significant—pointed silences. These have been built up over the millennia as (who can say?) snarls, growls, and love murmurs gathered meaning and dignity with long use, to end up perhaps as the worn coinage of trite expression.

Consider the Anglo-Saxon tradition of preserving one's calm. The American is taught by his culture to suppress his feelings. He is conditioned to regard emotion as generally bad (except in weak women who can't help themselves) and a stern self-control as good.

The more important a matter, the more solemn and outwardly dispassionate he is likely to be. A cool head, granite visage, dispassionate logic—it is no accident that the Western story hero consistently displays these characteristics.

In the Middle East it is otherwise. From childhood, the Arab is permitted, even encouraged, to express his feelings without inhibition. Grown men can weep, shout, gesture expressively and violently, jump up and down—and be admired as sincere.

The modulated, controlled Anglo-Saxon is likely to be regarded with suspicion—he must be hiding something, practicing to deceive.

The exuberant and emotional Arab is likely to disturb the Anglo-Saxon, cause him to writhe inwardly with embarrassment—for isn't this childish behavior? And aren't things getting rather out of hand?

Then, again, there is the matter of how loudly one should talk.

In the Arab world, in discussions among equals, the men attain a decibel level that would be considered aggressive, objectionable, and obnoxious in the United States. Loudness connotes strength and sincerity among Arabs; a soft tone implies weakness, deviousness. This is so "right" in the Arab culture that several Arabs have told us they discounted anything heard over the "Voice of America" because the signal was so weak!

Personal status modulates voice tone, however, even in Arab society. The Saudi Arab shows respect to his superior—to a sheik, say—by lowering his voice and mumbling. The affluent American may also be addressed in this fashion, making almost impossible an already difficult situation. Since in the American culture one unconsciously "asks" another to raise his voice by raising one's own, the American speaks louder. This lowers the Arab's tone more and increases the mumble. This triggers a shouting response in the American—which cues the Arab into a frightened "I'm not being respectful enough" tone well below audibility.

They are not likely to part with much respect for each other.

To Touch or Not to Touch?

How much physical contact should appropriately accompany social or business conversation?

In the United States we discourage physical contact, particularly between adult males. The most common physical contact is the handshake and, compared to Europeans, we use it sparingly.

The handshake is the most detached and impersonal form of greeting or farewell in Latin America. Somewhat more friendly is the left hand placed on another man's shoulder during a handshake. Definitely more intimate and warm is the *"doble abrazo"* in which two men embrace by placing their arms around each other's shoulders.

These are not difficult conventions to live with, particularly since the North American can easily permit the Latin American to take the initiative in any form of contact more intimate than the handshake. Far more difficult for the North American to learn to live with confortably are the less stylized forms of physical contact such as the hand on one's arm during conversation. To the North American this is edging toward what in his culture is an uncomfortable something—possibly sexual—which inhibits his own communication.

Yet there are cultures which restrict physical contact far more than we do. An American at a cocktail party in Java tripped over the invisible cultural ropes which mark the boundaries of acceptable behavior. He was seeking to develop a business relationship with a prominent Javanese and seemed to be doing very well. Yet, when the cocktail party ended, so apparently did a promising beginning. For the North American spent nearly six months trying to arrange a second meeting. He finally learned, through pitying intermediaries, that at the cocktail party he had momentarily placed his arm on the shoulder of the Javanese—and in the presence of other people. Humiliating! Almost unpardonable in traditional Javanese etiquette.

In this particular case, the unwitting breach was mended by a graceful apology. It is worth noting, however, that a truly cordial business relationship never did develop.

The Five Dimensions of Time

If we peel away a few layers of cultural clothing, we begin to reach almost totally unconscious reactions. Our ideas of time, for example, are deeply instilled in us when we are children. If they are contradicted by another's behavior, we react with anger, not knowing exactly why. For the businessman, five important temporal concepts are: Appointment time, discussion time, acquaintance time, visiting time, and time schedules.

Anyone who has traveled abroad or dealt at all extensively with nonAmericans learns that punctuality is variously interpreted. It is one thing to recognize this with the mind; to adjust to a different kind of *appointment time* is quite another.

In Latin America, you should expect to spend hours waiting in outer offices. If you bring your American interpretation of what constitutes punctuality to a Latin American office, you will fray your temper and elevate your blood pressure. For a 45-minute wait is not unusual—no more unusual than a five-minute wait would be in the United States. No insult is intended, no arbitrary pecking order is being established. If, in the United States, you would not be outraged by a five-minute wait, you should not be outraged by the Latin-American's 45-minute delay in seeing you. The time pie is differently cut, that's all.

Further, the Latin American doesn't usually schedule individual appointments to the exclusion of other appointments. The informal clock of his upbringing ticks more slowly and he rather enjoys seeing several people on different matters at the same time. The three-ring circus atmosphere which results, if interpreted in the American's scale of time and propriety, seems to signal him to go away, to tell him that he is not being properly treated, to indicate that his dignity is under attack. Not so. The clock on the wall may look the same but it tells a different sort of time.

The cultural error may be compounded by a further miscalculation. In the United States, a consistently tardy man is likely to be considered undependable, and by our cultural clock this is a reasonable conclusion. For you to judge a Latin American by your scale of time values is to risk a major error.

Suppose you have waited forty-five minutes and there is a man in his office, by some miracle alone in the room with you. Do you now get down to business and stop "wasting time"?

If you are not forewarned by experience or a friendly advisor, you may try to do this. And it would usually be a mistake. For, in the American culture, *discussion* is a means to an end: the deal. You try to make your point quickly, efficiently, neatly. If your purpose is to arrange some major affairs, your instinct is probably to settle the major issues first, leave the details for later, possibly for the technical people to work out.

For the Latin American, the discussion is a part of the spice of life. Just as he tends not to be overly concerned about reserving you your specific segment of time, he tends not as rigidly to separate business from nonbusiness. He runs it all together and wants to make something of a social event out of what you, in your culture, regard as strictly business.

The Latin American is not alone in this. The Greek businessman, partly for the same and partly for different reasons, does not lean toward the "hit-and-run" school of business behavior, either. The Greek businessman adds to the social element, however, a feeling about what length of discussion time constitutes good faith. In

America, we show good faith by ignoring the details. "Let's agree on the main points. The details will take care of themselves."

Not so the Greek. He signifies good will and good faith by what may seem to you an interminable discussion which includes every conceivable detail. Otherwise, you see, he cannot help but feel that the other man might be trying to pull the wool over his eyes. Our habit, in what we feel to be our relaxed and friendly way, of postponing details until later smacks the Greek between the eyes as a maneuver to flank him. Even if you can somehow convince him that this is not the case, the meeting must still go on a certain indefinite—but, by our standards, long—time or he will feel disquieted.

The American desire to get down to business and on with other things works to our disadvantage in other parts of the world, too; and not only in business. The head of a large, successful Japanese firm commented: "You Americans have a terrible weakness. We Japanese know about it and exploit it every chance we get. You are impatient. We have learned that if we just make you wait long enough, you'll agree to anything."

Whether this is literally true or not, the Japanese executive singled out a trait of American culture which most of us share and which, one may assume from the newspapers, the Russians have not overlooked, either.

By *acquaintance time* we mean how long you must know a man before you are willing to do business with him.

In the United States, if we know that a salesman represents a well-known, reputable company, and if we need his product, he may walk away from the first meeting with an order in his pocket. A few minutes conversation to decide matters of price, delivery, payment, model of product—nothing more is involved. In Central America, local custom does not permit a salesman to land in town, call on the customer and walk away with an order, no matter how badly your prospect wants and needs your product. It is traditional there that you must see your man at least three times before you can discuss the nature of your business.

Does this mean that the South American businessman does not recognize the merits of one product over another? Of course it doesn't. It is just that the weight of tradition presses him to do business within a circle of friends. If a product he needs is not available within his circle, he does not go outside it so much as he enlarges the circle itself to include a new friend who can supply the want. Apart from his cultural need to "feel right" about a new relationship, there is the logic of his business system. One of the realities of his life is that it is dangerous to enter into business with someone over whom you have no more than formal, legal "control." In the past decades, his legal system has not always been as firm as ours and he has learned through experience that he needs the sanctions implicit in the informal system of friendship.

Visiting time involves the question of who sets the time for a visit. George Coelho, a social psychologist from India, gives an illustrative case. A United States businessman received this invitation from an Indian businessman: "Won't you and your family come and see us? Come any time." Several weeks later, the Indian repeated the invitation in the same words. Each time the American replied that he would certainly like to drop in—but he never did. The reason is obvious in terms of our culture. Here "come any time" is just an expression of friendliness. You are not really expected to show up unless your host proposes a specific time. In India, on the contrary, the words are meant literally—that the host is putting himself at the disposal of his guest and really expects him to come. It is the essence of politeness to leave it to the guest to set a time at his convenience. If the guest never comes, the Indian naturally assumes that he does not want to come. Such a misunderstanding can lead to a serious rift between men who are trying to do business with each other.

Time schedules present Americans with another problem in many parts of the world. Without schedules, deadlines, priorities, and timetables, we tend to feel that our country could not run at all. Not only are they essential to getting work done, but they also play an important role in the informal communication process. Deadlines indicate priorities and priorities signal the relative importance of people and the processes they control. These are all so much a part of our lives that a day hardly passes without some reference to them: "I have to be there by 6:30." "If I don't have these plans out by 5:00 they'll be useless." "I told J. B. I'd be finished by noon tomorrow and now he tells me to drop everything and get hot on the McDermott account. What do I do now?"

In our system, there are severe penalties for not completing work on time and important rewards for holding to schedules. One's integrity and reputation are at stake.

You can imagine the fundamental conflicts that arise when we attempt to do business with people who are just as strongly oriented away from time schedules as we are toward them.

The Middle Eastern peoples are a case in point. Not only is our idea of time schedules no part of Arab life but the mere mention of a deadline to an Arab is like waving a red flag in front of a bull. In his culture, your emphasis on a deadline has the emotional effect on him that his backing you into a corner and threatening you with a club would have on you.

One effect of this conflict of unconscious habit patterns is that hundreds of American-owned radio sets are lying on the shelves of Arab radio repair shops, untouched. The Americans made the serious cross-cultural error of asking to have the repair completed by a certain time.

How do you cope with this? How does the Arab get another Arab to do anything? Every culture has its own ways of bringing pressure to get results. The usual Arab way is one which Americans avoid as "bad manners." It is needling.

An Arab businessman whose car broke down explained it this way:

> First, I go to the garage and tell the mechanic what is wrong with my car. I wouldn't want to give him the idea that I didn't know. After that, I leave the car and walk around the block. When I come back to the garage, I ask him if he has started to work yet. On my way home from lunch I stop in and ask him how things are going. When I go back to the office I stop by again. In the evening I return and peer over his shoulder for a while. If I didn't keep this up, he'd be off working on someone else's car.

If you haven't been needled by an Arab, you just haven't been needled.

A Place for Everything

We say that there is a time and place for everything, but compared to other countries and cultures we give very little emphasis to place distinctions. Business is almost a universal value with us; it can be discussed almost anywhere, except perhaps in church. One can even talk business on the church steps going to and from the service. Politics is only slightly more restricted in the places appropriate for its discussion.

In other parts of the world, there are decided place restrictions on the discussion of business and politics. The American who is not conscious of the unwritten laws will offend if he abides by his own rather than by the local rules.

In India, you should not talk business when visiting a man's home. If you do, you prejudice your chances of ever working out a satisfactory business relationship.

In Latin America, although university students take an active interest in politics, tradition decrees that a politician should avoid political subjects when speaking on university grounds. A Latin American politician commented to anthropologist Allan Holmberg that neither he nor his fellow politicians would have dared attempt a political speech on the grounds of the University of San Marcos in Peru—as did Vice-President Nixon.

To complicate matters further, the student body of San Marcos, anticipating the visit, had voted that Mr. Nixon would not be welcome. The university rector had issued no invitation, presumably because he expected what did, in fact, happen.

As a final touch, Mr. Nixon's interpreter was a man in full military uniform. In Latin American countries, some of which had recently overthrown military dictators, the symbolism of the military uniform could hardly contribute to a cordial atmosphere. Latin Americans need no reminder that the United States is a great military power.

Mr. Nixon's efforts were planned in the best traditions of our own culture: He hoped to improve relations through a direct, frank, and face-to-face discussion with students—the future leaders of their country. Unfortunately, this approach did not fit in at all with the culture of the host country. Of course, elements hostile to the United States did their best to capitalize upon this cross-cultural misunderstanding. However, even Latin Americans friendly to us, while admiring the vice-president's courage, found themselves acutely embarrassed by the behavior of their people and ours in the ensuing difficulties.

Being Comfortable in Space

Like time and place, differing ideas of space hide traps for the uninformed. Without realizing it, almost any person raised in the United States is likely to give an unintended snub to a Latin American simply in the way we handle space relationships, particularly during conversations.

In North America, the "proper" distance to stand when talking to another adult male you do not know well is about two feet, at least in a formal business conversation. (Naturally at a cocktail party, the distance shrinks, but anything under eight to ten inches is likely to provoke an apology or an attempt to back up.)

To a Latin American, with his cultural traditions and habits, a distance of two feet seems to him approximately what five feet would to us. To him we seem distant and cold; to us, he gives an impression of pushiness.

As soon as a Latin American moves close enough for him to feel comfortable, we feel uncomfortable and edge back. We once observed a conversation between a Latin and a North American which began at one end of a 40-foot hall. At intervals we noticed them again, finally at the other end of the hall. This rather amusing displacement had been accomplished by an almost continual series of small backward steps on the part of the American, trying unconsciously to reach a comfortable talking distance, and an equal closing of the gap by the Latin American as he attempted to reach his accustomed conversation space.

Americans in their offices in Latin America tend to keep their native acquaintances at our distance—not the Latin American's distance—by taking up a position behind a desk or typewriter. The barricade approach to communication is practiced even by old hands in Latin America who are completely unaware of its cultural significance. They know only that they are comfortable without realizing that the distance and equipment unconsciously make the Latin American uncomfortable.

How Class Channels Communication

We would be mistaken to regard the communication patterns which we observe around the world as no more than a miscellaneous collection of customs. The communication pattern of a given society is part of its total culture pattern and can only be understood in that context.

We cannot undertake here to relate many examples of communication behavior to the underlying culture of the country. For the businessman, it might be useful to mention the difficulties in the relationship between social levels and the problem of information feedback from lower to higher levels in industrial organizations abroad.

There is in Latin America a pattern of human relations and union-management relations quite different from that with which we are familiar in the United States. Everett Hagen of MIT has noted the heavier emphasis upon line authority and the lesser development of staff organizations in Latin American plants when compared with North American counterparts. To a much greater extent than in the United States, the government becomes involved in the handling of all kinds of labor problems.

These differences seem to be clearly related to the culture and social organization of Latin America. We find there that society has been much more rigidly stratified than it has with us. As a corollary, we find a greater emphasis upon authority in family and the community.

This emphasis upon status and class distinction makes it very difficult for people of different status levels to express themselves freely and frankly in discussion and argument. In the past, the pattern has been for the man of lower status to express deference to his superior in any face-to-face contact. This is so even when everyone knows that the subordinate dislikes the superior. The culture of Latin America places a great premium upon keeping personal relations harmonious on the surface.

In the United States, we feel that it is not only desirable but natural to speak up to your superior, to tell the boss exactly what you think, even when you disagree with him. Of course, we do not always do this, but we think that we should, and we feel guilty if we fail to speak our minds frankly. When workers in our factories first get elected to local union office, they may find themselves quite self-conscious about speaking up to the boss and arguing grievances. Many of them, however, quickly learn to do it and enjoy the experience. American culture emphasizes the thrashing-out of differences in face-to-face contacts. It deemphasizes the importance of status. As a result, we have built institutions for handling industrial disputes on the basis of the local situation, and we rely on direct discussion by the parties immediately involved.

In Latin America, where it is exceedingly difficult for people to express their differences face-to-face and where status differences and authority are much more strongly emphasized than here, the workers tend to look to a third party—the government—to take care of their problems. Though the workers have great difficulty in thrashing out their problems with management, they find no difficulty in telling government representatives their problems. And it is to their government that they look for an authority to settle their grievances with management.

Status and class also decide whether business will be done on an individual or a group basis.

In the United States, we are growing more and more accustomed to working as members of large organizations. Despite this, we still assume that there is no need to send a delegation to do a job that one capable man might well handle.

In some other parts of the world, the individual cannot expect to gain the respect necessary to accomplish this purpose, no matter how capable he is, unless he brings along an appropriate number of associates.

In the United States, we would rarely think it necessary or proper to call on a customer in a group. He might well be antagonized by the hard sell. In Japan—as an example—the importance of the occasion and of the man is measured by whom he takes along.

This practice goes far down in the business and government hierarchies. Even a university professor is likely to bring one or two retainers along on academic business. Otherwise people might think that he was a nobody and that his affairs were of little moment.

Even when a group is involved in the United States, the head man is the spokesman and sets the tone. This is not always the case in Japan. Two young Japanese once requested an older American widely respected in Tokyo to accompany them so that they could "stand on his face." He was not expected to enter into the negotiation; his function was simply to be present as an indication that their intentions were serious.

Adjustment Goes Both Ways

One need not have devoted his life to a study of various cultures to see that none of them is static. All are constantly changing and one element of change is the very fact that United States enterprise enters a foreign field. This is inevitable and may be constructive if we know how to utilize our knowledge. The problem is for us to be aware of our impact and to learn how to induce changes skillfully.

Rather than try to answer the general question of how two cultures interact, we will consider the key problem of personnel selection and development in two particular intercultural situations, both in Latin cultures.

One United States company had totally different experiences with "Smith" and "Jones" in the handling of its labor relations. The local union leaders were bitterly hostile to Smith, whereas they could not praise Jones enough. These were puzzling reactions to higher management. Smith seemed a fair-minded and understanding man; it was difficult to fathom how anyone could be bitter against him. At the same time, Jones did not appear to be currying favor by his generosity in giving away the firm's assets. To management, he seemed to be just as firm a negotiator as Smith.

The explanation was found in the two men's communication characteristics. When the union leaders came in to negotiate with Smith, he would let them state their case fully and freely—without interruption, but also without comment. When they had finished, he would say, "I'm sorry. We can't do it." He would follow this blunt statement with a brief and entirely cogent explanation of his reasons for refusal. If the union leaders persisted in their arguments, Smith would paraphrase his first statement, calmly and succinctly. In either case, the discussion was over in a few minutes. The union leaders would storm out of Smith's office complaining bitterly about the cold and heartless man with whom they had to deal.

Jones handled the situation differently. His final conclusion was the same as Smith's—but he would state it only after two or three hours of discussion. Furthermore, Jones participated actively in these discussions, questioning the union leaders for more information, relating the case in question to previous cases, philosophizing about labor relations and human rights and exchanging stories about work experience. When the discussion came to an end, the union leaders would leave the office, commenting on how warmhearted and understanding he was, and how confident they were that he would help them when it was possible for him to do so. They actually seemed more satisfied with a negative decision from Jones than they did with a hard-won concession with Smith.

This was clearly a case where the personality of Jones happened to match certain discernible requirements of the Latin American culture. It was happenstance in this case that Jones worked out and Smith did not, for by American standards both were top-flight men. Since a talent for the kind of negotiation that the Latin American considers graceful and acceptable can hardly be developed in a grown man (or perhaps even in a young one), the basic problem is one of personnel selection in terms of the culture where the candidate is to work.

The second case is more complicated because it involves much deeper intercultural adjustments. The management of the parent United States company concerned had learned—as have the directors of most large firms with good-sized installations overseas—that one cannot afford to have all of the top and middle-management positions manned by North Americans. It is necessary to advance nationals up the overseas-management ladder as rapidly as their abilities permit. So the nationals have to learn not only the technical aspects of their jobs but also how to function at higher levels in the organization.

Latin culture emphasizes authority in the home, church, and community. Within the organization this produces a built-in hesitancy about speaking up to one's superiors. The initiative, the acceptance of responsibility which we value in our organizations had to be stimulated. How could it be done?

We observed one management man who had done a remarkable job of building up these very qualities in his general foremen and foremen. To begin with, he stimulated informal contacts between himself and these men through social events to which the men and their wives came. He saw to it that his senior North American assistants and their wives were also present. Knowing the language, he mixed freely with all. At the plant, he circulated about, dropped in not to inspect or check up, but to joke and to break down the great barrier that existed in the local traditions between authority and the subordinates.

Next, he developed a pattern of three-level meetings. At the top, he himself, the superintendents, and the general foreman. At the middle level, the superintendents, general foremen, and foremen. Then the general foremen, foremen, and workers.

At the top level meeting, the American management chief set the pattern of encouraging his subordinates to challenge his own ideas, to come up with original thoughts. When his superintendents (also North Americans) disagreed with him, he made it clear that they were to state their objections fully. At first, the general foreman looked surprised and uneasy. They noted, however, that the senior men who argued with the boss were encouraged and praised. Timorously, with great hesitation, they began to add their own suggestions. As time went on, they more and more accepted the new convention and pitched in without inhibition.

The idea of challenging the boss with constructive new ideas gradually filtered down to the second and third level meetings. It took a lot of time and gentle handling, but out of this approach grew an extraordinary morale. The native general foremen and foremen developed new pride in themselves, accepted new responsibilities, even reached out for more. They began to work to improve their capacities and to look forward to moving up in the hierarchy.

Conformity or Adjustment?

To work with people, must we be just like them? Obviously not. If we try to conform completely, the Arab, the Latin American, the Italian, whoever he might be, finds our behavior confusing and insincere. He suspects our motive. We are expected to be different. But we are also expected to respect and accept the other people as they are. And we may, without doing violence to our own personalities, learn to communicate with them by observing the unwritten patterns they are accustomed to.

To be aware that there are pitfalls in cross-cultural dealings is the first big step forward. And to accept the fact that our convictions are in no respect more eternally "right" than someone else's is another constructive step.

QUESTIONS FOR DISCUSSION

1. According to Hall and Whyte, how important, in understanding and misunderstanding between people of different cultures, is the failure to speak another person's language?
2. Are politeness and honesty in communication related? Discuss how politeness and honesty might affect each other and the potential outcomes of cross-cultural interactions.
3. What are "the five dimensions of time"? Give examples which illustrate the cross-cultural differences in each dimension.
4. Does the case of Smith and Jones illustrate that in cross-cultural communication situations the person who spends more time and exchanges more stories about the problem under discussion will often be perceived as the better negotiator? What does it illustrate?
5. To what extent should we attempt to be like the members of another culture or expect them to be like us?
6. Suggest a method for introducing cultural change in an organization, which has worked in at least one case.

Mass communication messages contribute to the content of many interpersonal conversations. Going-to-the-movies and watching-television are two activities that provide the setting for interpersonal communication among friends and family, respectively.

A *gate-keeper* is any person who controls or influences the content of the news, such as a reporter or an editor. These individuals control certain "gates" through which a news item must pass on its way to becoming (or not becoming) an item that is printed in the newspaper or broadcast on radio or television. *News diffusion* research attempts to discover the path or paths that a news item takes from its initial printing or broadcasting by the mass media until it reaches everyone in the population who will eventually hear it, or hear of it. Some news items are heard directly from the media themselves while others are first heard from a friend or overheard from someone else's conversation.

The two step flow of communication is a theory of how people are affected by mass communication messages. The traditional view has been that people simply watch television or listen to the radio and are *directly* affected by the messages they receive. The two-step flow suggests that the influence of the media on a person's beliefs and actions is *not* direct but involves interpersonal communication with other persons who are called *opinion leaders:* influence flows from the media to opinion leaders and then from these opinion leaders to the majority of the persons who eventually hear the story. While many do see or hear the item directly in the media, the two-step flow hypothesis holds that the major effect of the item comes from discussing it with others whom the receiver perceives to be slightly more qualified than he is to discuss the content of the message.

19

tHE iNTERACTiNG AudiENCE: iNTERpERSONAL ASpECTS of MASS COMMUNiCATiON

John Dimmick

On a Wednesday morning at 5:59:30, the clock radio in the bedroom of 14-G, Greensward Apartments, clicks on completely inaudible to the sleeper. Promptly at six o'clock the strains of the "Star-Spangled Banner" by the United States Air Force Band soar across the room and assault the sleeping form of Professor William Urban. Radio station WEST, Westville, has begun its broadcast day.

Urban writhes briefly under the electric blanket then extricates himself from its folds and crosses the bedroom to the bathroom. Through the open door he listens to the local news, pausing once, razor in midstroke, to attend closely to a news item. The appointment of a new chancellor has been announced by the board of trustees of Westville University. The story is brief. Just the man's name, no details.

Back in the bedroom Urban dresses as WEST's morning DJ raps out the traffic and weather report. Traffic is moving slowly on the freeways. A light snowfall is expected in the evening. The temperature is thirty-nine degrees.

In the kitchen, Bill Urban plugs in the percolator and switches on a Sony portable TV. On the small screen, an ABC newsman on the "Today Show" interviews Iran's ambassador to the United Nations as Urban cooks eggs and makes toast. He carries the food to the breakfast bar and opens the morning paper, the *Westville Gazette and Chronicle*. While eating, he scans the news columns for a story about the newly

John Dimmick is assistant professor in the mass communication area of the Department of Speech and Theatre at the University of Illinois, Chicago Circle. Mr. Dimmick's article was prepared especially for this book.

appointed chancellor. The search is unrewarded; he flips to the editorial page and, finally, to the comics.

At 6:55 the beep of a Volvo's horn interrupts a third cup of coffee. Professor Urban dons his coat, picks up his briefcase, and steps outside. Opening the Volvo's door he is greeted by muted "good mornings" from its three occupants, members of the faculty car pool. As the door closes the opening chords of the Number One record in Westville burst from the car's radio.

As the Volvo enters the stream of freeway traffic, the four men talk about the weather, deplore an obnoxious guest on the previous night's Johnny Carson Show, and speculate about the character of the new university chancellor, oblivious to the familiar garish billboards that line the freeway and the neon signs that blink or stare into the grey morning.

Conversation is abruptly drowned as the driver turns up the radio volume. The DJ's voice has interrupted the music. Listeners are told to stand by for a weather bulletin from the WEST newsroom. A short silence and then the controlled tones of a newscaster: a traveler's warning is in effect for midafternoon; the snow will arrive earlier; and snow accumulation will be heavier than predicted. The newsman's voice is followed by music, radio volume subsides, and conversation resumes.

The four men talk about an early return home that evening. They refer to the blizzard of '67 when twenty-four inches of snow fell in thirty hours. Hundreds were stranded in the city; hotels were booked solid; people slept in lobbies or dozed on bar stools. A short discussion and it is decided. The schedules of three of the men permit them to leave for home at three o'clock. Urban has a three o'clock meeting; he will take a bus home.

At 7:55, Bill Urban unlocks his office door, removes his coat, takes a set of lecture notes from the briefcase and scans them. At eight o'clock he enters lecture room F-3 where his Introduction to Communication class meets, approaches the lectern and begins a lecture on interpersonal communication. He finishes at 8:49. In the scant minute remaining before the bell sounds, he reminds the students that tomorrow he will begin a series of lectures on mass communication.

At 3:39, the professor locks the office and walks in the burgeoning snowstorm to the bus stop. Most of Professor Urban's day was spent communicating. In the morning, he lectured. In the early afternoon, he worked on the draft of a paper he planned to submit to a journal for publication. Later, he went to a meeting of the department faculty to review applications for a new position. The meeting ended early because of the impending storm.

If he were asked to describe his day in terms of his communication activities, Professor Urban might begin by saying that he had engaged in both written and oral communication. If pressed further, he might recall the lecture, the faculty meeting, the morning newspaper, the radio, and the discussion with the members of the car pool. He might say, then, that he had engaged in communication behaviors which included mass communication, a speaker-audience situation, and small group discussion.

Such a description of his day in terms of these categories would be somewhat accurate. True enough, the lecture is a speaker-audience situation, the article he worked on is a form of written communication, and the faculty meeting had involved discussion in a small group. Portions of his day, however, are not so easily and neatly categorized. Actually, there was considerable interplay between the communication activities in which he engaged.

During breakfast, the radio news story concerning the newly appointed chancellor had triggered a search for further information in the morning newspaper. In the car that morning, mass media content—the Johnny Carson Show, the radio weather forecast, and the announcement of the appointment of the new chancellor—provided topics for casual conversation, the substance of interpersonal interaction with members of the car pool. The weather bulletin on the car radio resulted in a small-group discussion.

Despite the interplay between mass communication and interpersonal communication in his everyday life, Professor Urban delivers separate lectures on these subjects. But, as his rather mundane day illustrates, mass communication and the various forms of interpersonal communication are not separate and discrete activities but are interwoven in the fabric of daily living.

The following pages will show that the distinction between mass and interpersonal communication is, indeed, an academic one. The many ways in which mass and interpersonal communications interact has not been a major or persistent theme in communication theory and research. Nevertheless, sufficient research evidence has accumulated to document the importance of the interpersonal aspects of mass communication. Research evidence, for example, has accumulated to document the influence of interpersonal relationships on the **gate-keepers** who select what we see and hear on television and radio news programs and what we read in newspapers.[1] In addition, studies of **news diffusion**[2] and the **"two-step flow"** of communication[3] have demonstrated that people retransmit information they have seen or heard in the media to their friends, families and acquaintances. The purpose here, however, is not to review the literature on what might be called mass-personal communication. Rather, the objective is to introduce the student to some of the basic ways in which people use the media in their day-to-day relationships with others.

Mass Media and Interpersonal Needs

There is no word in contemporary language to describe a person who willfully shuns all contact with the mass media. Women-haters we call misogynists, haters of humans we term misanthropes, but we have no word to describe the likes of Mark Harris who wrote "The Last Article."

> I seldom read a newspaper and you shouldn't read one either; I seldom watch television, seldom pick up a popular magazine. . . . People addicted to the daily amusement of the media become extremely angry with me for tampering with their addiction. They stare at me. They mistrust their ears. They have believed from childhood that it is a civic duty to read the newspapers, a good man "keeps up with the news," just as a good man bathes regularly and slows his car at school crossings.[4]

Obviously, most people don't share Harris's view. If they did, tear stains would blur the digits in newspaper publishers' profit and loss statements, and today's television network executives might be tomorrow's bartenders. Harris is probably right, though. We are addicted, for addiction implies need for the addictive substance and twentieth-century Americans seem to "need" the mass media. The extent of our addiction is usually demonstrated by pointing out that most Americans spend a substantial portion of their leisure time watching television, listening to radio, and reading popular books and magazines. A more dramatic illustration of our need for the media is what Maxwell McCombs called the "Principle of Relative Constancy."[5] McCombs's analysis of economic data shows that spending by American consumers on the mass media is so consistent even in times of depression or recession that, economically, the media can be considered a staple commodity much like food, clothing, and shelter. In the years 1929-1968, McCombs found that people allocated a rather

- - -

constant proportion of their income, around three percent of total consumer spending, to the mass media. When people have less money they spend less on media. When finances improve they often spend more, but the *proportion* of consumer dollars devoted to spending on media is rather stable and constant. Such economic stability indicates that the mass media serve very important and basic needs in our lives.

Many of the basic human needs served by the mass communication media are related to interpersonal contact and communication. A unique study of the personal and social needs served by the media for people in Israel was conducted by Katz, Gurevitch and Haas.[6] Only those results which seem generalizable to American society will be reviewed here. Katz and his associates observe that most of the needs served by media are, first of all, self-needs such as tension reduction and, second, needs related to the immediate social environment such as contact with family and friends. Third, the media serve needs related to the society as a whole such as knowledge of actions of the country's leaders. The focus here, however, will be on Katz et al.'s findings as they relate to the satisfaction of interpersonal needs by the media.

Katz and his colleagues found that the need for contact with family was best served by television. As in American homes, the television set was the focus of Israeli family gatherings in the evening. On the other hand, the need for contact with friends was fulfilled by attending movies, while the need to participate in discussions with friends was best fulfilled by newspapers and books. Films provided an excuse for friends to get together. However, when friends met, the content of their conversation—what they actually talked about—was provided by the print media.

As a final note, Katz and his colleagues point out that, of course, not all needs are satisfied by the mass media. Some needs are better satisfied by interpersonal relationships or by participation in cultural events. Indeed, the terms "mass" communication and "mass" audience conceal more than they reveal about the nature of the people who watch television, read newspapers, and attend movies. People who are members of the "mass" audience are also members of families; they have a circle of friends and acquaintances; they belong to formal organizations such as clubs, professional associations, and political and religious groups. The interpersonal interaction which takes place among members of these social groups has an influence on an individual's selection of mass media content, his interpretation and his use of the content in daily life.

The Interpersonal Setting

A mass audience usually consists of groups of individuals who listen or watch together, not isolated individuals. Reading is usually a solitary and individual activity, but many mass communication messages such as TV programs are received in an interpersonal setting where two or more persons are present.

In an early study by Freidson, boys in grade school were asked whether they watched TV, went to the movies, or read comic books alone, with peers, or with family members.[7] Freidson found that watching television was something the boys did with their families, while movie-going was largely done with peers. By contrast, the boys in this study read comics when they were alone.

The interpersonal setting of mass communication is also illustrated in a study of 330 seventh-graders in Ann Arbor, Michigan.[8] Each adolescent was asked to describe the setting in which he usually listened to the radio or records, watched television and attended movies. The results are presented in Table 1.

TABLE 1

Percentage adolescents exposed to four mass media in personal and interpersonal settings. (N=330)

	With friends	By myself	With family	Only with brothers & sisters	No answer	TOTAL
When I listen to records, I usually listen	32%	**42%**	8%	12%	6%	100%
When I listen to the radio, I usually listen	11%	**62%**	12%	11%	4%	100%
When I watch TV, I usually watch	4%	20%	**52%**	19%	5%	100%
When I go to a movie, I usually go	**68%**	3%	18%	8%	3%	100%

For a majority of these adolescents (52%), television viewing takes place in an interpersonal setting with members of their families. This tendency weakens somewhat in later years. Older adolescents in a study by Lyle and Hoffman[9] watched TV with their families less than younger adolescents and watched more TV by themselves. Like TV viewing, movie attendance is primarily a group activity for the Ann Arbor students but it is a peer group activity, something that is done with one's friends. Over two-thirds of these youngsters usually attended movies with their friends. Radio listening, on the other hand, tends to be a much more "individual" activity. Roughly two-thirds of the adolescents listen to radio by themselves. Record listening is either done alone or in the company of friends. Thus, only radio listening for these youngsters is a predominantly "individual" activity.

The Interacting Audience

Many of the casual conversations as well as heated debates with our friends, family, and professional associates involve a movie we've seen, current events as reported in the newspaper or on television or radio news programs, and the entertainment programs we've watched on television. For friends and family, chatting about a TV show provides a way to pass the time while we enjoy each other's company. Conversely, when strangers meet, talking about the same TV show may serve as a sort of "neutral" territory wherein communication is restricted until (or if) one or the other is willing to talk about less public matters. As Leo Bogart observed, talking about media may make for companionship among people who have little in common except what they see on television or read in the newspaper.[10]

Much of our talk about the entertainment content of the media is casual and incidental; it is used to fill the gaps in our activities. Bogart's study of the role played by the newspaper comic strips in the conversations of residents of an urban lower-income neighborhood illustrates this point. The answers to Bogart's question concerning the situations in which people talked about the comics reveal this incidental and casual nature. He writes that

> conversation about the comics occurs typically among adult males—at work, at the street corner; down by the garage; when we're on our way to work; in the shop; with my friends; barroom talk; with a bunch of fellows on the corner.[11]

Newspaper stories are also major topics of conversation. This fact emerged from two studies of what people missed in their newspapers during newspaper strikes.[12] In both studies a major finding was the extent to which the news was used in conversation. For example, Kimball found that people said things like: "The radio is no substitute for a newspaper. I like to be able to make intelligent conversation!" or "You talk about the news with your friends."[13] Depriving people of their newspaper evidently leaves them without a routine topic of conversation. Similarly, depriving people of their TV sets would deprive them of an opportunity to talk and interact.

Some critics have depicted the American family as they sit nightly in front of the TV set as being an inert and apathetic group, struck mute in the presence of the "boob tube." The critics have charged that watching television stifles communication and conversation in the family. The evidence, however, does not support this contention. Lyle and Hoffman found that people do talk to each other when they watch television. Over two-thirds of the boys and girls in this study (sixth-graders and tenth-graders) said they talked with their families when they watched TV "sometimes" or "quite a bit." In addition, the conversations among families concern not just the program they're watching but other topics as well. Research has not yet documented the extent of conversation during such activities as record-listening. However, it is clear that the content of the media provides ample topics of conversation.

In the Lyle and Hoffman study, the media were a frequent topic of conversation for young people. When they talked with each other, television and movies were the most frequent topics of conversation. In talks with parents, the print media such as magazines, newspapers, and books, as well as news on TV, were additional subjects of conversation. These findings suggest that different media facilitate discussion with different persons.[14]

The results of the Ann Arbor study concerning media as topics of conversation parallel Lyle and Hoffman's findings. The Ann Arbor adolescents were asked to indicate how well certain statements described their conversations with friends about television, newspapers, and magazines. The results are shown in Table 2.

The data in Table 2 show opposite trends for TV and the print media as topics of conversation. Eighty percent responded that talking about TV shows was either "a lot like me" or "a little like me." Conversely, seventy percent said that talking about newspapers and magazines with their friends was only "a little like me" or "not at all like me."

As in Lyle and Hoffman's study, television is a more important topic of conversation for these seventh-graders than newspapers or magazines.

TABLE 2
Frequency of talking with friends
About TV and magazines and newspapers   (N=330)

1. "I often talk with my friends about the TV shows I watch."

a lot like me	39%
a little like me	41%
not at all like me	15%
No answer	5%
	100%

2. "My friends and I often talk about things we read in magazines or newspapers."

a lot like me	26%
a little like me	40%
not at all like me	30%
No answer	4%
	100%

In addition, the Ann Arbor youngsters spent a good deal of time watching TV and relatively less time with newspapers and magazines. Over two-thirds said they spent two, three, or four hours on a given day watching television. On the other hand, two-thirds of the students spent an hour or less of a specific day reading newspapers while ninety-one percent spent an hour or less reading magazines. These adolescents spent more time watching TV than reading magazines or newspapers and talked with their friends more about TV than about the print media. This parallels Clarke's finding that the amount of reading about popular music among young people correlates highly with the amount of talking about music with their friends.[15]

We do not know if it is true, in general, that people talk more about the content of the mass medium that they use most often. If it does hold true, then one would expect older, more educated people, who make greater use of newspapers and magazines, also to make greater use of the print media in their conversations.[16]

The Role of the Media in Family and Peer Relationships

The importance of peers or friends as an influence on our uses of the mass media was first recognized by Riley and Riley[17] and by Riley and Flowerman.[18] The Rileys began their study by observing that while most children belong to family groups, children vary in their membership in peer groups or circles of friends. Some children will have a large circle of friends, some a smaller group of friends, while others are relatively isolated from other children. The Rileys were interested in the ways in which media were used by peer group members and by children who were not members of peer groups. One difference these investigators found was that peer group members selected media content in ways which were useful in their everyday lives as group members. For example, boys who were members of peer groups used the stories in the "Lone Ranger" comics in their play with friends. Similarly, older girls who were peer group members read love comics because they contained practical information on the "nuts-and-bolts" of romance such as how to behave when going out with a boy. The nonmembers of groups in the Rileys' study used the same media, but merely for entertainment or escape.[19]

Freidson's study provides further evidence on the influence of peer groups on media use. Freidson reasoned that since the importance of the peer group increases with age, the older boys should prefer the mass medium which gave them the greatest opportunity for contact with their friends. This hypothesis was supported. The older boys in the higher primary grades were more likely to name movies as their favorite or most preferred medium. Recall that in Freidson's study movie-going was a peer group activity. On the other hand, the younger boys in the lower grades were more likely to say that TV, a family activity, was their favorite mass medium.[20]

The Rileys use the term "social utility" to denote the selection of media content which is useful in group relationships.[21] More recently, Tipton used the term "communicatory utility" to refer to "information seeking which stems from an intent to use that content later in one's own communication."[22] Tipton's term is more general than the Rileys', in that it doesn't focus exclusively on group-related use of information. In addition, by employing the term "search" in his definition, Tipton distinguishes between acquiring information as a by-product of passive media use and an active, purposive search for information.

Clarke clarifies the interpersonal uses of information-seeking and sharing. *Information-seeking,* according to Clarke refers to a search for information outside the social systems of which we are members such as family and peer groups. Information-seeking is directed towards sources like the media or institutional sources such as libraries. *Information-sharing,* on the other hand, refers to the exchange of information and opinions within the social systems of which one is a member.[23]

A study by Clarke illustrates the processes of information-seeking and sharing.[24] Clarke's major hypothesis predicted that information-seeking about entertainment will depend on the extent to which either family members or peers are believed to enjoy the entertainment.

Clarke obtained information from seventh, ninth and eleventh-grade students who had attended a symphony concert. The adolescents were asked, first of all, whether there was anything they wanted to know about symphony music. They were also asked whether there was anyone whose musical taste they believed they knew, who this person was, and whether the adolescent thought the person liked the music (if the person had attended the concert) or would have liked the music (if the person hadn't attended the concert). At the end of the questionnaire was a postcard the adolescents could mail if they wanted booklets containing information on symphony music or symphony musicians.

The results confirmed the general hypothesis that information-seeking—in this case mailing the postcard to request the booklets—would depend on the adolescents' belief that someone else, either a peer or a parent, had a favorable attitude toward the concert. In answer to the question about their need for information about symphony music or musicians, those adolescents who were aware of someone who might view the concert favorably were more likely to express a need for information about symphony. Similarly, those who were aware of someone they believed liked symphony music were more likely to write for the booklets. Further, teenagers who perceived that *both* a peer and a parent were favorable were more likely to request a booklet than those who perceived that *either* a peer or a parent held favorable attitudes toward symphony.

The implication of the study is that people engage in information-seeking behavior, such as sending for the booklet, because they are aware of someone in a social system (peer or family) of which they are a member who is interested in the topic. Presumably, the information gained is then shared with others, either peers or family. As Clarke points out, such information-seeking could occur regardless of the teenagers' own attitude toward music. *The belief that another person or persons, either friend or family member, held favorable attitudes toward symphony was a stronger predictor of information-seeking in this study than owning a musical instrument, playing in a band, or other variables related to an interest in music.*

The family, in some cases, exercises direct influence and control on members' media use. Parents sometimes prohibit their children from watching certain TV shows they consider harmful. Conversely, parents may encourage children to watch programs such as "Sesame Street" which they believe will benefit the child. Nor does the influence flow only in one direction, from parent to child. For example, in a study by Clarke (1963) of family TV viewing, the programs watched in about forty percent of the cases had either been selected or recommended by the teenager in the family.[25]

In addition to these direct influences of the family on the selection of media content, there is evidence that what Chaffee, McLeod, and Atkin call the "communicatory environment" in the family is a rather subtle and indirect influence on media use. These authors have distinguished between two general types of communicatory environments or family communication patterns. The first general pattern they term a *socio-orientation*. "In families that stress this socio-orientation the child is encouraged to maintain harmonious personal relations, avoid controversy, and repress his feelings on extrapersonal topics."[26] On the other hand, in homes that stress what they call the *concept orientation*, "the child is stimulated to express his ideas; he is exposed to controversy and encouraged to join it."[27]

Media use, Chaffee, McLeod, and Atkin found, is related to the type of communicatory environment in the family. Children and adolescents in homes that stress the concept orientation tend to spend more time reading newspapers, magazines, and watching TV news and relatively less time watching entertainment programs on television. Conversely, children and adolescents in homes stressing the socio-orientation, tend to spend more time watching entertainment programs and devote less time to the news media. The child or teenager in the concept oriented home, where he is encouraged to express ideas and engage in debate and discussion, finds the news media compatible with his interest. To the child or teenager in a home stressing the socio-orientation such media content has less "social utility" since it doesn't help him to get along with others.

The study by Katz et al., cited earlier, shows that television viewing in a family setting serves a need for family contact and togetherness. The Ann Arbor study provides data to illustrate the notion that family television watching, at least for younger adolescents, may be due to a need for contact with family members. The finding that families view TV together could simply be explained by the fact that there is only one TV set in the home. Or, if there is more than one set in the home, family viewing might result from the congregating of parents and children around the more preferred color set. During the Ann Arbor survey, respondents were asked how many working television sets were in the homes. In addition, if there were more than two

TV sets in the home, the adolescents were asked to indicate if they and their parents watched the same or different sets. Table 3 shows how they responded to these two questions.

TABLE   3

Percent multiple sets in household
And percentage watching same or different sets   (N=330)

1. "How many working television sets are there in your home?"

Number of Sets	
0	5%
1	23%
2	42%
3	26%
4	1%
No answer	3%
	100%

2. "If there are two or more TV sets in your home, do you and your parents watch the *same* TV or different ones?"

Watch same set	50%
Watch different sets	20%
Less than 2 TV's	28%
No answer	2%
	100%

As the data in Table 3 show, even in the households with more than one set the majority of families watch the same TV set. The percentages in Table 2 are computed for all the respondents including those without sets or those with only one set. The tendency for parents and children to watch the same set in households with multiple sets is even more striking when only the multiple set households are considered. Of the multiple set households, seventy-one percent of the respondents said they and their parents watched the same set while twenty-nine percent said they watched different sets.

Another indication that family TV viewing served the need for family contact is provided by the responses to an attitude question which the Ann Arbor students were asked. In response to the statement, "Watching TV is something I like to do with my family," seventy-six percent said the statement was "a lot like me," or "a little like me." Only twenty percent said the statement was "not at all like me."

If family TV viewing serves a need for contact among family members, it also provides an occasion for conflict. There is evidence to suggest that many of the TV programs watched by the family are the result of an interpersonal negotiation or bargaining process. In every home that has at least one more person than TV sets, there is the potential for disagreement over which TV shows will be watched. This is especially true in the evening hours when most family members are at home. If disagreements or conflicts arise, the family must find ways to resolve them. This interpersonal decision-making process which goes on nightly in millions of homes is largely unstudied and should be of interest to students of decision or game theory and those interested in small group communication, in addition to students of mass communication.

Wand found considerable conflict over TV program choice in Canadian households in which there was only a single television set. There were more disagreements in larger families and in families with older children.[28] Disagreements, however, are not limited to households with a single set. Streicher and Bonney found that among children in homes with an average of three sets, there was still a considerable amount of conflict.

In homes with multiple sets, one might expect that the availability of other sets might be used to settle disputes when they arise. However, Streicher and Bonney report that this was the method used for settling disputes in only twenty percent of the cases in their study. These authors found that the most frequent methods of resolving conflict included such rules as *first-come, first served,* meaning whoever gets to the TV set first chooses the program. In addition, *taking a vote* among family members and *compromise* were other strategies used to settle disputes.[29]

Two other studies of television viewing bear on the question of family decision-making. Smith found that *general agreement* was the second most frequent mode of choosing TV programs for family viewing in the evening.[30] Similarly, Niven found that a *family decision* was the most frequent method of choosing a program during prime time. Unfortunately, we do not know what kinds of decision-making behavior is included in such general categories as *general agreement* or *family decision*.[31] Aside from the limited data provided by Streicher and Bonney, we do not know how these decisions are reached.

SUMMARY

The audiences of the mass media are interacting audiences who use the media in a number of ways in their day-to-day relationships. The economic stability of the media—the fact that Americans allocate a rather constant proportion of their consumer spending to media—indicates that the media serve a rather stable set of personal and interpersonal needs.

Like the rest of us, Prof. William Urban does not engage in separate, distinct activities called "interpersonal" or "mass" communication. Rather, he inhabits what might be called a *communication environment*. This environment includes a network of interpersonal relationships with friends, family and co-workers, as well as the mass media. Bill Urban's needs—personal and interpersonal—account, in large part, for the attention he pays to the media, for what he remembers and what he forgets. For example, he attended closely to the story about the new chancellor, sought further information, and later shared his knowledge with his colleagues in the car pool. On the other hand, he ignored the billboards and neon signs on the way to work, and he couldn't, if his life depended on it, recall what Iran's ambassador to the United Nations said that morning on the "Today Show."

Further, within this communication environment, there is continual interplay between the media and interpersonal relationships. As the Rileys pointed out, our group affiliations affect our use of the media. People talk to each other about what they read in the newspaper. Friends go to a movie as an excuse for getting together. Children and adolescents watch television with their families partially just to be together even though there are disagreements over program choice. If Chaffee et al. are correct, the *communicatory environment* in the family shapes the child's pattern of media use and this pattern will persist when the child matures into an adult. As the Clarke study suggests, we may seek information about a topic from the media or other sources not because we are personally interested, but because we plan to share the information with someone we know who is interested in the subject.

These are some of the interpersonal aspects of mass communication. Other aspects await the attention of researchers and theorists in the field we call human communication.

QUESTIONS FOR DISCUSSION

1. What is the "Principle of Relative Consistency"? Give some reasons why this principle might work.
2. What kinds of needs are served by the mass media? Which media seem to best serve which needs?
3. Which interpersonal activities seem to go with the use of which media?
4. How would you respond to someone who suggests that television has driven conversation out of family life?
5. When do people seek more information about a topic?
6. In families with more than one TV set, what are the most commonly used methods of resolving conflicts over what program to watch?
7. Discuss the relationships between mass communication and interpersonal communication as presented by Dimmick.

NOTES

1. J. Dimmick, "The Gate-Keeper: An Uncertainty Theory," *Journalism Monographs* 37 (November 1974).
2. B. Greenberg, "Diffusion of News of the Kennedy Assassination," *Public Opinion Quarterly* (Summer 1964), pp.225-232.
3. N. Lin, "Information Flow, Influence Flow and the Decision Making Process," *Journalism Quarterly* 48 (Spring 1971), pp.33-40.
4. M. Harris, "The Last Article," *The New York Times Magazine* (October 6, 1974), p.20.
5. M. McCombs, "Mass Media in the Marketplace," *Journalism Monographs* 24 (August 1972).
6. E. Katz, M. Gurevitch, and H. Haas, "On the Use of the Mass Media for Important Things," *American Sociological Review* 38 (April 1973), pp.164-181.
7. E. Freidson, "The Relation of the Social Situation of Contact to the Media in Mass Communications," *Public Opinion Quarterly* 17 (Summer 1953), pp.230-238.
8. The data reported here and in later sections of the paper are from the first wave of a longitudinal study of mass media and youth in which the author participated. The study was directed by F. Gerald Kline of the Department of Journalism and Program in Mass Communication at the University of Michigan.
9. J. Lyle and H. Hoffman, "Children's Use of Television and Other Media," in E. Rubenstein et al., eds. *Television and Social Behavior*, (U.S. Government Printing Office, 1971), pp.129-256.

10. L. Bogart, "Adult Talk About Newspaper Comics," *American Journal of Sociology*, 61 (1955), pp.26-30.
11. *Ibid*, p.27.
12. B. Berelson, "What Missing the Newspaper Means," in Paul Lazarsfeld and Frank Stanton, eds. *Communications Research 1948-1949* (New York: Harper Brothers, 1949), pp.111-129; and P. Kimball, "People Without Papers," *Public Opinion Quarterly* 23 (Fall 1959), pp.389-398.
13. *Ibid*, p.39.
14. Lyle and Hoffman.
15. P. Clarke, "Teenagers Coorientation and Information Seeking About Pop Music," *American Behavioral Scientist* (March-April 1973), pp.551-566.
16. J. Robinson, "Mass Communication and Information Diffusion," in F.G. Kline and P.J. Tichenor, eds. *Current Perspectives in Mass Communication Research* (Beverly Hills: Sage Publications, 1972), pp.71-93.
17. M. Riley and J. Riley, "A Sociological Approach to Communications Research," *Public Opinion Quarterly*, 15 (Fall 1951), pp.444-460.
18. M. Riley and S. Flowerman, "Group Relations As a Variable in Communications Research," *American Sociological Review*, 16 (April 1951), pp.174-180.
19. Riley and Riley.
20. Freidson.
21. Riley and Riley.
22. L. Tipton, "Effects of Writing Tests on Utility of Information and Order of Seeking," *Journalism Quarterly*, 47 (Summer 1970), p. 309.
23. P. Clarke, "Children's Response to Entertainment," *American Behavioral Scientist* (January-February 1971), pp.353-370.
24. *Ibid*.
25. P. Clarke, "An Experiment to Increase the Audience for Educational Television," unpublished Ph.D. dissertation, University of Minnesota, 1963.
26. S. Chaffee, J. McLeod, and C. Atkin, "Parental Influence on Adolescent Media Use," *American Behavioral Scientist*, 14.
27. *Ibid*.
28. B. Wand, "Television Viewing and Family Choice Differences," *Public Opinion Quarterly*, 32 (Spring 1968), pp.84-94.
29. L. Streicher and N. Bonney, "Children Talk About Television," *Journal of Communication*, 24 (Summer 1974), pp.54-61.
30. D. Smith, "The Selectors of TV Programs," *Journal of Broadcasting*, 6 (1961-1962), pp.35-44.
31. H. Niven, "Who in the Family Selects the TV Program," *Journalism Quarterly*, 37, (Winter 1960), pp.110-111.

SEVEN

SOME PRACTICAL advice

This article discusses *serial communication* or communication in a straight line from A to B to C. Very few communication situations are purely straight line transfers of messages, but all communication involves some straight line transfer, at least from person A to person B.

Some of the most dramatic illustrations of the importance of accurate serial transmission occur in organizational settings where one person is responsible for accurately relaying a message between two other persons. One day in June of 1975, several pilots landing at Kennedy Airport in Queens, New York reported very windy conditions to the air traffic controller at Kennedy. One of them, a pilot for Flying Tiger Airlines, reported "a tremendous windshear" on final approach and urged the controller to change runways. One pilot of an Eastern Air Line flight found conditions so windy he aborted the attempted landing and landed instead at Boston's Logan Airport. As another plane approached Kennedy, Eastern's Flight 66 from New Orleans, the air traffic controller radioed Flight 66 that "the only problems reported have been a windshear on final approach." This played down the seriousness of previous warnings, left out the word "tremendous," and did not mention how many pilots had had problems or what actions they had taken or urged should be taken. More than one hundred persons died when Flight 66 crashed short of the runway.

There is far more to communication than serial transmission, but Haney's article provides some good guidelines to remember.

20

SERiAL COMMUNiCATiON
of iNFORMATiON
iN ORGANiZATiONS

William V. Haney

An appreciable amount of the communication which occurs in business, industry, hospitals, military units, government agencies—in
short, in chain-of-command organizations—consists of serial transmissions. *A* communicates a message to *B*; *B* then communicates *A*'s
message (or rather his *interpretation* of *A*'s message) to *C*; *C* then
communicates his interpretation of *B*'s interpretation of *A*'s message to
D; and so on. The originator and the ultimate recipient of the message[1]
are separated by "middle men."

"The message" may often be passed down (but not necessarily all
the way down) the organization chain, as when in business the chairman acting on behalf of the board of directors may express a desire to
the president. "The message" begins to fan out as the president, in
turn, relays "it" to his vice-presidents; they convey "it" to their respective subordinates; and so forth. Frequently "a message" goes up (but
seldom all the way up) the chain. Sometimes "it" travels laterally.
Sometimes, as with rumors, "it" disregards the formal organization
and flows more closely along informal organizational lines.

Regardless of its direction, the number of "conveyors" involved,
and the degree of its conformance with the formal structure, serial
transmission is clearly an essential, inevitable form of communication
in organizations. It is equally apparent that serial transmission is
especially susceptible to distortion and disruption. Not only is it

William V. Haney is professor in the School of Business at Northwestern University.
William V. Haney, "Serial Communication of Information in Organizations," in *Concepts
and Issues in Administrative Behavior*, Sidney Mailick and Edward H. Van Ness, eds., ©
1962. Reprinted by permission of Prentice-Hall, Inc.

subject to the shortcomings and maladies of "simple" person-to-person communication but, since it consists of a series of such communications, the anomalies are often *compounded*.

This is not to say, however, that serial transmissions in organizations should be abolished or even decreased. We wish to show that such communications *can be improved* if communicators are able (1) to recognize some of the patterns of miscommunication which occur in serial transmissions; (2) to understand some of the factors contributing to these patterns; (3) to take measures and practice techniques for preventing the recurrence of these patterns and for ameliorating their consequences.

I shall begin by cataloguing some of the factors which seemingly influence a serial transmission.[2]

Motives of the Communicators

When B conveys A's message to C he may be influenced by at least three motives of which he may be largely unaware.

The Desire to Simplify the Message

We evidently dislike conveying detailed messages. The responsibility of passing along complex information is burdensome and taxing. Often, therefore, we unconsciously simplify the message before passing it along to the next person.[3] It is very probable that among the details most susceptible to omission are those we already knew or in some way presume our recipients will know without our telling them.

The Desire to Convey a "Sensible" Message

Apparently we are reluctant to relay a message that is somehow incoherent, illogical, or incomplete. It may be embarrassing to admit that one does not fully understand the message he is conveying. When he receives a message that does not quite make sense to him he is prone to "make sense out of it" before passing it along to the next person.[4]

The Desire to Make the Conveyance of the Message As Pleasant and/or Painless as Possible for the Conveyor

We evidently do not like to have to tell the boss unpleasant things. Even when not directly responsible, one does not relish the reaction of his superior to a disagreeable message. This motive probably accounts for a considerable share of the tendency for a "message" to lose its harshness as it moves up the organizational ladder. The first-line supervisor may tell his foreman, "I'm telling you, Mike, the men say that if this pay cut goes through they'll strike—and they mean it!" By the time "this message" has been relayed through six or eight or more echelons (if indeed it goes that far) the executive vice-president might express it to the president as, "Well, sir, the men seem a little concerned over the projected wage reduction but I am confident that they will take it in stride."

One of the dangers plaguing some upper managements is that they are effectively shielded from incipient problems until they become serious and costly ones.

Assumptions of the Communicators

In addition to the serial transmitter's motives we must consider his assumptions—particularly those he makes about his communications. If some of these assumptions are fallacious and if one is unaware that he holds them, his communication can be adversely affected. The following are, in this writer's judgment, two of the most pervasive and dangerous of the current myths about communication:

The Assumption That Words Are Used in Only One Way

A study[5] indicates that for the 500 most commonly used words in our language there are 14,070 different dictionary definitions—over 28 usages per word, on the average. Take the word *run*, for example:

Babe Ruth scored a *run*.
Did you ever see Jesse Owens *run*?
I have a *run* in my stocking.
There is a fine *run* of salmon this year.
Are you going to *run* this company or am I?
You have the *run* of the place.
Don't give me the *run* around.
What headline do you want to *run*?
There was a *run* on the bank today.
Did he *run* the ship aground?
I have to *run* (drive the car) downtown.
Who will *run* for President this year?
Joe flies the New York-Chicago *run* twice a week.
You know the kind of people they *run* around with.
The apples *run* large this year.
Please *run* my bath water.

We could go on at some length—my small abridged dictionary gives eighty-seven distinct usages for *run*. I have chosen an extreme example, of course, but there must be relatively few words (excepting some technical terms) used in one and in only one sense.

Yet communicators often have a curious notion about words *when they are using them*, i.e., when they are speaking, writing, listening, or reading. It is immensely easy for a "sender" of a communication to assume that words are used in only one way—the way he intends them. It is just as enticing for the "receiver" to assume that the sender intended his words as he, the receiver, happens to interpret them at the moment. When communicators are unconsciously burdened by the assumption of the mono-usage of words they are prone to become involved in the pattern of miscommunication known as *bypassing*.

A foreman told a machine operator he was passing: "Better clean up around here." It was ten minutes later when the foreman's assistant phoned: "Say, boss, isn't that bearing Sipert is working on due up in engineering pronto?"

"You bet your sweet life it is. Why?"

"He says you told him to drop it and sweep the place up. I thought I'd better make sure."

"Listen," the foreman flared into the phone, "get him right back on that job. It's got to be ready in twenty minutes."

. . . What the foreman had in mind was for Sipert to gather up the oily waste, which was a fire and accident hazard. This would not have taken more than a couple of minutes, and there would have been plenty of time to finish the bearing.[6]

Bypassing: Denotative and Connotative. Since we use words to express at least two kinds of meanings there can be two kinds of bypassings. Suppose you say to me, "Your neighbor's grass is certainly green and healthy looking, isn't it?" You could be intending your words merely to *denote*, i.e., to point to or to call my attention, to the appearance of my neighbor's lawn. On the other hand, you could have intended your words to *connote*, i.e., to imply something beyond or something other than what you were ostensibly denoting. You might have meant any number of things: that my own lawn needed more care; that my neighbor was inordinately meticulous about his lawn; that my neighbor's lawn is tended by a professional, a service you do not have and for which you envy or despise my neighbor; or even that his grass was not green at all but, on the contrary, parched and diseased; and so forth.

Taking these two kinds of meanings into account it is clear that bypassing occurs or can occur under any of four conditions:

1. *When the sender intends one denotation while the receiver interprets another.*
   (As in the case of Sipert and his foreman.)

2. *When the sender intends one connotation while the receiver interprets another.*
   A friend once told me of an experience she had had years ago when as a teenager she was spending the week with a maiden aunt. Joan had gone to the movies with a young man who brought her home at a respectable hour. However, the couple lingered on the front porch somewhat longer than Aunt Mildred thought necessary. The little old lady was rather proud of her ability to deal with younger people so she slipped out of bed, raised her bedroom window, and called down sweetly, "If you two knew how pleasant it is in bed, you wouldn't be standing out there in the cold."

3. *When the sender intends only a denotation while the receiver interprets a connotation.*
   For a brief period the following memorandum appeared on the bulletin boards of a government agency in Washington:
   Those department and sections heads who do not have secretaries assigned to them may take advantage of the stenographers in the secretarial pool.

4. *When the sender intends a connotation while the receiver interprets a denotation only.*
   Before making his final decision on a proposal to move to new offices, the head of a large company called his top executives for a last discussion of the idea. All were enthusiastic except the company treasurer who insisted that he had not had time to calculate all the costs with accuracy sufficient to satisfy himself that the move was advantageous. Annoyed by his persistence, the chief finally burst out:
   "All right, Jim, all right! Figure it out to the last cent. A penny saved is a penny earned, right?"
   The intention was ironic. He meant not what the words denoted but the opposite—forget this and stop being petty. For him this was what his words connoted.
   For the treasurer "penny saved, penny earned" meant exactly what it said. He put several members on his staff to work on the problem and, to test the firmness of the price, had one of them interview the agent renting the proposed new quarters without explaining whom he represented. This indication of additional interest in the premises led the agent to raise the rent. Not until the lease was signed, did the agency discover that one of its own employes had, in effect, bid up its price.[7]

The Assumption That Inferences Are Always
Distinguishable from Observations

It is incredibly difficult, at times, for a communicator (or anyone) to discriminate between what he "knows" (i.e., what he has actually observed—seen, heard, read, etc.) and what he is only inferring or guessing. One of the key reasons for this lies in the character of the language used to express observations and inferences.

Suppose you look at a man and observe that he is wearing a white shirt and then say, "That man is wearing a white shirt." Assuming your vision and the illumination were "normal" you would have made a statement of *observation*—a statement which directly corresponded to and was corroborated by your observation. But suppose you now say, "That man bought the white shirt he is wearing." Assuming you were not present when and if the man bought the shirt that statement would be *for you a statement of inference*. Your statement went *beyond* what you observed. You inferred that the man bought the shirt; you did not observe it. Of course, your inference may be correct (but it could be false: perhaps he was given the shirt as a gift; perhaps he stole it or borrowed it; etc.).

Nothing in the nature of our language (the grammar, spelling, pronunciation, accentuation, syntax, inflection, etc.) prevents you from speaking or writing (or thinking) a statement of inference *as if* you were making a statement of observation. Our language permits you to say, "Of course, he bought the shirt" with certainty and finality, i.e., with as much confidence as you would make a statement of observation. The effect is that it becomes exceedingly easy to confuse the two kinds of statements and also to confuse inference and observation on nonverbal levels. The destructive consequences of acting upon inference as if acting upon observation can range from mild embarrassment to tragedy. One factual illustration may be sufficient to point up the dangers of such behavior.

THE CASE OF JIM BLAKE[8]

Jim Blake, 41, had been with the Hasting Co. for ten years. For the last seven years he had served as an "inside salesman," receiving phone calls from customers and writing out orders. "Salesman," in this case, was somewhat of a euphemism as the customer ordinarily knew what he wanted and was prepared to place an order. The "outside salesmen," on the other hand, visited industrial accounts and enjoyed considerably more status and income. Blake had aspired to an outside position for several years but no openings had occurred. He had, however, been assured by Russ Jenkins, sales manager, that as senior inside man he would be given first chance at the next available outside job.

Finally, it seemed as if Jim's chance had come. Harry Strom, 63, one of the outside men, had decided in January to retire on the first of June. It did not occur to Jenkins to reassure Blake that the new opening was to be his. Moreover, Blake did not question Jenkins because he felt his superior should take the initiative.

As the months went by Blake became increasingly uneasy. Finally, on May 15 he was astonished to see Strom escorting a young man into Jenkins's office. Although the door was closed Blake could hear considerable laughing inside. After an hour the three emerged from the office and Jenkins shook hands with the new man saying, "Joe, I'm certainly glad you're going to be with us. With Harry showing you around his territory you're going to get a good start at the business." Strom and the new man left and Jenkins returned to his office.

Blake was infuriated. He was convinced that the new man was being groomed for Strom's position. Now he understood why Jenkins had said nothing to him. He angrily cleaned out his desk, wrote a bitter letter of resignation and left it on his desk, and stomped out of the office.

Suspecting the worst for several months, Blake was quite unable to distinguish what he had inferred from what he had actually observed. The new man, it turned out, was being hired to work as an inside salesman—an opening which was to be occasioned by Blake's moving into the outside position. Jenkins had wanted the new man to get the "feel" of the clientele and thus had requested Strom to take him along for a few days as Strom made his calls.

Trends in Serial Transmission

These assumptions,[9] the mono-usage of words, and the inference-observation confusion, as well as the aforementioned motives of the communicators, undoubtedly contribute a significant share of the difficulties and dangers which beset a serial transmission. Their effect tends to be manifested by three trends: omission, alteration, and addition.

Details Become Omitted

It requires less effort to convey a simpler, less complex message. With fewer details to transmit the fear of forgetting or of garbling the message is decreased. In the serial transmissions even those final versions which most closely approximated the original had omitted an appreciable number of details.

There are Eagles in front of the frat house at the State University. It cost $75 to $100 to remove paint each year from the eagles.

The essential question, perhaps, which details *will be retained*? Judging from interviewing the serial transmitters after the demonstrations these aspects will *not* be dropped out:

Details the transmitter wanted or expected to hear.

Details which "made sense" to the transmitter.

Details which seemed important *to the transmitter*.

Details which for various and inexplicable reasons seemed to stick with the transmitter—those aspects which seemed particularly unusual or bizarre; those which had special significance to him; etc.

Details Become Altered

When changes in detail occurred in the serial transmissions, it was often possible to pinpoint the "changers." When asked to explain why they had changed the message, most were unaware that they had done so. However, upon retrospection some admitted that they had changed the details in order to simplify the message, "clarify it," "straighten it out," "make it more sensible," and the like. It became evident, too, that among the details most susceptible to change were the qualifications, the indefinite. Inferential statements are prone to become definite and certain. What may start out as, "The boss seemed angry this morning" may quickly progress to, "The boss was angry."

A well-known psychologist once "planted" a rumor in an enlisted men's mess hall on a certain Air Force base. His statement was: "Is it true that they are building a tunnel big enough to trundle B-52's to—(the town two miles away)?" Twelve hours later the rumor came back to him as: "They are building a tunnel to trundle B-52's to—." The "Is-it-true" uncertainty had been dropped. So had the indefinite purpose ("big enough to").

It became obvious upon interviewing the serial transmitters that bypassing (denotative and connotative) had also played a role. For example, the "president" in the message about the "eagles" was occasionally bypassed as the "President of the U.S." and sometimes the rest of the message was constructed around this detail.

The White House was in such a mess that they wanted to renovate it but found that the cost would be $100 to $75 to paint the eagle so they decided not to do it.

Details Become Added

Not infrequently details are added to the message to "fill in the gaps," "to make better sense," and "because I thought the fellow who told it to me left something out."

The psychologist was eventually told that not only were they building a tunnel for B-52's but that a mile-long underground runway was being constructed at the end of it! The runway was to have a ceiling slanting upward so that a plane could take off, fly up along the ceiling and emerge from an inconspicuous slit at the end of the cavern! This, he admitted, was a much more "sensible" rumor than the one he had started, for the town had no facilities for take-offs and thus there was nothing which could have been done with the B-52's once they reached the end of the tunnel!

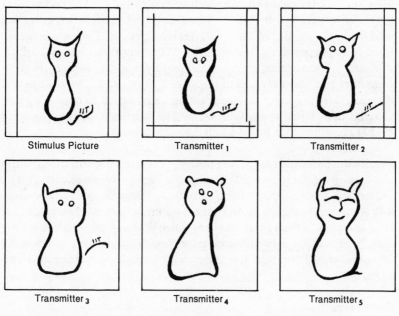

| Stimulus Picture | Transmitter 1 | Transmitter 2 |
| Transmitter 3 | Transmitter 4 | Transmitter 5 |

Figure 20

Pictorial Transmission

An interesting facet about serial transmission is that the three trends—omission, alteration, and addition—are also present when the "message" is pictorial as opposed to verbal. Our procedure was to permit the "transmitter" to view the stimulus picture (upper left corner of Figure 20) for thirty seconds. He then proceeded to reproduce the picture as accurately as possible from memory. When he finished his drawing he showed it to transmitter$_2$ for thirty seconds, who then attempted to reproduce the first transmitter's drawing from memory, etc. Drawings 1 through 5 represented the work of a fairly typical "team" of five transmitters.

Details Become Omitted. Note the progressive simplification of the configuration in the lower right and the eventual omission of it altogether. Note the omission of the border.

Details Become Altered. The border is an interesting example of alteration. The original border is quite irregular, difficult to remember. Transmitter$_1$ when interviewed afterward said, "I remembered that the frame was incomplete somehow but couldn't remember just how it was incomplete." Note how indefinitely irregular his border is. So subtle, in fact, that Transmitter$_2$ said he never recognized it as purposefully asymmetrical: "I thought he was just a little careless." Transmitter$_2$ drew a completely regular border—easy to remember but also easy to fail to notice. Transmitter$_3$ was surprised afterwards to discover that the drawing he had tried to memorize had had a border. It had apparently seemed so "natural," so much a part of the background, that he had failed to attend to it.

Details Become Added. Transmitter$_1$ perceived the stimulus picture as a cat and a cat it remained through the series. When shown that he had added a nose Transmitter$_4$ admitted, "You know, I knew there was something missing from that cat—I knew it had a body, a head, ears, and eyes. I thought it was the mouth that was missing but not the nose." Providing everything *except* a mouth was far too enticing for Transmitter$_5$: "I thought the other fellow made a mistake so I corrected it!"

Correctives[10]

Even serial transmissions, as intricate and as relatively uncontrolled communications as they are, can be improved. The suggestions below are not sensational panaceas. In fact, they are quite commonplace, common sense, but uncommonly used techniques.

Take Notes. Less than five percent of the serial transmitters took notes. Some said that they assumed they were not supposed to (no such restriction had been placed upon them), but most admitted that they rarely took notes as a matter of course. In the cases where all transmitters on a team were instructed to take notes the final versions were manifestly more complete and more accurate than those of the non-notetakers.

Give Details in Order. Organized information is easier to understand and to remember. Choose a sequence (chronological, spatial, deductive, inductive, etc.) appropriate to the content and be consistent with it. For example, it may suit your purpose best to begin with a proposal followed by supporting reasons or to start with the reasons and work toward the proposal. In either case take care to keep proposals and reasons clearly distinguished rather than mixing them together indiscriminately.

Be Wary of Bypassing. If you are the receiver, query (ask the sender what he meant) and paraphrase (put what you think he said or wrote into your own words and get the sender to check you). These simple techniques are effective yet infrequently practiced, perhaps because we are so positive we *know* what the other fellow means; perhaps because we hesitate to ask or rephrase for fear the other fellow (especially if he is the boss) will think less of us for not understanding the first time. The latter apprehension is usually unfounded, at least if we can accept the remarks of a hundred or more executives questioned on the matter during the last four years. "By all means," they have said almost to a man, "I *want* my people to check with me. The person who wants to be sure he's got it straight has a sense of responsibility and that's the kind of man (or woman) I want on my payroll."

Although executives, generally, may take this point of view quite sincerely, obviously not all of them practice it. Querying and paraphrasing are *two-way* responsibilities, and the sender must be truly approachable by his receivers if the techniques are to be successful.

This check-list may be helpful in avoiding bypassing:

Could he be denoting something other than what I am?
Could he be connoting something other than what I am?
Could he be connoting whereas I am merely denoting?
Could he be merely denoting whereas I am connoting?

Distinguish Between Inference and Observation. Ask yourself sharply: Did I *really* see, hear, or read this—or am I guessing part of it? The essential characteristics of a statement of observation are these:

It can be made only by the observer.

(What someone tells you as observational is still inferential for you if you did not observe it.)

It can be made only *after* observation.

It stays with what has been observed; does not go beyond it.

This is not to say that inferential statements are not to be made—we could hardly avoid doing so. But it is important or even vital at times to know *when* we are making them.

Slow Down Your Oral Transmissions. By doing so, you give your listener a better opportunity to assimilate complex and detailed information. However, it is possible to speak *too* slowly so as to lose his attention. Since either extreme defeats your purpose, it is generally wise to watch the listener for clues as to the most suitable rate of speech.

Simplify the Message. This suggestion is for the *originator* of the message. The "middlemen" often simplify without half trying! Most salesmen realize the inadvisability of attempting to sell too many features at a time. The customer is only confused and is unable to distinguish the key features from those less important. With particular respect to oral transmission, there is impressive evidence to indicate that beyond a point the addition of details leads to disproportionate omission. Evidently, you can add a straw to the camel's back without breaking it, but you run the decided risk of his dropping two straws.

Use Dual Media When Feasible. A message often stands a better chance of getting through if it is reinforced by restatement in another communication medium. Detailed, complex, and unfamiliar information is often transmitted by such combinations as a memo follow-up on a telephone call or a sensory aid (slide, diagram, mockup, picture, etc.) accompanying a written or oral message.

Highlight the Important. Presumably the originator of a message knows (or should know) which are its important aspects. But this does not automatically insure that his serial transmitters will similarly recognize them. There are numerous devices for making salient points stand out as such, e.g., using underscoring or capitals in writing, using vocal emphasis or attention-drawing phrases ("this is the main point," "here's the crux," "be sure to note this") in speaking.

Reduce the Number of Links in the Chain. This suggestion has to be followed with discretion. Jumping the chain of command either upward or downward can sometimes have undesirable consequences. However, whenever it is possible to reduce or eliminate the "middlemen," "the message" generally becomes progressively less susceptible to aberrations. Of course, there are methods of skipping links which are commonly accepted and widely practiced. Communication downward can be reduced to person-to-person communication, in a sense, with general memos, letters, bulletins, group meetings, and so forth. Communication upward can accomplish the same purpose via suggestion boxes, opinion questionnaires, or "talk-backs."

Preview and Review. A wise speech professor of mine used to say: "Giving a speech is basically very simple if you do it in three steps: First, you tell them what you're going to tell them; then you tell; then, finally, you tell them what you've told them." This three-step sequence is often applicable whether the message is transmitted by letter, memo, written or oral report, public address, telephone call, or by other means.

SUMMARY

After the last suggestion I feel obliged to review this article briefly. We have been concerned with serial transmission—a widespread, essential, yet susceptible form of communication. Among the factors which vitiate a serial transmission are certain of the communicator's motives and fallacious assumptions. When these and other factors are in play the three processes—omission, alteration, and addition—tend to occur. The suggestions offered for strengthening serial transmission will be more or less applicable, of course, depending upon the communication situation.

An important question remains: What can be done to encourage communicators to practice the techniques? They will probably use them largely to the extent that they think the techniques are needed. But *do* they think them necessary? Apparently many do not. When asked to explain how the final version came to differ so markedly from the original, many of the serial transmitters in my studies were genuinely puzzled. A frequent comment was, "I really can't understand it. All I know is that I passed the message along the same as it came to me." If messages *were* passed along "the same as they came," of course, serial transmission would no longer be a problem. And so long as the illusion of fidelity is with the communicator it is unlikely that he will be prompted to apply some of these simple, prosaic, yet effective techniques to his communicating. Perhaps a first step would be to induce him to question his unwarranted assurance about his communication. The controlled serial transmission experience appears to accomplish this.

QUESTIONS FOR DISCUSSION

1. Discuss, in terms of your own experience, the motives and assumptions Haney lists as leading to inaccuracies in serial transmission. Give an example of each motive and assumption in *your own* past communication behavior.
2. Which of the "correctives" listed by Haney would be of greatest help in face-to-face interpersonal situations?

References

1. Allport, G.W., and Postman, L., "The Basic Psychology of Rumor," *Transactions of the New York Academy of Sciences*, Series II, 8 (1945), pp.61-81.
2. Allport, G.W. and Postman, L., *The Psychology of Rumor*. (New York: Holt, Rinehart & Winston, 1947.)
3. Asch, S., "Group Forces on the Modification and Distortion of Judgments," *Social Psychology*. (Englewood Cliffs, N.J.: Prentice-Hall, 1952.)
4. Back, K.W., "Influence through Social Communication," in Swanson, Newcomb, and Hartley, eds. *Readings in Social Psychology*. (New York: Holt, Rinehart & Winston, 1952.)
5 Back, K.W. et al. "A Method of Studying Rumor Transmission," in Festinger et al., *Theory and Experiment in Social Communication*. (Ann Arbor, Mich: Research Center for Group Dynamics, University of Michigan, 1950.)
6. Borst, M., "Recherches experimentales sur l'éducabilité et la fidèlité du témoignage," *Archives de Psychologie*, 3 (1904), pp.204-314.
7. Bruner, J.S., "The Dimensions of Propaganda," *Journal of Abnormal and Social Psychology*, 36 (1941), pp.311-37.
8. Bruner, J.S., and Postman, L., "Emotional Selectivity in Perception and Reaction," *Personality*, 16 (1947), pp.69-77.
9. Cantril, H., Goudet, H., and Herzog, H., *The Invasion from Mars*. (Princeton: Princeton University Press, 1940.)

10. Carmichael, L., Hogan, H.P., and Walter, A.A., "An Experimental Study of the Effect of Language on the Reproduction of Visually Perceived Form," *Journal of Experimental Psychology*, 15 (1932), pp. 73-86.

11. Carter, L.F., and Schooler, K., "Value, Need, and Other Factors in Perception," *Psychological Review*, 56 (1949), pp.200-207.

12. Claparède, E., "Expériences sur le témoignage: témoignage simple; appréciation; confrontation," *Archives de Psychologie*, 5 (1906), pp. 344-87.

13. *Communicating with Employees*, Studies in Personnel Policy No. 129. (New York: National Industrial Conference Board, 1952.)

14. De Fleur, M.L., and Larsen, O.N., *The Flow of Information*. (New York: Harper and Brothers, 1958.)

15. Gardiner, Riley W., and Lohrenz, Leander J., "Leveling-Sharpening and Serial Reproduction of a Story," *Bulletin of the Menninger Clinic*, 24 (November 1960).

16. Haney, W.V., *Measurement of the Ability to Discriminate Between Descriptive and Inferential Statements*. Unpublished doctoral dissertation, Northwestern University, 1953.

17. Higham, T.M., "The Experimental Study of the Transmission of Rumor," *British Journal of Psychology, General Section*, 42 (1951), pp.42-55.

18. Irving, J.A., "The Psychological Analysis of Wartime Rumor Patterns in Canada," *Bulletin of the Canadian Psychological Association*, 3 (1943), pp.40-44.

19. Jacobson, D.J., *The Affairs of Dame Rumor* (New York: Holt, Rinehart and Winston, 1948).

20. Katz, D., "Psychological Barriers to Communication," in Schramm, ed., *Mass Communications* (Urbana, Ill.: University of Illinois Press, 1949).

21. Katz, E., and Lazarsfeld, P., *Personal Influence: The Part Played by People in the Flow of Mass Communications*. (Glencoe, Ill.: The Free Press, 1955.)

22. Knapp, R.H., "A Psychology of Rumor," *Public Opinion Quarterly*, 8 (1944), pp.23-37.

23. Otto, M.C., "Testimony and Human Nature," *Journal of Criminal Law and Criminology*, 9 (1918), pp.98-104.

24. Postman, L., and Bruner, J.S., "Perception under Stress," *Psychological Review*, 55 (1948), pp.313-23.

25. Postman, L., Bruner, J.S., and McGinnies, E., "Personal Values as Selective Factors in Perception," *Journal of Abnormal and Social Psychology*, 43 (1948), pp.142-54.

26. Smith, G.H., "The Effects of Fact and Rumor Labels," *Journal of Abnormal and Social Psychology*, 42 (1947), pp.80-90.

27. Stefansson, V., *The Standardization of Error*. (London: Routledge and Kegan, Paul, 1928.)

28. Whipple, G.M., "The Observer as Reporter: A Survey of the 'Psychology of Testimony,'" *Psychological Bulletin*, 6 (1909), pp. 153-70.

NOTES

1. "The message," as already suggested, is a misnomer in that what is being conveyed is not static, unchanging, and fixed. I shall retain the term for convenience, however, and use quotation marks to signify that its dynamic nature is subject to cumulative change.

2. During the past three years I have conducted scores of informal experiments with groups of university undergraduate and graduate students, business and government executives, military officers, professionals, and so on. I would read the "message" (below) to the first "conveyor." He would then relay his interpretation to the second conveyor who, in turn, would pass along his interpretation to the third, etc. The sixth (and final member of the "team") would listen to "the message" and then write down his version of it. These final versions were collected and compared with the original.

   > Every year at State University, the eagles in front of the Psi Gamma fraternity house were mysteriously sprayed during the night. Whenever this happened, it cost the Psi Gams from $75 to $100 to have the eagles cleaned. The Psi Gams complained to officials and were promised by the president that if ever any students were caught painting the eagles, they would be expelled from school.*

   > *Adapted from "Chuck Jackson" by Diana Conzett, which appears in Irving J. Lee's *Customs and Crises in Communication* (New York: Harper & Bros., 1954), p.245. Reprinted by permission.

3. On an arbitrary count basis the stimulus message used in the serial transmission demonstrations described in footnote 2 contained 24 "significant details." The final versions contained a mean count of approximately 8 "significant details"—a "detail loss" of 65%.

4. The great majority (approximately 93%) of the final versions (from the serial transmission demonstrations) made "sense." Even those which were the most bizarre and bore the least resemblance to the original stimulus were in and of themselves internally consistent and coherent.
   For example,

   > "At a State University there was an argument between two teams—the Eagles and the Fire Gems in which their clothing was torn."

   > "The Eagles in front of the university had parasites and were sprayed with insecticide."

   > "At State U. they have many birds which desecrate the buildings. To remedy the situation they expelled the students who fed the birds."

5. Lydia Strong, "Do You Know How to Listen?" *Effective Communication on the Job*, Dooher and Marquis, eds. (New York: American Management Association, 1956), p.28.

6. Reprinted from *The Foreman's Letter* with permission of National Foremen's Institute, New London, Conn.

7. Robert Froman, "Making Words Fit the Job," *Nation's Business* (July 1959). Copyright 1959 by NATION'S BUSINESS, Chamber of Commerce of the United States. Reprinted by permission of the publisher.

8. The names have been changed.

9. For a more detailed analysis of these assumptions and for additional methods for preventing and correcting their consequences, see William V. Haney, *Communication: Patterns and Incidents* (Homewood, Ill.: Irwin, 1960), chs. III, IV, V.

10. Most of these suggestions are offered by Irving J. and Laura L. Lee, *Handling Barriers in Communication* (New York: Harper & Bros., 1956), pp.71-74.

Two common situations in which much interpersonal communication occurs are the work setting and the home or family setting. Haney's article discussed serial transmission problems that are likely to occur in work situations. Virginia Satir discusses communication in a family setting. She believes that interpersonal communication is best described as a request-making process. Her article emphasizes the difference between the common meanings that people share for a message (she calls this the *denotative level*) and the qualifications and changes in meanings provided by additional comments about the message, both verbal and nonverbal. A comment about a message, or communication about communication, is called a *metacommunication.* Metacommunication was discussed earlier by Bender and Hocking.

21

COMMUNICATION: A VERBAL ANd NONVERbAL PROCESS of MAKING REQUESTS of THE RECEIVER

Virginia Satir

1. When judging whether a communication is clear, one must also remember that people communicate in a variety of ways in addition to using words.

   A person simultaneously communicates by his gestures, facial expression, body posture and movement, tone of voice, and even by the way he is dressed.

   And all this communication occurs within a context. When does it take place? Where? With whom? Under what circumstances? What is the contract between the persons carrying on the interchange?

2. Because of all these factors, communication is a complex business. The receiver must assess all the different ways in which the sender is sending messages, as well as being aware of his own receiving system, that is, his own interpretation system.

   When A talks, B assesses the verbal meaning of A's message.
   He also listens to the tone of voice in which A speaks.
   He also watches what A does; he notes the "body language" and facial expressions which accompany A's message.
   He also assesses what A is saying within a social context.
   The context may be how B has seen A respond to him and to

Virginia Satir is a consultant and lecturer on family therapy, interpersonal relations, and human communication. Reprinted by permission of the author and the publisher. From Virginia Satir, *Conjoint Family Therapy,* Revised edition, Science and Behavior Books, 1967.

others in the past. It may also be B's expectations about what the requirements of the situation are.

In other words, the receiver (B) is busy assessing both the verbal and the nonverbal content of A's message so that he can come to some judgment about what A meant by his communication.

3.   What A meant by his communication can be said to have at least two levels:

The denotative level: the literal content.

The metacommunicative level: a comment on the literal content as well as on the nature of the relationship between the persons involved.

4.   Animals other than man can send metacommunications. For example, as Gregory Bateson describes it:

Cats may go through all their battery of fighting motions yet at the same time withhold their claws.

By this metacommunication the cat clues other cats as well as people to the fact that he is not "really" fighting; he is playing at fighting. (1)

5.   Metacommunication is a message *about* a message.

It conveys the sender's attitude toward the message he just sent: "The message I sent was a friendly one."

It conveys the sender's attitude toward himself: "I am a friendly person."

It conveys the sender's attitude, feelings, intentions toward the receiver: "I see you as someone to be friendly with."

6.   Humans are especially versatile at metacommunication.

Humans, like other animals, can send nonverbal metacommunications. But the variety of these is wide; humans can frown, grimace, smile, stiffen, slump. And the context in which humans communicate is, itself, one way of communicating.

As a matter of fact, humans cannot communicate without, at the same time, metacommunicating. Humans cannot *not* metacommunicate.

Humans can also send verbal metacommunications. They can verbally explain their message-sending.

7.   When a person verbally explains his message-sending, he is thus denotatively speaking at a metacommunicative level. And these

verbal metacommunications are, themselves, at various abstraction levels.

A person can label what kind of message he sent telling the receiver how seriously he wishes him to receive it and how he should respond to it. He can say:

"It was a joke." (laugh at it)
"It was just a passing remark." (ignore it)
"It was a question." (answer it)
"It was a request." (consider it)
"It was an order." (obey it)

He can say why he sent the message, by referring to what the other did.

"You hit me. So I hit you back."
"You were kind to me. I was returning the favor."

He can say why he sent the message, by referring to what he thinks the other's wishes, feelings, intentions toward him are.

"I thought you were mad and were going to hurt me."
"I thought you were tired and wanted me to help you."
"I thought you were discouraged and wanted me to reassure you."

He can say why he sent the message by referring to a request made by the other:

"You were ordering me to do something, and I don't take orders."
"You were requesting something from me, and I was considering it."

He can say why he sent the message by referring to the kind of response which he was trying to elicit from the other:

"I was trying to get your goat."
"I was trying to get you to love me."
"I was trying to get you to talk."
"I was trying to make you laugh."
"I was trying to get you to agree with me."

He can say why he sent the message by specifically referring to what he was trying to get the other to do or say or *not* do and *not* say:

"I wanted you to go to the store for me."
"I was asking you to phone her for me."
"I was asking you to leave the room."
"I didn't want you to tell her about my illness."
"I wanted you to tell him that I was home."

8. Since humans can "metacommunicate" both verbally and non-verbally, they can give the receiver quite an assortment of messages to sort and weigh, as he tries to figure out what is meant by the communication.

Perhaps A makes the following denotative statement: "The dog is on the couch."
He automatically comments, nonverbally, on this statement by the irritable tone in which he makes it.
He can then verbally explain what he meant by what he said. Out of the welter of choices, he may say: "I wanted you to take the dog off the couch."

9. The receiver of these messages (B) must balance what A said, with how he said it, with what he then said about it.

B balances the nonverbal and the verbal metacommunications (within the context) and compares them to the denotative statement.
If they are all congruent (seem to jibe with each other) he has little difficulty in deciding that A meant what he said he meant.
Whether or not they jibe, he will attend more to the nonverbal metacommunications and to context than he will to the verbal metacommunications. For one thing, the nonverbal is a less clear or explicit communication, so it requires greater attention.

10. Whenever a person communicates he is not only making a statement, he is also asking something of the receiver and trying to influence the receiver to give him what he wants. This is the "command aspect" of a message. Such requests, however, may have various degrees of explicitness and intensity.
The sender may be simply asking the receiver to show, by response, that his message was heard: "Just listen to me."
Or he may be asking for a specific kind of response: "Tell me where the store is" or, "Go to the store for me."

11. The receiver, in turn, must respond, because people cannot *not* communicate.

Even if the receiver remains silent, he is still communicating. And, incidentally, symptoms are one way of communicating in a nonverbal way.

12. But even though all messages have requests in them, they are not always expressed verbally. Thus, the receiver must rely on metacommunications for his clues as to what the sender wants. He asks himself:

What is the sender verbally saying?
What, specifically, is he requesting? Is the request fully expressed at the denotative level?
If not, perhaps the way in which he communicates and the context in which he is communicating will give me clues to what he is asking of me.

13. If the communication, or message, and the metacommunication or metamessage do not fit, the receiver must somehow translate this into a single message. In order to do this satisfactorily he needs to be able to comment on the presence of the discrepancy.
Let us take a trivial example. A husband who is working on a household fixture says, in an irritable tone, "Damn it, the fixture broke!" The wife, in this relationship, may go through the following process (with greater agility and speed, of course, than the snail's pace described here):

He is telling me about the condition of the electrical fixture he is working on.
But he is doing more than that. He is telling me that he is irritated. His "Damn it," along with his tone, helps me decide this.
Is he criticizing me? Is he telling me that I am responsible for the condition of the fixture?
If he is criticizing me, what does he want me to do? Take over the job for him? Apologize? Or what?
Or is he criticizing himself, irritated that he is having a frustrating time with the job, and that he only has himself to blame for the fact that the fixture broke?
If he is primarily criticizing himself, what is he asking me to do? Sympathize with him? Listen to him? Or what?
I know, from living with him, that he prides himself on his tool dexterity and that he considers electrical maintenance his special forte. Evidently, his view of himself is being put to the

test. So he must be criticizing himself. And he must primarily be asking me to sympathize with him.

But sympathize *how*? Does he want me to help him with the job, bring him coffee, or what? What behavior on my part that he could see and hear would mean to him that I am sympathizing with him?

14. Let us take another example. A husband says, in an irritable tone, "The dog is on the couch." The wife, in this relationship, may go through the following process:

He is telling me where the dog is.
But he is doing more than that. He sounds irritated.
Why is he telling me about his irritation? Is he criticizing me for the fact that the dog is on the couch?
If he is not criticizing me, what does he want me to do? Just listen to him? Sympathize with his irritation? Take the dog off the couch? Or what?
I wanted a dog. He didn't. I went ahead and got one without his agreement. Now, when he shows his irritation at the dog, he is complaining about what I did. He is criticizing me for disobeying him. He undoubtedly wants me to take the dog off the couch, but does he also want me to get rid of the dog and apologize to him for going against his wishes?

15. Let us return to the first example. Instead of saying, "Damn it, the fixture broke," the husband could say, "Damn it, I'm having a hard time with this job. Bring me a cup of coffee." The wife, in this case, would have little trouble assessing his message. He would be telling her overtly what he wanted from her and why. In other words, his request that she sympathize with him by bringing coffee would be clear.

16. In the second example, instead of saying, "The dog is on the couch," the husband could say, "Take the dog off the couch and get rid of him. You never should have bought a dog. I told you I didn't want one." The wife in this case would have little trouble assessing his message.

He would be telling her specifically what he wanted from her and why. In other words, his request that she agree to obey him would be clear.

In both cases, the wife is still in the position of deciding whether or not to agree to her husband's request that she obey him. But at least she is in no doubt about what it really is that her husband wants of her.

17. In other words, the request, which is part of every message, may or may not be expressed denotatively. And there are degrees to which requests can be spelled out denotatively.

"Damn it, the fixture broke," and, "The dog is on the couch," are very indirect requests, requests not expressed at the denotative level.

"Bring me a cup of coffee," and, "Take the dog off the couch and get rid of him," are direct requests, requests expressed at the denotative level.

Or, if these specific requests had been expressed at a more abstract level, they would also be direct: "Sympathize with me" or, "Do what I want."

18. However, all messages, when viewed at their highest abstraction level can be characterized as "Validate me" messages. These are frequently interpreted as "Agree with me," "Be on my side," "Validate me by sympathizing with me," or, "Validate me by showing me you value me and my ideas."

19. When people communicate, they rarely go around verbally requesting that others agree with them or requesting that others want what they want. They don't, because they are forced by the wish to be valued, and by the wish for cooperation, to persuade or at least try to elicit the wished-for response. Many persons feel embarrassed about their wish to get validation from outside themselves.

As I have said, communication is a necessarily incomplete process. But we can now see why this process becomes even more incomplete than pure logic or inadequacy of words would dictate.

Incomplete (indirect) communication can serve many interpersonal purposes which are not necessarily dysfunctional.

It can help camouflage such requests.

It can prevent embarrassment in case one's requests (of any kind) are refused.

20. Up to now, I have been discussing the problems posed for human
     receivers by the complexity and the incompleteness of human
     communication.

     Just because this communication *is* complex and incomplete to
        differing degrees, all receivers are required to fill in or complete
        the sender's message by clairvoyance or guesswork.
     Receivers can and do achieve this, sometimes with amazing accu-
        racy, considering all the fancy footwork they have to go
        through.
     But there are times when even the most clairvoyant of receivers
        guesses incorrectly. When this happens, the sender's next
        message usually lets him know his error.

21. The messages I have listed in this chapter have all been relatively
     congruent within the context; they have jibed with each other.

     A congruent communication is one where two or more messages
        are sent via different levels but none of these messages seri-
        ously contradicts any other. For example, the husband says,
        "The dog is on the couch" in an irritable tone, in a context
        which tells the wife that he is irritated and why he is irritated.
     An incongruent communication is one where two or more mes-
        sages, sent via different levels, seriously do contradict each
        other. One level of communication is context itself. For exam-
        ple, the husband says, in a delighted tone, that the dog is on the
        couch, but from the context the wife knows that he hates dogs;
        whether they are on couches or anywhere else.

22. Simple contradictory communication is where two or more mes-
     sages are sent in a sequence via the same communication level
     and oppose each other.

     Perhaps A says the following:

        "Come here . . . No, go away."
        "I love you . . . No, I hate you."
        "I'm happy . . . No, I'm sad."
        "My wife is tall . . . No, my wife is short."

     Perhaps A does the following:

        Pushes B away. Pulls B back.
        Buys a ticket to the movie, but doesn't go see it.
        Puts his coat on, then takes it off.

23.   But such simple contradictions cannot occur without some accompanying metacommunication, since one cannot *not*
metacommunicate.

Although the self-contradictions listed above are relatively clear,
they are also accompanied by smiles or frowns or tone of voice,
and in a context.
When contradictions occur between different levels of communication, they become *incongruent*. "Incongruent" refers to a discrepancy between the report and the command aspects of a
message.

24.   Messages differ in the degree to which they are incongruent.
Relatively simple incongruent communication sounds and looks
like this:

A says, "It's cold in here," and takes off his coat.
A says, "I hate you," and smiles.
A wears an evening dress to a funeral.
A wears tennis shoes to a board of directors' meeting.
A says, "Come closer, darling," and then stiffens.

25.   Incongruent communication can become even more so when the
sender's nonverbal metacommunication does not jibe with his
verbal metacommunication.

The sender may say "Come closer, darling," then stiffen, and
then say, "I want to make love."

In this case, should the receiver respond to the sender's denotative statement ("Come closer, darling")?
Or should he respond to the sender's nonverbal statement (the
stiffness)?
Or should he respond to the sender's words explaining his
intentions ("I want to make love")?
This is called being presented with a double-level message.

As usual, the receiver relies heavily on context and on the nonverbal signals to help him in his clairvoyance process. In this
case, the nonverbal signals and the context contradict each
other. But, being an especially trusting and courageous receiver, he says to himself:

"Let's see. The sender and I are courting. Yet other people are
around.

"I have learned from past experience with the sender that she is
nervous about showing amorous feelings publicly. But that
doesn't mean she doesn't have amorous feelings toward me.

"I will live dangerously and ignore her nonverbal metacommunication in this case. I will rely on context alone and
accept her verbally-stated intention.

"In other words, her verbal statement, 'I want to make love'
carries greater weight with me. All I do is add to it the
proviso which she did not add: '. . . but other people are
around, so I am just nervous.' In other words, the sender is
willing to be nervous, with a little assistance."

The freedom to comment and question immediately takes the
receiver out of the clairvoyant dilemma. When this freedom is
not present, the chances for misunderstanding are great. In
the case of a child, as we have seen, there is a likelihood that
such messages will be built up to the point where a "double
bind" occurs.

26.   Incongruent communication like that just described puts an extra
burden on the receiver. But, whether or not the sender's message
is incongruent, the receiver can still go through various
checking-out procedures in order to find out what is being reported, what requested, and why.

For example, when the wife heard her husband say, in an irritable
tone, "Damn it, the fixture broke," she could have decided that
she still didn't have enough data, even from the content of the
message, to find out what her husband was requesting from
her and why.

She might have gone to where he was and stood there for a
minute, continuing to pick up clues from him.

If she had done this, she would, of course, have been communicating with him. By her presence she would be saying:
"I heard you. I am attending."

He would also continue to communicate with her, as he jabbed
at the fixture, grunted, sighed, and so forth.

The wife might then have asked, "Is there anything I can do?"
The minute she did this, she would be asking her husband to be
specific in what he was requesting.

Perhaps he would have said, "No, I just have to work it out."
By this response, the wife would have succeeded in narrowing

her unknowns. She would now be more certain that he was distressed with himself but she still could not be sure what he specifically wanted from her. Did he want her to listen? Attend? Sympathize?

The wife might go on to ask, "Would you like a cup of coffee?" And he might answer, "Yes, damn it, I would." The communication sequence would now be relatively closed or complete. (Of course, it is more complete if she actually brings the coffee!)

27. If, instead, the wife had been fairly confident about her clairvoyance, she might have simply assumed that she knew what his implied request was. She might have put it in words herself and seen how he responded.

She could have asked outright, "Would you like a cup of coffee?" and he might have said, "Yes, damn it, I would." If she had guessed correctly enough, the sequence would have been relatively closed.

But he might have said, "Hell, no, what would I want coffee for, at a time like this?" Then she would have known that her clairvoyance process wasn't working very well. She would have been required to check out further, perhaps by going through the clue-getting procedures already described.

28. Receivers vary in their ability to perceive the needs and wishes of others.

Although all receivers put great weight on the metacommunicative aspects, they vary in their ability to assess what the sender is asking of them.

The wife may mistake her husband's irritation with himself for a criticism of her, and end up trying to take over the job for him instead of sympathizing with him.

The wife may mistake her husband's criticism of her for irritation over the specific behavior of the dog, and end up trying to sympathize with him instead of taking the dog off the couch or getting rid of the dog.

The lover, in the third example, may mistake the woman's stiffening for distaste, and end up rejecting her instead of making love.

We even have psychiatric labels for people who are not able to accurately weigh a message for its meaning. They are not able to guess attitudes, intentions, feelings (as expressed in metacommunication) accurately.

If this wife, in all contexts, in all relationships, and at all times within a relationship, decides that senders are criticizing her or praising her, we would readily label her paranoid or egocentric.

Also, although receivers put great weight on the metacommunicative aspects to help tell them what the sender is requesting, they vary in their ability to attend to denotation in spite of, or along with, metacommunication. For example, perhaps a person attends a lecture for the purpose of receiving denotative content from the speaker. But perhaps the speaker speaks in such a frightened tone that the receiver cannot hear what the speaker is saying because he is so concerned about the speaker's fright.

29. Senders vary in their ability to send clear requests, so that the receiver has to guess as little as possible.

For example, let us say that a wife wants to see a movie with her husband. If she communicates in a functional way, she might say, "Let's see a movie," or, more overtly, "I would like to see a movie with you."

But, if she communicates in a dysfunctional way, she might say any of the following things:

"You would like to see a movie, *wouldn't* you."
"It would do you good to see a movie."
"If you want to see a movie, we'll see one."
"We might as well see a movie. It's Saturday night."
"There's a new movie house down the street."
"My voices are ordering me to see a movie."

30. These are some of the covert ways in which this wife can request something from her husband without acknowledging that she is making a request.

She does not clearly label her wish which is behind her request, as *her* wish.

Or, she may fail to label her wish *as a wish*. It becomes not a wish but a "must," something one is commanded to do. (The commander may be the other person or people in general, or "one's duty" or "voices" or something foreign inside of the self.)

Or, she may label her wish as not a wish but as "the lesser of two evils."

31. The husband, in this case could do some checking out. He could say: "Do *you* want to see a movie?" or "Do you want to see a movie *with me?*"

   But here is what can happen if the husband does ask his wife what she meant by her communication. She might go on to explain her message in any one of the following statements:

   "No, I thought *you* wanted to go."
   "No, I just thought we *should.*"
   "No, I don't necessarily want to go. I want to do what you want."
   "There are times when I want to see a movie, but this isn't one of them."
   "I don't particularly want to go. My voices are ordering me."

32. By denying that she had a wish, the wife is also denying that her wish expressed toward her husband. She denies that she has made a request of him. If he pursues his questions, she may go on to deny further.

   "You can go or not. I don't care."
   "If you want to be a stay-at-home, that's your business."
   "If you go to the movies, you go to the movies."
   "Nobody asked you to go. If you want to go, then go."

33. The wife, when replying to her husband's request (in this case, a request to clarify), denies any or all parts of her message.

   The Bateson group, and Jay Haley, in particular, has defined four parts of every message:

   I (the sender)
   am saying something (message)
   to you (the receiver)
   in this situation (context). (3)

   All messages are requests, yet the wife may deny this, in so many words, by saying:

   "I didn't care one way or the other." (*I* didn't request anything.)

"I just threw out a suggestion for whatever it was worth." (I didn't *request* anything.)

"Whether or not you go to the movies is immaterial to me." (I didn't request anything *of you*.)

"At one time, I might have wanted to go with you. But I know better now." (I didn't request anything of you *just now*.)

34. We note how defensive the wife is, as she sends her highly incomplete message. (These messages are incomplete because they do not clearly label "*I, want this, from you, in this situation.*") She makes it hard for her husband to find out what she wants.

    She covers herself as she sends her request, almost as though she anticipated refusal.

    "Voices are ordering me. . ."
    "I am doing this for you. . ."
    "There's a new movie house down the street."

    She covers herself after she is asked to clarify: "I thought *you* wanted me to go," or, "Nobody asked you to go."

35. We also note how offensive the wife is, as she sends her request and responds to requests to clarify. She makes it hard for her husband to want to do what she wants.

    She disparages him in anticipation of refusal:

    "A person should see a movie at least once a month if he professes to be cultured."
    "We might as well see a movie. I'm bored."

    She disparages him after he asks her to clarify (and this very disparagement reveals her disappointment over the fact that he does not seem influenceable):

    "I can't *make* you do anything."
    "You'll do exactly what you *feel* like doing."
    "Ask anything of you?th I know better!"

36. One could decide, on first thought, that this wife is a dysfunctional communicator and that she puts unnecessary burdens on her functional husband who, in this case, tries to check out the meaning of her message.

But when people communicate, they are sending a message to a receiver.

The wife tailors her message to the way she thinks her husband will respond to it.

Once we note how he does respond to her, we will see that her messages are tailored to a kind of response which she has learned to expect from her husband.

Her husband, in his response, does the same.

37. One cannot view messages separate from interaction, as I have been doing, and receive the full picture.

One must at least note what A says, how B responds, how A responds to B's response. Communication is a two-sided affair: senders are receivers; receivers are also senders.

One must note whether or not these interaction sequences repeat themselves over time and in different content areas.

If they do repeat themselves, these sequences represent how these two people characteristically communicate with one another.

38. However, before analyzing interaction, one can profit from analyzing isolated messages. Such an analysis:

Highlights different principles about messages and message-sending.

Highlights the kinds of problems which highly defensive communication poses for the receiver.

Helps document inferences about what inner wishes and fears dictate and how they perpetuate dysfunctional communication.

39. This husband's communication does have something to do with the wife's characteristic way of asking for something from him.

But even before analyzing this, we can guess that this wife fears that her husband will reject her request.

Behind her denials that she has a wish and has made a request, is the wish that her husband would not only want to go to the movies with her, but would want to do what she wants because he loves her: "You'll do what you *feel* like doing."

She is not unusual in having this want. But if she cannot come to terms with it, she can easily trap herself and her husband in an impossible dilemma.

No two people think alike on everything.
No two people feel the same way at all times within a relation-
    ship.
No two people want the same things or want them at the same
    time. People operate from different timetables.
We are, in fact, autonomous, different, and unique beings.
Yet we are, at the same time, dependent on others. We need
    them to help us get many of the things we want (or not
    prevent us from getting them). We are also dependent on
    others to validate our existence and worth.

40. Therefore, even though people are making requests of others
     when they communicate, there are some things that cannot be
     requested. Yet these are the very things people also want.

We cannot ask that others feel as we do or as we want them to. As
    Bateson and Watzlawick have pointed out, feelings are spon-
    taneous; they are not subject to self-request or to the requests of
    others. (1, 7)

All we can do is try to elicit feelings.
Failing to elicit, we can accept our disappointment and try
    again.

We cannot ask that others think as we do. Thoughts are not
    subject to the requests of others.

All we can do is try to persuade others, and present our argu-
    ments in the clearest, most cogent form possible.
Failing to persuade, we can accept our disappointment and
    compromise, or "agree to disagree."

We can, of course, *demand* that others say or do (or not say or not
    do) what we want. But if we succeed in this, our success will be
    questionable.

We shall have validated our power but not our lovability or
    worth, since we have "had to ask."
Also, since such a tactic challenges the other's autonomy, it is
    likely that he will feel devalued and will devalue back.

41. Evidently man is insatiable. He can never be loved enough,
     valued enough. Yet he can never be safe enough, powerful
     enough.

These two wants are contradictory if viewed on the same continuum. Man seems to have a built-in potential for defeating
himself.

If he sees these two wants as an either/or proposition, he puts
them in conflict with each other and loses out on both.
If he allows them to coexist, each in its proper time and place,
he will not only gain both, but will find that each enhances
the other.

The way he communicates with other persons will take its form
from whichever of these two approaches he adopts.

If he takes the first approach, it indicates that he will handle the
different-ness of others in terms of *war* and *who is right*.
If he takes the second, he will handle different-ness on the basis
of *exploration* and *what fits*.
The former leads to stalemating, retardation and pathology.
The latter leads to growth, individuality and creativity.

References

1. Bateson, G. "A Theory of Play and Fantasy", *Psychiat. Res. Rep.*, 2 (1955).
   39-51.
2. Bateson, G.; Jackson, D.D.; Haley, J., and Weakland, J.H. Toward a
   Theory of Schizophrenia, *Behavioral Science*, 1 (1956), 251-264.
3. Haley, J. "The Family of the Schizophrenic: A Model System," *Journal of
   Nervous and Mental Disease*, 129 (1959), 357-374.
4. Haley, J. "Control in the Psychotherapy of Schizophrenics," *Archives of
   General Psychiatry*, 5 (1961), 340-353.
5. Jackson, D.D. "Family Interaction, Family Homeostasis, and Some Implications for Conjoint Family Psychotherapy", In J. Masserman, ed., *Individual and Familial Dynamics* (New York: Grune & Stratton, 1959).
6. Jackson, D.D.; Riskin, J., and Satir, V.M., "A Method of Analysis of a
   Family Interview" *Archives of General Psychiatry*, 5 (1961), 321-339.
7. Watzlawick, P. *An Anthology of Human Communication* (Palo Alto, Calif:
   Science and Behavior Books, 1963).

QUESTIONS FOR DISCUSSION

1. If you want to be precise, what is wrong with saying, "What is
   meant by the communication"? How does Satir intend us to
   interpret those words?

2. Satir says that "all messages have requests in them." Another way of phrasing this would be to say that all messages are persuasive in nature. Do you agree with Satir or disagree? State your reasons.
3. What is a "validate me" message?
4. According to Satir, if a wife just stands by her husband, she is communicating with him. How would Berlo's definition of communication classify such an act?
5. Why does Satir suggest that "one cannot view messages separate from interaction . . . and receive the full picture"? What kinds of information might we get about a communication interaction by noting *responses* to *responses* and *patterns repeated over time*?

David Ralph discusses the steps involved in constructing a message. This message may be a public speech at a political convention or a request for a favor from a friend. Although the steps may prove more useful in a formalized speaking situation, the steps and the principles involved are the same for both settings. People assume that communication is an automatic process in which the meanings of one person are transferred directly to the mind of another. As the preceding chapters have emphasized, this assumption is incorrect. But people often behave as though they believed it to be true. They produce messages without considering the possible or even the probable effects of those messages on receivers. Such messages are often "clear only if known." That is, if you already know what the source of the message intended, then the message will appear quite clear to you. But in that case, you didn't really need the message— you gained no information. Messages that are "clear only if known" are of little help to a receiver who is trying to sort out the many possible meanings a source may have intended. If the source remembers that messages do not carry meaning but only help the receiver to discriminate between many possible meanings he already possesses, the sources may construct messages that are more easily understood.

22

fIRST STEPS
iN COMMUNiCATiNq ORAlly

David C. Ralph

This book aims to help you improve in your ability to communicate orally with other people. The principles of communication it employs (verbal and nonverbal) have been developed over thousands of years and, in recent times, have been tested and refined through scientific research. It is important for you to realize that the development or improvement of the skills of *communicating* will require a substantial effort over a considerable period of time—the principles of communicating effectively are neither few enough nor simple enough to learn overnight.

But your need to communicate will not wait while you master these pages—while you relate principles with practice. This very day, for example, you will deliver many, many messages: most of them probably brief; the great majority of them informal, without much time given to thinking about the message or its consequences; many of them unimportant and purposeless; but many of them vital to your moment-by-moment existence. True, you will probably be receivers much more often than sources of messages; but in a normal waking day you may give directions, inquire into the health of your neighbor, exchange quips concerning the latest activities on Capitol Hill, exert influence (or attempt to) upon your boss or a co-worker, explain why you failed to accomplish a certain task, discuss the apparent meaning of a passage with your teacher or with other students, cope with the

David C. Ralph is Professor of Communication at Michigan State University. From *Principles of Speaking*, Third Edition, by Kenneth G. Hance, David C. Ralph, and Milton J. Wiksell. Copyright © 1975 by Wadsworth Publishing Company. Reprinted by permission of the publisher.

wounded feelings of a young child, wriggle evasively out of a direct response to an embarrassing question, report on a project to your superior or a team of consultants, seek advice from a lawyer, wrestle with a group of other interested citizens over various solutions to a local problem, argue that pot smoking is no worse than getting drunk, achieve an understanding with your living companion concerning some philosophical point, and on and on.

Some of these messages will be "prepared," that is, thought about in advance, some will be off the cuff (and some regretted), some will be spoken in a dyad (a one-to-one conversation), some in a group, and some may be delivered to people who have gathered for the purpose of listening to your words. Messages will vary in length.

But they will be messages and most of them will be oral (what many people call "speakin' "). And, what is especially significant to our purpose, they will all be based upon one set of communication principles, drawn from what we have been able to develop of communication theory. This book directs those principles to the comprehensive development of your skills as an oral communicator. This chapter offers an interim and brief look at the steps you will take in preparing and presenting a message.

Although some of these steps apply mainly to situations that call for a planned, carefully prepared message, most of them apply to the daily, informal messages that make up the bulk of our communication:

1. Decide the why and what of your message.
2. Analyze your receiver's potential response to your message.
3. Construct a basic, abbreviated plan for your message.
4. Discover, create, gather, interpret, and evaluate materials for your message.
5. Organize your message.
6. Deliver your message.
7. Evaluate your message.

Communicating for a purpose, as we have described it, results from some kind of exigence[1]—a need, an event, a stimulus, a demand, a raison d'être, a cause, a situation. The process of communicating is, of course, much more involved than the simple list of steps (above) might suggest. However, this list is workable for the beginning speaker, and the order of the steps is probably the most workable order for him or her. As he attains the freedom that comes with experience and success, the communicator will learn (for both formal and informal occasions) to vary the order of preparation and the degree of emphasis upon the steps.

Step 1: Decide the Why and What of Your Message

Why are you communicating and what will you make known? These questions should pop into your mind the instant you feel the urge to open your mouth—at least in any situation where you are speaking for a purpose. The questions are significant, urgent, whether your message is an almost instantaneous reply to a demand of your environment (an exigence) or whether it is a carefully prepared and rehearsed formal statement. Any further preparation, ranging from quick, unrehearsed decisions concerning the content of a brief message to extensive research for supporting evidence, depends upon the answers to the questions, "Why am I communicating?" and, "What do I want to say?"

First of all, as a beginning student of communication, you should determine your *specific purpose* for speaking. Make a concise and accurate statement of what you want to accomplish—or, to put the matter in behavioral terms, state what you want your listeners to do or believe or understand. This is your *purpose sentence,* and you should refer to it throughout the preparation of your message so that you never lose track of why you are speaking.

If your message is a formal one, involving time and effort for preparation, you should write down your purpose sentence at the top of the page on which you are planning your message. If the message is informal or must be presented quickly, with no time to set your thoughts on paper, "file" the purpose sentence in the front of your mind, where you can refer to it often and quickly as the message develops. In many instances you will actually use it in the presentation of your message: perhaps when you wish to declare what you are talking about; perhaps when you offer arguments or evidence in support of your purpose, or present key explanations of your purpose; perhaps at the conclusion, when you may wish to remind your listeners of the reasons for your speech.

Your purpose sentence, written down or not, should be as specific as you can make it: "The new federal regulations in the field of automotive safety are intended to reduce automotive accidents in three major ways."[2] "Extensive development of mass transportation between nearby metropolitan areas must be begun *now*" is an example of a specific purpose sentence for a message advocating a specific course of action. "The Beatles are gone—but never forgotten" does not sound terribly specific, but it may sum up precisely what you feel about hard rock music on radio.

Sometimes you feel a compulsion to originate a message—either as a reply to one that has just been aimed at you or as the result of some thinking on your part, and you may, therefore, want to ask yourself, "What is my *general purpose*, or goal, in speaking on this occasion?" Viewed from one perspective, the purpose of communication is affective—that is, you communicate in order to affect the behavior of others. This motivation suggests at least three approaches to communicative situations: (1) You may want to advocate a change, or try to get your listeners to agree with your position on a controversial subject. (2) You may want to explain something, or enlighten your listeners on a subject you think they should know more about. (3) You may want to amuse others. You may even want to do all these things in the same message.

Sometimes formal opportunities or exigences may occur calling for the delivery of a prepared message on a subject of your own choice; or you may be enrolled in a course in communication or public speaking where either you will be assigned a topic or subject area for investigation and oral report or you will be asked to choose your own topic. The following hints will apply to these situations, but they are also useful as study points for conversational or daily communication behavior:

Hints for the Beginning Student

1. Choose a worthwhile subject. No one enjoys listening to someone talk about a subject that neither of them feels is important. Most listeners want to get something worth remembering, or at least worth thinking about, in return for making the effort to listen. Talk about ideas, issues, controversies, doubts, unresolved questions that affect our lives.

2. Choose a subject your listeners will find interesting. Don't be afraid to be a little ambitious. Think about what your listeners like, what they do, how they feel. If they can identify their own interests in your talk, it is a safe bet they will enjoy it.

3. Choose a subject in which *you* are interested. Your listeners will seldom care any more about a topic than you do. You will find that your best speaking in any situation—formal speech making or coffee-break conversation—happens when you stick to subjects that interest you and fit your beliefs. Even though your interests can never be identical with those of your listeners, people gathered in one group usually have many things in common—that is why they are there. If your interests are very different from theirs, they may just be uninformed about your particular subject, and you may kindle their interest.

4. Choose a topic you understand. If you don't understand it, you can hardly expect your listeners to. As you become more experienced in speaking to people, you will find yourself tackling subjects you know little about and discovering new ideas and viewpoints. But as a beginner, *talk about something you know*.

5. Choose that aspect of the assigned topic that you understand best or believe in most. If the subject under consideration is "Peace," you might choose to show how "Peace Begins in the Heart of an Individual."

6. Choose that aspect you think will be most enjoyable or most useful to your listeners. Don't try to cover the whole subject in a few minutes.

7. After your topic is chosen and limited, analyze your listeners' probable reactions. Will they be interested or bored, receptive or hostile, apathetic? If it seems unlikely that your subject will receive some kind of positive reaction, now is the time to choose a new one.

Step 2: Analyze Your Receiver's Potential Response to Your Message

In Chapter 1 we discovered that the receiver is as much a part of the communication process as is the source. In fact, in many—if not most—daily communication exchanges (interpersonal communication, for instance), speaker and listener exchange and share roles so frequently that a spy in the corner often could not distinguish between the two. It follows, then, that the speaker should give as much consideration to his audience as he does to what he is saying; and the time, place, and conditions under which he speaks deserve no less careful thought.

Analysis of (and adaptation to) the receiver's potential response takes place throughout the life of the particular communication event, beginning at the moment of the exigence or the decision to create a message is made, and continuing throughout the preparation, during the actual presentation, and certainly during whatever evaluation circumstances permit.

Significant decisions are made during the analysis and adaptation phases of your message preparation and delivery. You may elect to plunge ahead with your original ideas and message structure, to modify them, to alter language, to change your basic mode of communication (from directly persuasive to explanatory, for example), or even to abandon the message altogether.

It is most important to remember that listener analysis and adaptation are not restricted to formal messages prepared in advance. In almost any communication situation, verbal and nonverbal cues will be given off by your receiver, cues that will help you to discover (1) whether you're getting the message across, (2) whether you are convincing your hearer (or whether he is accepting your explanation), or (3) when he wants to respond or present a message of his own.

Moreover, adapting your message to improve its chance of getting across is not necessarily evil or tricky or unethical—unless you deliberately choose to become so. Understanding between two human beings through communication is the first step toward consensus, whether consensus means that you have persuaded the other to your views or that the two of you can agree to respect each other's beliefs.

While the following hints are intended primarily for the speaker who has some time *in advance of the presentation* to analyze and adapt to his listener and to the occasion of the message, careful study will show you that some of them can fit even the most informal and spontaneous communication situations.

Hints for the Beginning Student

1. Note the physical conditions of the place in which you will communicate and adjust your method of presentation accordingly. Is the room large? Speak loudly. Small? Use ordinary conversational volume. Will you be speaking from a stage or platform, in an office, or in a family living room? Whatever conditions are present in the room— shape, size, and so on—take note of them and adapt accordingly.

2. Learn the purpose of the meeting. If the audience is coming to hear *you* speak, prepare your message with this in mind. If the meeting is more a round-table discussion, a seminar, or a committee meeting, prepare your message with an eye to contributing what you can to the meeting's intent.

3. Learn as much as you can about the people you will communicate with. In most impromptu, everyday speaking situations, you probably already know something about your listeners from having worked or talked with them, and conscious adaptation will sometimes be unnecessary; it will have become almost automatic. However, when you are presenting a prepared speech or are speaking to strangers, it will help you to know in advance the sex and age groups of the listeners, their occupations and life styles, their education, interests. It will help you to know something about their political or religious affiliations, cultural inclinations, and views on current controversial issues. These things help reveal the personalities, attitudes, beliefs, and behaviors of your listeners, and they assist you in deciding what kind of language and ideas you'll need to use to get your messages across most effectively. When you prepare your message, spend a

little time finding out about your audience; when you communicate without specific preparation, give these items a little thought before you open your mouth—and throughout the duration of your communication. Chances are you know your listeners better than you think you do and can speak to *them* (and, most importantly, *with them*), not just hear yourself speak.

Step 3: Construct a Basic, Abbreviated Plan for Your Message

If your message is to be spontaneous, informal, or otherwise unshaped for specific circumstances, you will, of course, not plan it out in advance. However, lack of opportunity for planning does not excuse the communicator from communicating as clear and effective a message as possible. You should, therefore, even in the brief time it takes to clear your throat, shuffle your feet, or otherwise signify your intention of communicating, think out a basic plan of what you intend to say and the order of your main points.

As we shall demonstrate in Step 5, it is convenient to think of a prepared message as consisting of four parts: *purpose sentence, introduction, body,* and *conclusion.* Even in an impromptu, interpersonal message, it is usually possible to ask yourself, "What do I want to say? Why?" The answers to those questions constitute your purpose sentence. You also will probably have time to ask, "Shall I hit the matter directly or work up to it slowly and indirectly?" The answer to this question produces the basic structure of your message—the direct approach we call "deductive" and the indirect approach "inductive"—and it also tells you something about your introduction and your conclusion. (Remember that all of this is going through your head in a split second, or while you are blowing your nose or lighting a cigarette or otherwise stalling for a little time!)

For example, if your message is to be short and direct, you may want no introduction other than some word or nonverbal sign to assure the attention of your listener. But, because you did launch into your main point first, you may wish to say it again at the end of your message (conclusion), to make sure your receiver remembers it. On the other hand, an indirect message usually demands a beginning that will capture the listener's attention and a general theme that will lead into your "gut" point. In this case, the statement of the main point may also be the end or conclusion of the message.

Obviously, many interpersonal messages and others of the off-the-cuff variety (and that accounts for most of our communication) fail to get through because the communicator either didn't understand or ignored the principle of order or structure—after all, if we can't follow the message, we can't understand it.

Hints for constructing a plan are found in Step 5. With a little study, they can be adapted and abbreviated to fit the message that cannot wait for formal planning. And by the way, what better procedure for the composer of the formal message to follow than to include Step 3 in *his* preparation, as well? You cannot really wait until you have gathered up all the material for your formal speech to start thinking about how you intend to order it. So you, too, should compose a basic, abbreviated plan for your message, early in your preparation stage.

Step 4: Discover, Create, Gather, Interpret, and Evaluate Materials for Your Message

The stuff of which talk is made—the materials of speaking—can be classified as three kinds: *personal proof* (to raise or maintain our credibility with our listeners), *materials of development* (to carry the sense of our message), and *materials of experience* (to help our listeners associate our experience with their experiences). As situations and audiences differ, they demand different uses of and emphases on the materials; and even within one speaking situation, you may have to change your emphasis from time to time as you analyze your listeners. Some of these materials are just waiting for you to find and use them. Others you must create with your own reasoning abilities and imagination. Or you must put old wine in a new skin—that is, put together materials from an outside source into your own patterns. Of course, the more time you have to prepare, the greater use you can make of these materials; but persistent and careful study will enable you to employ them even in informal, impromptu, and interpersonal speaking situations (which is just another way of saying that the more attention we pay to what is going on around us, the more effective we become in the art of communication).

Hints for the Beginning Student

1. Use personal proof. Try to show your listeners that you are interested in them, that you know your subject, that you really *want* to share your ideas with them. The *you* in speaking will work wonders in putting your message across.

2. Use materials of development. Your listeners will not "get" your message unless you back up your statements with evidence and reasoning, and make clear to them points they may not understand immediately.

3. Use experience and sensory materials. Help your listeners feel what you feel, experience (vicariously) what you have experienced, and become as interested in your talk as you are. Use words and phrases that appeal to the "doors of perception"—the senses—and your listeners will feel actively engaged in your talk.

4. As you gather materials, consider how much you know about your subject and how much more you need to know to accomplish your speaking purpose.

5. Talk with other people who have information about your topic.

6. Learn about your subject by firsthand observation.

7. Read as much as you can on your subject. Make good use of libraries, and exploit any other research facilities you can.

8. Record all your findings accurately and clearly so that they will be available as you prepare your speech.

Step 5: Organize Your Message

Now that you have all the basic parts of your message—the materials—you will want to make some sense of them; that is, you will want to put them together, in outline form, according to a speech plan. But first, you will have to decide how you will start and in what direction you will develop your message. Normally, the most useful plan is one that has four parts: the *purpose sentence*, the *introduction*, the *body* of the message, and the *conclusion*.

When circumstances demand a carefully prepared speech, you should organize your materials into a form that will show what you are going to say, how you will say it, what you will emphasize, and in what order you will present the points of your message. There is no substitute for a thorough job of organization, using an outline. Without an outline, it is extremely difficult to present your message step by step in coherent and understandable development; instead, you may find yourself punctuating your presentation with apologies and excuses for not having said something earlier, for having said something prematurely, and for other evidences of carelessness and disorganized thinking.

In impromptu discourse, too, you will discover that by learning the principles of outlining and organization you will do a better job of speaking without conscious and deliberate preparation.

Hints for the Beginning Student

1. Suppose you wish to develop your plan according to your *specific purpose*. Let's say that you want to tell about the history of acupuncture. You might start with the ancient Chinese; next show how the outside world responded to this technique down the years, and then bring the history up to date with attitudes and developments following the recognition of Red China.

2. Suppose you wish to set up your plan according to your *general* purpose. In speaking to inform, for example, you might start with some fundamental background material and then develop toward more complex and detailed material.

3. For first attempts at formal oral communication, use as simple a plan as possible, such as the chronological plan for speaking of the history of a movement. It may be more effective to combine a chronological plan with one that shows cause-and-effect relationships, but save the more complicated plans for later, when you have had more experience.

4. First prepare your purpose sentence (placing it in the plan at the point where you want to tell the purpose of your speech); then prepare the body, the conclusion, and, finally , the introduction. (Since the introduction introduces the message, you cannot logically prepare it until you know what the message is all about!)

5. Follow the instructions for outlining. Don't take shortcuts; you may forget your original intention if you do.

6. Remember that outlining and organizing are different—outlining gives form and order to the plan.

7. An outline that shows part-to-whole relationships is best for speaking to inform, at least for the beginner. Speaking to advocate requires an outline that shows reasons and evidence (proof) in support of your main contentions.

8. An outline can be made of words, simple phrases, or complete sentences, depending on its purpose. Each form has its advantages and limitations. Your instructor will tell you what he wants.

9. The outline is useful both in preparation and in presentation of your formal message. It is the product of your thinking and a reminder of what you thought.

Step 6: Deliver Your Message

In most communication situations, which do not permit much advance preparation, Step 6 will follow immediately after Step 3, in which you constructed a brief mental plan of the message to be delivered. In other communication situations, however, you have had an opportunity to prepare—that is, to acquire information and to design arguments or explanations that add strength to the message (Step 4); and you have organized all this material into a speech plan, employing one or more forms of the outline (Step 5). Whether prepared or unprepared, however, your moment of truth has arrived: No preparation, little preparation, much preparation—you have no message, you have no oral communication until you open your mouth and breathe life into the thoughts in your head or the words on your paper.

This brief discussion concerning delivery is designed primarily for the more complicated forms of oral communication, the prepared speech or talk (it follows that the more complicated the communication situation is, the more complex and detailed are the principles of delivery involved). *However, and this is important, the basic principles of delivery are the same for all oral communication, and by studying and mastering the principles of formal delivery of speeches, you will learn the necessary principles of delivery for informal, everyday communication. With experience and thought it will be simple for you to abstract those principles that apply to the communication situation in which you find yourself.*

Suggestions about *what to do* to present your message cover four problem areas associated with delivery: (1) the modes of delivery, (2) conversational quality in speaking, (3) stage fright, and (4) language.

The Modes of Delivery. There are four modes, or methods, of delivering a talk: *impromptu, extemporaneous, reading a manuscript,* and *memorizing the speech.* We will concentrate on the first two, impromptu and extemporaneous, because they are most frequently used.

By far the most frequent mode of oral communication is the *impromptu.* This method is the one you use to tell a stranger how to find the post office, to report on the progress of a project in business, to tell a younger brother and his friends how to play chess, and to rap with friends about the current political situation. Except for those concerned with deliberate preparation, the steps we have outlined so far apply to impromptu speaking in the sense of mentally running through them in the brief moment before you speak. Some of the preparation can be accomplished during communication. You can recall certain bits of information and knowledge or improve upon your organization as you go along; one idea will call to mind a related idea that may be important. Experience in more formal speaking will help you become familiar with the steps of preparation, and they will eventually become almost automatic in your handling of daily communication encounters.

In most situations in which you will be expected to present a *prepared* talk, the *extemporaneous* method will be well received because it seems most natural to your listener and offers you greater freedom for development and flexibility. Extemporaneous speeches are not memorized word for word; after careful preparation, the speaker, frequently using brief notes to remind himself of the emphasis and order of his ideas, just talks to his listeners. If your first classroom exercise is to be an extemporaneous speech, don't try to memorize it, thinking that you can later learn extemporaneous speaking as you become more proficient. Since the requirements of contemporary communication situations (and of your speech or communication teacher) will force you sooner or later to make the decision to talk from notes instead of from memory or manuscript, you might as well do it right away.

Conversational Quality in Formal Speaking. One of the best ways to approach speaking to a group is to think of the situation as an *expanded conversation*. Depending on your listeners, certain adaptations will be necessary in language and manner, because conversation is often filled with irrelevant materials and private language is usually somewhat disorganized. However, conversations are ordinarily marked by enthusiasm, animation, excitement, and naturalness; and it is these qualities that can be carried over into the speaking situations discussed here. This principle was illustrated well by James A. Winans, one of the foremost teachers of speaking:

> Here comes a man who has seen a great race, or has been in a battle, or perhaps is excited about his new invention, or on fire with enthusiasm for a cause. He begins to talk with a friend on the street. Others join them, five, ten, twenty, a hundred. Interest grows. He lifts his voice that all may hear; but the crowd wishes to hear and see the speaker better. "Get up on this truck!" they cry; and he mounts the truck and goes on with his story or his plea.
>
> A private conversation has become a public speech; but under the circumstances imagined it is thought of only as a conversation, an enlarged conversation. It does not seem abnormal, but quite the natural thing.

When does the converser become a speech-maker? When ten persons gather? Fifty? Or is it when he gets on the truck? There is, of course, no point at which we can say the change has taken place. There is no change in the nature or the spirit of the act; it is essentially the same throughout, a conversation adapted as the speaker proceeds to the growing number of his hearers. . . .

I wish you to see that speech-making, even in the most public place, is a normal act which calls for no strange, artificial methods, but only for an extension and development of the most familiar act, conversation.[3]

Conversational quality, of course, does not mean slipshod grammar, sloppy diction, confused thinking, or addled organization. It does mean that the speaker can add to his speaking in public the freedom, the relative informality, the friendliness, the sincerity, and the honesty of conversation.

Stage Fright. Almost everyone is nervous before speaking in a formal setting. Even in impromptu situations, you may find that your hands are shaking a little, the room is suddenly too warm, and you are at a loss for words—for a moment. Sometimes your palms itch or you get a slight feeling of nausea. On the other hand, you may experience none of these symptoms or only one or two of them, or possibly nothing but a little self-conscious nervousness. These feelings—commonly called stage fright—may stay with you throughout life, every time you encounter a situation that demands some sort of connected discourse, but you can learn to live with them and still be able to communicate effectively.

Perhaps the knowledge that this tension is good rather than harmful will help to dispel some of the discomfort of stage fright. A football coach who walks into the locker room just before a game to find his players relaxed and contented is likely to have a fit. They are *supposed* to be a little nervous; in order to play well, they must be keyed up. Likewise, the speaker who is a little keyed up will speak more effectively—unless his nervousness is so great that he cannot move his lips or finds his throat too dry to make a sound. In any case, stage fright is a perfectly natural phenomenon. Nature has provided us with the kind of energy we need to meet challenging situations; the skillful speaker can exploit the nervous energy that nature provides.

Moreover, it should help you to know that your listeners perceive much less nervousness than you are experiencing. If, however, you find that your nervousness makes you unable to speak clearly and keep track of your ideas, you must give some attention to curbing it. Here are some suggestions that should help establish the confidence you need in order to overcome excessive nervousness.

Choose a topic in which you are interested. When you are vitally interested, your mind will be full of ideas about your subject and you won't have much time to think about yourself. (Stage fright stems from excessive self-consciousness.) Even when you've had little option in selecting the subject, keep your attention on your ideas and the listeners instead of on yourself. Use materials that will sustain the listeners' interest, and you will be more interested in the talk, too.

Prepare thoroughly. When you are excessively nervous, you risk forgetting something. Don't let this frighten you; simply prepare enough material beforehand so that even if you forget part of it, you will be able to keep your listeners with you. Find out more than you need to know; a frequent cause of stage fright is the fear that you don't have enough to say.

Beware of attempting to memorize your speech. Nothing promotes stage fright so quickly as trying to memorize a speech that is supposed to be extemporaneous. You can't fake it, unless you are a real pro. And if you fill your mind with fear of being exposed as a fake, instead of filling your mind with your subject, you deserve all the stage fright you will inevitably have.

Relax. There *are* ways to relax, and they can be learned. Two of the simplest are: (1) Take a few deep, long breaths just before you rise to face your listeners. (2) Take your time in getting ready to speak—look at your listeners, smile at them, appreciate them, discover that they, like you, are human beings. Take a moment to get set to speak. No one's in a hurry.

In recent years a new technique for reducing anxiety in speaking, "systematic desensitization," has been developed and is being used in a number of colleges and universities with considerable success. The procedure is not difficult to learn, under proper supervision, and you should take advantage of this opportunity to learn relaxation while communicating, if a school near you offers it.[4]

Channel nervous energy into movement and gestures. Walk around; use the chalkboard; demonstrate objects; even arrange your notes. At first you may be a little stiff with these actions and gestures; but, if you let yourself do what feels natural and right, these bits of nonverbal communication behavior will help you to put your message across and to use energy that might otherwise manifest itself in quaking knees and trembling hands. After all, you probably use your face, hands, and body when you communicate informally with another person—why not let these natural actions become a part of your more formal messages?

Language. Obviously, language is what you use to express your ideas and feelings, for the most part. Therefore, you should take the trouble, whenever you communicate orally, to use the kind of language that you believe will best convey your message to your listeners. The situation will determine the degree of formality that is appropriate for the occasion. For your first formal attempts at oral communication, the best and safest suggestion is to concentrate upon maintaining clarity and precision. Vague phrasing usually leads to greater complications than precise phrasing does, even though precision seems to take more effort at first.

Hints for the Beginning Student

1. How does an extemporaneous speech grow from accumulated ideas into spoken words? The fact is, preparing to speak extemporaneously begins with Step 1 and continues through Step 7. If you will regard planning, outlining, organizing, and practicing your speech as steps in the *speaking* process, you will find that, by the time you are required to speak, you will be ready. As you plan, you are really deciding upon and committing to memory the basic order of your remarks. As you outline and organize, you are preparing and memorizing the key points of your speech. As you practice, you are *not* practicing to remember individual words but to remember thought sequences, to find transitions from one idea to another, and to improve the clarity of your thinking. If you do this and compose a new and shorter set of notes each time you practice, you will discover that your speech is ready and that you can deliver it with little worry about words and little or no reference to notes. This is an effective way to learn to speak, and countless speech teachers around the country will testify that *it really works.*

2. Use audio-visual aids with your prepared speeches; they will help put your message across, arouse and maintain your listeners' interest, and use up some excess energy that might otherwise come out as stage fright.

3. The visible impression you make on your listeners is part of your presentation. Be sure your appearance and posture will earn their respect.

4. Body movement, gestures, and facial expression can contribute a lot to your listeners' understanding and acceptance of your message. A smile or slight laugh before a humorous comment, for example, will let them know what's coming—but don't "lead" the laughter!

5. Pay close attention to articulation, pronunciation, and loudness; your listeners do not want to work harder than they have to in order to figure out what you're saying. Speak more loudly—and articulate more carefully—in a large room than in a small one.

6. Vary the pitch of your voice to keep it from tiring the listeners. A monotonous voice always seems to be talking about a boring idea.

7. Vary your rate of speaking according to the size of the audience and the acoustics of the room, the emphasis you wish to make, and the complexity of your ideas. Slow down a little for ideas that are new, particularly important, or difficult to understand.

A world-renowned concert pianist was strolling around the neighborhood of Carnegie Hall one evening, so the story goes, to relax a bit before his performance. An eager young man approached him, obviously in a hurry, and asked, "Pardon me, sir, I'm a stranger to New York. Can you tell me how to get to Carnegie Hall?" The pianist's answer: "Practice, my boy, practice."

The same advice applies to successful formal oral communication. If you want to get your message across as effectively as you can, you must practice. Moreover, the more attention you can give to practicing speeches, the better your informal communication will be—but here are a few more hints.

Hints for Practicing Your Formal Message

1. Allow enough time to practice your message thoroughly. Don't put it off until the last minute and dash into the room jotting the last item on the end of your speech plan.

2. Practice the entire message. Sometimes you will be tempted to neglect the conclusion, thinking that it is bound to "come off" well because the rest of the speech leads up to it; more often than not, however, your conclusion will fall flat unless you have given it the same care and attention as the introduction and the body.

3. Practice your message aloud. Most beginning speakers have no idea how they sound; practicing will give you a chance to listen to yourself. Later on, you may practice silently; or you may want to continue to practice aloud because it lets you adjust the sound of your voice in advance.

4. Find your own best means and your own best place for practicing. This is a matter of personal preference; what seems best for one communicator may not work out for another. Try this method for practicing extemporaneous talks. First, find some privacy; shut yourself into a room alone or go down by the river or out behind your dorm or house. Take your plan with you. Then simply start talking about your subject as if your listeners were there. As you talk, jot a few notes on your plan—like "Need to say more here," or "Belaboring the obvious." Remember, you are trying only to learn what your ideas are and in what order they fall as you practice. You are not trying to decide on exact words; the words of your message, except for specialized terms, are conceived at the moment of delivery. Each time you practice, try to reduce your dependence on the speech plan and try to cut down on the notes. In this way you will develop the ability to speak extempore and lessen your dependence on notes. For the actual speaking appearance, leave your speech plan behind; use only a very *few* note cards, *and type your notes in all caps, triple spaced.*

5. Do not practice your message too many times. It is possible to wear out your interest in it; and if you do, your audience will sense—and share—your boredom. Practice until you know it well, and no more.

Step 7: Evaluate Your Message

The advantages of learning something about the effect that your oral communication has upon the person or persons with whom you are communicating are obvious. We most often communicate for a purpose, and whatever the purpose is, it is more likely to be achieved if we can receive and accurately interpret feedback from our message.

Most well-known speakers try to evaluate their public speaking during delivery and afterward. Many have this evaluation done for them by competent critics, and often elaborate polls and other devices are employed to ascertain listener reaction. Experienced speakers recognize what every beginning speaker and every communicator should come to know: that only through evaluation can one learn to improve his speaking.

Hints for the Beginning Student

1. Make an effort to evaluate listener reactions *while you are speaking.* Try to learn which ideas, words, sentences, and movements achieve the effects you want and which ones do not. Study audience feedback— the way the audience reveals its reactions often provides a reliable

guide to evaluation. Try to discover the meanings of facial expressions, yawns, and body movements, because these reveal reactions to what you are saying. *And you can improve your message while you are communicating it.*

2. If you are about to give a prepared speech and a tape recorder is available, record your message—*before* you present it, if possible. In this way you can find weaknesses and correct them ahead of time. Listening to your taped speech *after* the event is perhaps the best way to assimilate the criticism you have received.

3. If you are in a speech-communication class in which students communicate messages under some direction, you will be fortunate enough to receive the evaluations of your instructor and sometimes of your fellow students. They have the advantage of being able to concentrate on all the aspects of your performance while you are talking. If, by some chance, they do not offer actual appraisal, ask for it.

4. Finally, never avoid criticism and evaluation; this is what you paid your money for. Ask for evaluation, take it in good grace, and then evaluate the evaluation. Do not be depressed when the criticism reveals your faults. Use it to become a better communicator.

QUESTIONS FOR DISCUSSION

1. People usually are more nervous about speaking in front of a group in a formal situation than about talking with people informally. List the differences between the two types of situation that usually lead to increased apprehension in the more formal situation.
2. Compare the steps outlined by David Ralph with the list you compiled in Question 1. Which steps might help to decrease which sources of apprehension?
3. Distinguish between *impromptu* speaking and *extemporaneous* speaking.
4. Ralph suggests that you memorize some elements of the speech. What are these elements? What does he suggest should *not* be memorized?
5. How much practice is best before a speech is actually given?
6. A speech cannot transfer ideas from the speaker to the audience. It can only elicit meanings that are already within the audience. How might this communication concept influence your construction of a speech?

NOTES

1. See Lloyd F. Bitzer, "The Rhetorical Situation." *Philosophy and Rhetoric*, Vol. 1. (January 1968), pp.1-14.
2. This sentence is probably *not* one you will say to your listeners, in an informal, unrehearsed situation, until you have developed and presented the entire message. There is nothing more embarrassing than to promise your listeners three points and then be able to deliver only one or two of them!
3. James A. Winans, *Speech-Making* © 1938, pp. 11 and 12. Reprinted by permission of Prentice-Hall.
4. You or your communication-speech instructor may wish to read a description of SD and the results of experimental work in this area in James C. McCroskey, David C. Ralph, and James E. Barrick, "The Effect of Systematic Desensitization on Speech Anxiety," *The Speech Teacher*, 19 (January 1970), pp. 32-36.

Barker presents suggestions for improving the amount of information it is possible to gain from another person's messages. Listening, like talking and walking, is something we all do from an early age. Why should we need special instruction in something a five-year-old can do? The answer may be that many of us have learned little about listening since we were five and still listen in much the same fashion as we did then. Most people can talk and most can hear; but far fewer can communicate well, and fewer still are good listeners.

23

listening behavior

Larry L. Barker

Some "Common Sense" about Listening

This is a "how to do it" [discussion]. The suggestions that follow are gleaned from a variety of sources. They are based on personal experiences, observation, and descriptive and experimental research. However, most of them might be classified as "common sense" suggestions. They are ideas to which you probably will say to yourself upon reading, "Everybody knows that—that's just common sense." This observation will be entirely accurate. The only purpose for including such suggestions . . . at all is that often we tend to forget them or neglect to utilize them. . . . In fact, the suggestions found here should serve primarily to stimulate thinking about the general process of listening improvement and help you discover additional common sense suggestions on your own, which relate directly to your personal listening behaviors. The relationship between reading these suggestions and implementing them is similar to the relationship between getting solutions and solving problems. It is relatively easy to discover a variety of solutions to any problem you may encounter. However, solving the problem by implementing the best solution(s) is quite a different matter. Just as a problem is not solved until the solutions are successfully implemented, listening improvement does not occur until suggestions are successfully implemented in actual listening settings. Review the suggestions included [here], but most important, *apply* them to your own listening behavior.

Larry L. Barker is Professor of Communication at Florida State University. Larry L. Barker, *Listening Behavior*, © 1971, pp. 73-84. Reprinted by permission of Prentice-Hall.

Before the *specific* suggestions to improve your listening behavior are presented, two general suggestions to help you become a better listener should be emphasized. The first is simply to be constantly aware that listening is vital to communication. . . .

The second general suggestion is to review the bad listening habits . . . and attempt to modify or correct those which you recognize in your own listening behavior. . . .

Some Specific Suggestions for Listening Improvement

(1) Be Mentally and Physically Prepared to Listen

This suggestion may be obvious, but active listening involves being physically and mentally "in shape." We take for granted that athletes involved in active competition must prepare their minds and bodies for the sport in which they are engaged. However, few people view listening as an activity which demands being in condition. Your attention span is directly related to your physical and mental condition at a given moment. If you are tired, your capacity to listen actively and effectively is reduced.

(2) Think About the Topic in Advance When Possible

In the case of classroom lectures it is often possible to read ahead about the lecture topic and devote some conscious thought to the issues in advance. The same holds true, to a lesser extent, when you plan to attend a public speech or public discussion. You should try to provide an opportunity to review in your mind considerations regarding the topic about which you will be listening. This suggestion is based on learning research, which supports the contention that, if you are somewhat familiar with a topic before you attempt to learn more about it, your learning takes place more efficiently and is generally longer lasting.

(3) Behave as You Think a Good Listener Should Behave

A partial summary of desirable listening behaviors might include:
(a)   Concentrating all of your physical and mental energy on listening (see 7 in this section).
(b)   Avoiding interrupting the speaker when possible.
(c)   Demonstrating interest and alertness.

(d)   Seeking areas of agreement with the speaker when possible.

(e)   Searching for meanings and avoiding arguing about words (see 10 in this section).

(f)   Demonstrating patience because you understand that you can listen faster than the speaker can speak. . . .

(g)   Providing clear and unambiguous feedback to the speaker. . . .

(h)   Repressing the tendency to respond emotionally to what is said. . . .

(i)   Asking questions when you do not understand something.

(j)   Withholding evaluation of the message until the speaker is finished—and you are sure you understand the message (see 11-a in this section).

Try to imitate those behaviors which lead to effective listening. In addition, observe other people who are good listeners and model your own behavior in listening settings after them. In this particular instance, imitation not only may be a sincere form of flattery, it also may help you become a better listener.

(4) Determine the Personal Value of the Topic for You

This suggestion is designed to make you a "selfish listener." It is based upon the assumption that initial motivation to listen may not be sufficient without some added active effort on your part to perceive what may be gained by listening to the message. Search for ways in which you can use the information. Look for potential economic benefits, personal satisfaction, or new interests and insights. In other words, strive to make listening to the topic appear vital or rewarding for you.

(5) Listen for Main Points

The key word in this suggestion is "main." Look for those points which, in your estimation, represent the primary theme of the message, that is, the central idea the speaker is trying to impart. It is impossible to remember everything a speaker says. Therefore, try to isolate major points and do not attempt to memorize all of the subpoints. This suggestion, if followed, should help you begin to quickly identify important elements in the speaker's message while screening out less important points.

(6) Practice Listening to Difficult Expository Material

This is, perhaps, more of an exercise than a suggestion, but it has been found that by applying good listening habits to difficult listening, listening under normal circumstances can be improved. This same principle applies to other areas of mental and physical improvement. For example, if you practice shooting a basketball into a hoop smaller than regulation size, theoretically it should be easier to make baskets in a hoop of normal size. If you find you are an effective listener in extremely difficult listening settings, it is very probable you will be even more effective when listening under normal conditions.

(7) Concentrate—Do Not let Your Thoughts Wander

Listening is an activity which is usually performed at relatively high speeds. Speaking can be performed at a variety of speeds, most of them considerably lower than normal listening speeds.

The listener should be aware of the difference between the rate of speech and the rate of thinking and should use the time lag effectively rather than letting it destroy the listening process. Some specific suggestions can help the listener use this time lag constructively to enhance the listening process.

(a) *Identify the developmental techniques used by the speaker.* This means, look at examples used, order of arrangement, and the mechanics of the message itself in an attempt to determine how the message is constructed and how it combines a set of ideas into a coherent unit (or if it does not combine ideas into a coherent unit).

(b) *Review previous points.* Use the time lag to review in your mind the points the speaker has made already. This may help you learn the material more completely and reinforce ideas the speaker has made so you can relate them to other parts of his message.

(c) *Search for deeper meanings than you received upon hearing the message for the first time.* Some words may have secondary or connotative meanings which you did not identify at first. Search the message for words which may have hidden meanings and apply these new meanings to the rest of the speaker's message.

(d) *Anticipate what the speaker will say next.* This sort of second guessing could be a bad listening habit if the listener does not compare what the speaker actually says with what he anticipated was going to be said. . . . However, this suggestion can be useful if you try to evaluate what has been said, predict what will be said, and compare the actual message transmitted with that which you predicted. This active mental activity also can help reinforce the speaker's ideas in your mind and keep your attention focused on the message.

Obviously, you cannot engage in all four of these mental activities simultaneously. If you were to try, you probably would completely lose track of the speaker's message. You need to decide initially which of the activities should prove most beneficial in a given listening setting. This decision should be based, in part, on your specific purpose for listening.

(8) Build Your Vocabulary as Much as Possible

This suggestion has been stressed by educators for several years. Comprehension is directly related to a listener's having meaningful associations for the word symbols. In other words, listeners must have a sufficiently developed vocabulary to understand most of what the speaker is saying. In some instances it may even be necessary to learn a "new" vocabulary before attempting to listen. In the classroom you may need to review a new set of definitions or terms, or learn some key words which will be used throughout the course, in order to understand what the teacher is saying. A foreign language course provides a good example of the need to have a sufficient vocabulary in order to understand what is happening in class. This is why most language courses begin by having students memorize certain words; new words are then gradually added as they are used in the daily lesson.

(9) Be Flexible in Your Views

Do not be close-minded. Examine your own views. Make sure the views you hold that are inflexible are held for a very good reason; and try to keep in mind that there may be other, contradictory views which may have some merit even if you cannot give them total acceptance. If you approach all listening situations with an open mind, you can only profit.

(10) Compensate for Emotion-Rousing Words

Some words evoke "signal reactions" (i.e., reactions which are a function of habit or conditioning) as opposed to cognitive deliberation. We must be aware of those particular words which affect us emotionally—for example, "sex," "nigger," "teacher," and most "four-letter" words—and attempt to compensate at the cognitive level for them. Following are some specific suggestions to help compensate for emotion-rousing words. (a) *Identify, prior to listening, those words that affect you emotionally.* This step simply involves making yourself aware of specific words which you know stimulate signal reactions. (b) *Attempt to analyze why the words affect you the way they do.* What past experiences or encounters have created for you unique meanings for certain words? (c) *Try to reduce their impact upon you by using a "defense" mechanism.* One which is popularly suggested to help avoid emotional reactions to certain words is called "rationalization." Rationalization involves attempting to convince yourself that the word really is not such a bad word or it does not have any real referent. Another technique is to repress certain meanings of emotionally laden words and substitute new meanings. No matter what defense mechanisms you use, try to eliminate, insofar as possible, a conditioned or signal reaction to a word. Try to determine objectively what meaning the word holds for the speaker.

(11) Compensate for Main Ideas to Which You React Emotionally

This is similar to (10) in that there also are certain trains of thought, main points, or ideas to which we may react emotionally. For example, a listener may react very emotionally when the topic of compulsory arbitration in unions is discussed, because he is a long-standing union member. Students may react emotionally when the topic of grades is discussed, and so forth.

When you hear an issue being discussed to which you have an apparent emotional reaction, there are several suggestions which may help you compensate for your initial bias.

   (a) *Defer judgment.* This is a principle suggested by Osborn (1962) in his text *Applied Imagination.* He suggested that in order to be a creative thinker, problem solver, or listener you must learn to withhold evaluation of ideas until you have listened to everything the speaker has to say. This suggestion often is difficult to employ because of prior experiences, positive or negative, that you may have had with certain ideas. However, if you can successfully employ the principle of deferred judgment you will become a more effective and appreciated listener.
   (b) *Empathize.* This involves taking the speaker's point of view while you listen, and trying to discover why he says what he says. In essence, identify with the speaker, search for his reasons, views, and arguments which differ from your own but which, from his point of view, may nevertheless hold some validity.
   (c) *Place your own personal feelings in perspective.* Try to realize that your past experiences, including your cultural and educational back-

ground, have molded you into a unique human being. As a result, you hold certain views which may be different from the views that others hold. Nevertheless, you must evaluate your own perceptions and feelings in light of those the speaker is trying to communicate. If you can critically evaluate your own views and feelings, you may be able to discover how they relate to or differ from those of the speaker.

Keep These Points in Mind When You Listen

The previous eleven suggestions relate to specific aspects of listening improvement. Following are some questions you should constantly keep in mind in all listening settings. If you can answer all of them at the end of each listening experience, the probability is high that you have listened successfully.

(1) *What does the speaker really mean?* This question was implied earlier, but is important to ask at all listening levels. Since you hold different meanings for words than the speaker as a result of differing past experiences, you must search actively to discover what message the speaker really is trying to communicate through his word symbols.

(2) *Have some elements of the message been left out?* People often speak without paying careful attention to the way they use certain words. Similarly, they often take for granted that the listener will fill in missing information in the message. The omission of information may be intentional or it may be subconscious on the part of the speaker. Therefore, you, the listener, have to take the active role in finding out what elements the speaker may have left out, which might help clarify and add meaning to his message.

(3) *What are the bases for the speaker's evidence?* This question implies that you must evaluate critically the reasons why a speaker advocates certain points. Is his evidence based on firsthand observation (perhaps this class of data may be called "facts") or is it based primarily on personal opinion? If on opinion, is the speaker an expert (thought to have a valued opinion on the subject) or are his opinions based on inferences or secondhand observations? Is the speaker's evidence consistent with what you may know? Is it based on careful study or cursory observation? All of these considerations contribute to the validity of the speaker's arguments. As you begin to search and evaluate the speaker's evidence, you become more critically aware of the quality and importance of his ideas.

Some Hints for Note Taking

Closely related to the listening process is the process of taking notes. Note taking is employed frequently in classroom settings, but also may be exercised in other public speaking or semiformal listening situations. Below are several suggestions designed to improve your note taking ability.

(1) Determine Whether or Not to Take Notes

Notes may be useful in some settings, but unnecessary, and even distracting, in others. Your purpose for listening should determine whether or not you need to take notes. If you feel you may need to refer to the information at a future time, the notes probably are necessary. However, if the information is for immediate use (e.g., announcements about the day's schedule at a summer workshop), it may be more effective simply to listen carefully without taking notes. Your own ability to comprehend and retain information is a variable which also must be taken into account. If you have high concentration and retention abilities, you probably will need to take relatively few notes. However, if you have difficulty remembering information the day after it is presented, you probably should get out the notepad.

(2) Decide What Types of Notes Are Necessary

There are at least three different types of notes which people may elect to take. They differ in purpose and specificity. These three common types are key words, partial outline, and complete outline.

(a) *Key words.* When you primarily want to remember some specific points in the message, key word notes are probably the most efficient. For example, if you wanted to remember an entertaining story about a member of Students for a Democratic Society who attended a meeting of the John Birch Society by mistake, so you could retell it later, you might elect to write the key words, "SDS at Birch meeting," on your notepad. Key words are used to help provide cues for ideas which were presented during the listening setting. However, unless you can positively associate the meaning with the key words , they are not of value.

(b) *Partial Outline.* If you decide that there are several important elements you should remember in a message, it probably is desirable to take notes in partial outline form. The points in the message which seem important to you are noted rather completely and other points which you do not deem important are not recorded. For example, if you are auditing a class on statistics and your professor illustrates how to compute a mean, median, and mode, you may decide that you want to remember only how to compute the mode. Consequently, you record in your notes only that portion of the lecture that relates to your specific interest. The notes you take are complete, but they do not represent all of the message that was presented.

(c) *Complete Outline.* In many lecture classes it is important to record most of what is presented in class. This is because you often will be expected to remember specific information later on tests. In such classes, and in other settings where you may need to have a complete record of what was said, a complete set of notes in outline form is necessary.

The key is to determine in advance what form of notes you will need to take in a given listening setting, and then adapt your note taking accordingly. If you modify your note taking according to the demands of the situation, you will make most efficient and effective use of your energy.

(3) Keep Notes Clear

This involves not only using brief sentences and statements of ideas which are understandable after you have written them, but involves such technical details as not cluttering the page, not scribbling, and not writing side comments. Use the paper efficiently; do not crowd words together.

(4) Keep Notes Brief

This suggestion speaks for itself. The briefer your notes, the less time you will be spending writing. This means you also will be less likely to miss what the speaker says.

(5) Note as Quickly as Possible the Organizational Pattern (or Lack of Pattern) of the Speaker

First, be aware of the fact that many speakers have no discernible organizational pattern. There is a tendency for some note takers to try to organize notes on the basis of their own organizational patterns rather than the speaker's. For example, you may prefer outlining with Roman numeral I, followed by A and B, 1 and 2, a and b, and so forth. However, if the speaker is simply talking in random fashion without much formal organization, artificially imposing an organizational pattern on his message may distort this message. Therefore, it is important to note quickly if the speaker is employing a formal organizational pattern and adapt your own note taking to his pattern.

(6) Review Your Notes Later

This suggestion is extremely important in a learning theory framework because by reviewing information frequently it is possible to retain information more permanently. Ideas that we hear once tend to be forgotten within twenty-four hours. Without some review they may be lost to us forever. Another reason for reviewing your notes soon after taking them is that you may remember some subtleties at that point which you might not remember when reading your notes at some future time.

Appreciative Listening Suggestions

The previous suggestions in this chapter refer primarily to critical and discriminative listening settings. The suggestions below are designed to improve appreciative listening behavior in social or informal settings.

1. *Determine what you enjoy listening to most.* This suggestion requires a self-analysis to discover those listening situations in which you find yourself most frequently involved by choice.
2. *Analyze why you enjoy these listening settings.* Determining the reasons why you enjoy particular situations may help you more fully understand your listening preferences.
3. *Compare your own likes in listening with those of others.* By comparing your own likes with those of others you can derive some social reinforcement for the types of listening you enjoy.
4. *Be curious.* Have an inquisitive mind about everything you hear. Try to be constantly creative and noncritical in the way you approach listening settings.
5. *Read and consult to learn more about those areas in which you enjoy listening.* Find out as much as you can about the subject (or music) to which you like to listen. Get more out of listening by being mentally prepared regarding the subject prior to engaging in listening.

An Ideal Environment for Listening

In some situations you may have control over the listening environment. The following suggestions may be helpful in structuring the environment for effective listening. Teachers generally have control over classroom listening environments; consequently, several of the specific suggestions that follow are derived from classroom listening.

(1) *Establish a comfortable, quiet, relaxed atmosphere in the room.* Listening is usually more successful when there are few physical

distractions. It is possible to create an atmosphere that is so comfortable that the listener may become sleepy or drowsy. However, it is more probable that noise and other elements in the environment will distract the listener. These elements should be controlled. (2) *Make sure the audience senses a clear purpose for listening.* This may involve a brief explanation or preview on your part of what is ideally supposed to take place in the listening setting. The reason for this suggestion is obvious. When motivation is present (that is, perception of personal purpose), listening effectiveness is increased. (3) *Prepare the listeners for what they are about to hear.* This involves more than just providing them with a purpose for listening. It involves giving them some background in the content area of the message—e.g., define critical terms or provide a conceptual framework for the message. (4) *Break up long periods of listening with other activities.* How long a person can listen depends on many factors, such as his immediate physical condition, the air temperature, humidity, time of day, and so forth. For adult listeners a maximum time period for concentrated listening probably should be one hour, or less, if possible. If you are in control of a situation in which listening is to take place, you should intersperse other activities, hopefully involving physical action, so that the listeners can seek a diversion, become relaxed, and become mentally and physically prepared for the next listening session.

Many bad listening habits often are practiced simultaneously. Similarly, many of the suggestions in this discussion for improving your listening effectiveness interrelate. For example, when you concentrate hard on what the speaker is saying, (7), you also are likely to be searching for main points, (5), and behaving like a good listener should behave, (3). Similarly, if you are truly flexible in your views, (9), you are likely to try not to let yourself become overstimulated by emotional words, (10), or ideas, (11).

In conclusion, the suggestions in this [discussion] are intended primarily to provide a basis for listening improvement. They are by no means exhaustive, and all of them may not apply in every listening situation. The objectives of this [discussion] will have been realized if you have carefully examined each suggestion, applied it to your own personality and listening behavior, and assessed its usefulness. Remember, understanding concepts about listening without trying to improve your own listening behavior is of little value.

SUMMARY

Sensitivity to listening problems is probably the most effective means of improving listening behavior. However, several "common sense" suggestions also can help interested listeners become more effective in a variety of listening settings. Among the suggestions to help improve listening are the following: (1) be physically and mentally prepared to listen; (2) think about the topic in advance when possible; (3) behave as good listeners should behave; (4) determine the personal value of the topic for you; (5) listen for main points; (6) practice listening to difficult expository material; (7) concentrate—do not let your thoughts wander; (8) build your vocabulary as much as possible; (9) be flexible in your views; (10) compensate for emotion-rousing words; (11) compensate for main ideas to which you react emotionally.

Some general questions to keep in mind while listening are: (1) What does the speaker really mean? (2) Have some elements of the message been left out? (3) What are the bases for the speaker's evidence?

Some hints for note taking include: (1) determine whether or not to take notes; (2) decide what type of notes are necessary; (3) keep notes clear; (4) keep notes brief; (5) note as quickly as possible the organizational pattern (or lack of pattern) of the speaker; (6) review your notes later.

The previous suggestions relate primarily to critical and discriminative listening settings. The following suggestions relate to appreciative listening: (1) determine what you enjoy listening to most; (2) analyze why you enjoy these listening settings; (3) compare your own likes in listening with those of others; (4) be curious; (5) read and consult to learn more about those areas in which you enjoy listening.

When listeners have an opportunity to modify the listening environment to enhance the probability of effective listening they should (1) establish a comfortable and quiet, relaxed atmosphere in the room (but not too comfortable), (2) make sure the audience senses a clear purpose for listening, (3) prepare listeners for what they are about to hear, and (4) break up long periods of listening with other activities.

Note

Some of the suggestions in this section are derived, with some adaptation, from T. Lewis and R. Nichols, *Speaking and Listening: A Guide to Effective Oral-Aural Communication* (Dubuque, Iowa: William C. Brown, 1965).

QUESTIONS FOR DISCUSSION

1. Barker suggests that a person who is flexible in his views will retain more information from a message than will someone who is less flexible. Why should this be true?
2. We are often told that we should not attempt to repress our feelings. Why does Barker indicate that we should repress emotional reactions to words when listening?
3. When you listen, should you evaluate what is being said and make judgments about it, or should you defer judgments to a later time? Why—what problems does this prevent?
4. Why should you review any notes you take within twenty-four hours? Do you usually do this?

EIGHT

A REMINDER: COMMUNICATION IS AN INTERACTING PROCESS

Earlier readings stressed the concept of communication as a process, an interaction of many variables with no fixed beginning or end. Some of the later readings stray from a strict process viewpoint, discussing *the* source, *the* receiver, and *the* message. While these articles recognize that sources are also receivers, that *the message* is a multichannel event, and that there is a fundamental difference between an event in the physical world and a person's perception or experience of that event, the emphasis is on practical applications rather than on the process of communication itself. The next reading takes *behavior,* a physical event, and *experience,* an internal perceptual event, as starting points and discusses human interaction as a function of experiences-of-behavior and experiences-of-experience. It reemphasizes the process approach to the study of human communication which the book has attempted to stress.

One alternative to adjusting our communication behavior toward another person in order to change the other into what we would like him to become, is to change our beliefs about that person without any corresponding change in the person himself. We can act on our experience of the other person in place of acting to actually influence the other. This is a form of self deception similar to the notion of *projection* in clinical psychology. In projection the person comes to believe that the other possesses a characteristic that the person himself possesses but will not admit to himself that he possesses. I may be angry and say to you, "Why are you so angry?" Laing, Phillipson, and Lee discuss projection and the problems involved in overcoming it during interpersonal communication, when one is usually unaware of the other's standards and beliefs. They emphasize the importance of the *relationship* between one person's behaviors and another person's experience and interpretation of those behaviors in any description of a communication interaction.

24

INTERACTION AND INTEREXPERIENCE IN dyAds

Ronald D. Laing
Herbert Phillipson
A. Russell Lee

To a much greater extent than most of us realize, and any of us wish to believe, we have been "programmed" like computing machines to handle incoming data according to prescribed instructions. Often this has been accompained by meta-instructions against being aware that we are being instructed. This is an additional factor in the frequently great difficulty that many people have in opening their own "programming" to their own conscious reflection.

If each of us carries around a set of criteria by which we judge certain acts as loving and tender or hating and brutal, what may be a loving act to one person may be a hating act to another. For example, one woman may be delighted if her suitor uses a "caveman approach" with her; another woman may think of him as repugnant for just the same behavior. The woman who sees the caveman approach as loving may in turn interpret a more subtle approach as "weak," whereas the woman who is repelled by a caveman approach may see the more subtle approach as "sensitive." Thus behavior even of itself does not directly lead to experience. It must be perceived and interpreted according to some set of criteria. . . .

Let us take, for example, a situation in which a husband begins to cry. The behavior is crying. This behavior must now be experienced by his wife. It cannot be experienced without being inter-

Ronald D. Laing is a family therapist. He and Herbert Phillipson were formerly associated with the Tavistock Institute of Human Relations. A. Russell Lee was the Director of Mental Health Services of Emmanual Hospital, Turlock, Calif. Abridged from *Interpersonal Perception: A Theory and a Method of Research*, by R.D. Laing, H. Phillipson, and A.R. Lee, pp. 9-22. Published by Springer Publishing Company.

preted. The interpretation will vary greatly from person to person, from culture to culture. For Jill, a man crying is inevitably to be interpreted as a sign of weakness. For Jane, a man crying will be interpreted as a sign of sensitivity. Each will react to a greater or lesser extent according to a preconceived interpretive model which she may or may not be aware of. At its simplest level, Jill may have been taught by her father that a man never cries, that only a sissy does. Jane may have been taught by her father that a man can show emotion and that he is a better man for having done so. Frequently such intermediary steps . . . that contribute to the determination of the experience are lost to awareness. Jill simply experiences her husband as weak; Jane simply experiences hers as sensitive. Neither is clear why. They might even find it difficult to describe the kinds of behavior which have led them to their conclusions. . . .

Our experience of another entails a particular interpretation of his behavior. To feel loved is to perceive and interpret, that is, to experience, the actions of the other as loving. The alteration of my experience of my behavior to your experience of my behavior—there's the rub.

> I act in a way that is *cautious* to me, but *cowardly* to you.
> You act in a way that is *courageous* to you, but *foolhardy* to me.
> She sees herself as *vivacious*, but he sees her as *superficial*.
> He sees himself as *friendly*, she sees him as *seductive*.
> She sees herself as *reserved*, he sees her as *haughty and aloof*.
> He sees himself as *gallant*, she sees him as *phoney*.
> She sees herself as *feminine*, he sees her as *helpless and dependent*.
> He sees himself as *masculine*, she sees him as *overbearing and dominating*.

Experience in all cases entails the perception of the act *and* the interpretation of it. Within the issue of perception is the issue of selection and reception. From the many things that we see and hear of the other we select a few to remember. Acts highly significant to us may be trivial to others. We happen not to have been paying attention at that moment; we missed what to the other was his most significant gesture or statement. But, even if the acts selected for interpretation are the same, even if each individual perceives these acts as the same act, the interpretation of the identical act may be very different. She winks at him in friendly complicity, and he sees it as seductive. The act is the same, the interpretation and hence the experience of it disjunctive. She refuses to kiss him goodnight out of "self-respect," but he sees it as rejection of him, and so on.

A child who is told by his mother to wear a sweater may resent her as coddling him, but to her it may seem to be simply a mark of natural concern.

In one society to burp after a good meal is good manners; in another it is uncouth. Thus, even though the piece of behavior under consideration may be agreed upon, the interpretation of this behavior may be diametrically disagreed upon.

What leads to diametrically opposed interpretations? In general, we can say interpretations are based on our past learning, particularly within our family (i.e., with our parents, siblings and relatives) but also in the larger society in which we travel.

Secondly, the act itself is interpreted according to the context in which it is found. Thus, for example, the refusal of a goodnight kiss after one date may seem to be perfectly normal for both parties, but after six months' dating a refusal would seem more significant to each of them. Also a refusal after a previous acceptance will seem more significant. . . .

In dyadic relationships, any action on the other has effects on me, and any action on self affects the other. I may so act as to induce the other to experience me in a particular way. A great deal of human action has as its goal the induction of particular experiences in the other of oneself. I wish to be seen by the other as generous, or tough, or fair-minded. However, I may or may not know what it is that I have to do to induce the other to interpret my action and experience me as I desire, whether generous or tough or fair-minded. His criteria for making these evaluations may be diametrically opposed to my criteria, and this I may or may not be aware of. Thus a passively resistant person (e.g., a Gandhi) may seem to one person to be tough, whereas to another he may seem to be weak.

Further, the other may wittingly or unwittingly be set to interpret every possible action of mine as indicating a preconceived hypothesis (e.g., that I am hurtful). For example, at a conjoint therapy session a wife interpreted her husband's absence as proof that "he wished to hurt her." When he showed up late she quite calmly assumed that he had finally decided to come "in order to hurt her." This is a particularly difficult bind if at the same time the person implies that there is a right course of action that the other just hasn't found. In such a situation the covert operative set is that no matter what he does he intends to hurt, whereas the overt implication is that if he did not intend to hurt he would be doing the right thing.

I therefore tend to select others for whom I can be the other that I wish to be. . . .

We have already suggested that projection is one way of acting on the other by . . . not acting directly on him as a real person, but on one's experience of him. But if I convey to the other how I experience him I am certainly influencing him. Indeed, one of the most effective ways to affect the other's experience of me is to tell him how I experience him. Every flatterer knows that, all things being equal, one tends to like someone by whom one is liked. If I am ugly, I am not ugly only in my eyes, I see myself in the looking-glass of your eyes as ugly too. You are the witness of my ugliness. In fact, insofar as ugliness is relative, if you and everyone else saw me as beautiful, I might be ugly no more. If I cannot induce you to see me as I wish, I may act on my experience of you rather than your experience of me. I can invent your experience of me. Many projections, of course, are the apparently compulsive inventions of persons who see themselves as ugly, and wish to extrude this perception from their own self-self relation. . . .

In Zarathustra, the ugliest man abolishes God because he cannot stand an eternal witness to his ugliness, and replaces him with nothing.

Projection refers to a mode of experiencing the other in which one experiences one's outer world in terms of one's inner world. Another way of putting this is that one experiences the perceptual world in terms of one's phantasy system, without realizing that one is doing this. . . .

A husband and wife, after eight years of marriage, described one of their first fights. This occurred on the second night of their honeymoon. They were both sitting at a bar in a hotel when the wife struck up a conversation with a couple sitting next to them. To her dismay her husband refused to join the conversation, remained aloof, gloomy and antagonistic both to her and the other couple. Perceiving his mood, she became angry at him for producing an awkward social situation and making her feel "out on a limb." Tempers rose, and they ended in a bitter fight in which each accused the other of being inconsiderate. This was the extent of their report of the incident. Eight years later, however, we were able to tease out some of the additional factors involved. When asked why she had struck up the conversation with the other couple, the wife replied: "Well, I had never had a conversation with another couple as a wife before. Previous to this I had always been a 'girl friend' or 'fiancée' or 'daughter' or 'sister.' I thought of the honeymoon as a fine time to try out my new role as a wife, to have a conversation as a wife with my husband at my side. I had never had a husband before, either." She thus carried into the situation her expectancy that the honeymoon would be an opportunity to begin to socialize as a couple with other couples. She looked forward to this eagerly and joyfully. By contrast, her husband had a completely differing view of the honeymoon. When questioned about his aloofness during the conversation he said: "Of course I was aloof. The honeymoon to me was a time to get away from everyone—a time when two people could learn to take advantage of a golden opportunity to ignore the rest of the world and simply explore each other. I wanted us to be sufficient unto ourselves. To me, everyone else in the world was a complication, a burden and an interference. When my wife struck up that conversation with the other couple I felt it as a direct insult. She was telling me in effect that I was not man enough for her, that I was insufficient to fill her demands. She made me feel inadequate and angry."

Eight years later they were able to laugh at the situation. He could say, "If I had only known how you felt it would have made a great difference." The crucial point is that each interpreted the other's action as inconsiderate and even deliberately insulting. These attributions of inconsiderateness and insult and maliciousness were based on hidden discrepant value systems and discrepant expectations based on these value systems. . . .

[Suppose that we were to observe two people, Peter and Paul, who are talking with each other. Consider Peter's perception of Paul in relation to Paul's perception of Peter.] One might suppose that the easiest part of the circuit to become phantasized by Peter might be what was going on inside Paul, for here there is the minimum of validation available to Peter, except from the testimony of Paul.

Thus, Peter says, "I think you are unhappy inside."

Paul says, "No I'm not."

Peter may, however, attempt to validate his attribution about Paul's relation to Paul by watching the actions of Paul. He may say, "If *I* acted in that way I would be unhappy," or, "When mother acted that way she was unhappy." He may have nothing that he can "put his finger on," but "senses" that Paul is unhappy. He may be correctly reconstructing Paul's experience by succeeding in synthesizing many cues from Paul's behavior, or he may be "wrong" to construe Paul's behavior in his own terms (Peter's) rather than Paul's, or he may put inside Paul unhappiness that he is trying not to feel inside himself. It is not easy to discover criteria of validity here, because Peter may actually make Paul unhappy by "going on" about it. . . .

Paul may be seeking to deny his unhappiness. On the other hand, Peter may be attributing to Paul what he is denying himself. Furthermore, Peter may seek to avoid feeling unhappy himself by *trying to make Paul unhappy.* One of his ways of doing this may be to tell Paul that he or Paul is unhappy. Let us suppose he does the latter. Paul may accuse Peter of trying to make him unhappy by telling him he is. Very likely, Peter will repudiate this attribution in favor, perhaps, of one of the order, "I am only trying to help you."

Thus, if Peter becomes upset about something, Paul may hope to help him by remaining calm and detached. However, Peter may feel that this is just the wrong thing for Paul to be doing when he is upset. His feeling may be that a really friendly, helpful person would get upset with him. If Paul does not know this and Peter does not communicate it, Peter may assume that Paul is deliberately staying aloof to hurt him. Paul may then conclude that Peter is "projecting" angry feelings onto him. This, then, is a situation where projection is attributed by Paul to Peter, but it has not actually occurred. This commonly happens in analytical therapy when the analyst (Paul) assumes that a detached mirrorlike attitude is the most helpful stance he can adopt towards the patient (Peter). However, the patient may feel that only an open self-disclosing person could be of help, and if he goes on to interpret the analyst's stance as not only unhelpful in effect but unhelpful in intention, then the analyst may in turn counter-attribute "projection" to the patient. A vicious circle of mismatched interpretations, expectancies, experiences, attributions and counter-attributions is now in play.

It starts to whirl something like this:

Peter:	*Paul:*
1. I am upset.	1. Peter is upset.
2. Paul is acting very calm and dispassionate.	2. I'll try to help him by remaining calm and just listening.
3. If Paul cared about me and wanted to help he would get involved and show some emotion also.	3. He is getting even more upset. I must be even more calm.
4. Paul knows that this upsets me.	4. He is accusing me of hurting him.
5. If Paul knows that his behavior upsets me, he must be intending to hurt me.	5. I'm really trying to help.
6. He must be cruel, sadistic. Maybe he gets pleasure out of it, etc.	6. He must be projecting.

Attributions of this kind, based on a virtually inextricable mix of mismatched expectations and phantasy and perception, are the very stuff of interhuman reality.

QUESTIONS FOR DISCUSSION

1. Laing, Phillipson, and Lee suggest that we have been programmed to experience the behavior and other outside events we observe, through a set of criteria which we carry within us. What earlier readings have discussed this set of criteria? How are those readings related to this discussion of interpersonal perception?
2. List three possible reasons why two persons' experience of the same act may be different.
3. Is it possible to act in such a way that another person will experience your behavior in a particular way? Why is it so difficult to get others to perceive you as you wish to be perceived?
4. Suggest how the differences between behavior and experience which are discussed by Laing, Phillipson, and Lee affect the process of communication.